Dawn of the Arcana

XII

XI

X

IX

VIII

VII

VI

V

IIII

III

II

I

Story & Art by
Rei Toma

Dawn of the Arcana

Volume 4

XII
XI
X
IX
VIII
VII
VI

CONTENTS

characters

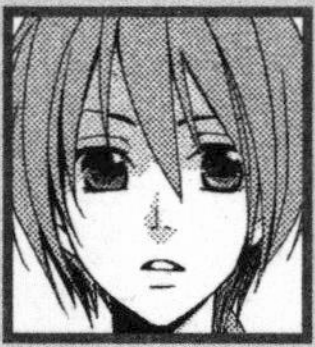

Nakaba
The princess royal of Senan. Strong of will and noble of spirit, she possesses a strange power.

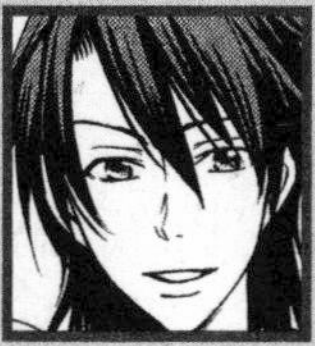

Caesar
The second-born prince of Belquat. Nakaba's husband through a marriage of political convenience. Headstrong and selfish.

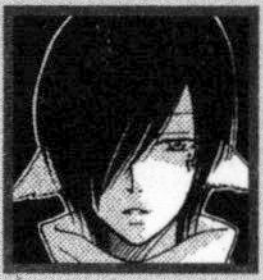

Loki
Nakaba's attendant. His senses of perception are unmatched.

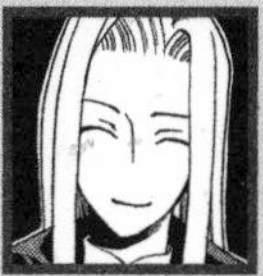

Bellinus
Caesar's attendant. Always cool and collected.

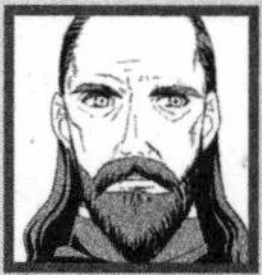

Guran
King of Belquat.

story

- Wed to Prince Caesar as a symbol of peace between their two countries, Nakaba is actually little more than a hostage. Unbeknownst to King Guran, she is a survivor of the race he tried to destroy for fear of their power.
- The political marriage between Nakaba and Caesar got off to a rocky start, but as they grew to know each other, the gulf between them began to close.

While visiting from the country of Lithuanel, a staunch ally of Belquat, Prince Akhil learned that Nakaba possesses the Arcana of Time. Together they discovered a Belquat plot that could plunge the realm into war!

Neighboring Kingdoms

Senan
A poor kingdom in the cold north of the island. Militarily weak.

Belquat
A powerful country that thrives thanks to its temperate climate.

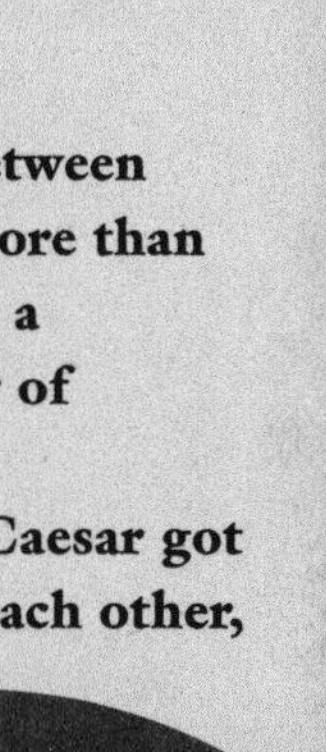
Senan
Belquat

Chapter 12

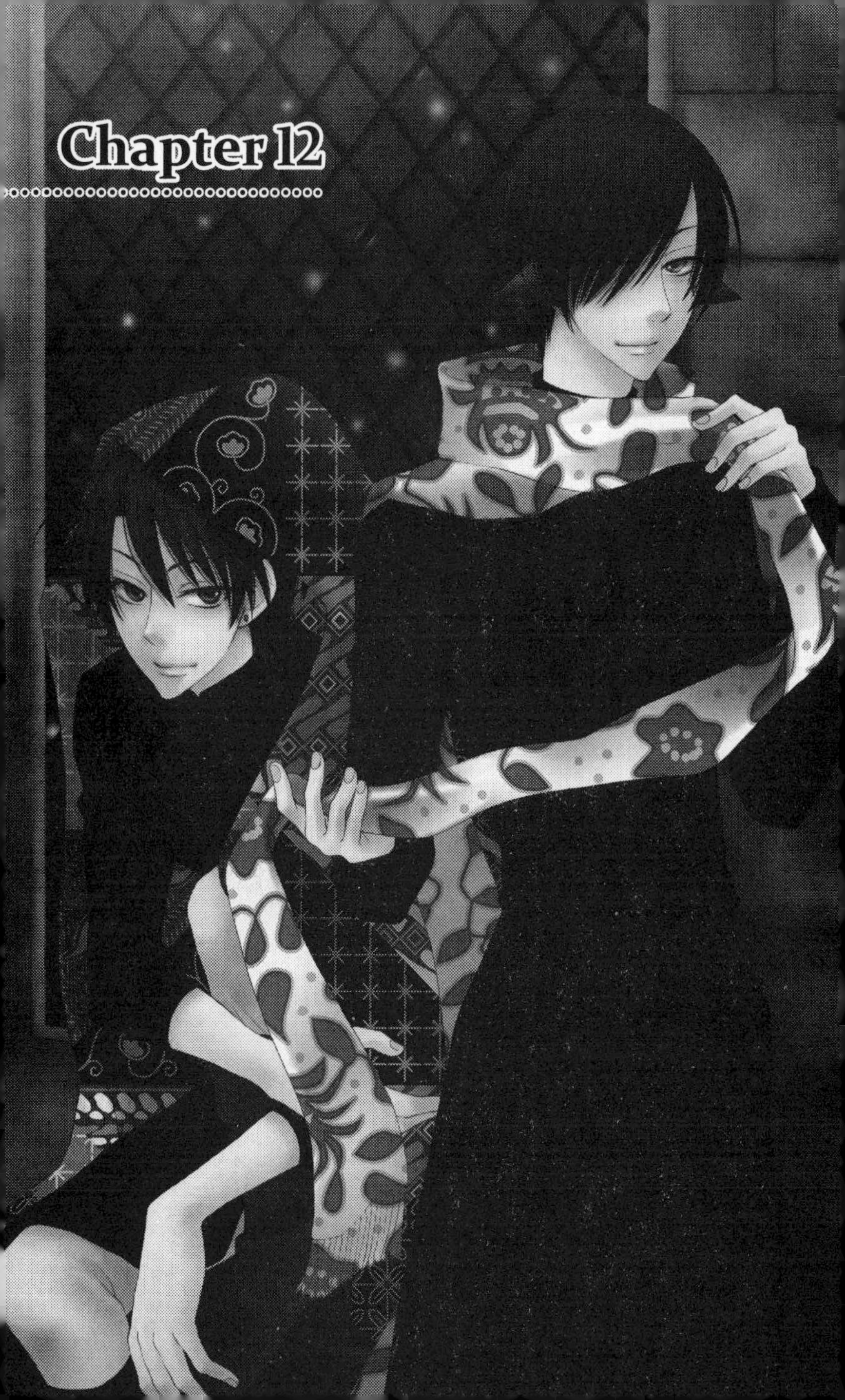

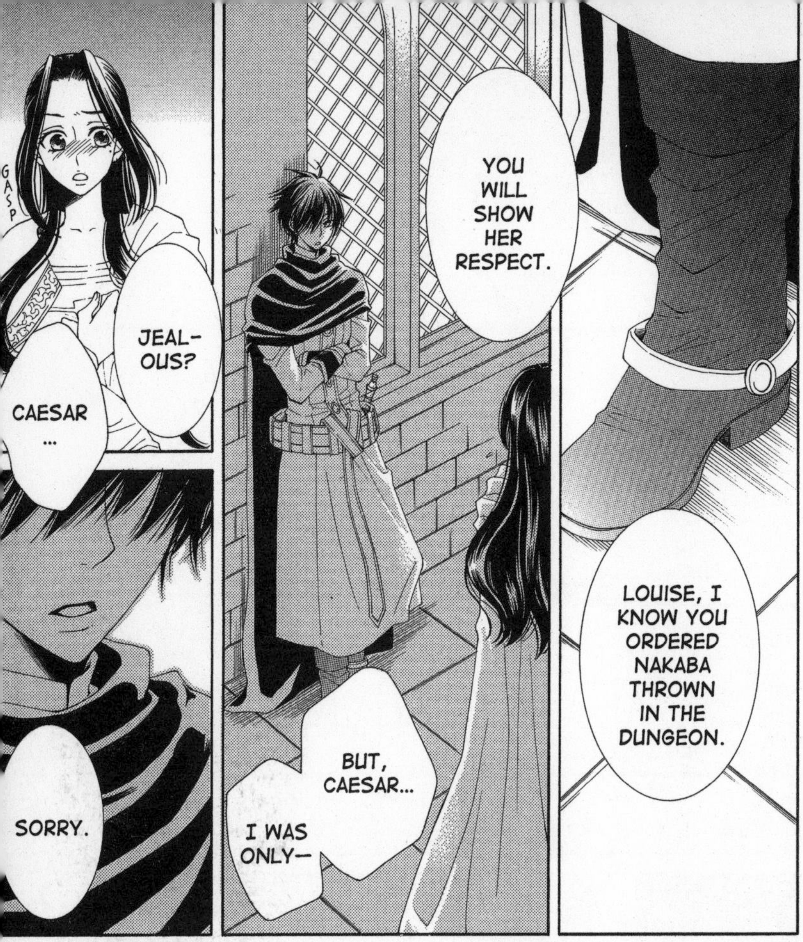
LOUISE, I KNOW YOU ORDERED NAKABA THROWN IN THE DUNGEON.
YOU WILL SHOW HER RESPECT.
BUT, CAESAR...
I WAS ONLY—
GASP
JEAL-OUS?
CAESAR ...
SORRY.

Dawn of the Arcana

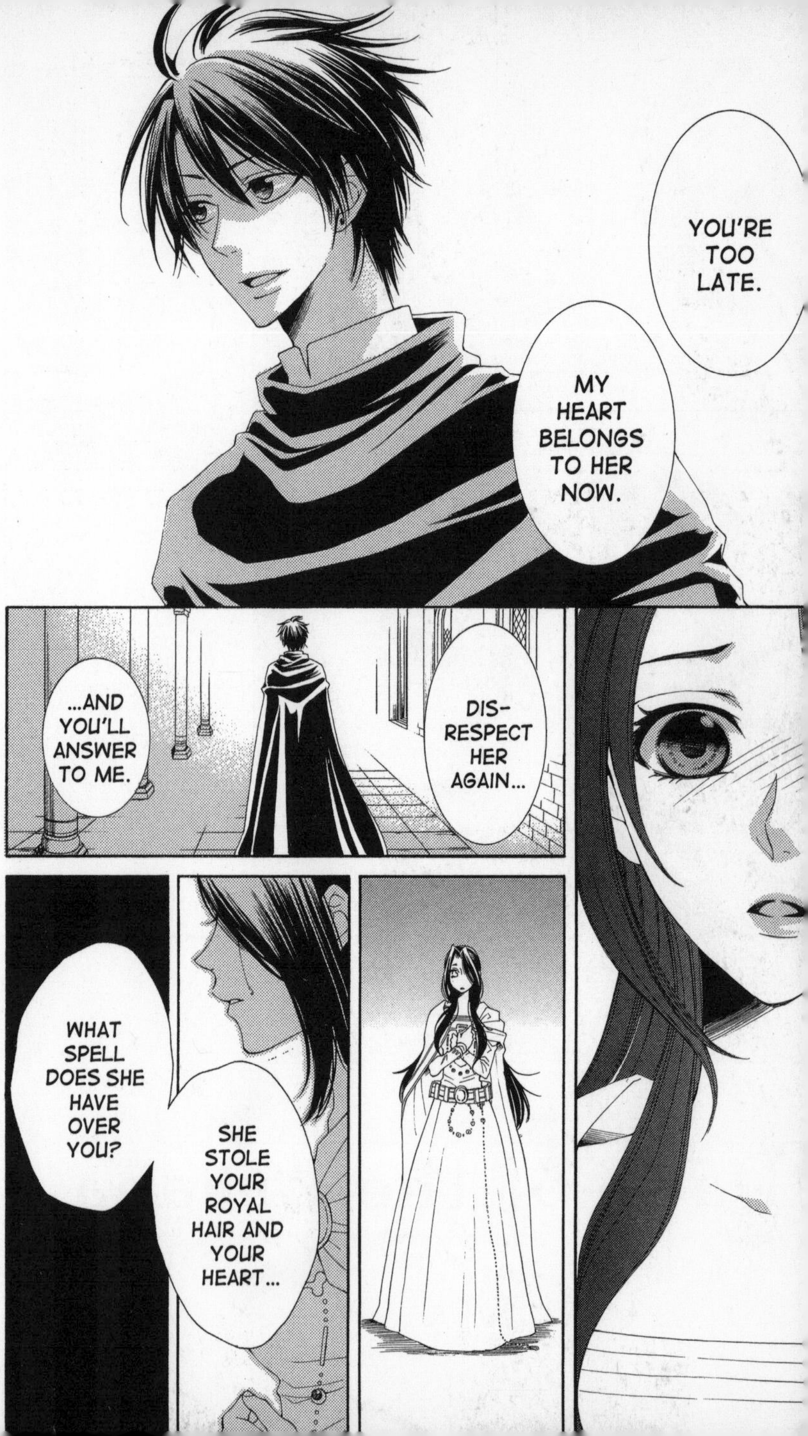
YOU'RE TOO LATE.
MY HEART BELONGS TO HER NOW.
DIS-RESPECT HER AGAIN...
...AND YOU'LL ANSWER TO ME.
SHE STOLE YOUR ROYAL HAIR AND YOUR HEART...
WHAT SPELL DOES SHE HAVE OVER YOU?

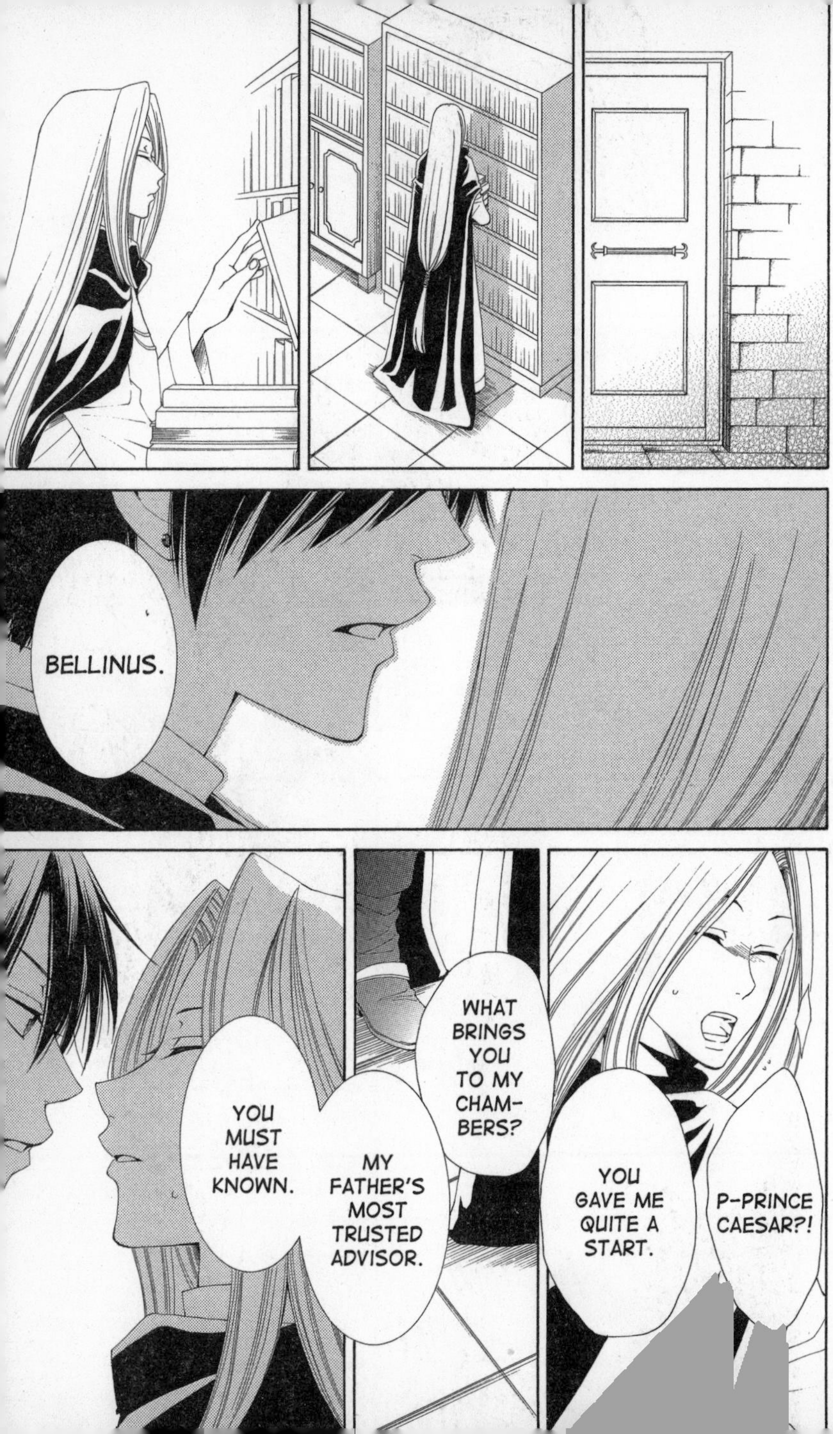
BELLINUS.
P-PRINCE CAESAR?!
YOU GAVE ME QUITE A START.
WHAT BRINGS YOU TO MY CHAMBERS?
MY FATHER'S MOST TRUSTED ADVISOR.
YOU MUST HAVE KNOWN.

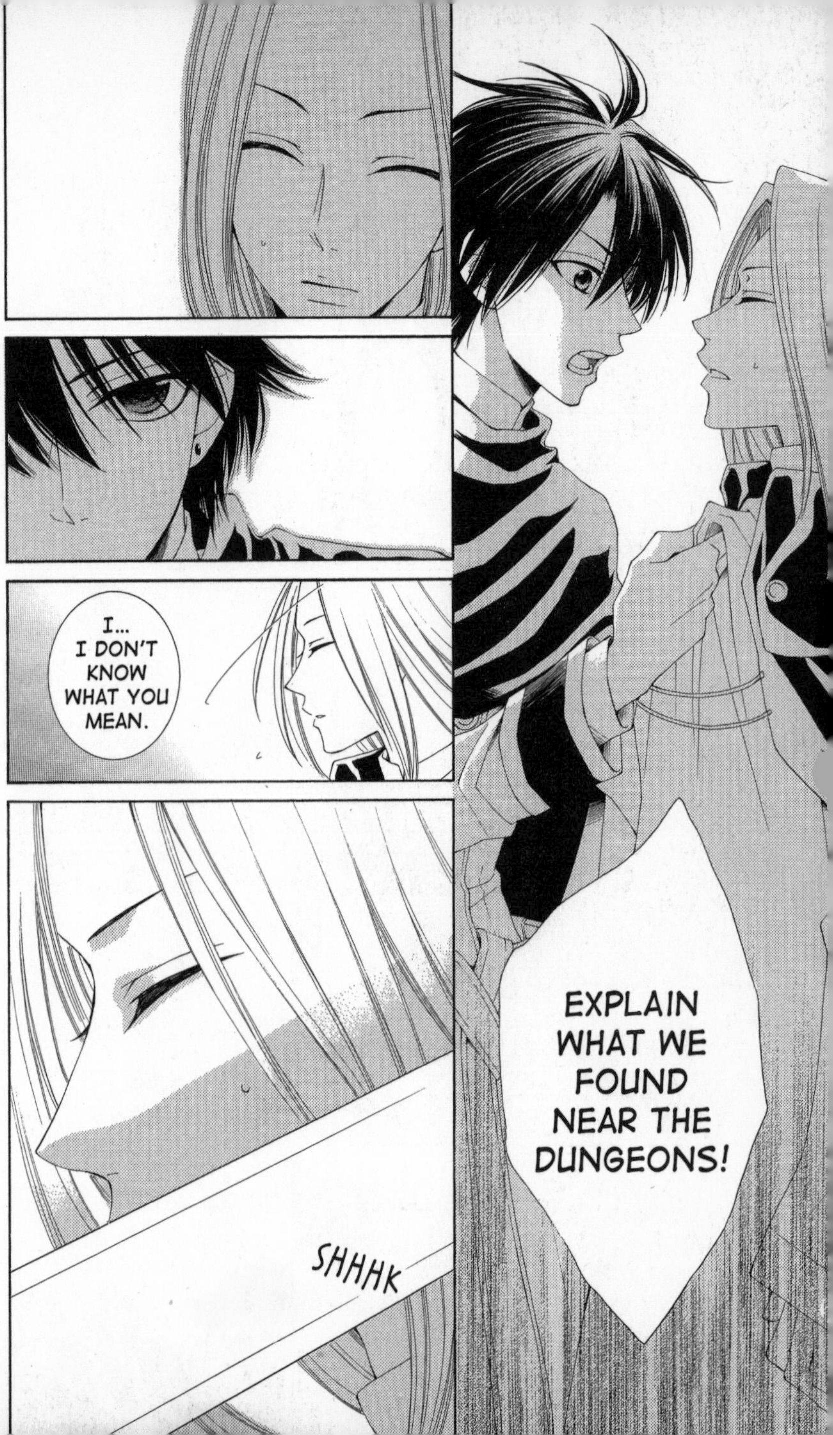
EXPLAIN WHAT WE FOUND NEAR THE DUNGEONS!
I... I DON'T KNOW WHAT YOU MEAN.
SHHHK

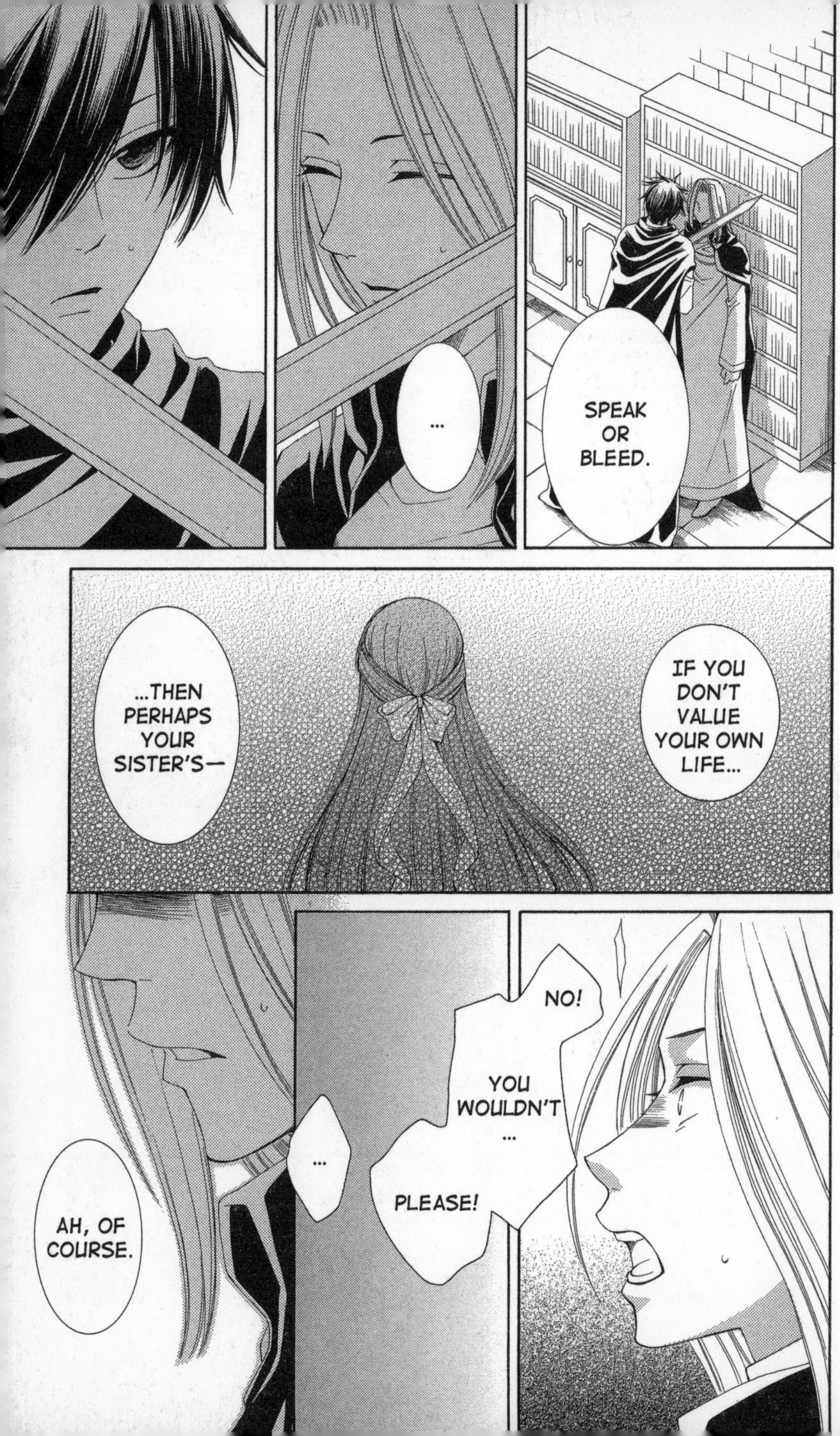
SPEAK OR BLEED.
...
IF YOU DON'T VALUE YOUR OWN LIFE...
...THEN PERHAPS YOUR SISTER'S—
NO!
YOU WOULDN'T ...
PLEASE!
...
AH, OF COURSE.

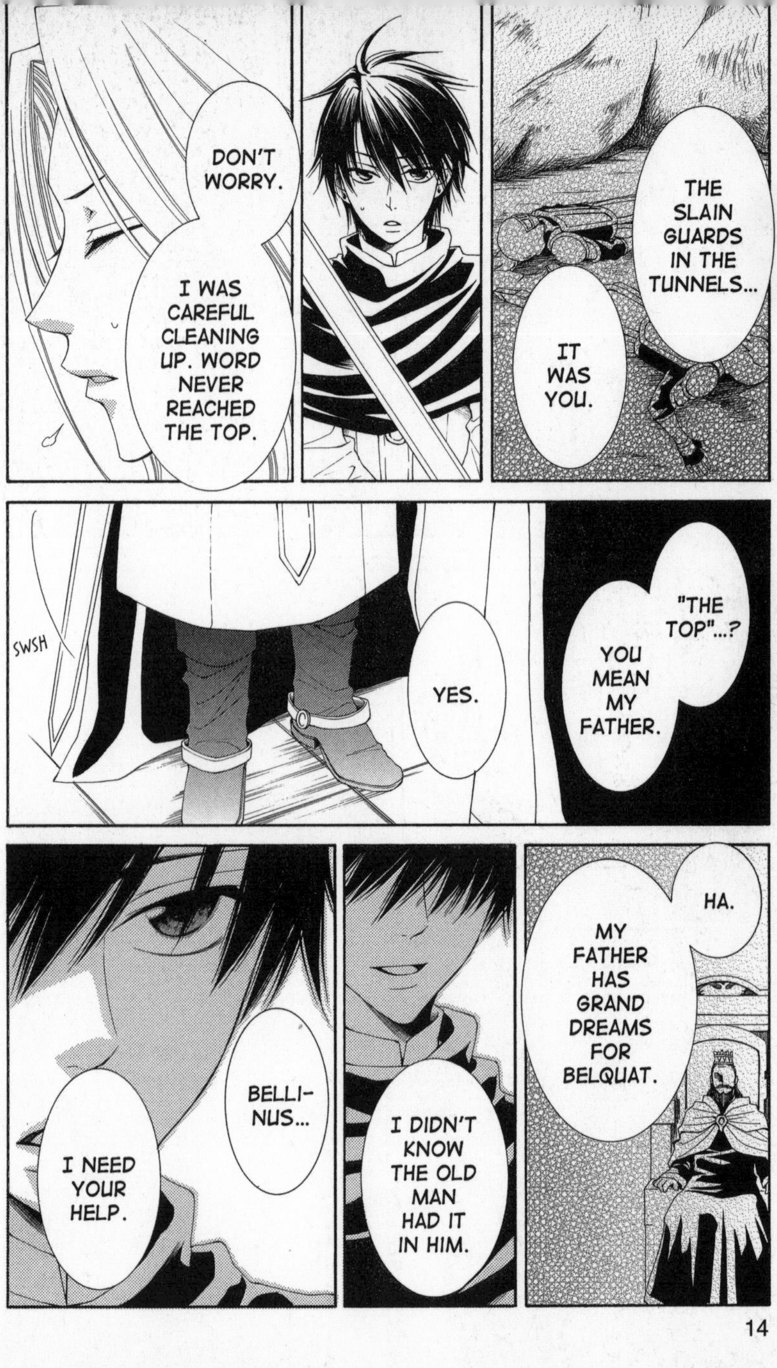
THE SLAIN GUARDS IN THE TUNNELS...
IT WAS YOU.
DON'T WORRY.
I WAS CAREFUL CLEANING UP. WORD NEVER REACHED THE TOP.
"THE TOP"...?
YOU MEAN MY FATHER.
YES.
SWSH
HA.
MY FATHER HAS GRAND DREAMS FOR BELQUAT.
I DIDN'T KNOW THE OLD MAN HAD IT IN HIM.
BELLI-NUS...
I NEED YOUR HELP.

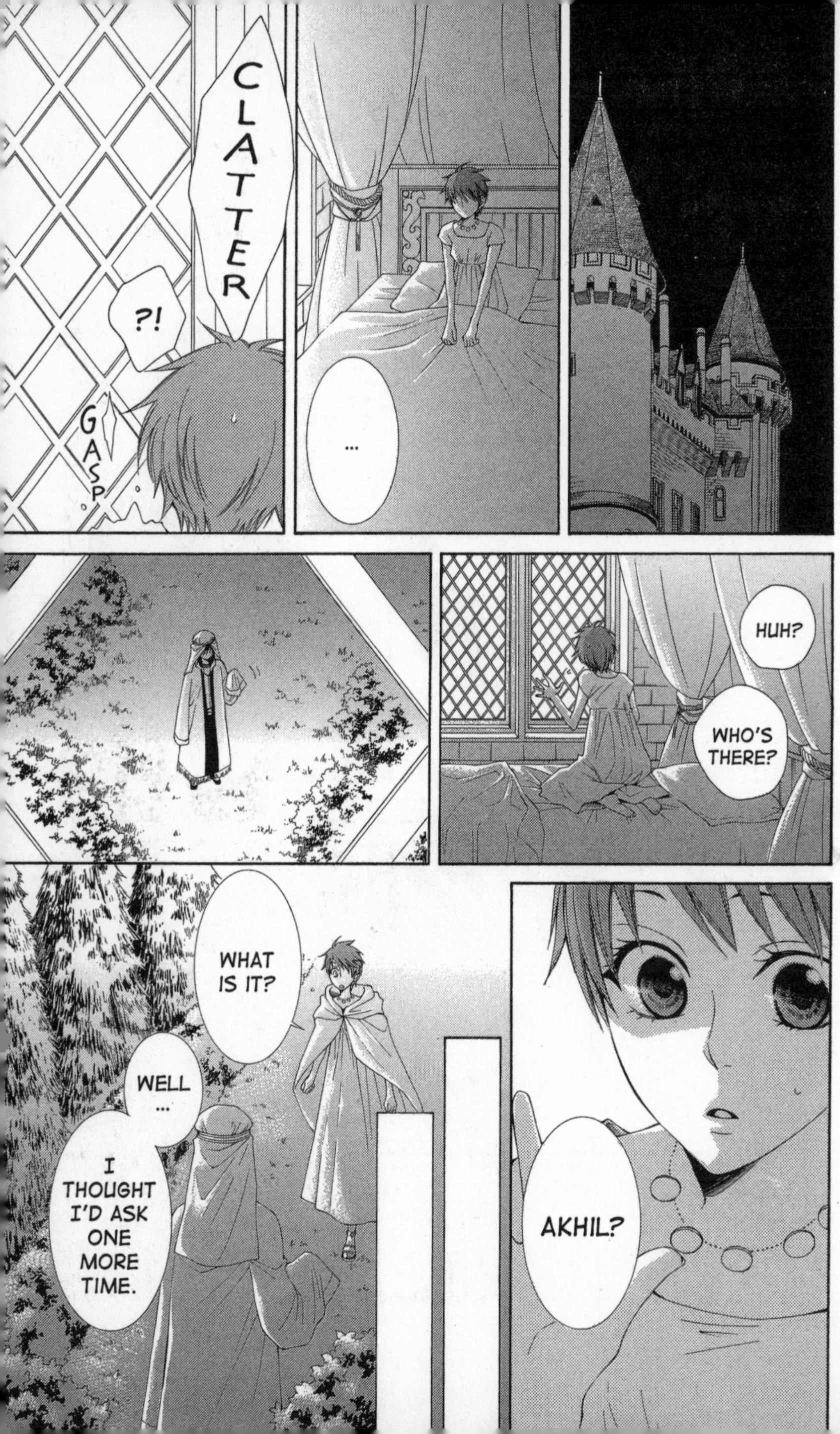
...
CLATTER
?!
GASP
HUH?
WHO'S THERE?
AKHIL?
WHAT IS IT?
WELL ...
I THOUGHT I'D ASK ONE MORE TIME.

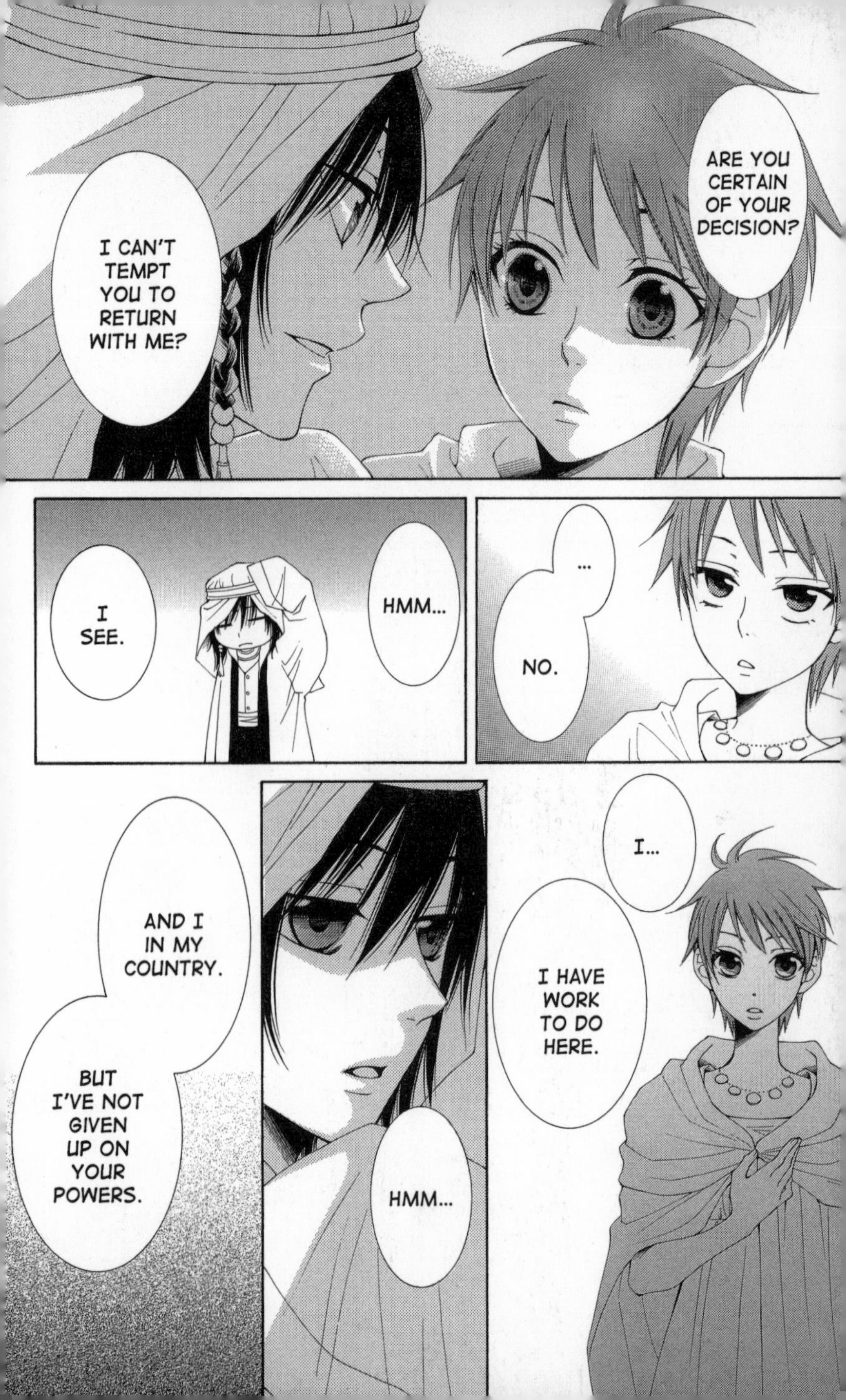
ARE YOU CERTAIN OF YOUR DECISION?
I CAN'T TEMPT YOU TO RETURN WITH ME?
...
NO.
HMM...
I SEE.
I...
I HAVE WORK TO DO HERE.
AND I IN MY COUNTRY.
BUT I'VE NOT GIVEN UP ON YOUR POWERS.
HMM...

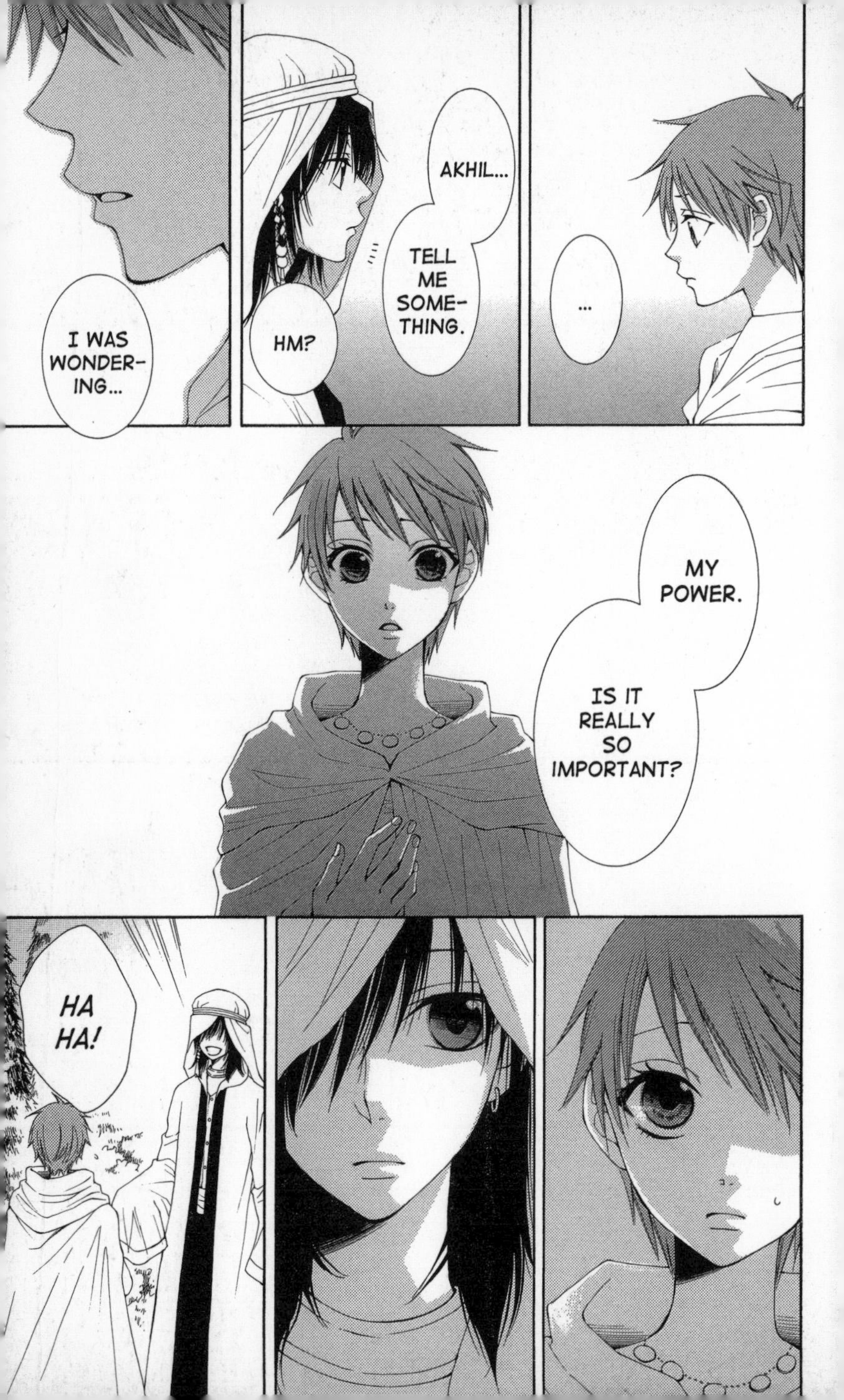
...
AKHIL...
TELL ME SOME-THING.
HM?
I WAS WONDER-ING...
MY POWER.
IS IT REALLY SO IMPORTANT?
HA HA!

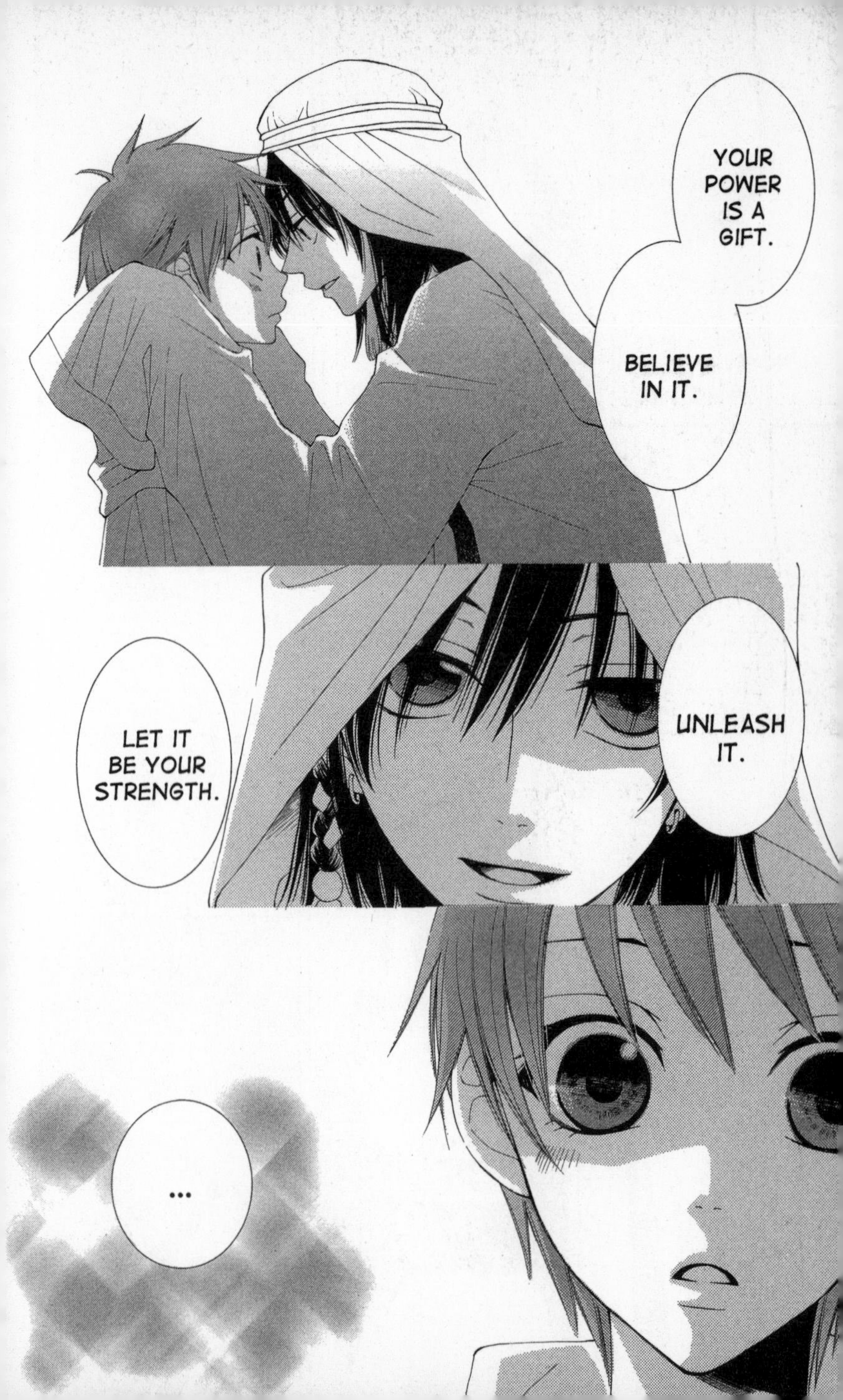
YOUR POWER IS A GIFT.
BELIEVE IN IT.
UNLEASH IT.
LET IT BE YOUR STRENGTH.
...

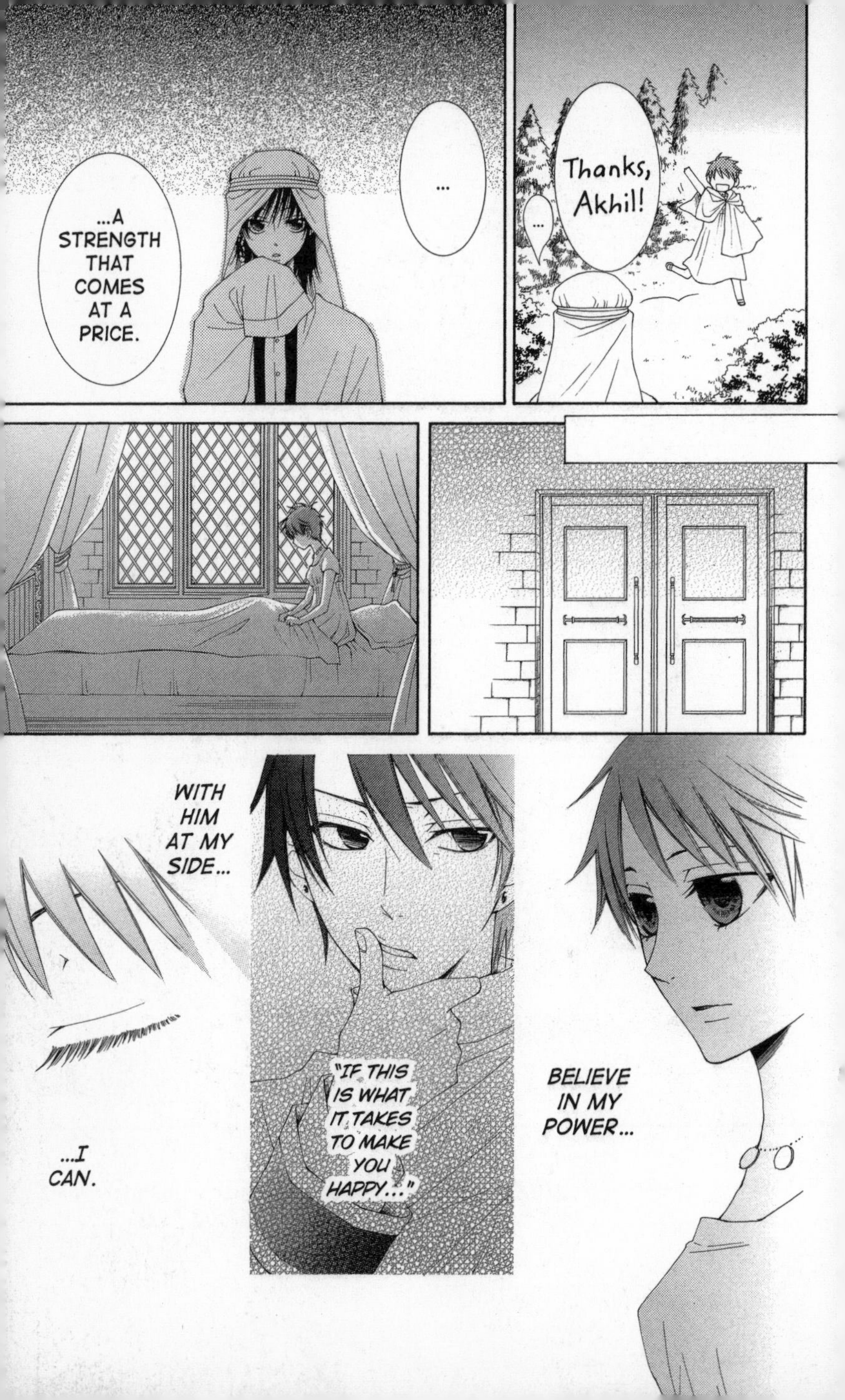
Thanks, Akhil!
...
...
...A STRENGTH THAT COMES AT A PRICE.
BELIEVE IN MY POWER...
"IF THIS IS WHAT IT TAKES TO MAKE YOU HAPPY..."
WITH HIM AT MY SIDE...
...I CAN.

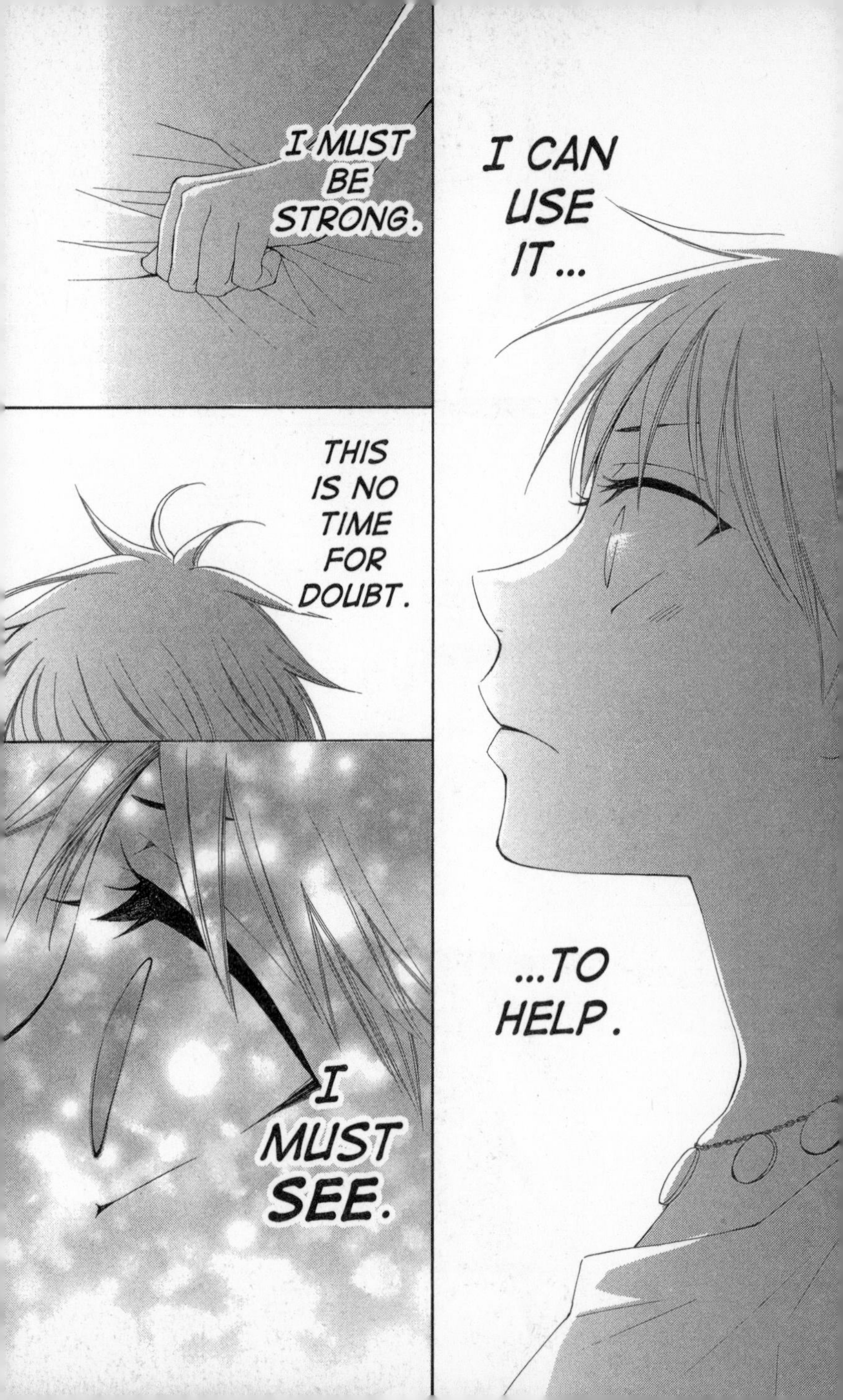
I CAN USE IT...
...TO HELP.
I MUST BE STRONG.
THIS IS NO TIME FOR DOUBT.
I MUST SEE.

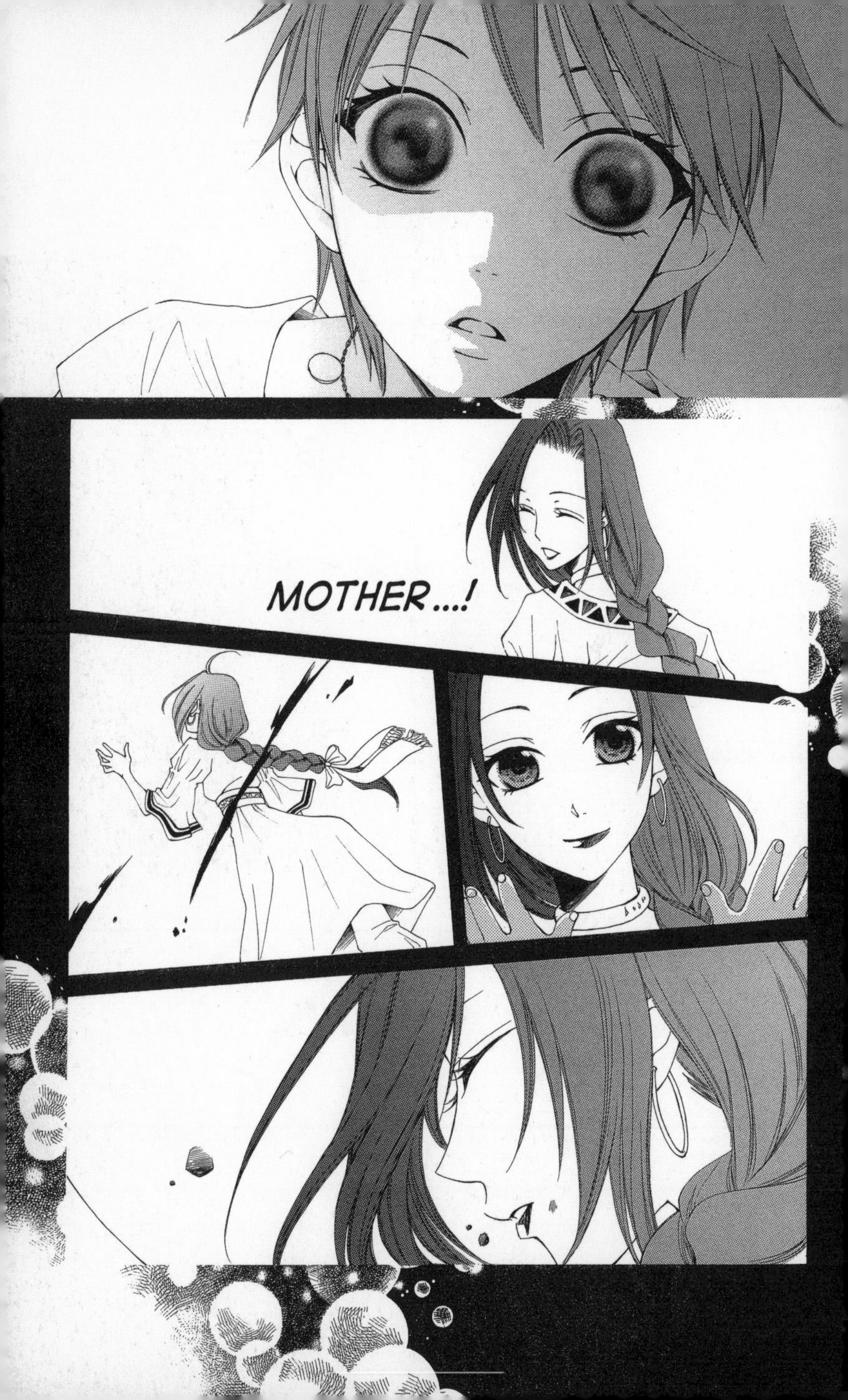
MOTHER...!

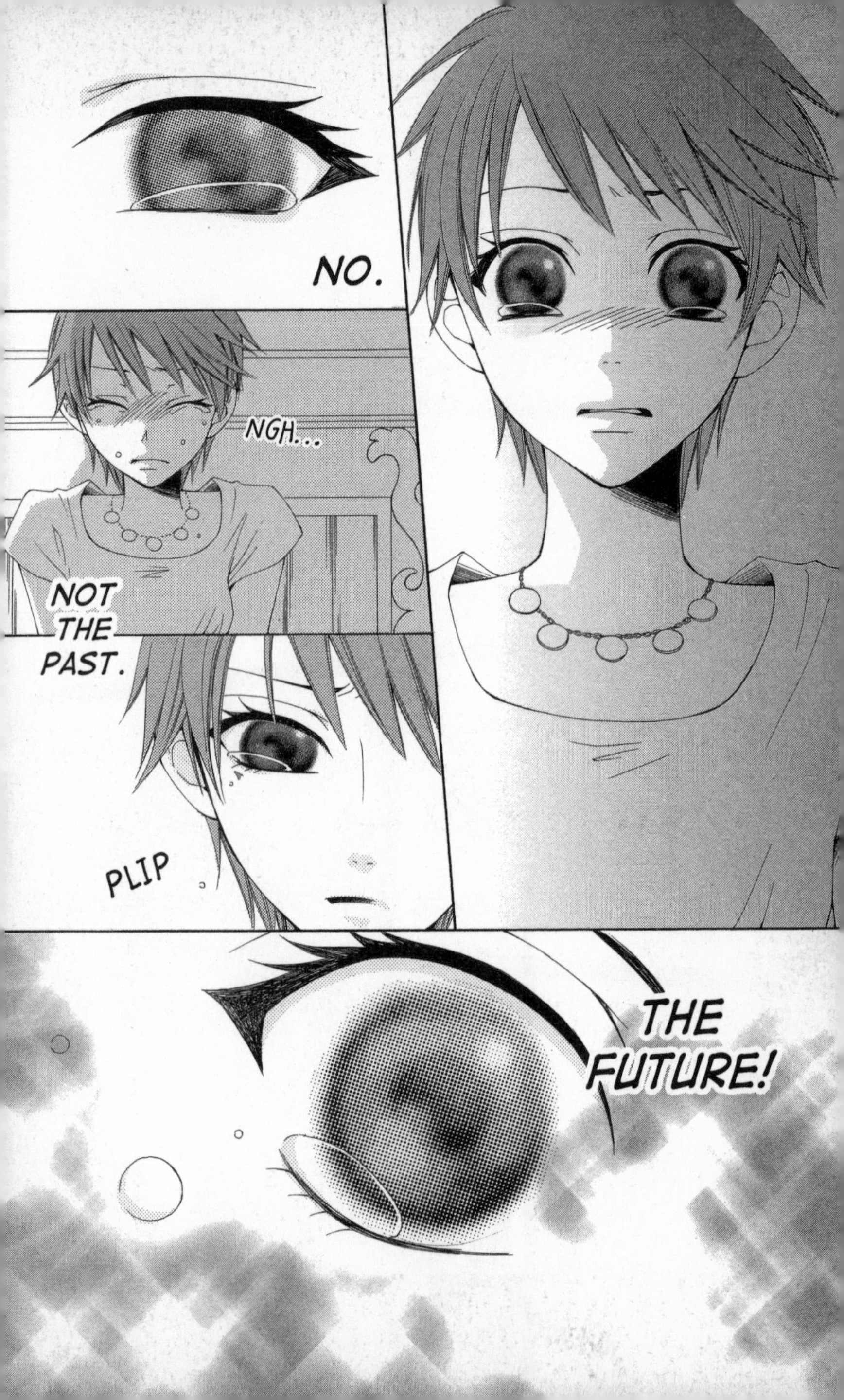
NO.
NGH...
NOT THE PAST.
PLIP
THE FUTURE!

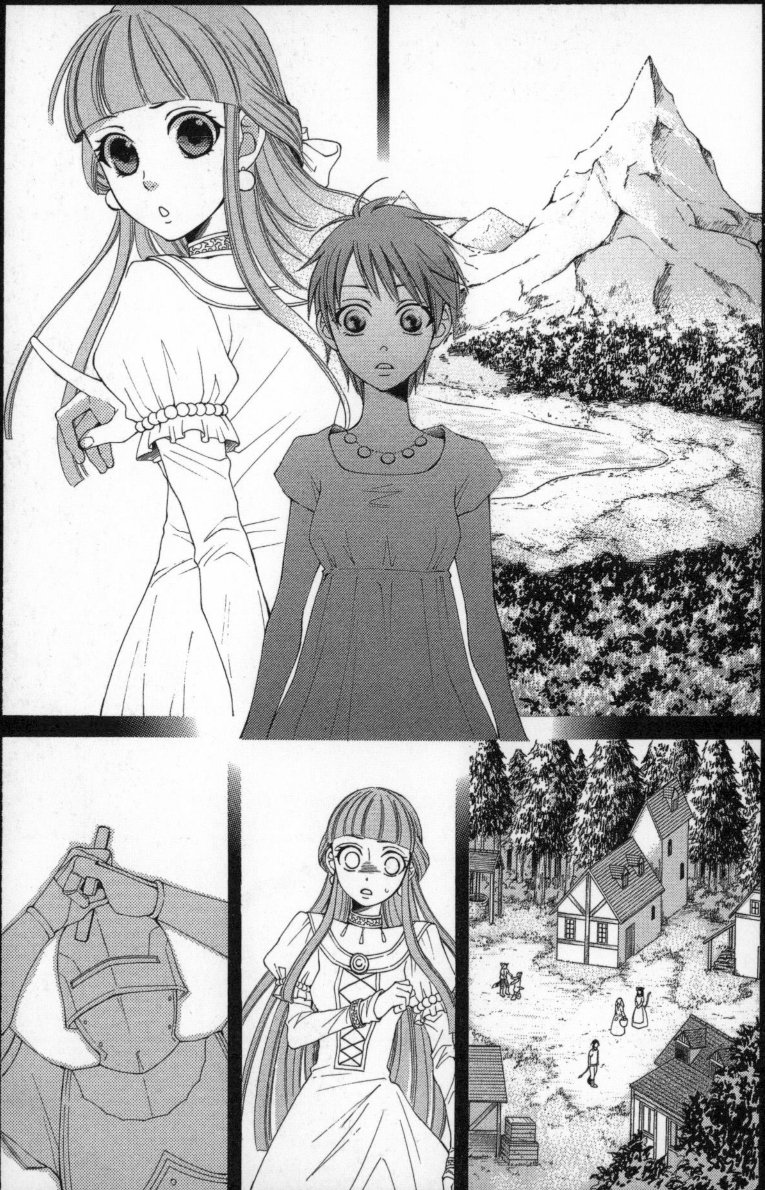

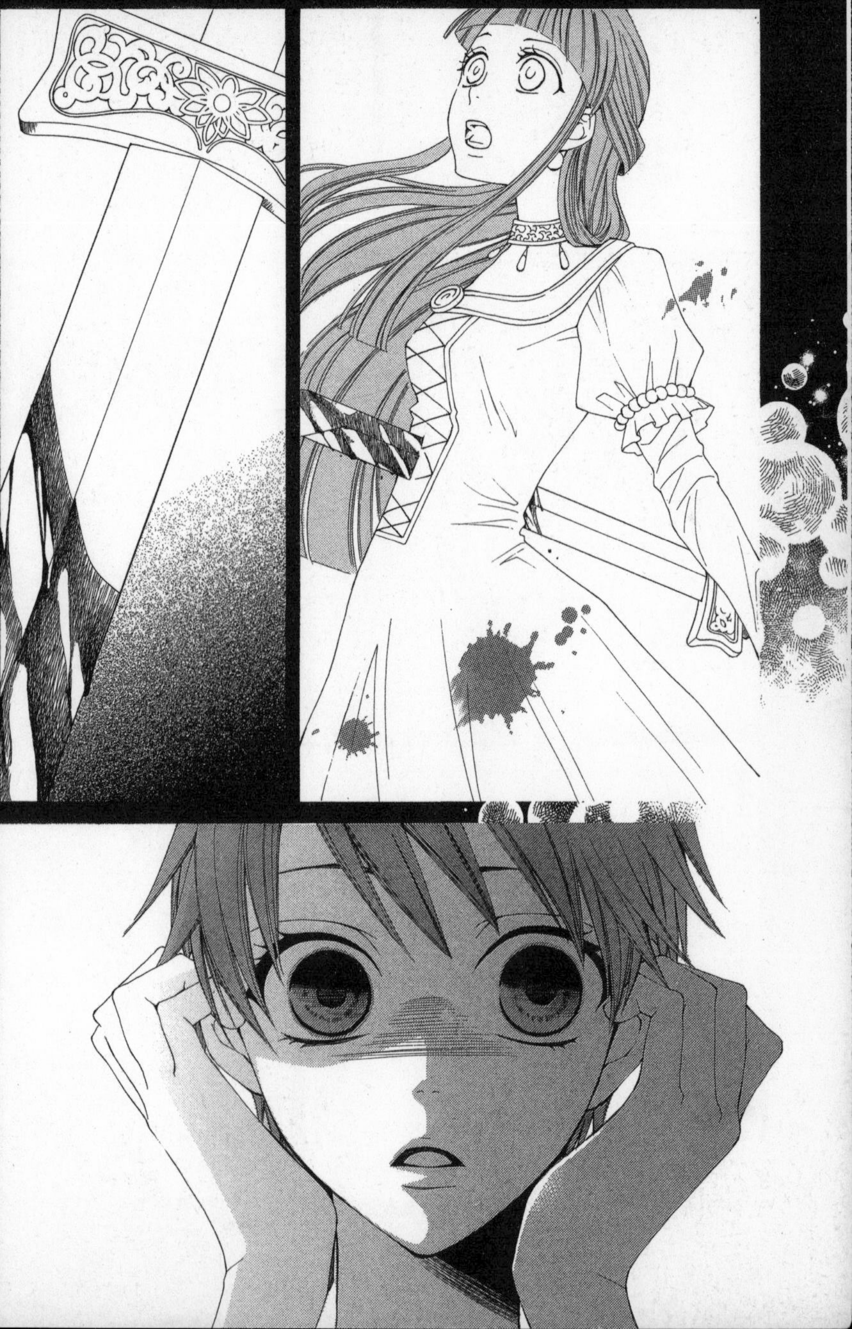

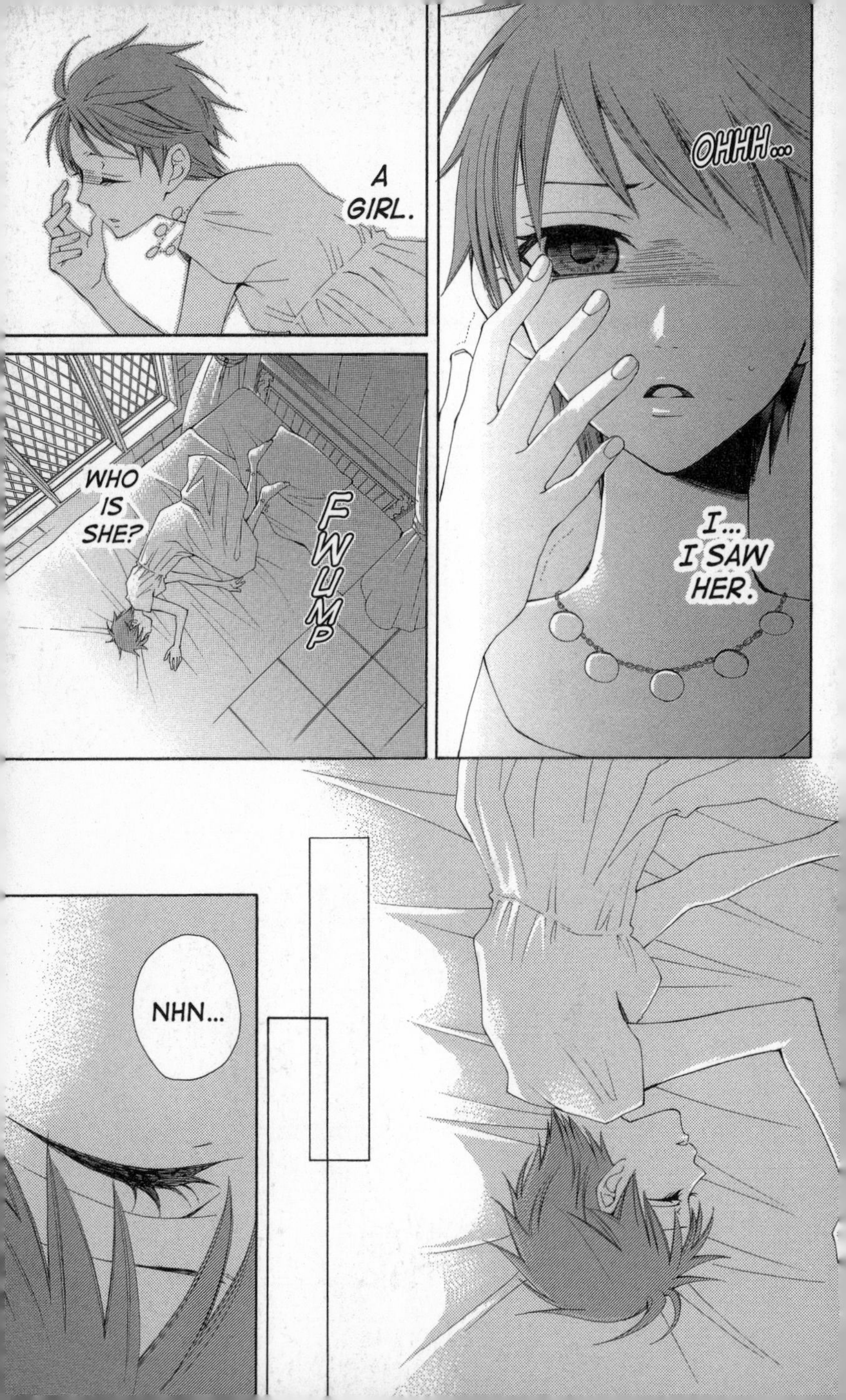
OHHH...
I...
I SAW HER.
A GIRL.
WHO IS SHE?
FWUMP
NHN...

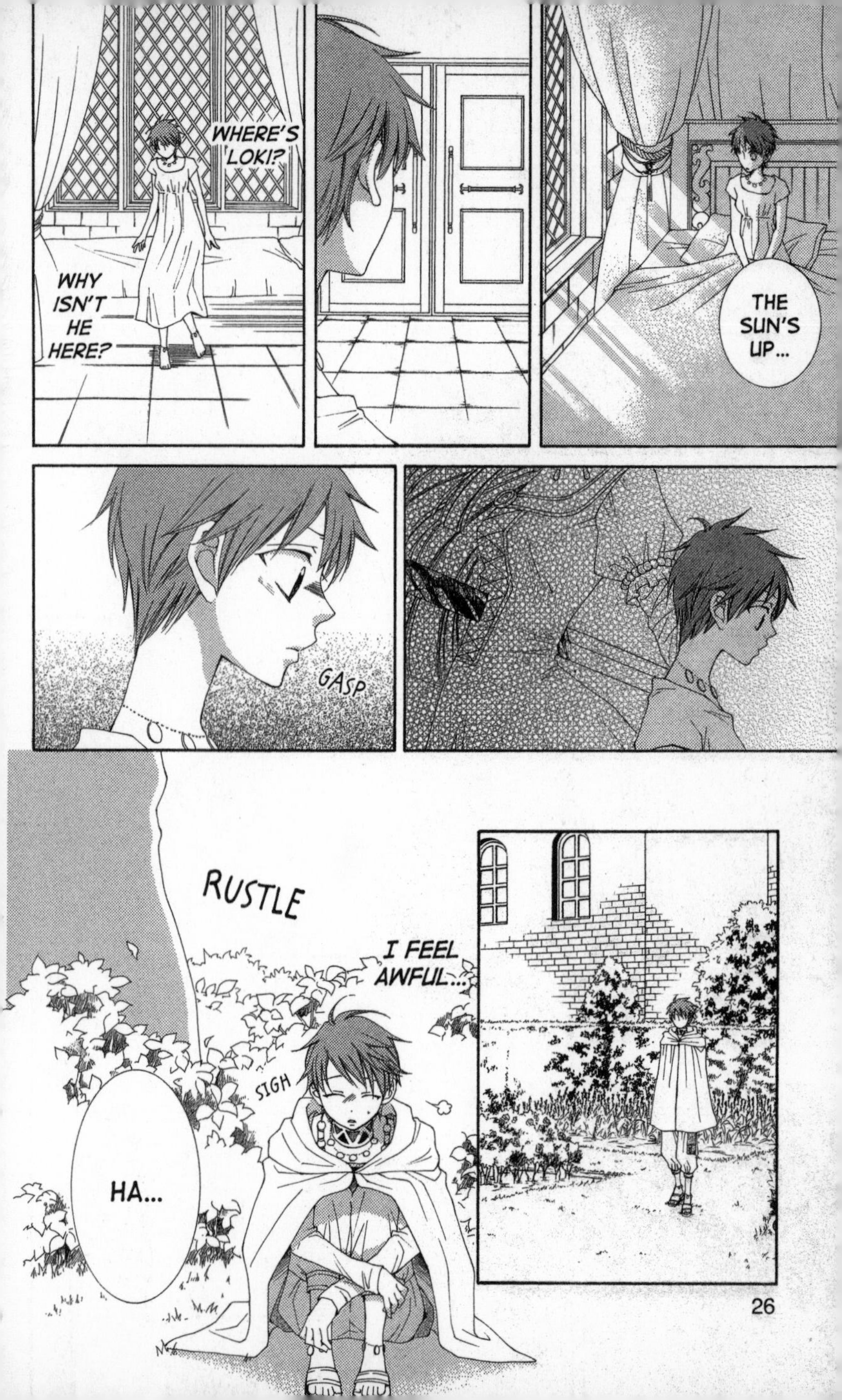
THE SUN'S UP...
WHERE'S LOKI?
WHY ISN'T HE HERE?
GASP
RUSTLE
I FEEL AWFUL...
SIGH
HA...

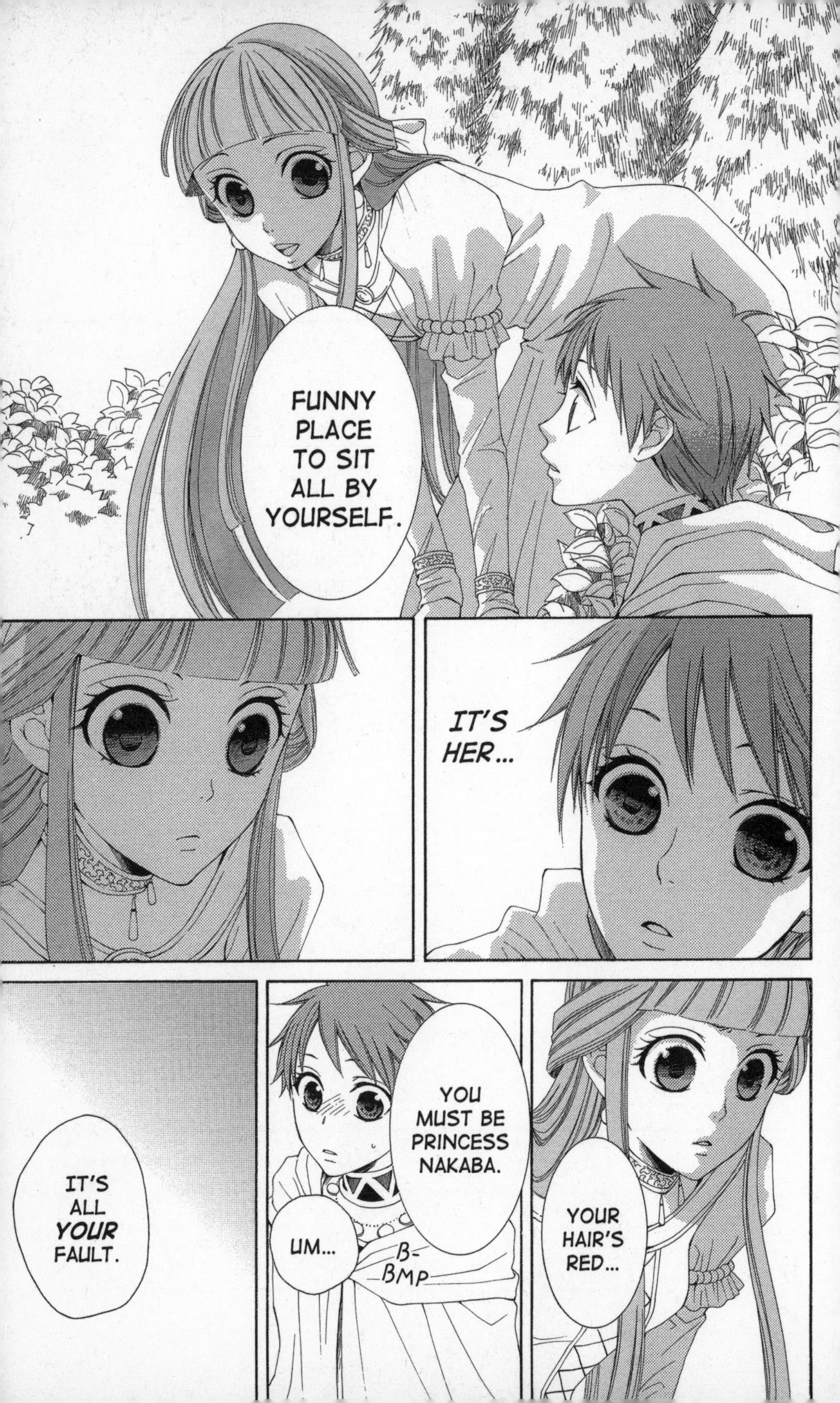
FUNNY PLACE TO SIT ALL BY YOURSELF.
IT'S HER...
YOUR HAIR'S RED...
YOU MUST BE PRINCESS NAKABA.
B-BMP
UM...
IT'S ALL *YOUR* FAULT.

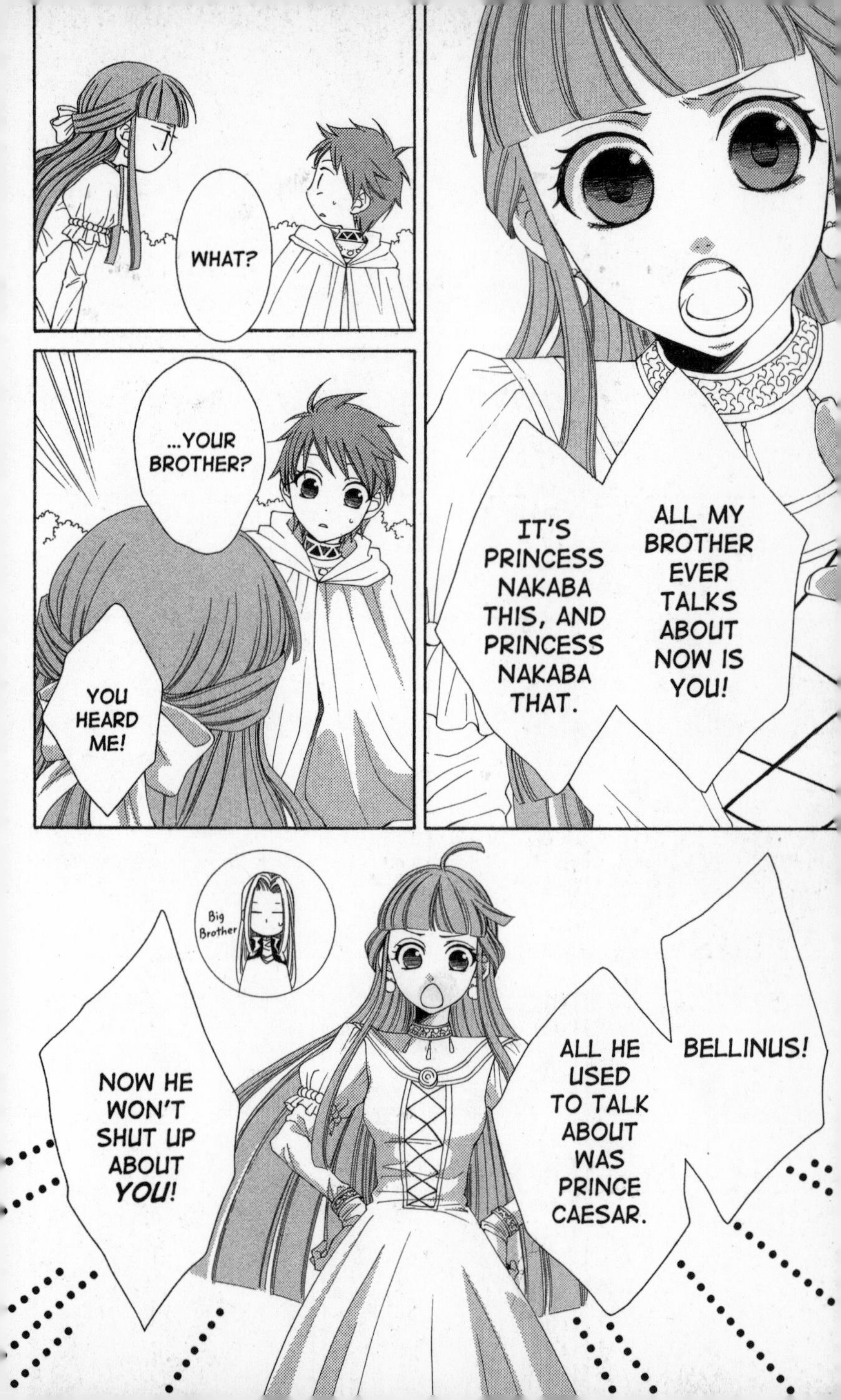
ALL MY BROTHER EVER TALKS ABOUT NOW IS YOU!
IT'S PRINCESS NAKABA THIS, AND PRINCESS NAKABA THAT.
WHAT?
...YOUR BROTHER?
YOU HEARD ME!
BELLINUS!
ALL HE USED TO TALK ABOUT WAS PRINCE CAESAR.
Big Brother
NOW HE WON'T SHUT UP ABOUT *YOU*!

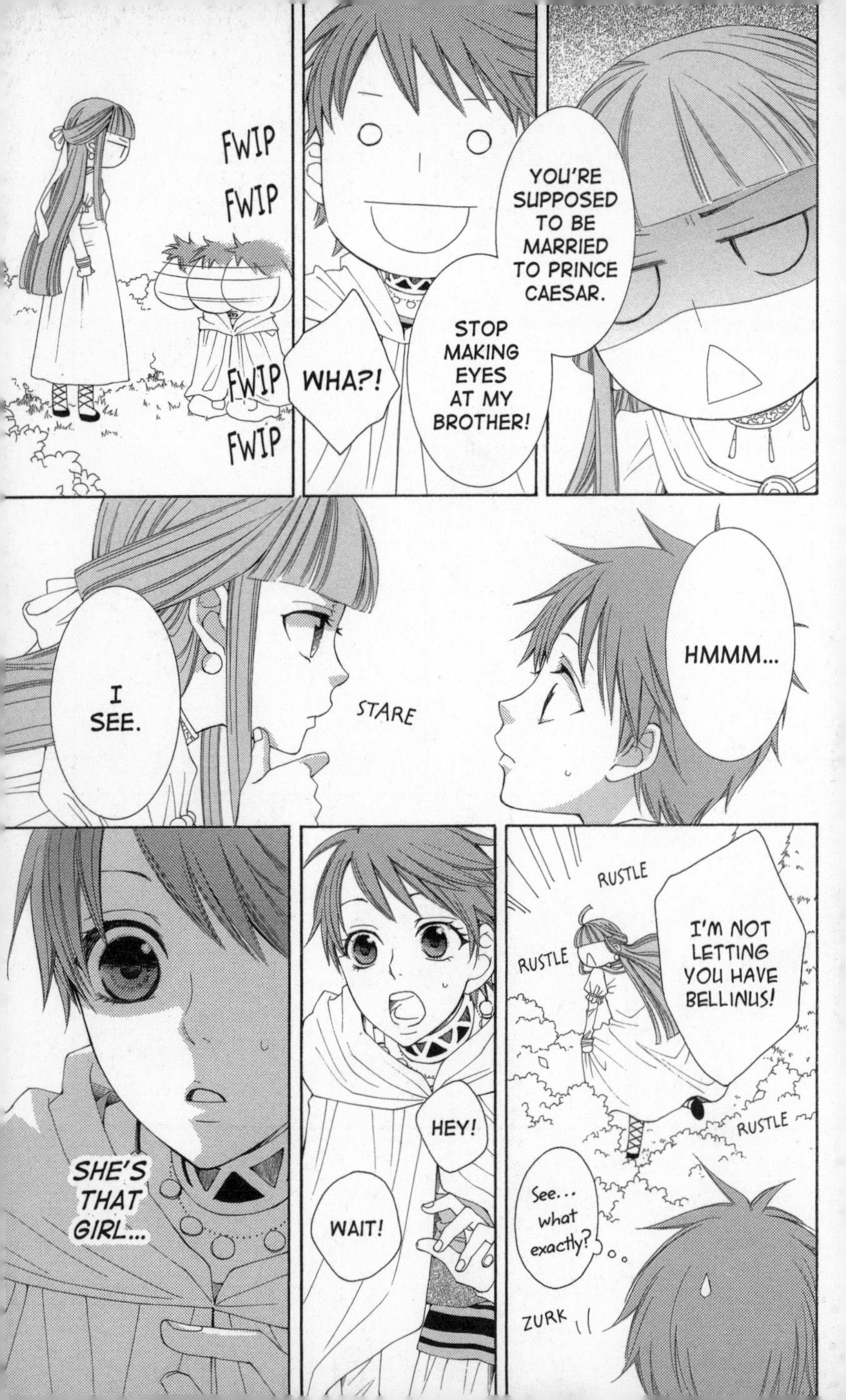

YOU'RE SUPPOSED TO BE MARRIED TO PRINCE CAESAR.
STOP MAKING EYES AT MY BROTHER!
WHA?!
FWIP
FWIP
FWIP
FWIP
HMMM...
STARE
I SEE.
RUSTLE
I'M NOT LETTING YOU HAVE BELLINUS!
RUSTLE
RUSTLE
See... what exactly?
ZURK
HEY!
WAIT!
SHE'S THAT GIRL...

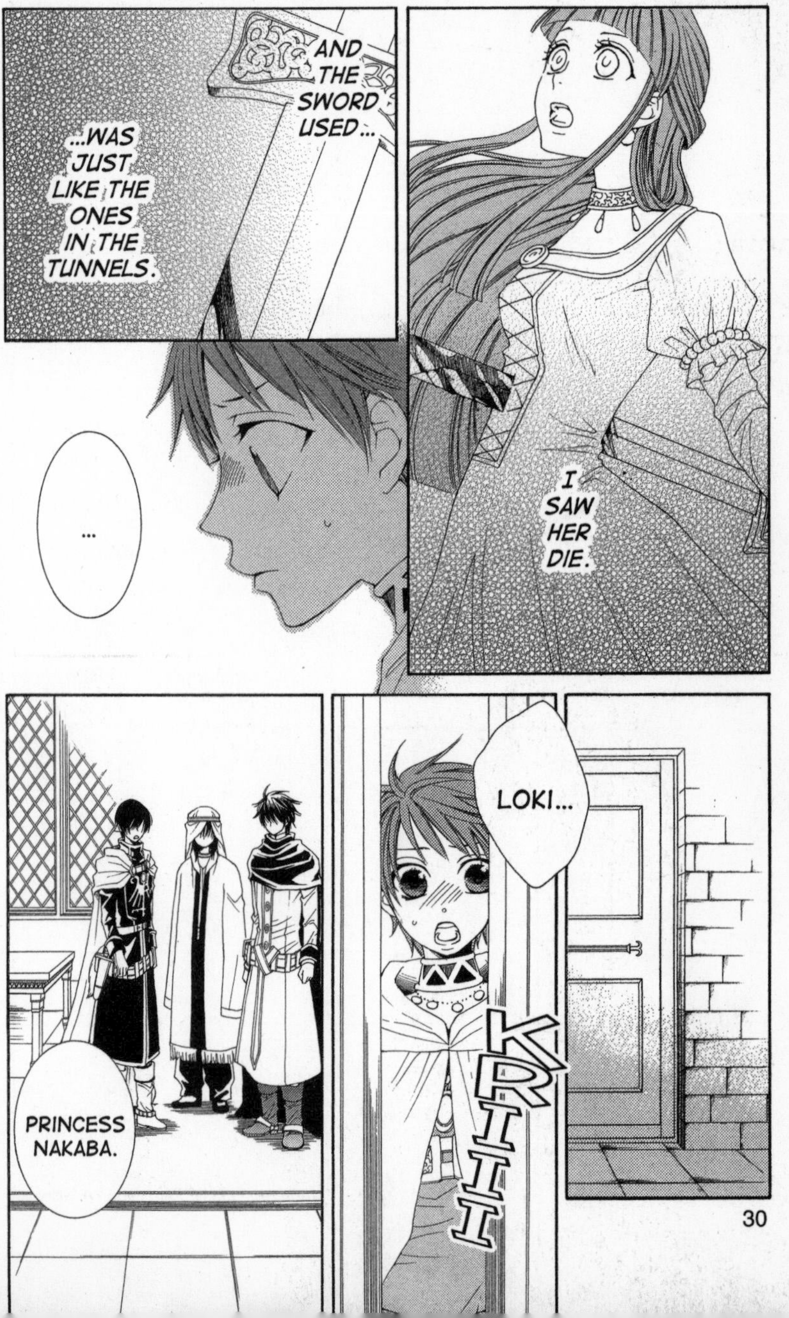
I SAW HER DIE.
AND THE SWORD USED...
...WAS JUST LIKE THE ONES IN THE TUNNELS.
...
LOKI...
KRIIII
PRINCESS NAKABA.

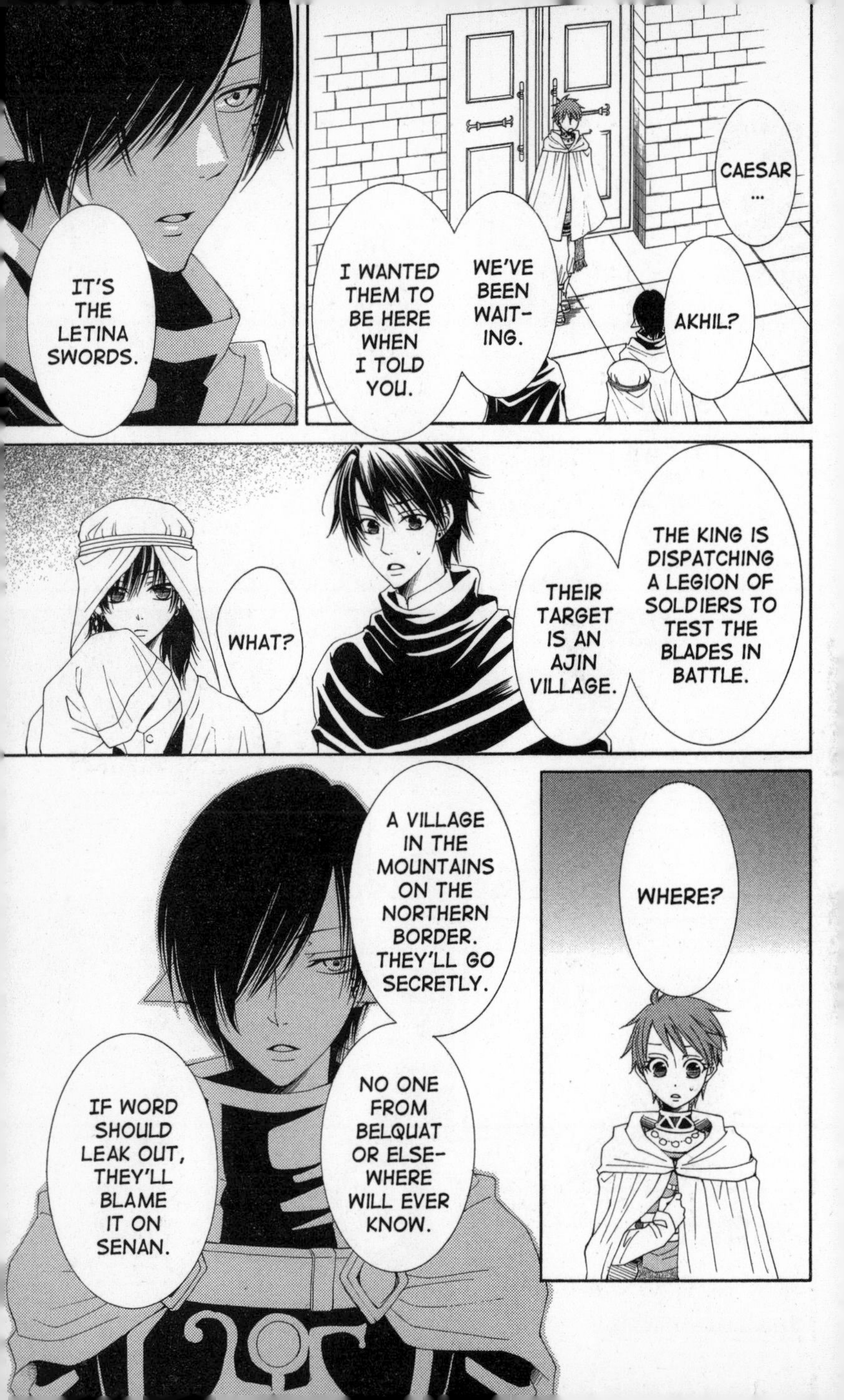

CAESAR...
AKHIL?
WE'VE BEEN WAITING.
I WANTED THEM TO BE HERE WHEN I TOLD YOU.
IT'S THE LETINA SWORDS.
THE KING IS DISPATCHING A LEGION OF SOLDIERS TO TEST THE BLADES IN BATTLE.
THEIR TARGET IS AN AJIN VILLAGE.
WHAT?
WHERE?
A VILLAGE IN THE MOUNTAINS ON THE NORTHERN BORDER. THEY'LL GO SECRETLY.
NO ONE FROM BELQUAT OR ELSEWHERE WILL EVER KNOW.
IF WORD SHOULD LEAK OUT, THEY'LL BLAME IT ON SENAN.

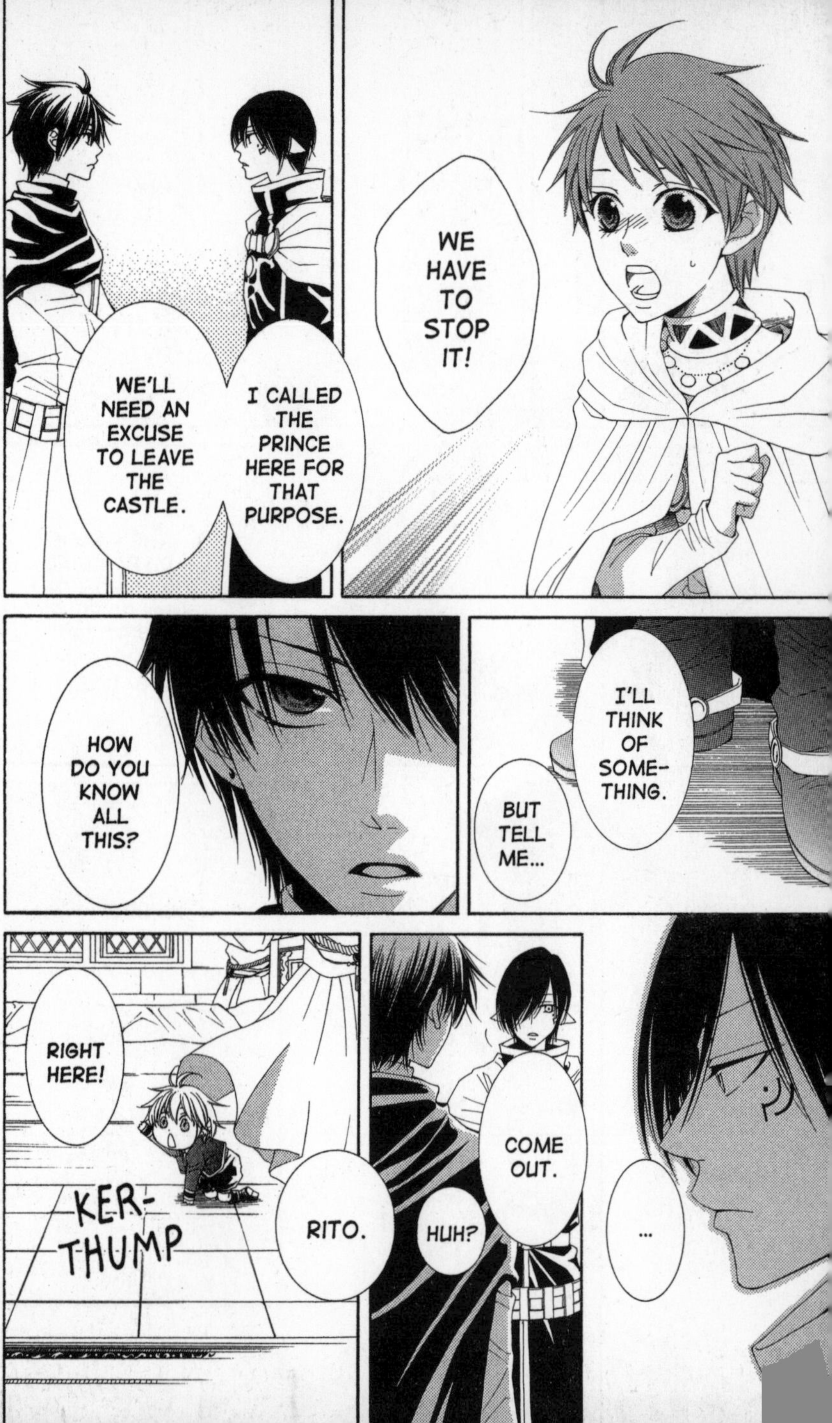
WE HAVE TO STOP IT!
I CALLED THE PRINCE HERE FOR THAT PURPOSE.
WE'LL NEED AN EXCUSE TO LEAVE THE CASTLE.
I'LL THINK OF SOME-THING.
BUT TELL ME...
HOW DO YOU KNOW ALL THIS?
...
COME OUT.
HUH?
RITO.
RIGHT HERE!
KER-THUMP

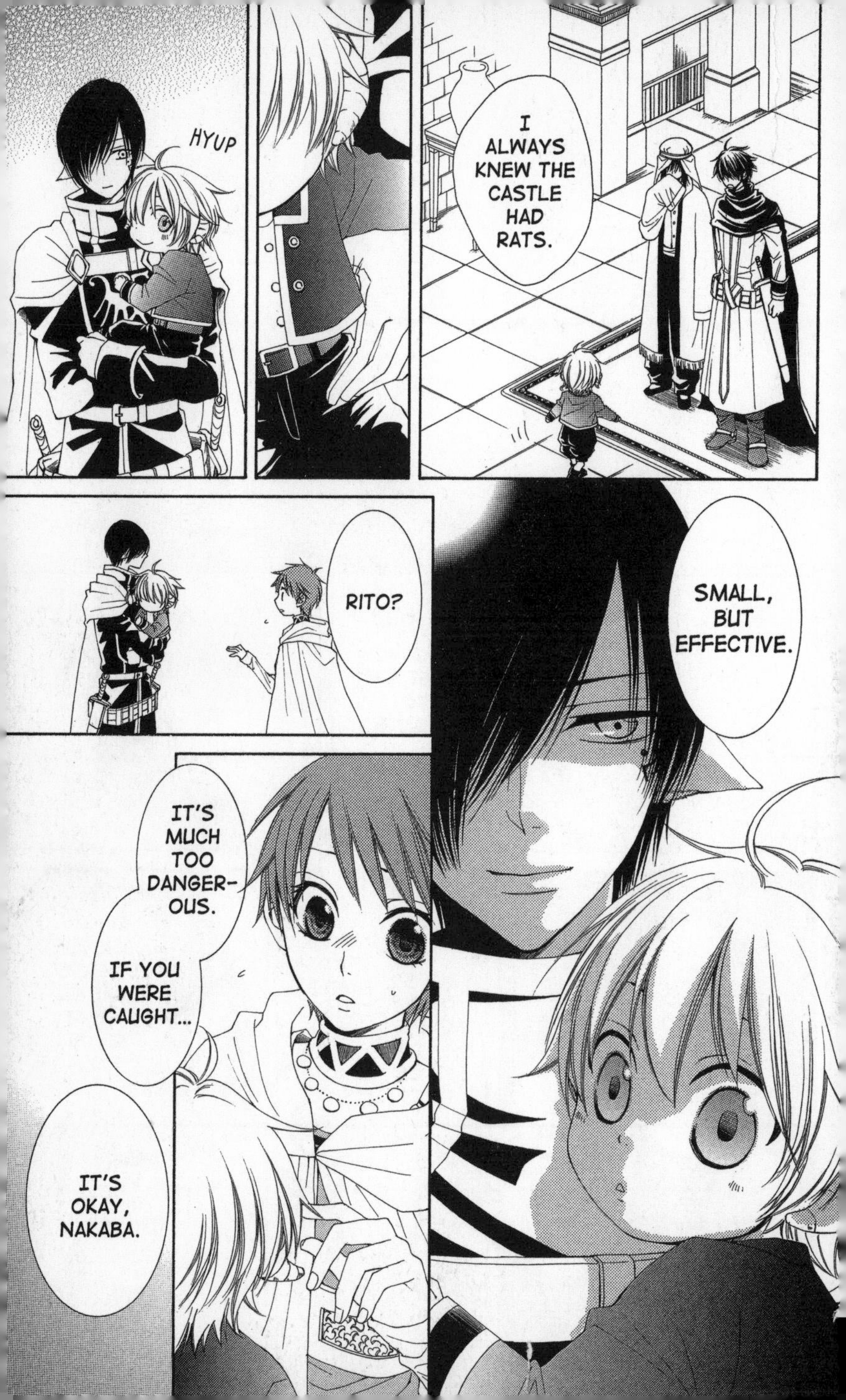
I ALWAYS KNEW THE CASTLE HAD RATS.
HYUP
SMALL, BUT EFFECTIVE.
RITO?
IT'S MUCH TOO DANGER-OUS.
IF YOU WERE CAUGHT...
IT'S OKAY, NAKABA.

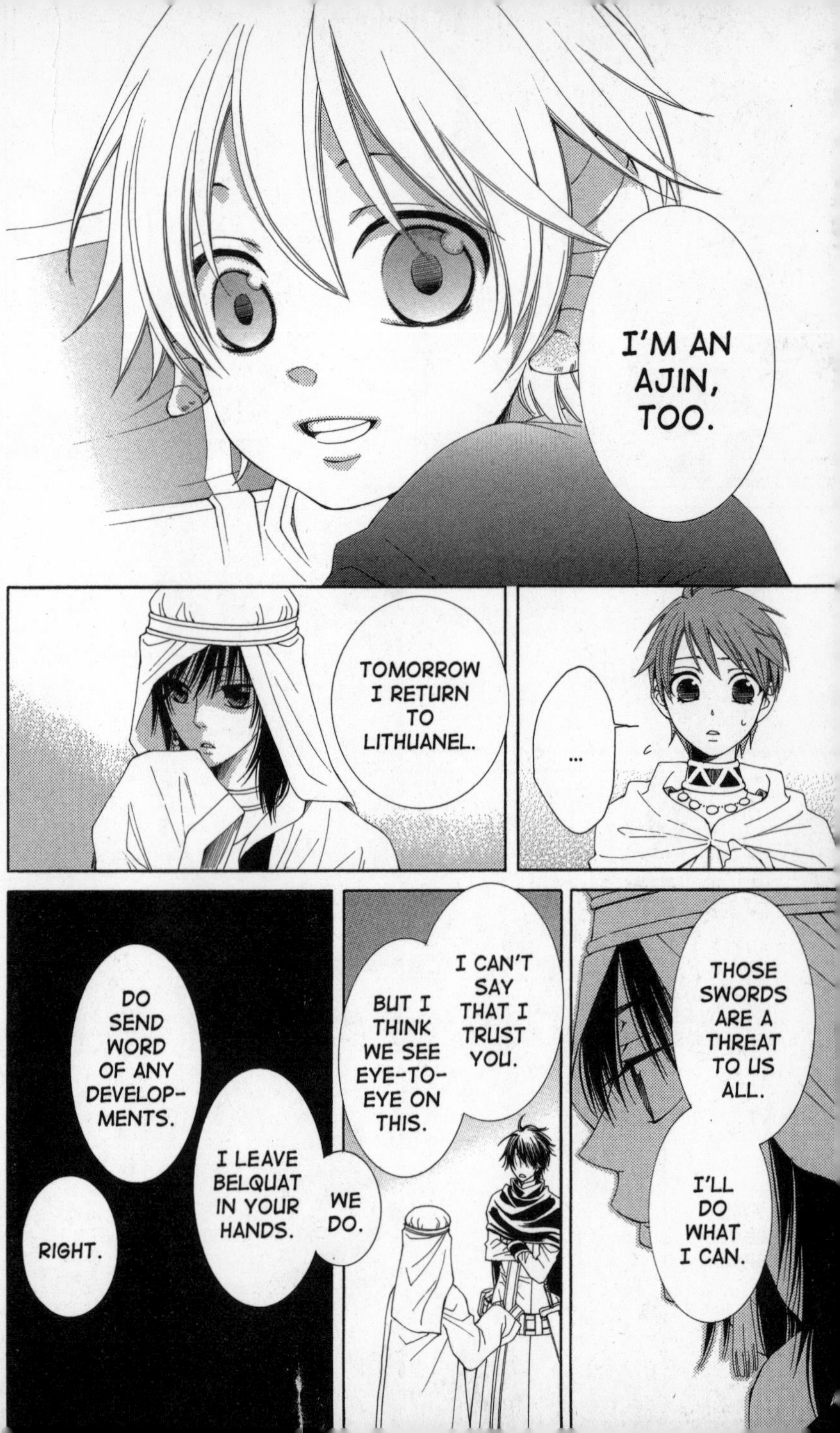
I'M AN AJIN, TOO.
...
TOMORROW I RETURN TO LITHUANEL.
THOSE SWORDS ARE A THREAT TO US ALL.
I'LL DO WHAT I CAN.
I CAN'T SAY THAT I TRUST YOU.
BUT I THINK WE SEE EYE-TO-EYE ON THIS.
WE DO.
I LEAVE BELQUAT IN YOUR HANDS.
DO SEND WORD OF ANY DEVELOP-MENTS.
RIGHT.

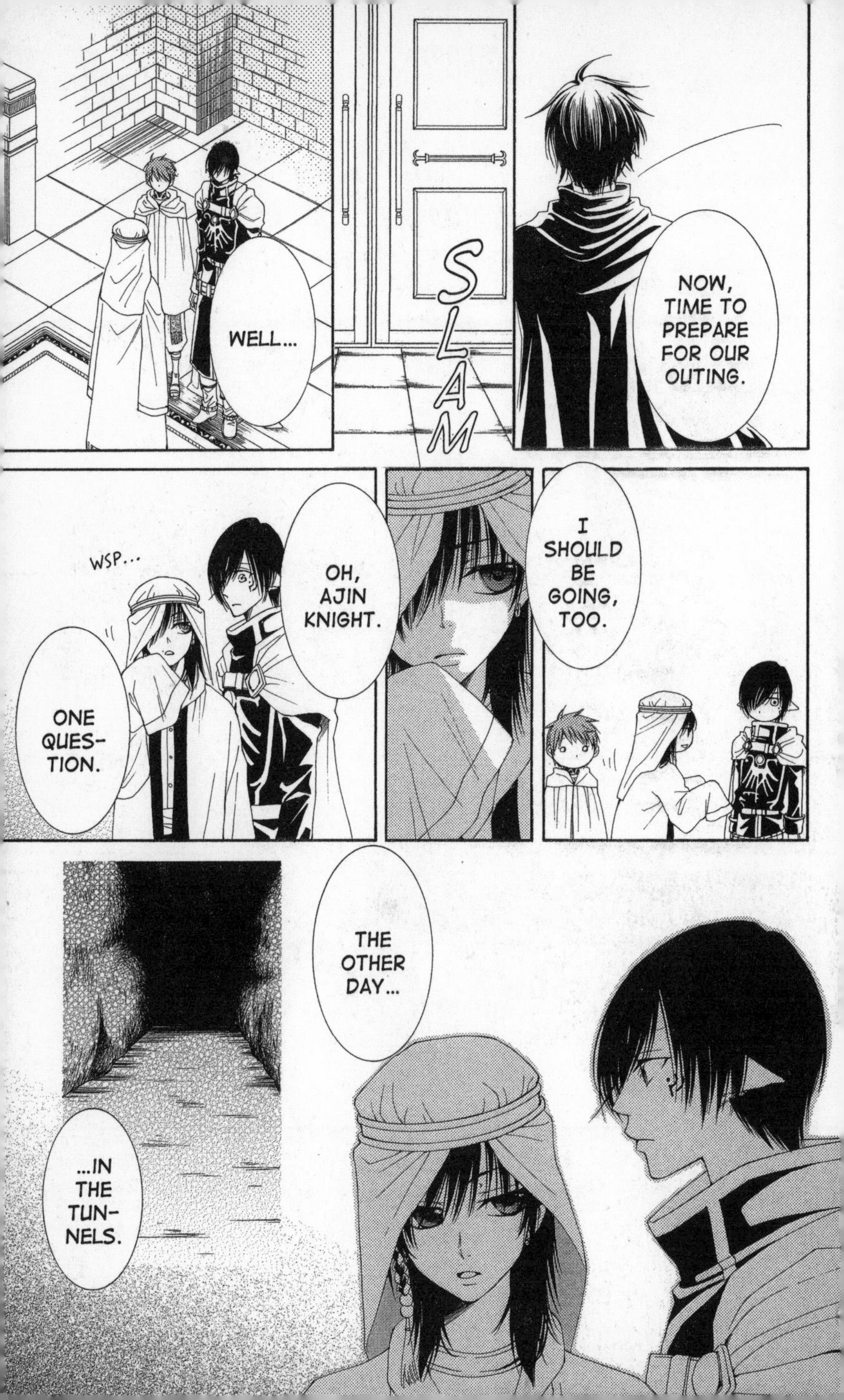
NOW, TIME TO PREPARE FOR OUR OUTING.
SLAM
WELL...
I SHOULD BE GOING, TOO.
OH, AJIN KNIGHT.
WSP...
ONE QUES-TION.
THE OTHER DAY...
...IN THE TUN-NELS.

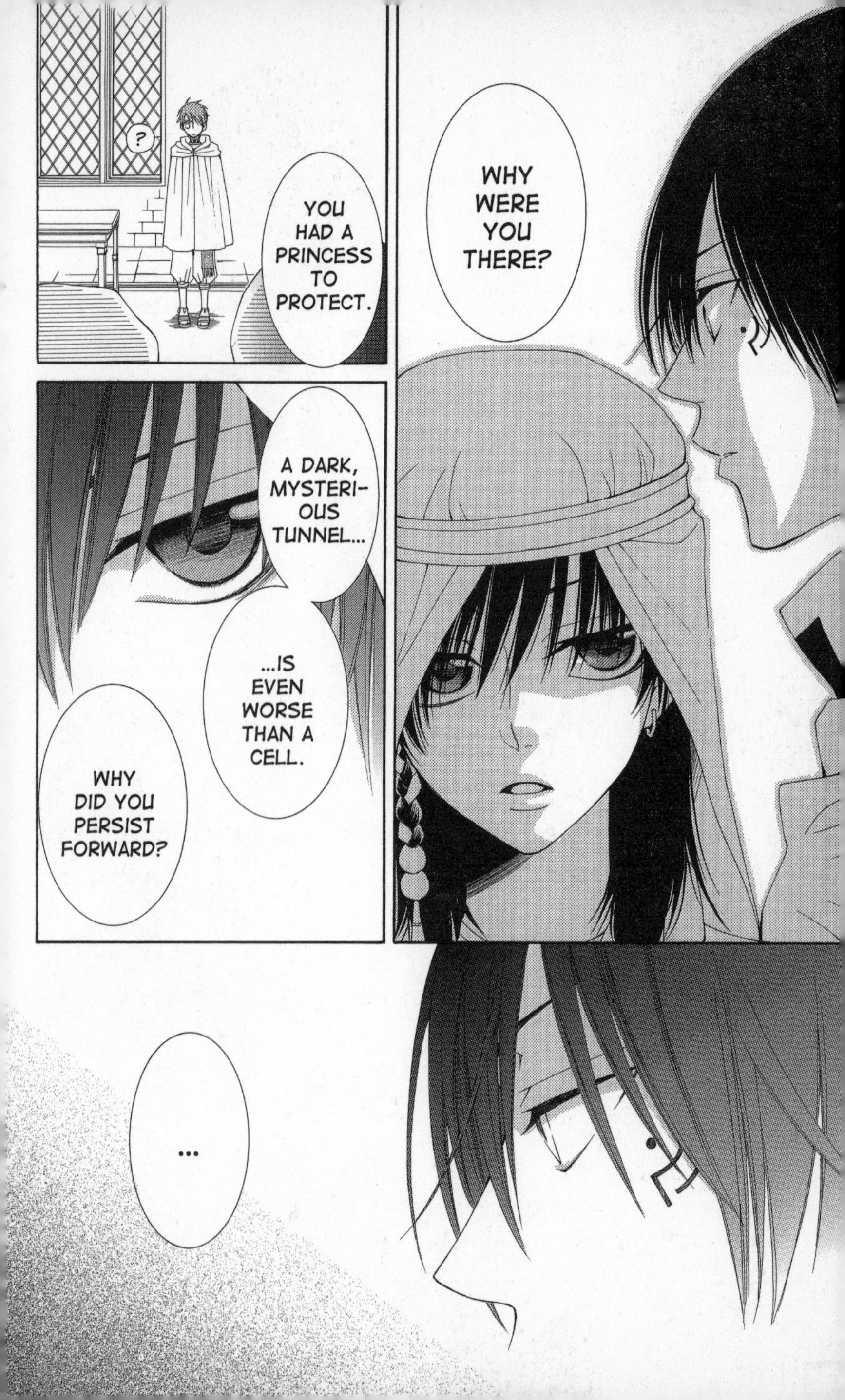
WHY WERE YOU THERE?
?
YOU HAD A PRINCESS TO PROTECT.
A DARK, MYSTERI-OUS TUNNEL...
...IS EVEN WORSE THAN A CELL.
WHY DID YOU PERSIST FORWARD?
...

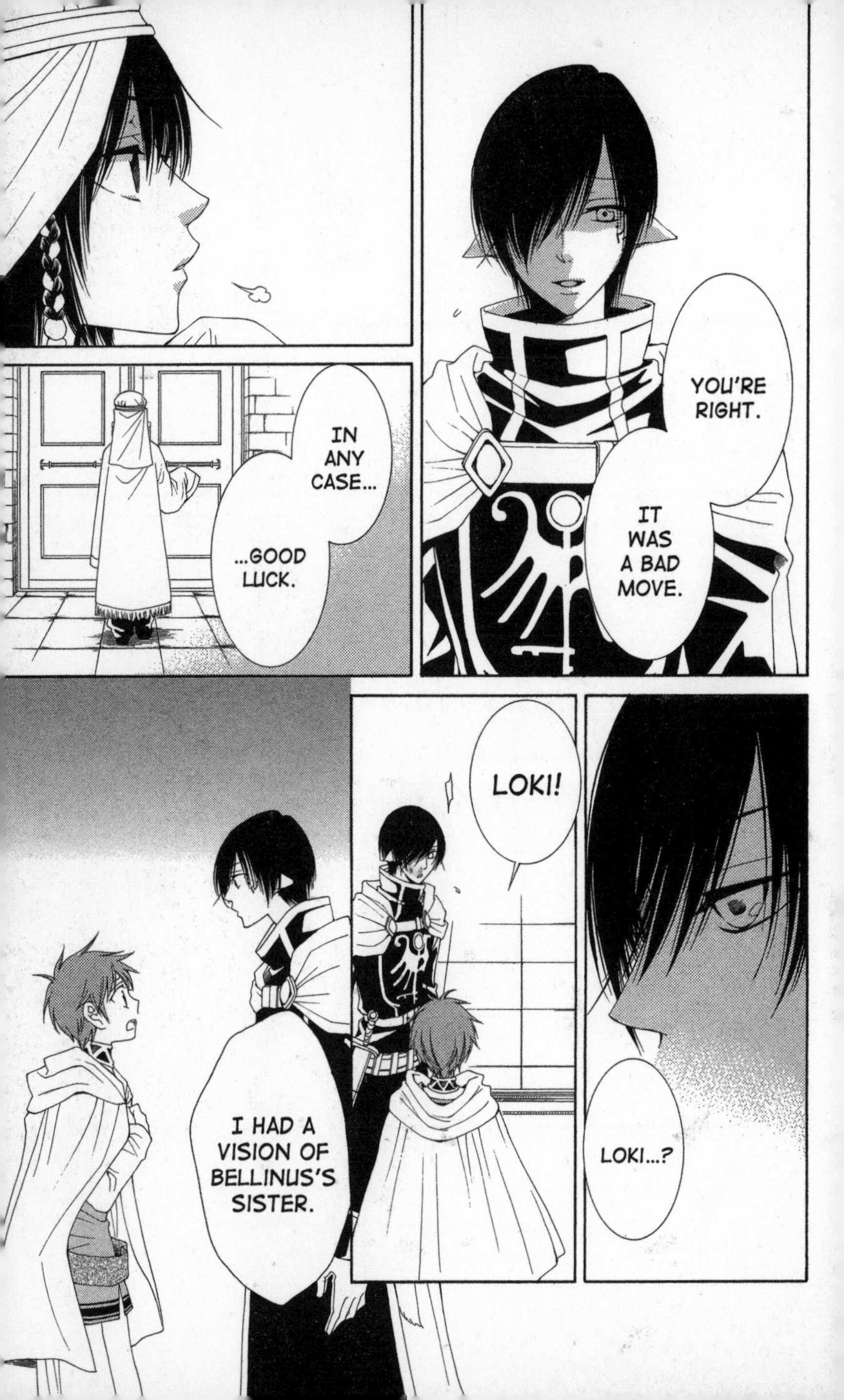
YOU'RE RIGHT.
IT WAS A BAD MOVE.
IN ANY CASE...
...GOOD LUCK.
LOKI...?
LOKI!
I HAD A VISION OF BELLINUS'S SISTER.

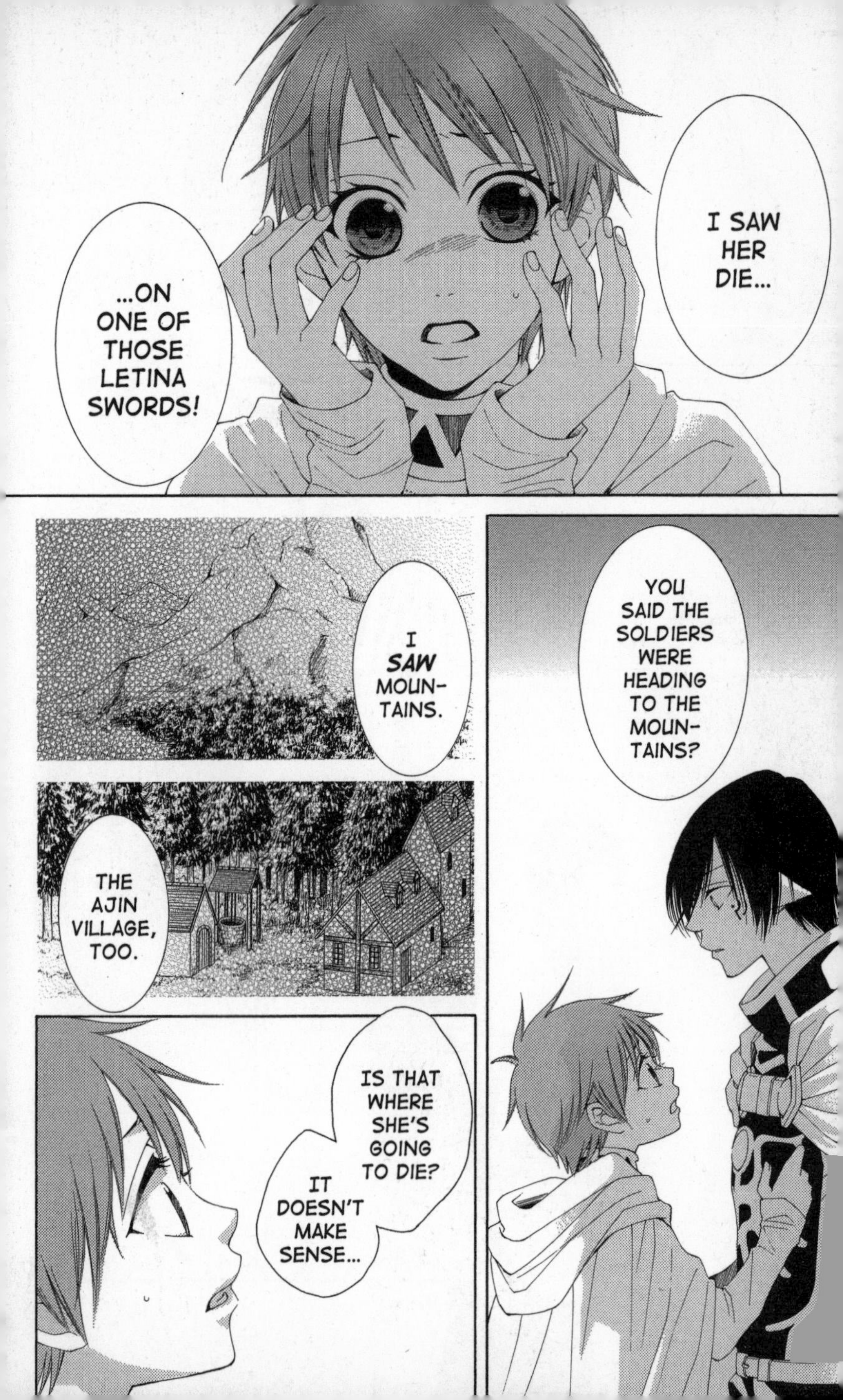
I SAW HER DIE...
...ON ONE OF THOSE LETINA SWORDS!
YOU SAID THE SOLDIERS WERE HEADING TO THE MOUN-TAINS?
I *SAW* MOUN-TAINS.
THE AJIN VILLAGE, TOO.
IS THAT WHERE SHE'S GOING TO DIE?
IT DOESN'T MAKE SENSE...

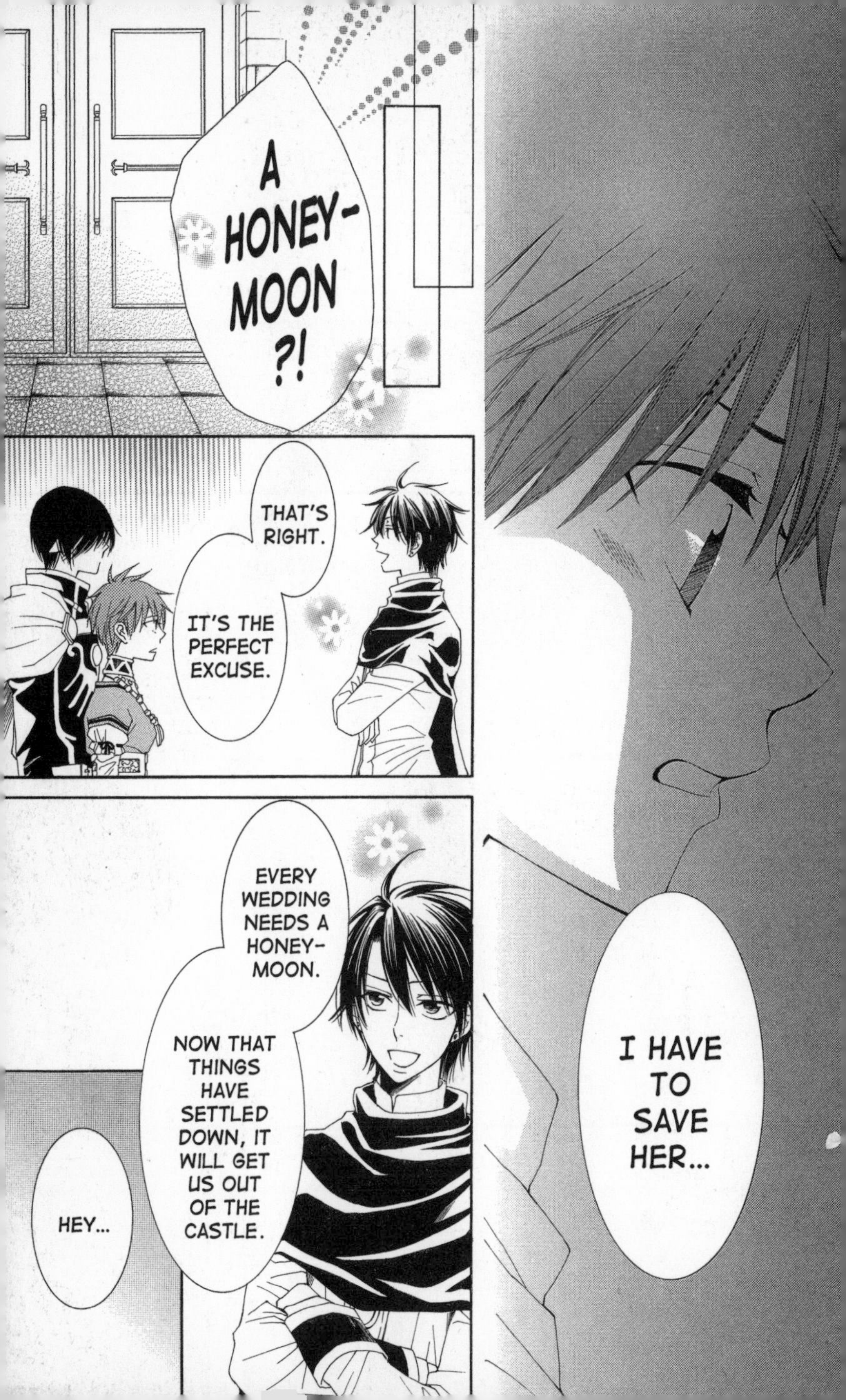
I HAVE TO SAVE HER...
A HONEY-MOON?!
THAT'S RIGHT.
IT'S THE PERFECT EXCUSE.
EVERY WEDDING NEEDS A HONEY-MOON.
NOW THAT THINGS HAVE SETTLED DOWN, IT WILL GET US OUT OF THE CASTLE.
HEY...

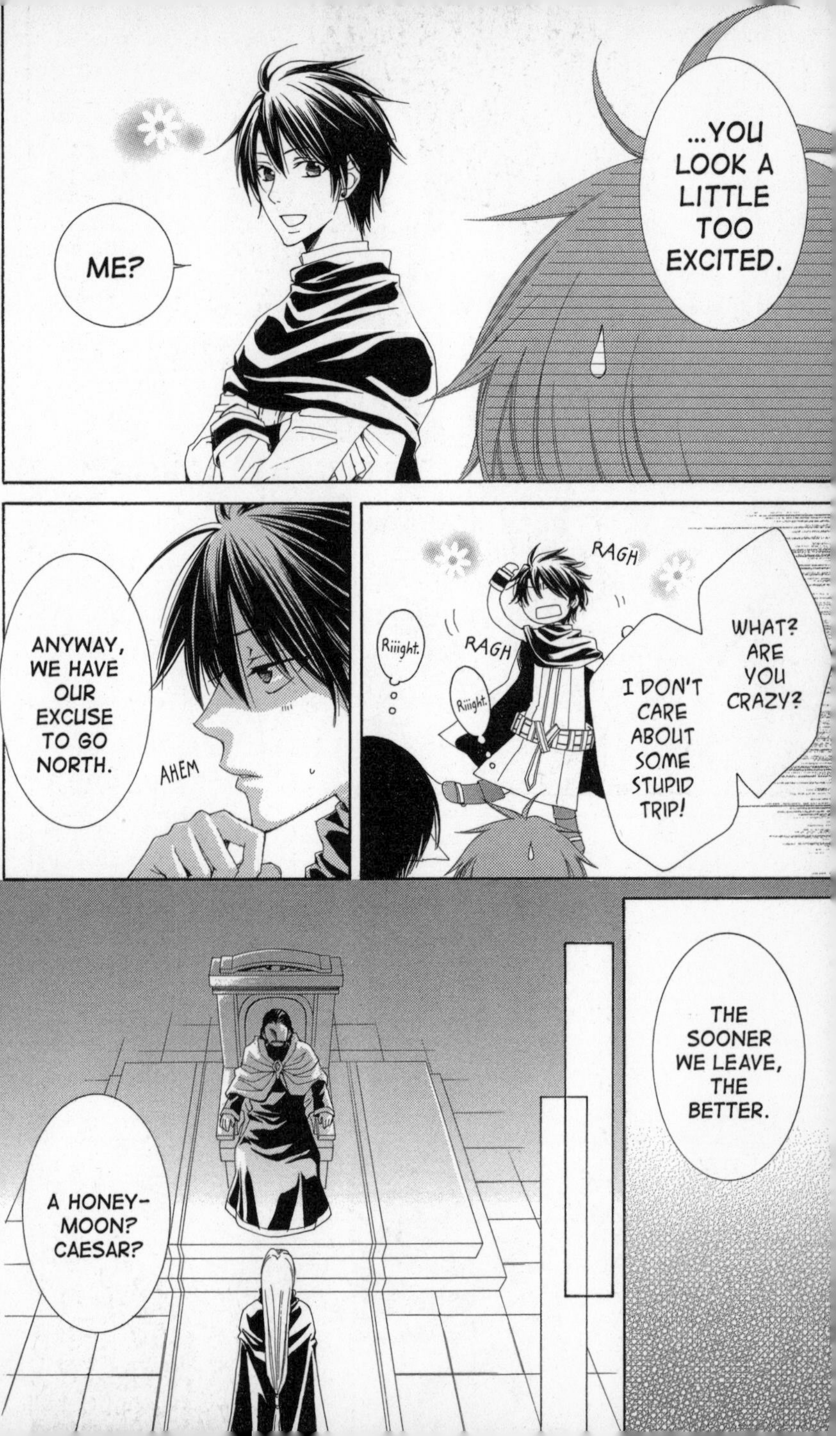
...YOU LOOK A LITTLE TOO EXCITED.
ME?
RAGH
WHAT? ARE YOU CRAZY?
I DON'T CARE ABOUT SOME STUPID TRIP!
RAGH
Riiight.
Riiight.
ANYWAY, WE HAVE OUR EXCUSE TO GO NORTH.
AHEM
THE SOONER WE LEAVE, THE BETTER.
A HONEY-MOON? CAESAR?

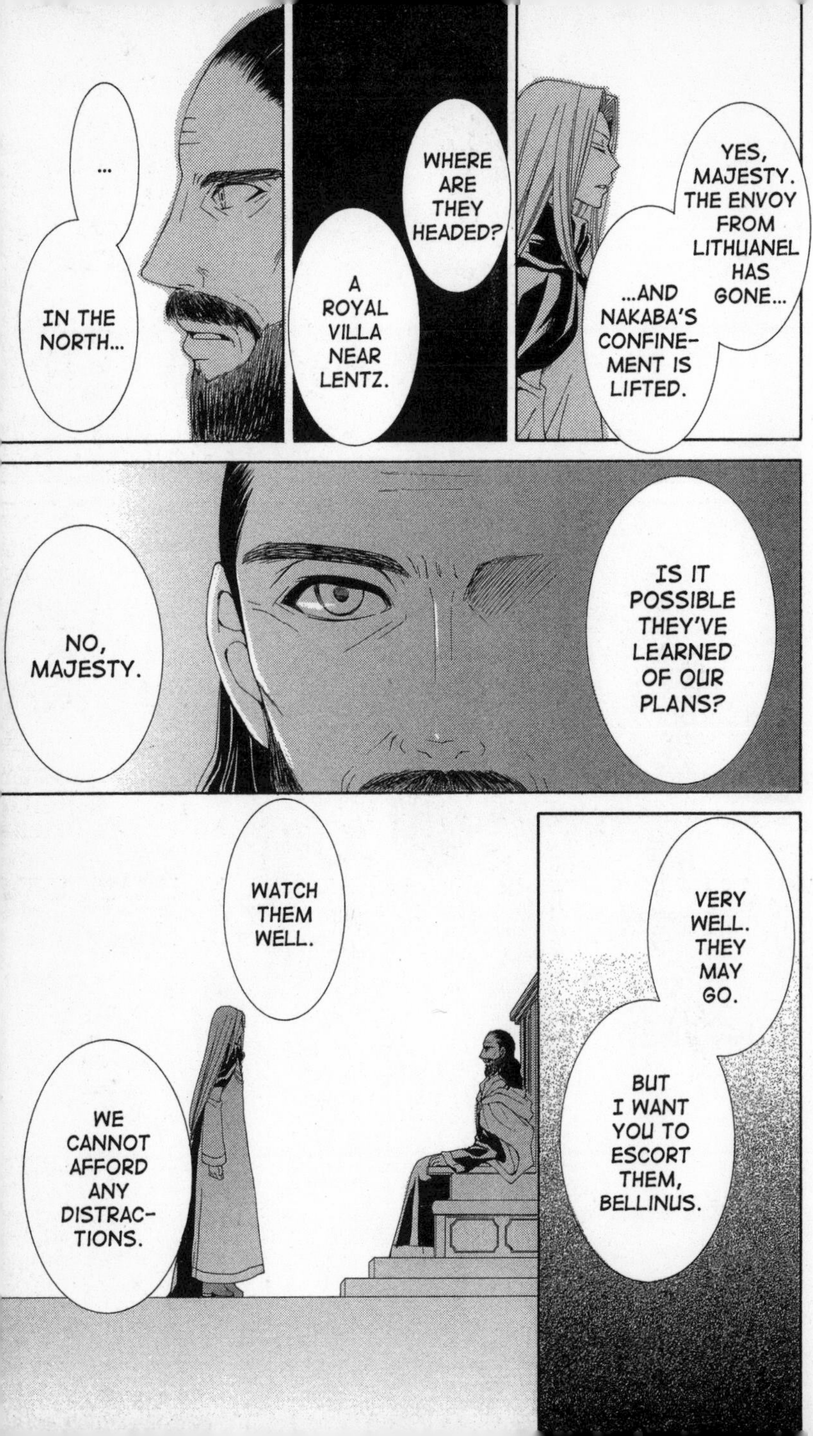
YES, MAJESTY. THE ENVOY FROM LITHUANEL HAS GONE...
...AND NAKABA'S CONFINEMENT IS LIFTED.
WHERE ARE THEY HEADED?
A ROYAL VILLA NEAR LENTZ.
...
IN THE NORTH...
IS IT POSSIBLE THEY'VE LEARNED OF OUR PLANS?
NO, MAJESTY.
VERY WELL. THEY MAY GO.
BUT I WANT YOU TO ESCORT THEM, BELLINUS.
WATCH THEM WELL.
WE CANNOT AFFORD ANY DISTRACTIONS.

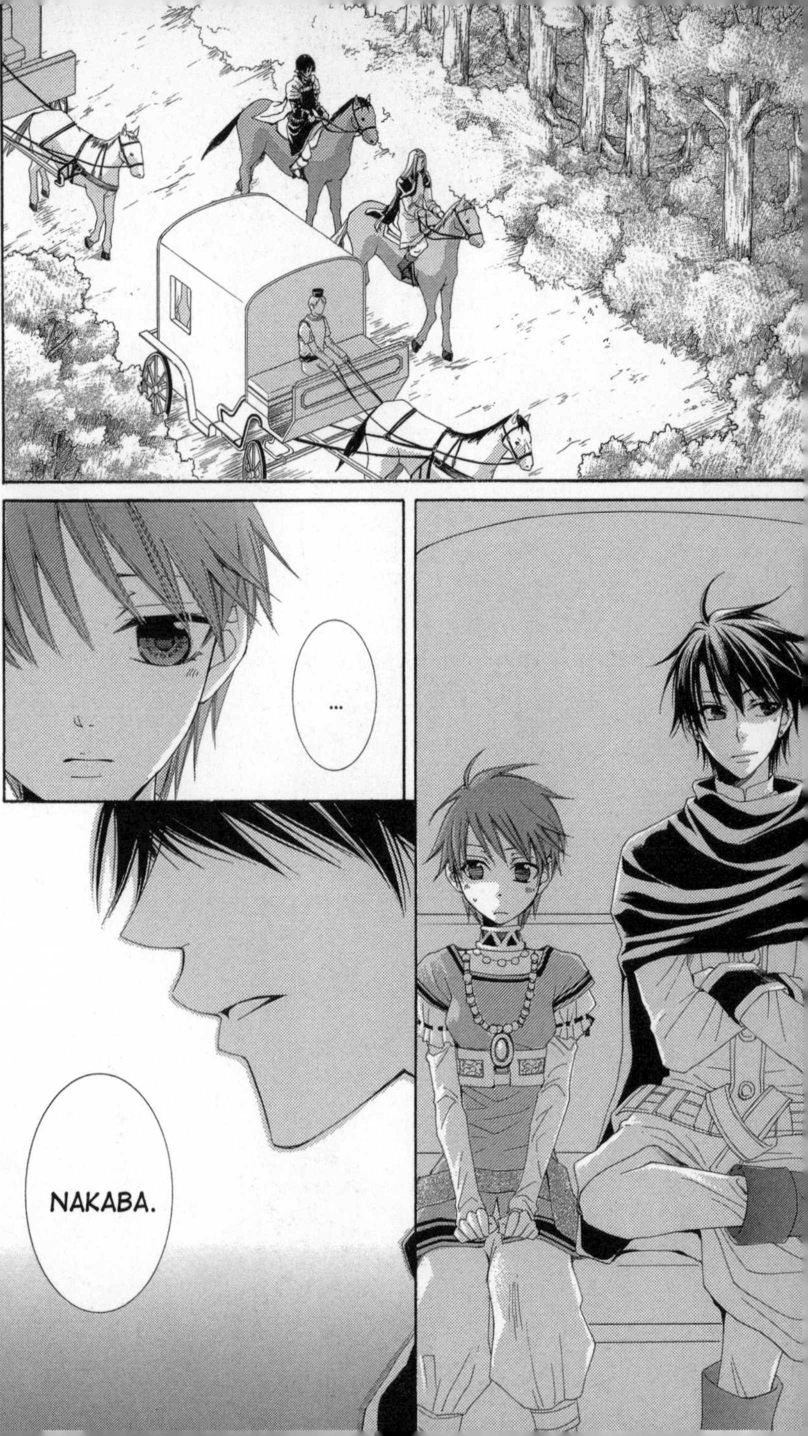
...
NAKABA.

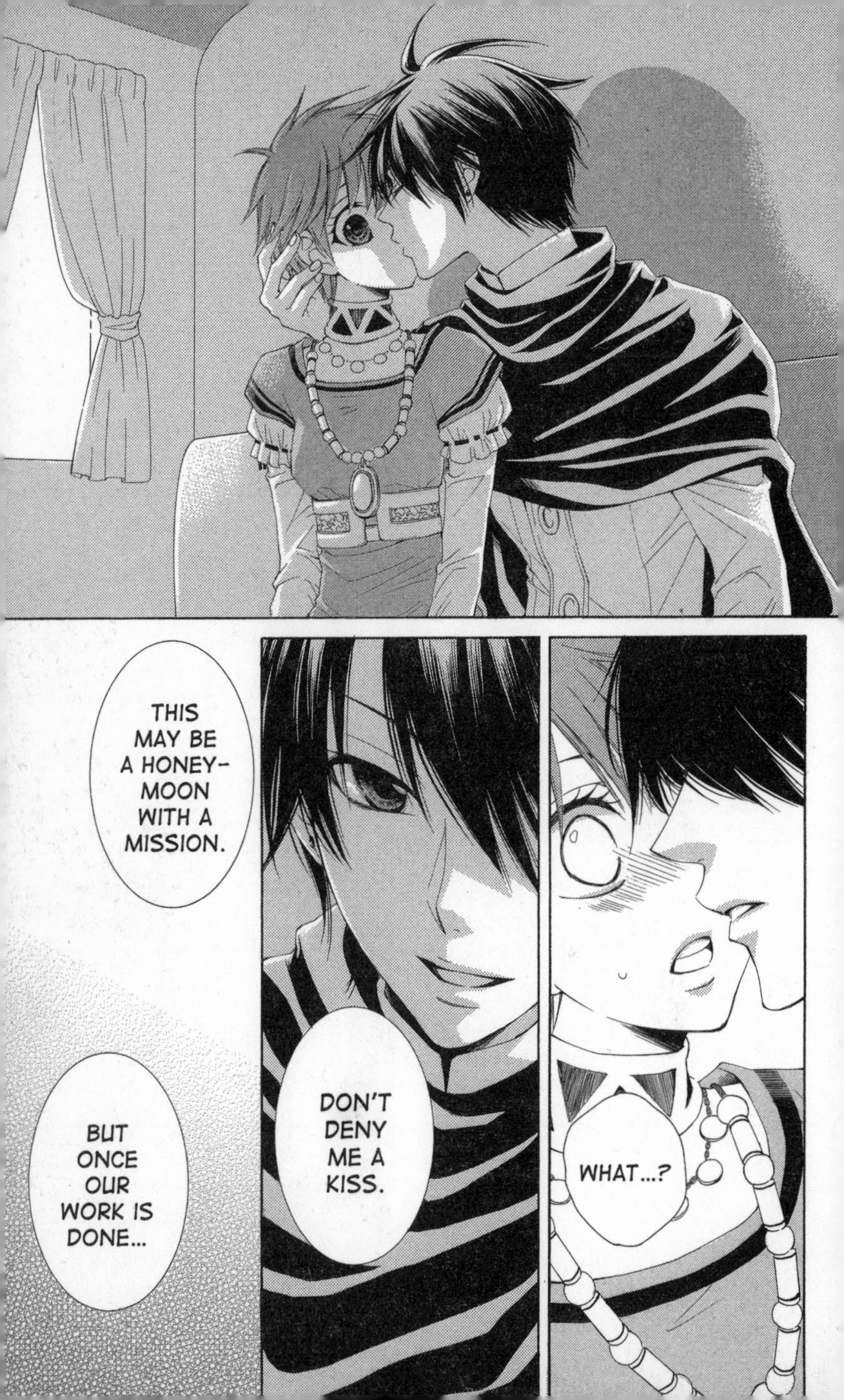
WHAT...?
THIS MAY BE A HONEY-MOON WITH A MISSION.
BUT ONCE OUR WORK IS DONE...
DON'T DENY ME A KISS.

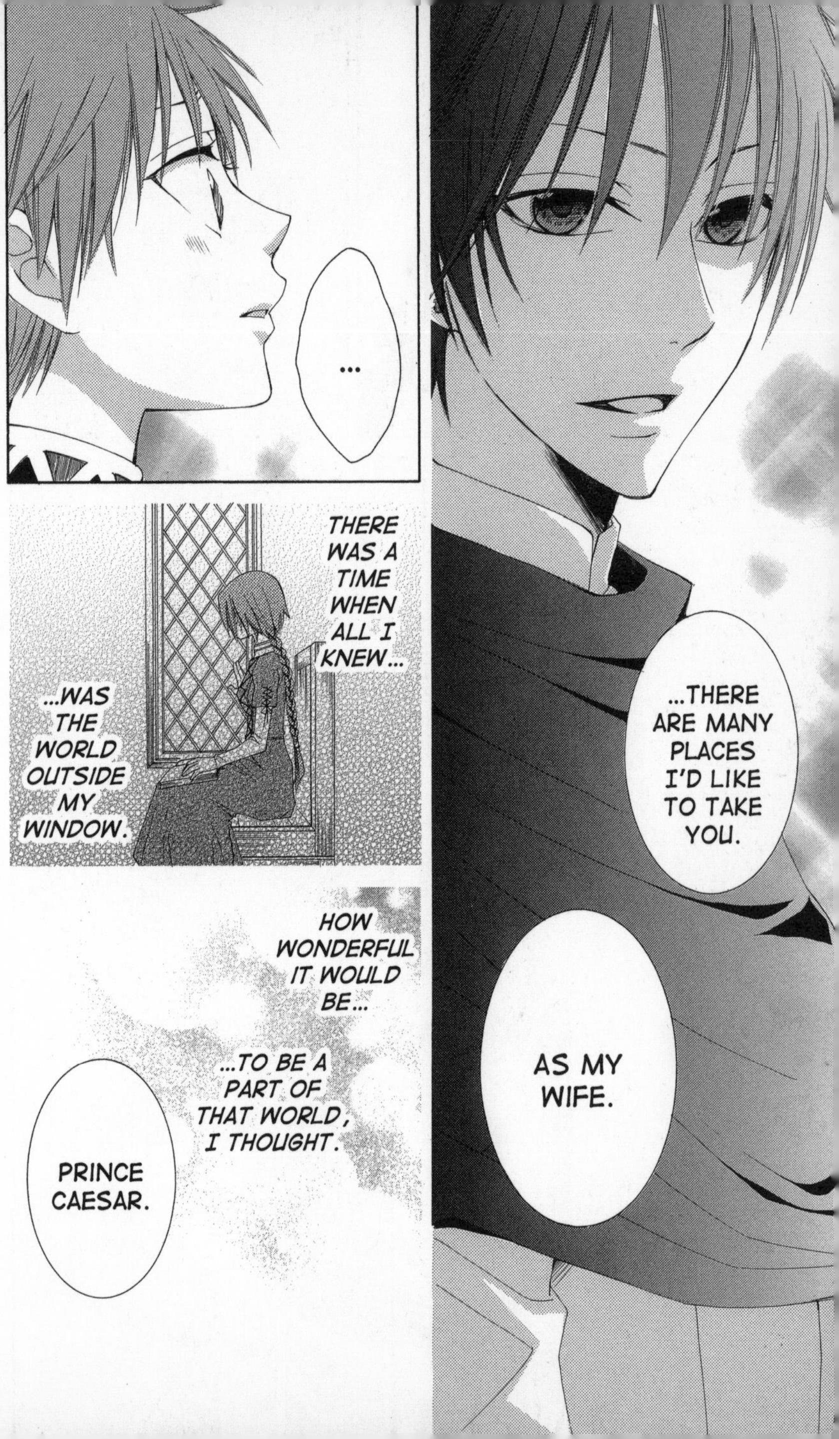
...THERE ARE MANY PLACES I'D LIKE TO TAKE YOU.
AS MY WIFE.
...
THERE WAS A TIME WHEN ALL I KNEW...
...WAS THE WORLD OUTSIDE MY WINDOW.
HOW WONDERFUL IT WOULD BE...
...TO BE A PART OF THAT WORLD, I THOUGHT.
PRINCE CAESAR.

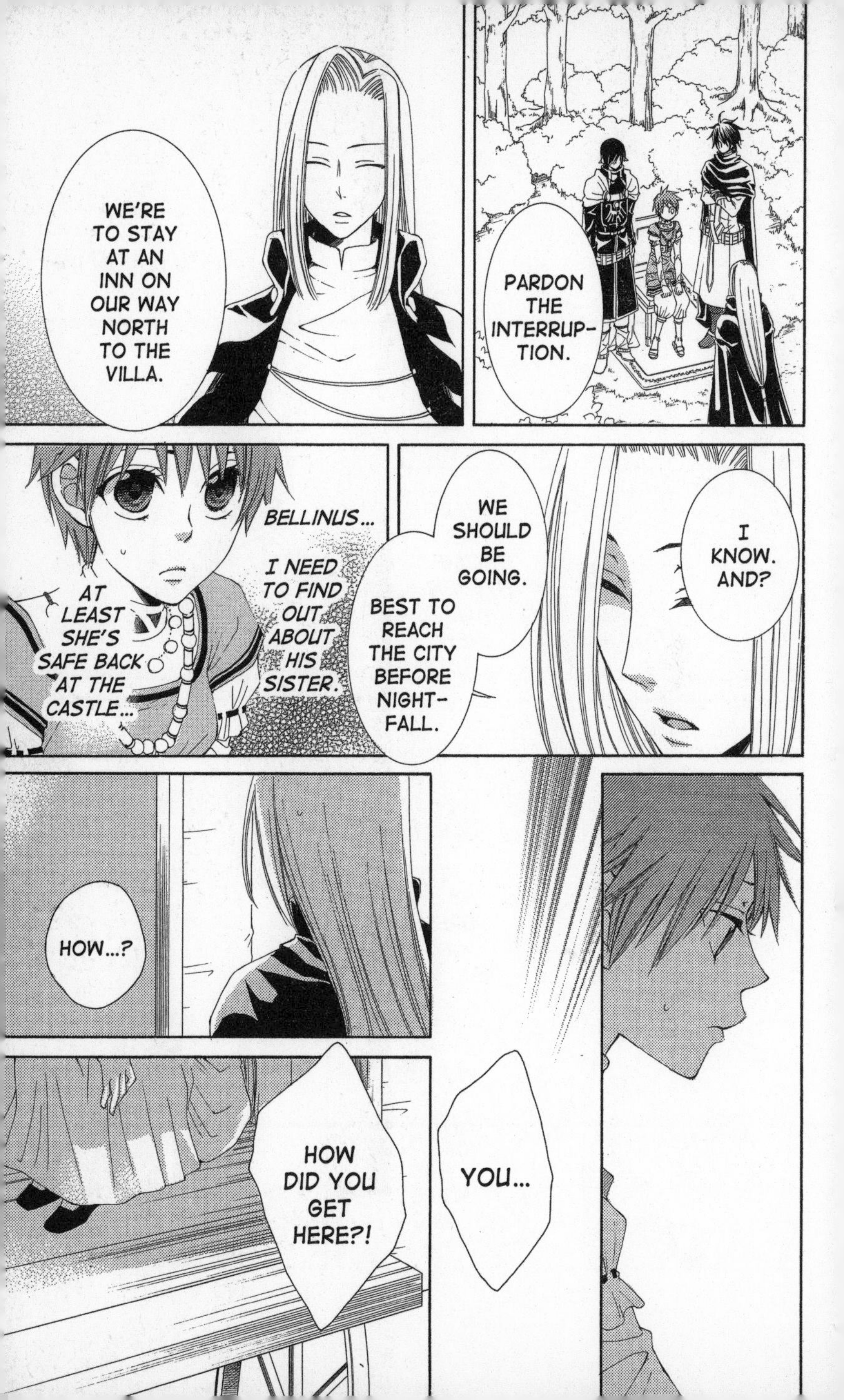
PARDON THE INTERRUP-TION.
WE'RE TO STAY AT AN INN ON OUR WAY NORTH TO THE VILLA.
I KNOW. AND?
WE SHOULD BE GOING.
BEST TO REACH THE CITY BEFORE NIGHT-FALL.
BELLINUS...
I NEED TO FIND OUT ABOUT HIS SISTER.
AT LEAST SHE'S SAFE BACK AT THE CASTLE...
HOW...?
YOU...
HOW DID YOU GET HERE?!

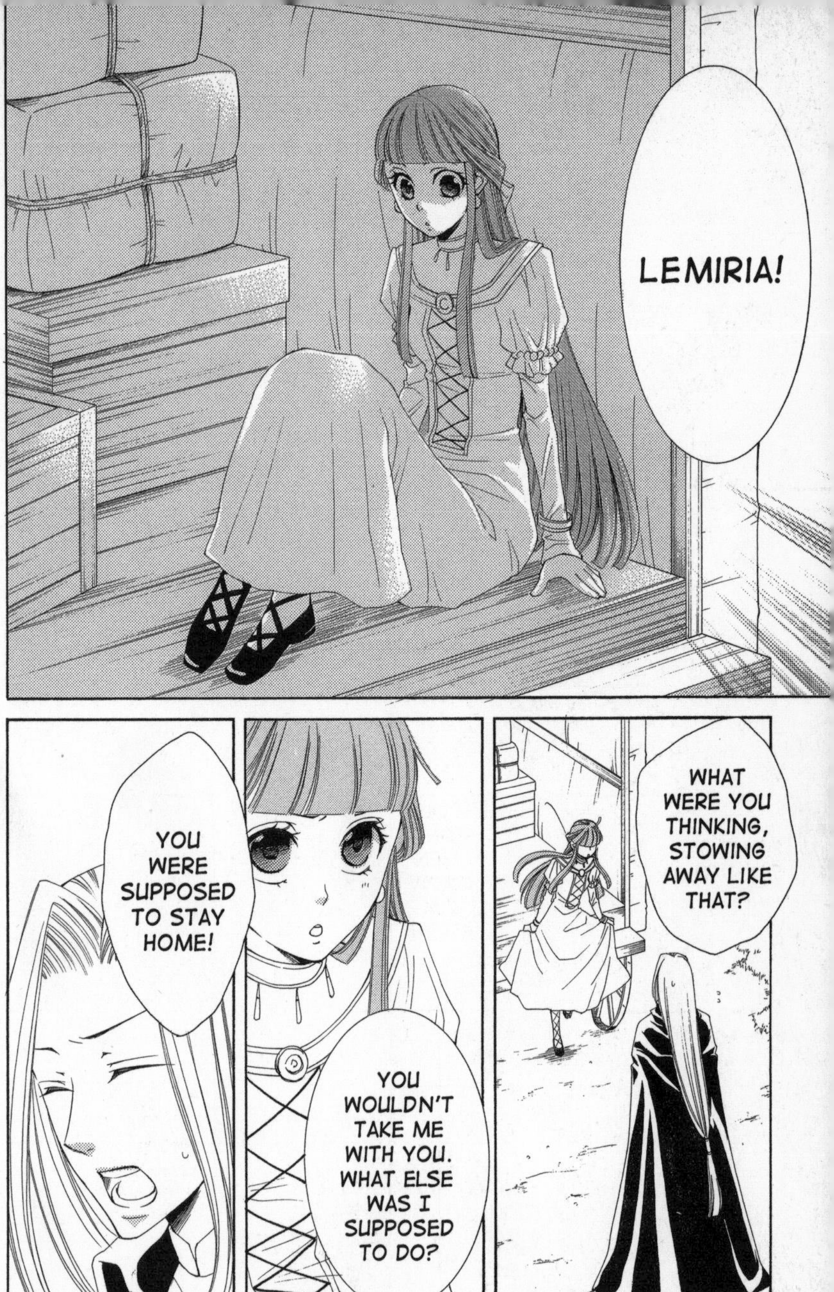
LEMIRIA!
WHAT WERE YOU THINKING, STOWING AWAY LIKE THAT?
YOU WOULDN'T TAKE ME WITH YOU. WHAT ELSE WAS I SUPPOSED TO DO?
YOU WERE SUPPOSED TO STAY HOME!

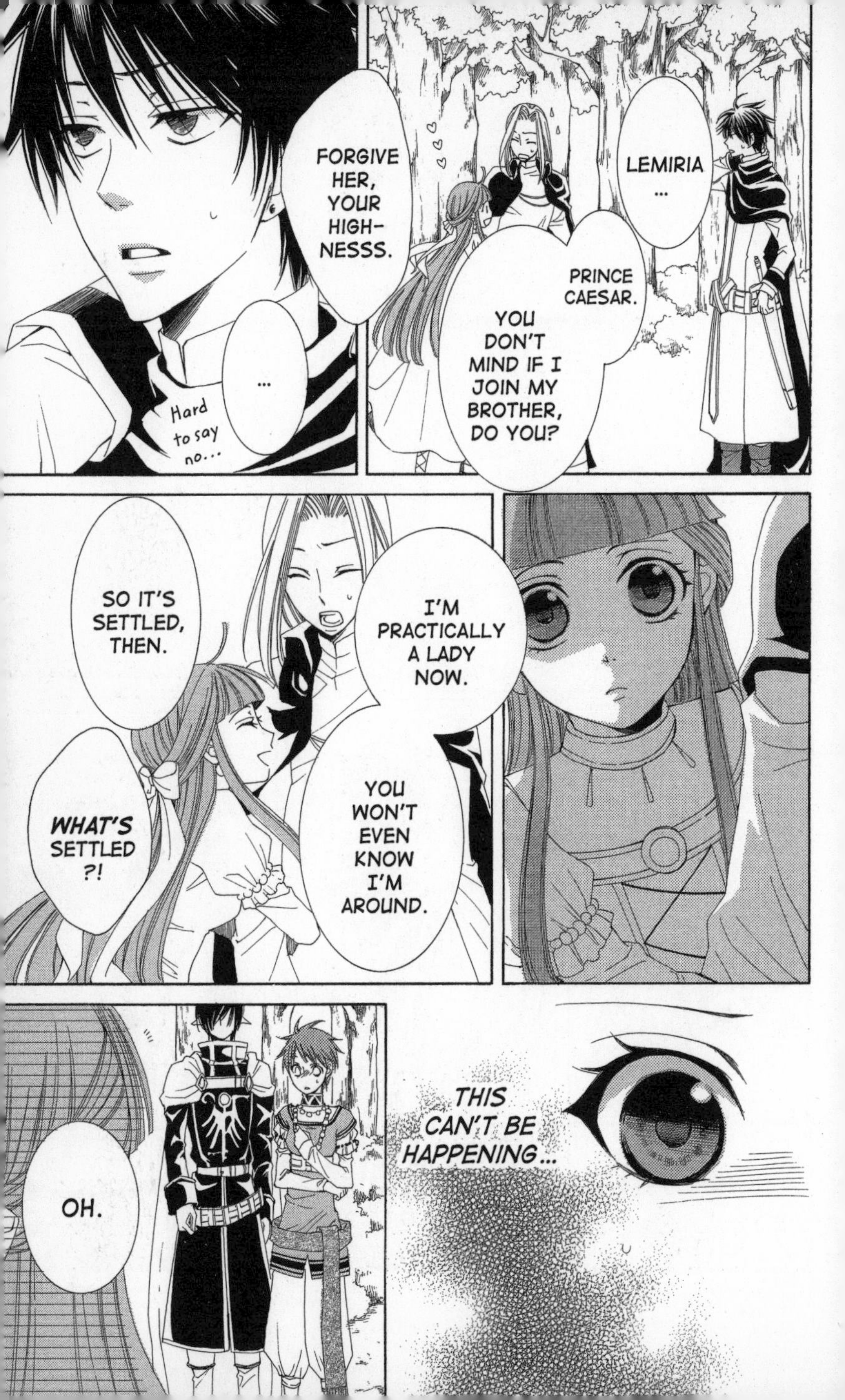
LEMIRIA ...
PRINCE CAESAR.
YOU DON'T MIND IF I JOIN MY BROTHER, DO YOU?
FORGIVE HER, YOUR HIGHNESSS.
...
Hard to say no...
I'M PRACTICALLY A LADY NOW.
YOU WON'T EVEN KNOW I'M AROUND.
SO IT'S SETTLED, THEN.
WHAT'S SETTLED?!
THIS CAN'T BE HAPPENING...
OH.

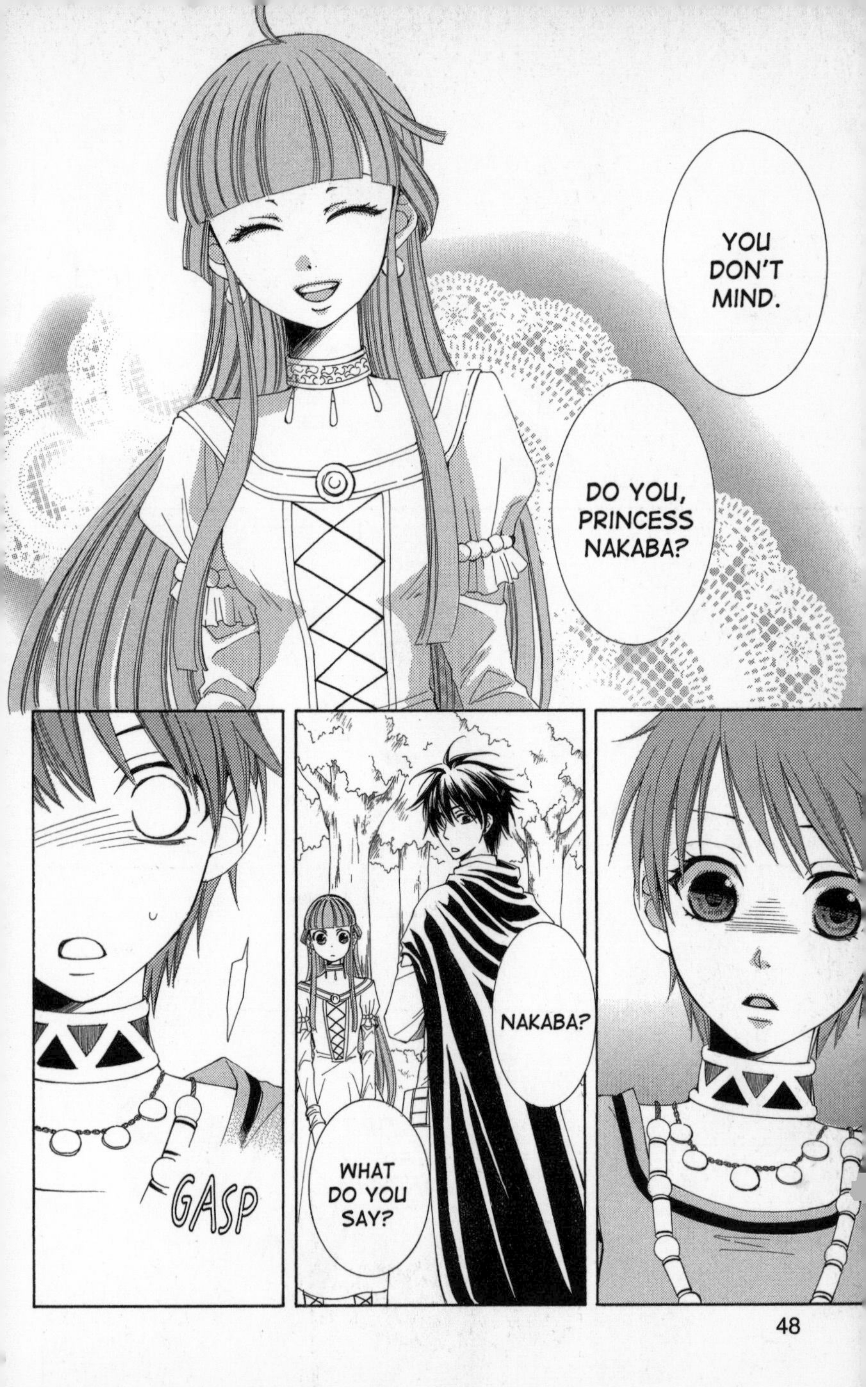
YOU DON'T MIND.
DO YOU, PRINCESS NAKABA?
NAKABA?
WHAT DO YOU SAY?
GASP

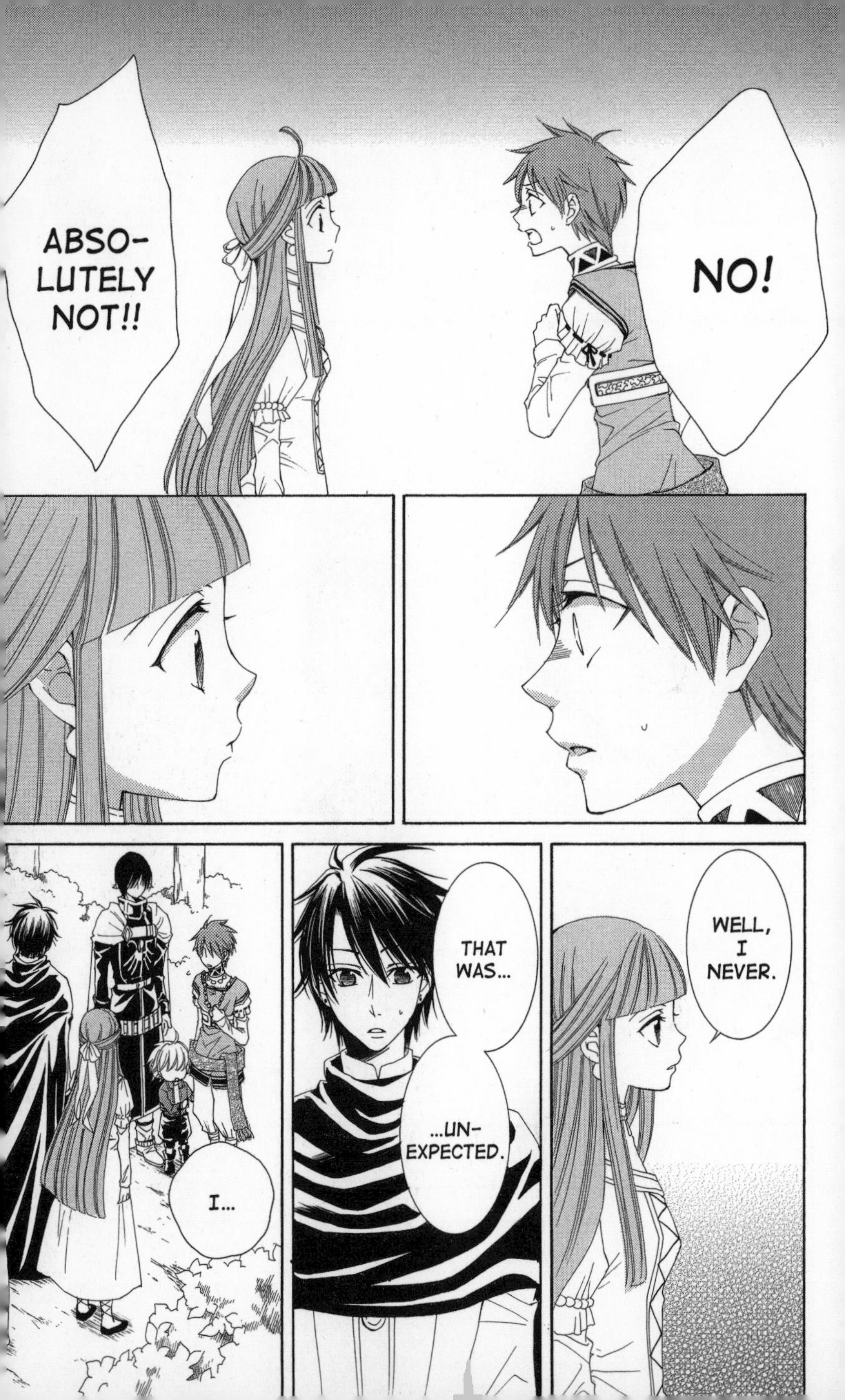
NO!
ABSO-LUTELY NOT!!
WELL, I NEVER.
THAT WAS...
...UN-EXPECTED.
I...

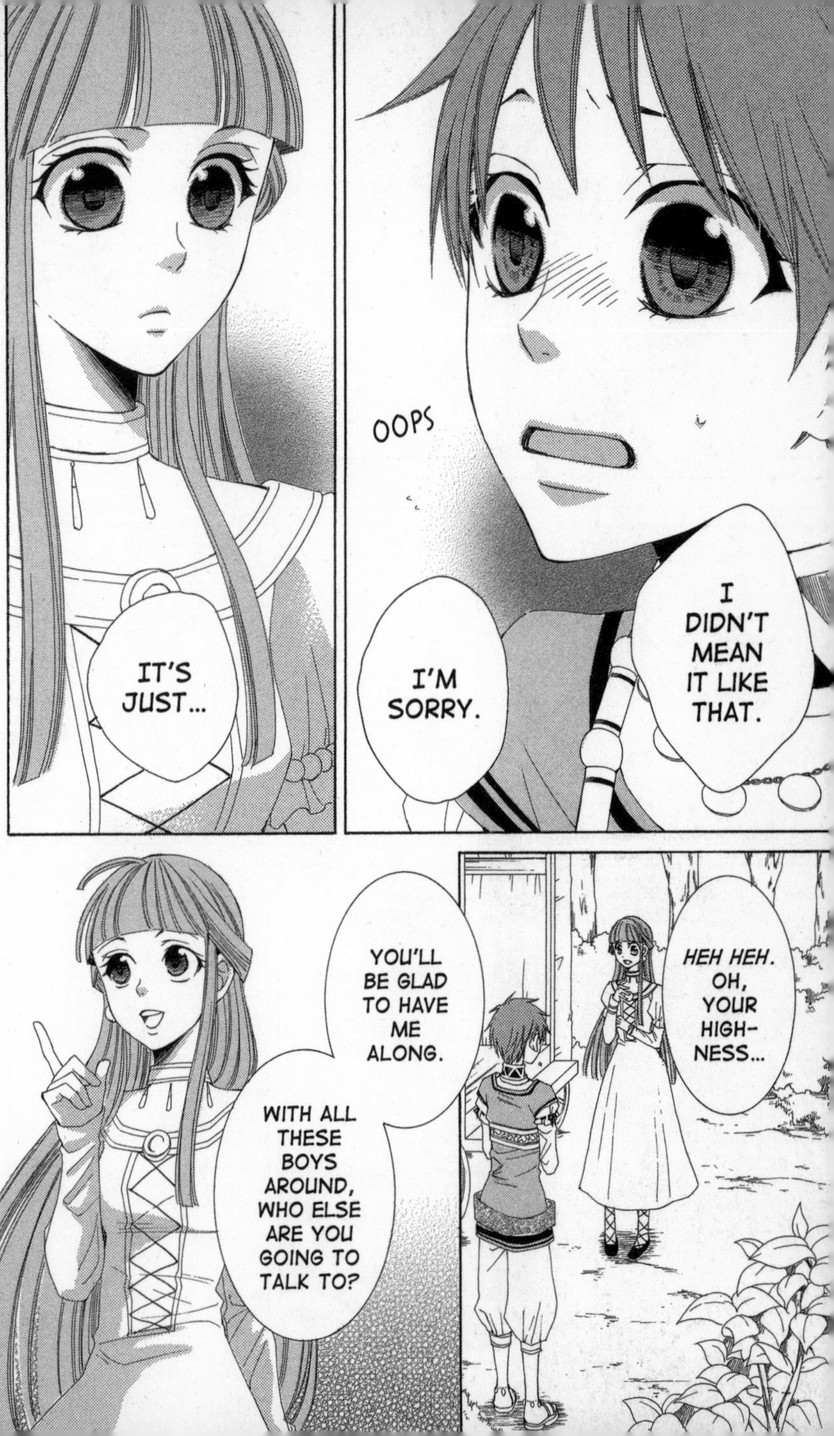
OOPS
I DIDN'T MEAN IT LIKE THAT.
I'M SORRY.
IT'S JUST...
HEH HEH. OH, YOUR HIGH-NESS...
YOU'LL BE GLAD TO HAVE ME ALONG.
WITH ALL THESE BOYS AROUND, WHO ELSE ARE YOU GOING TO TALK TO?

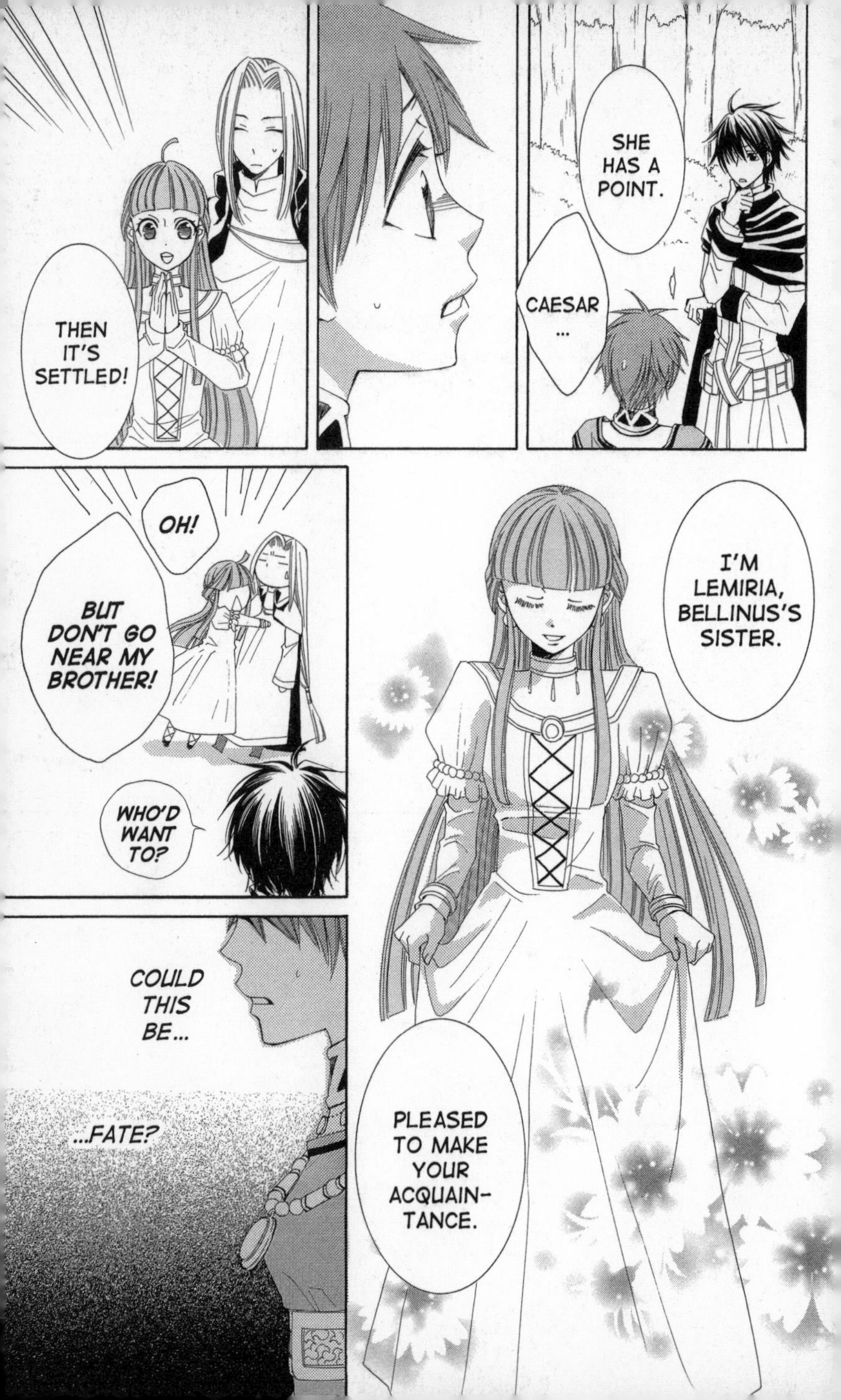
SHE HAS A POINT.
CAESAR...
THEN IT'S SETTLED!
I'M LEMIRIA, BELLINUS'S SISTER.
PLEASED TO MAKE YOUR ACQUAINTANCE.
OH!
BUT DON'T GO NEAR MY BROTHER!
WHO'D WANT TO?
COULD THIS BE...
...FATE?

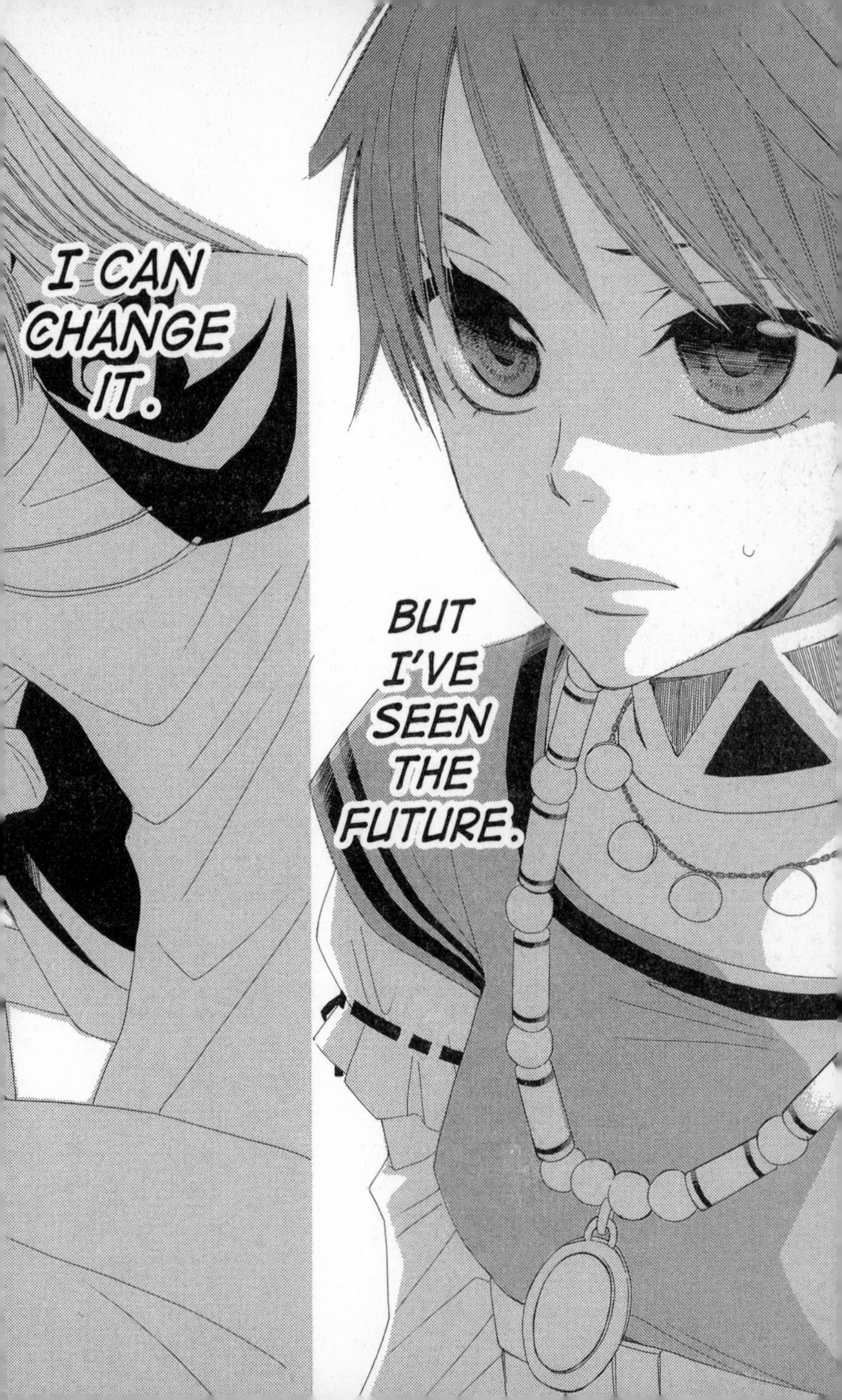
BUT I'VE SEEN THE FUTURE.
I CAN CHANGE IT.

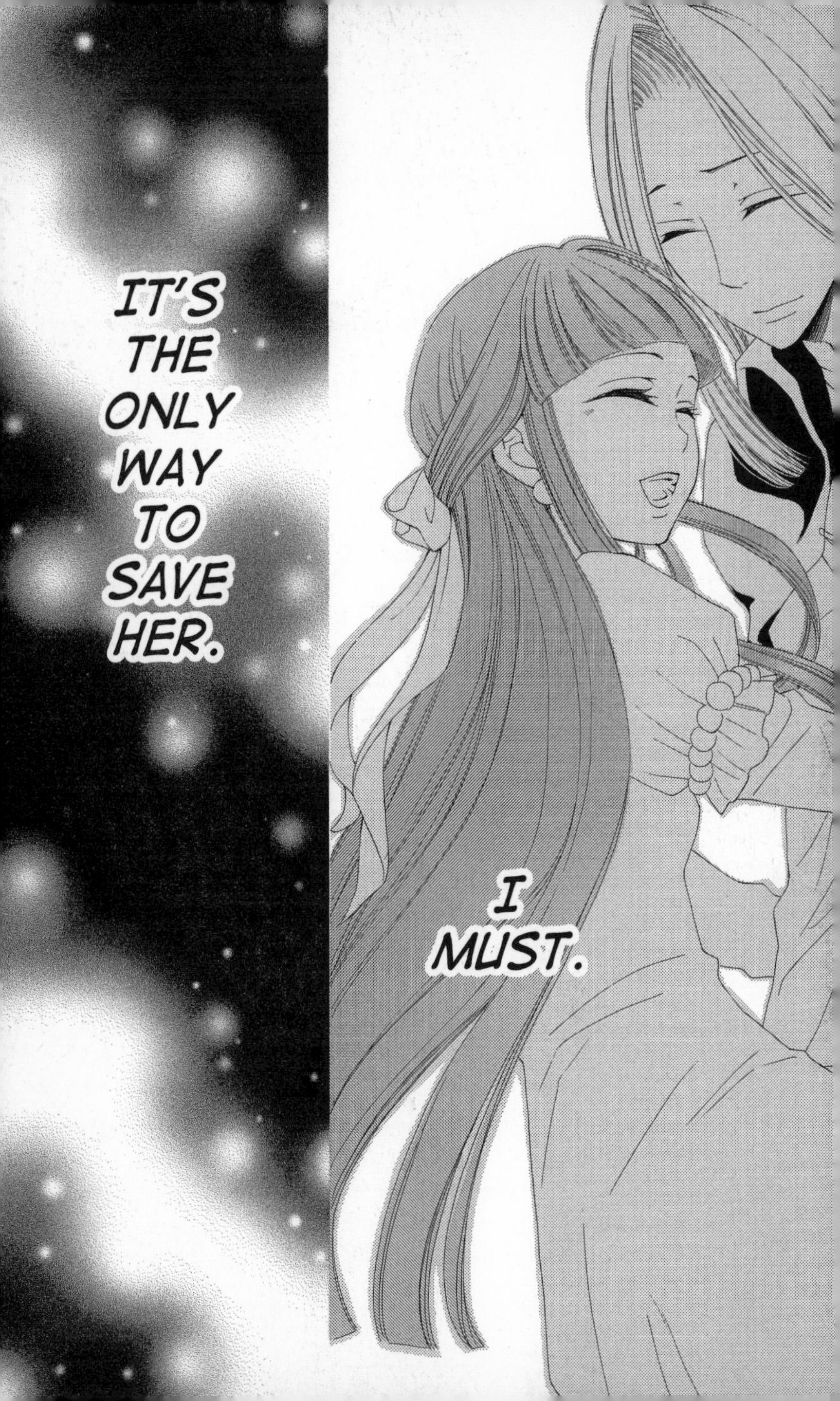
I MUST.
IT'S THE ONLY WAY TO SAVE HER.

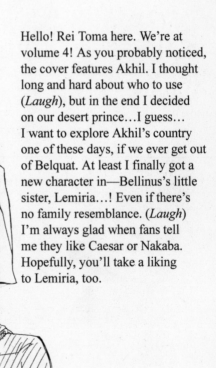

Hello! Rei Toma here. We're at volume 4! As you probably noticed, the cover features Akhil. I thought long and hard about who to use (*Laugh*), but in the end I decided on our desert prince…I guess… I want to explore Akhil's country one of these days, if we ever get out of Belquat. At least I finally got a new character in—Bellinus's little sister, Lemiria…! Even if there's no family resemblance. (*Laugh*) I'm always glad when fans tell me they like Caesar or Nakaba. Hopefully, you'll take a liking to Lemiria, too.

Chapter 13

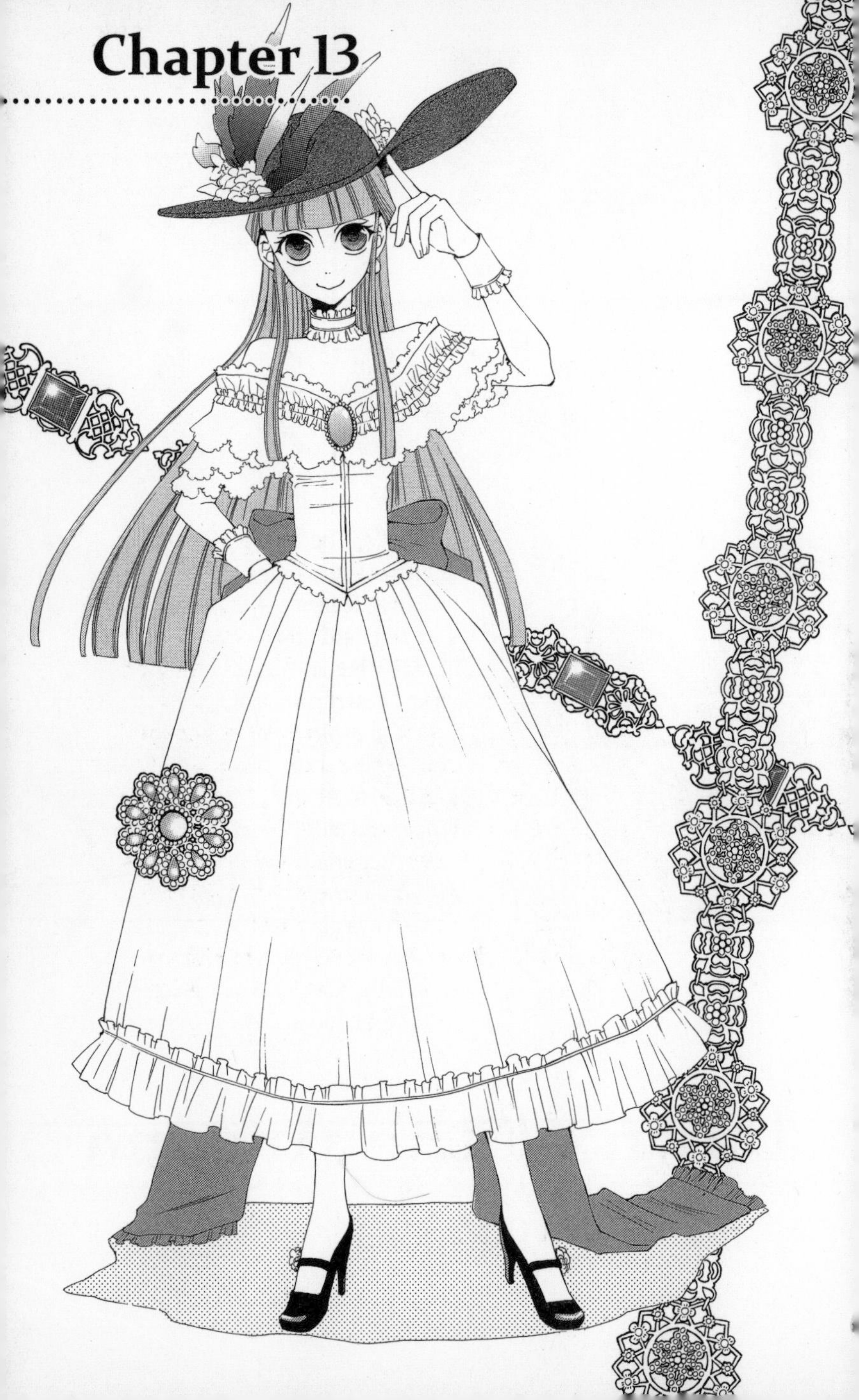

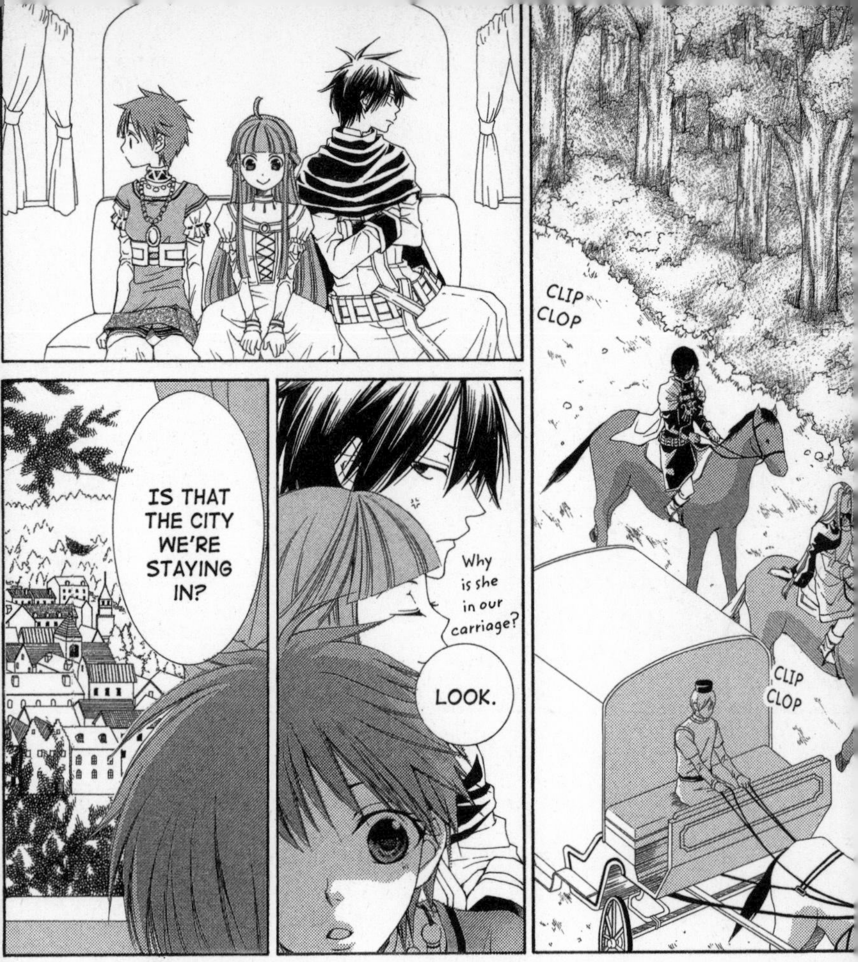
CLIP
CLOP
CLIP
CLOP
Why is she in our carriage?
LOOK.
IS THAT THE CITY WE'RE STAYING IN?

Dawn of the Arcana

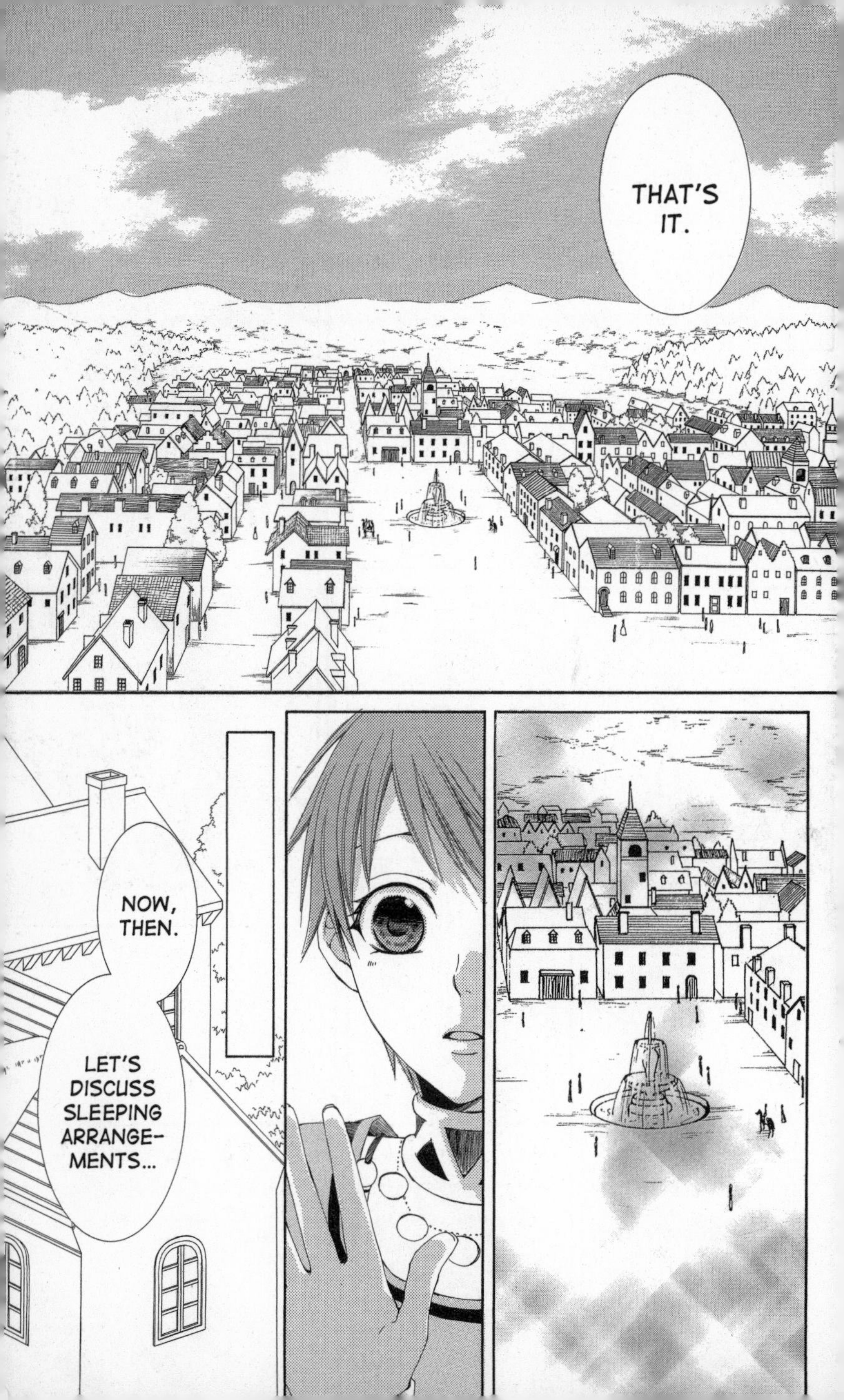
THAT'S IT.
NOW, THEN.
LET'S DISCUSS SLEEPING ARRANGE-MENTS...

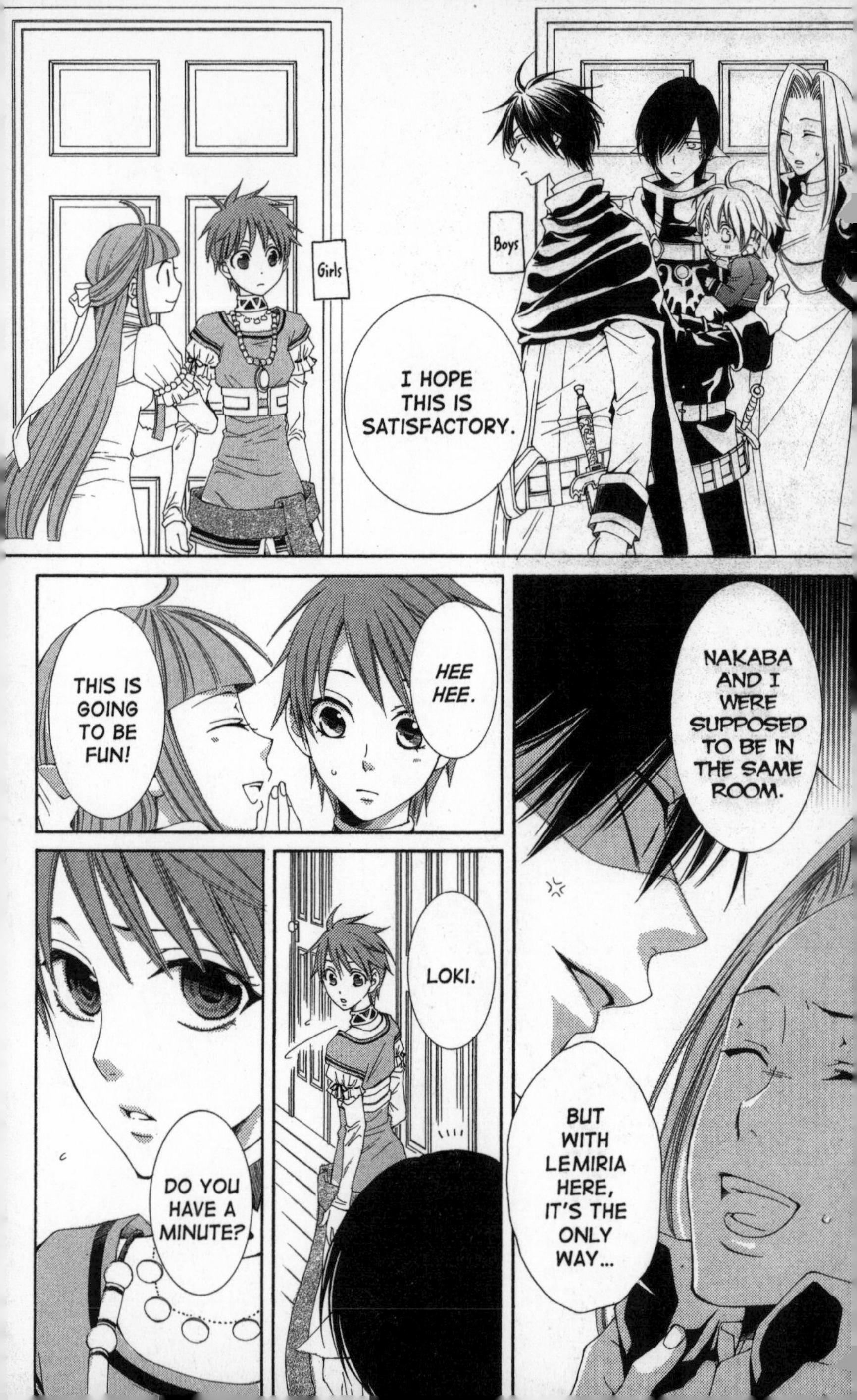
Boys
Girls
I HOPE THIS IS SATISFACTORY.
NAKABA AND I WERE SUPPOSED TO BE IN THE SAME ROOM.
BUT WITH LEMIRIA HERE, IT'S THE ONLY WAY...
HEE HEE.
THIS IS GOING TO BE FUN!
LOKI.
DO YOU HAVE A MINUTE?

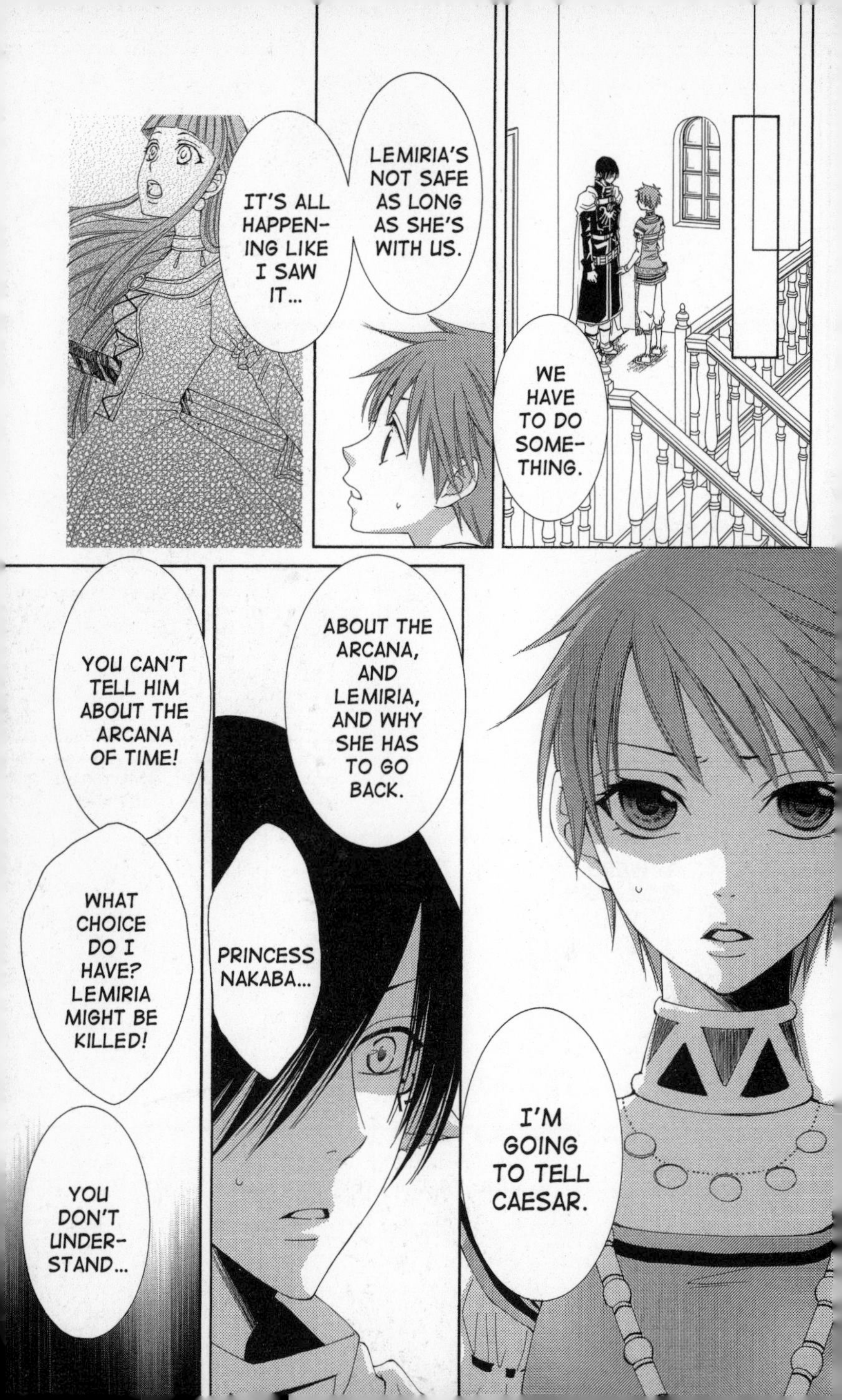
WE HAVE TO DO SOMETHING.
LEMIRIA'S NOT SAFE AS LONG AS SHE'S WITH US.
IT'S ALL HAPPENING LIKE I SAW IT...
I'M GOING TO TELL CAESAR.
ABOUT THE ARCANA, AND LEMIRIA, AND WHY SHE HAS TO GO BACK.
PRINCESS NAKABA...
YOU CAN'T TELL HIM ABOUT THE ARCANA OF TIME!
WHAT CHOICE DO I HAVE? LEMIRIA MIGHT BE KILLED!
YOU DON'T UNDERSTAND...

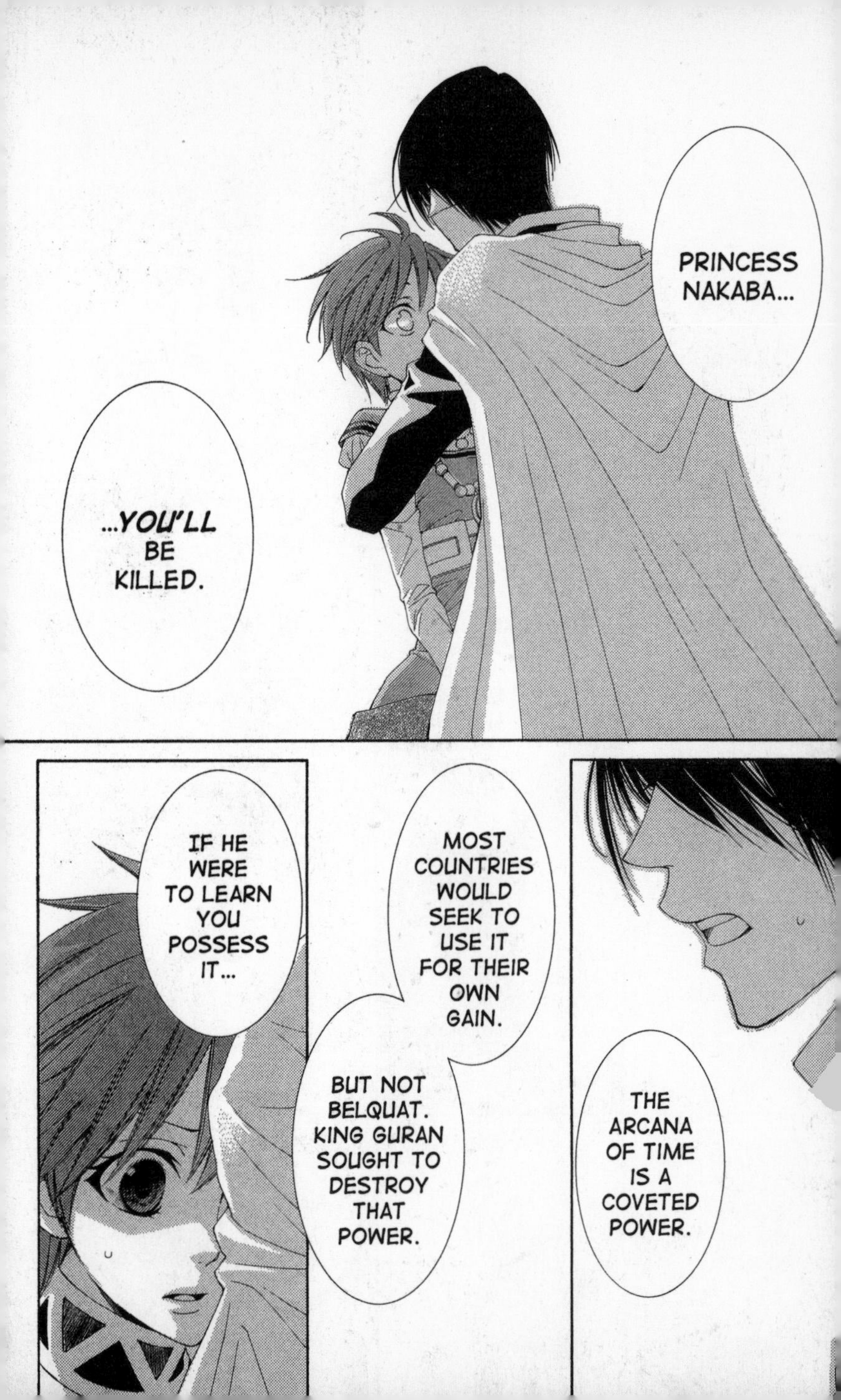
PRINCESS NAKABA...
...YOU'LL BE KILLED.
THE ARCANA OF TIME IS A COVETED POWER.
MOST COUNTRIES WOULD SEEK TO USE IT FOR THEIR OWN GAIN.
BUT NOT BELQUAT. KING GURAN SOUGHT TO DESTROY THAT POWER.
IF HE WERE TO LEARN YOU POSSESS IT...

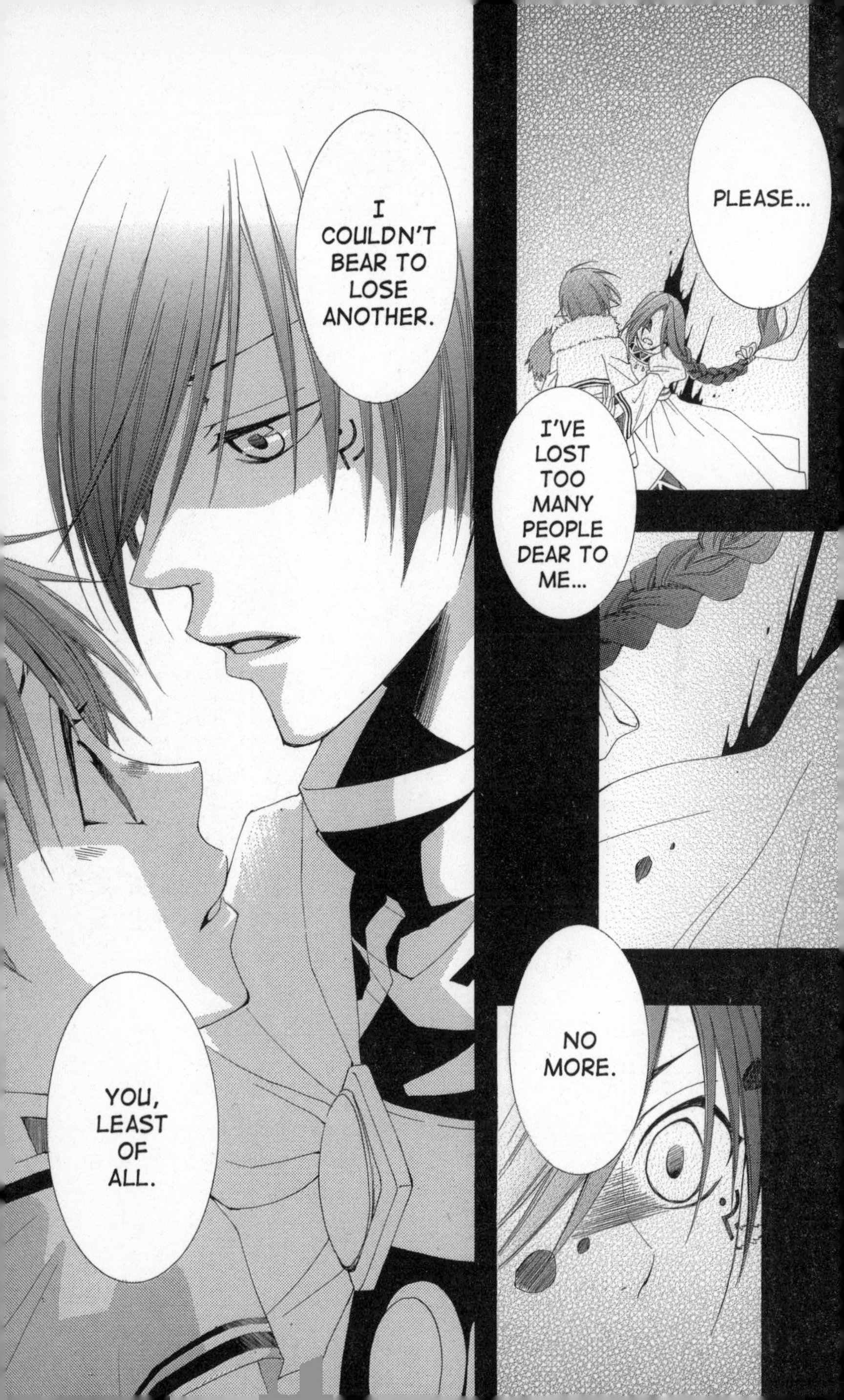
PLEASE...
I'VE LOST TOO MANY PEOPLE DEAR TO ME...
NO MORE.
I COULDN'T BEAR TO LOSE ANOTHER.
YOU, LEAST OF ALL.

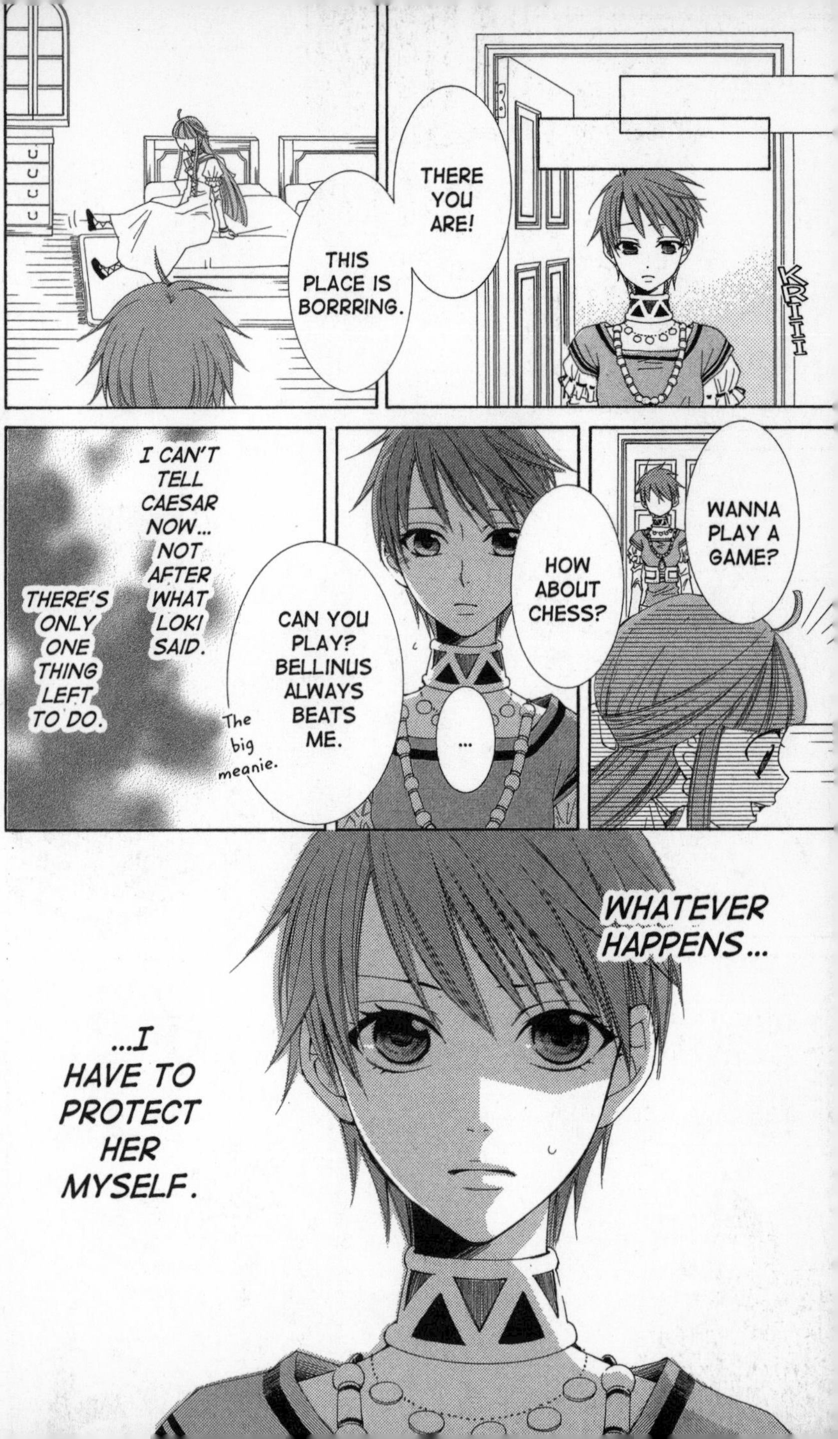
KRIIII
THERE YOU ARE!
THIS PLACE IS BORRRING.
WANNA PLAY A GAME?
HOW ABOUT CHESS?
CAN YOU PLAY? BELLINUS ALWAYS BEATS ME.
The big meanie.
...
I CAN'T TELL CAESAR NOW... NOT AFTER WHAT LOKI SAID.
THERE'S ONLY ONE THING LEFT TO DO.
WHATEVER HAPPENS...
...I HAVE TO PROTECT HER MYSELF.

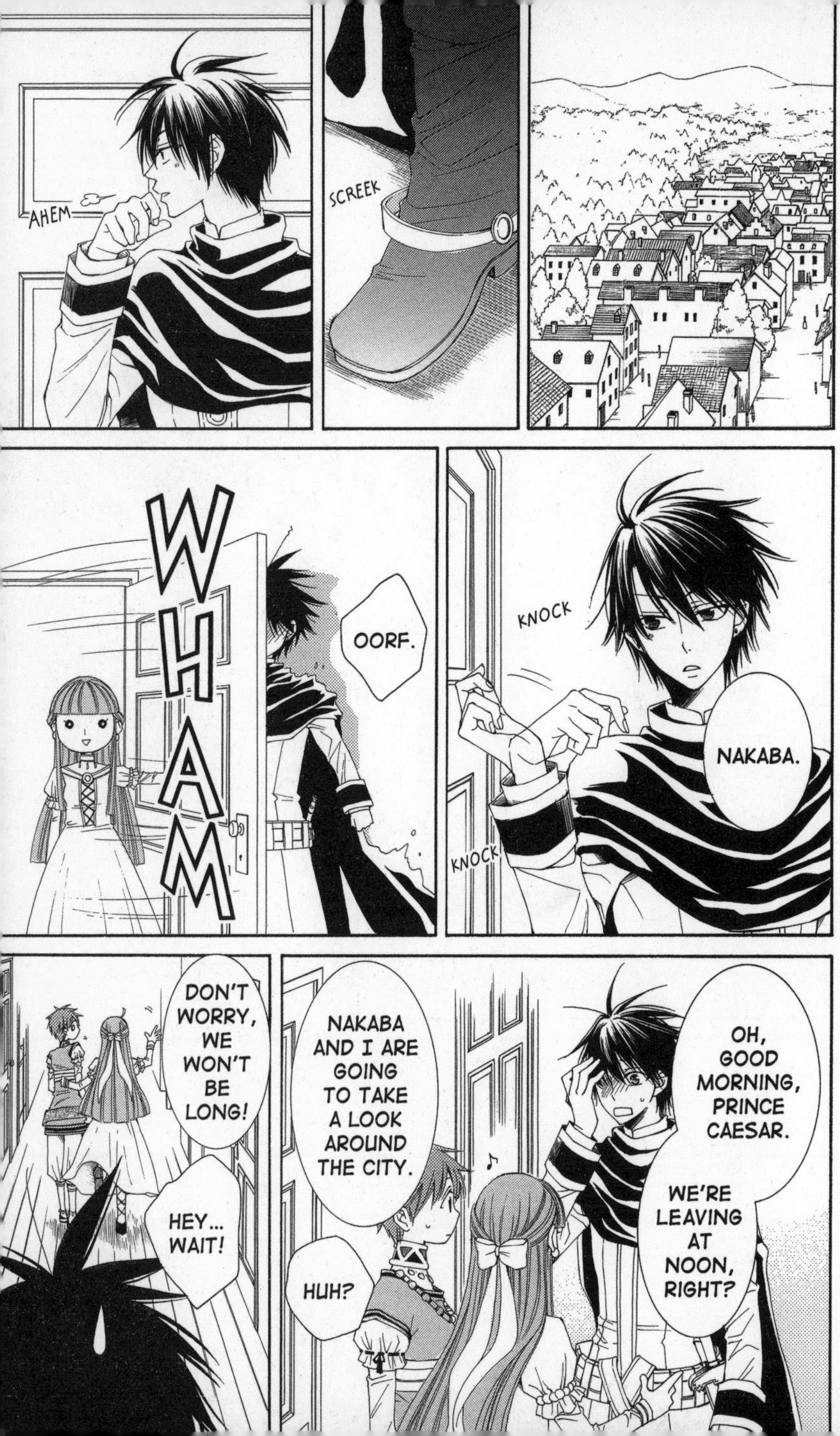
SCREEK
AHEM
KNOCK
NAKABA.
KNOCK
OORF.
WHAM
OH, GOOD MORNING, PRINCE CAESAR.
WE'RE LEAVING AT NOON, RIGHT?
NAKABA AND I ARE GOING TO TAKE A LOOK AROUND THE CITY.
HUH?
DON'T WORRY, WE WON'T BE LONG!
HEY... WAIT!

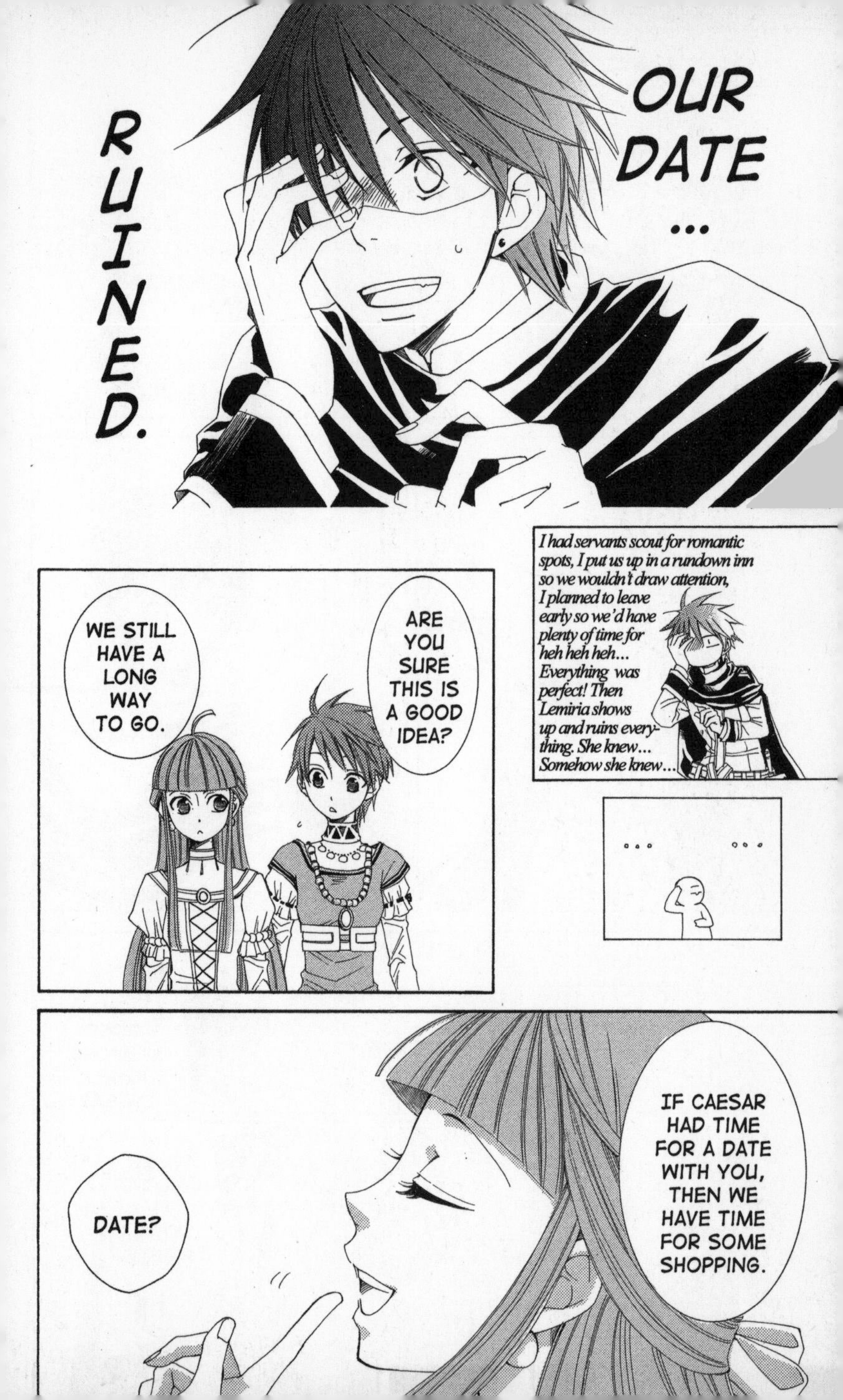
OUR DATE ...
RUINED.
I had servants scout for romantic spots, I put us up in a rundown inn so we wouldn't draw attention, I planned to leave early so we'd have plenty of time for heh heh heh... Everything was perfect! Then Lemiria shows up and ruins everything. She knew... Somehow she knew...
... ...
ARE YOU SURE THIS IS A GOOD IDEA?
WE STILL HAVE A LONG WAY TO GO.
IF CAESAR HAD TIME FOR A DATE WITH YOU, THEN WE HAVE TIME FOR SOME SHOPPING.
DATE?

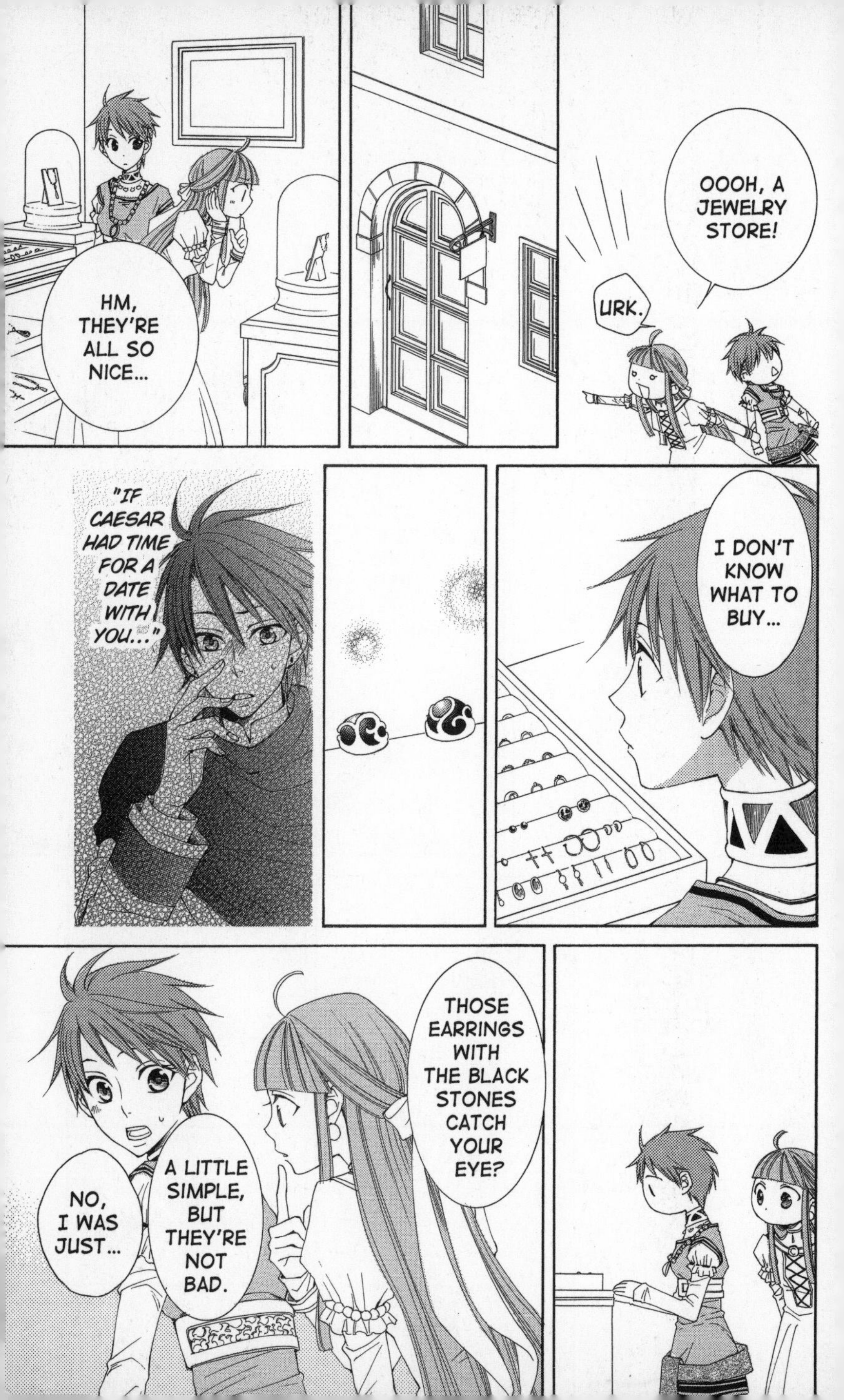
OOOH, A JEWELRY STORE!
URK.
HM, THEY'RE ALL SO NICE...
I DON'T KNOW WHAT TO BUY...
"IF CAESAR HAD TIME FOR A DATE WITH YOU..."
THOSE EARRINGS WITH THE BLACK STONES CATCH YOUR EYE?
A LITTLE SIMPLE, BUT THEY'RE NOT BAD.
NO, I WAS JUST...

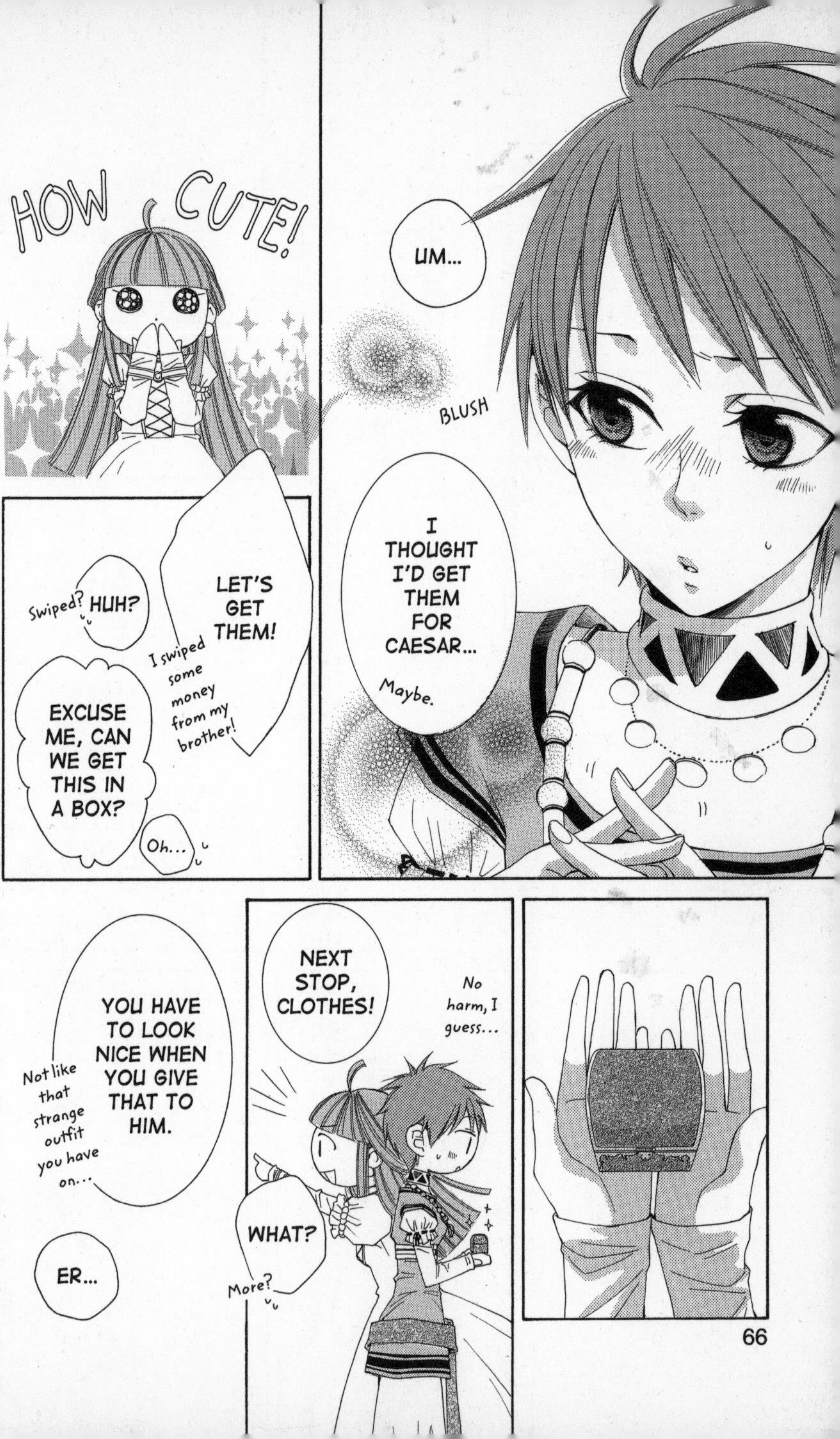
UM...
BLUSH
I THOUGHT I'D GET THEM FOR CAESAR...
Maybe.
HOW CUTE!
LET'S GET THEM!
I swiped some money from my brother!
HUH?
Swiped?
EXCUSE ME, CAN WE GET THIS IN A BOX?
Oh...
NEXT STOP, CLOTHES!
No harm, I guess...
WHAT?
More?
YOU HAVE TO LOOK NICE WHEN YOU GIVE THAT TO HIM.
Not like that strange outfit you have on...
ER...

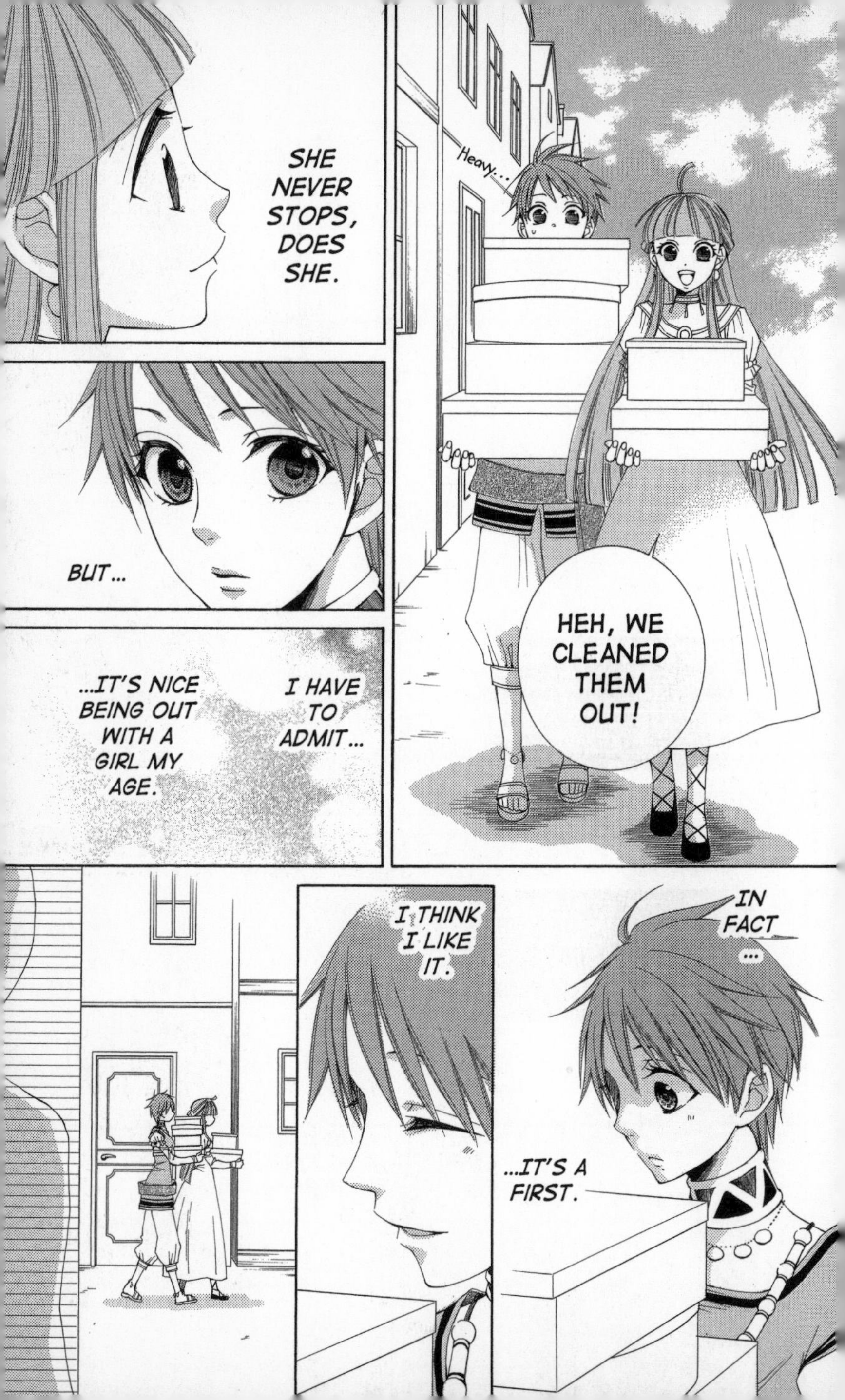
Heavy...
HEH, WE CLEANED THEM OUT!
SHE NEVER STOPS, DOES SHE.
BUT...
I HAVE TO ADMIT...
...IT'S NICE BEING OUT WITH A GIRL MY AGE.
IN FACT...
...IT'S A FIRST.
I THINK I LIKE IT.

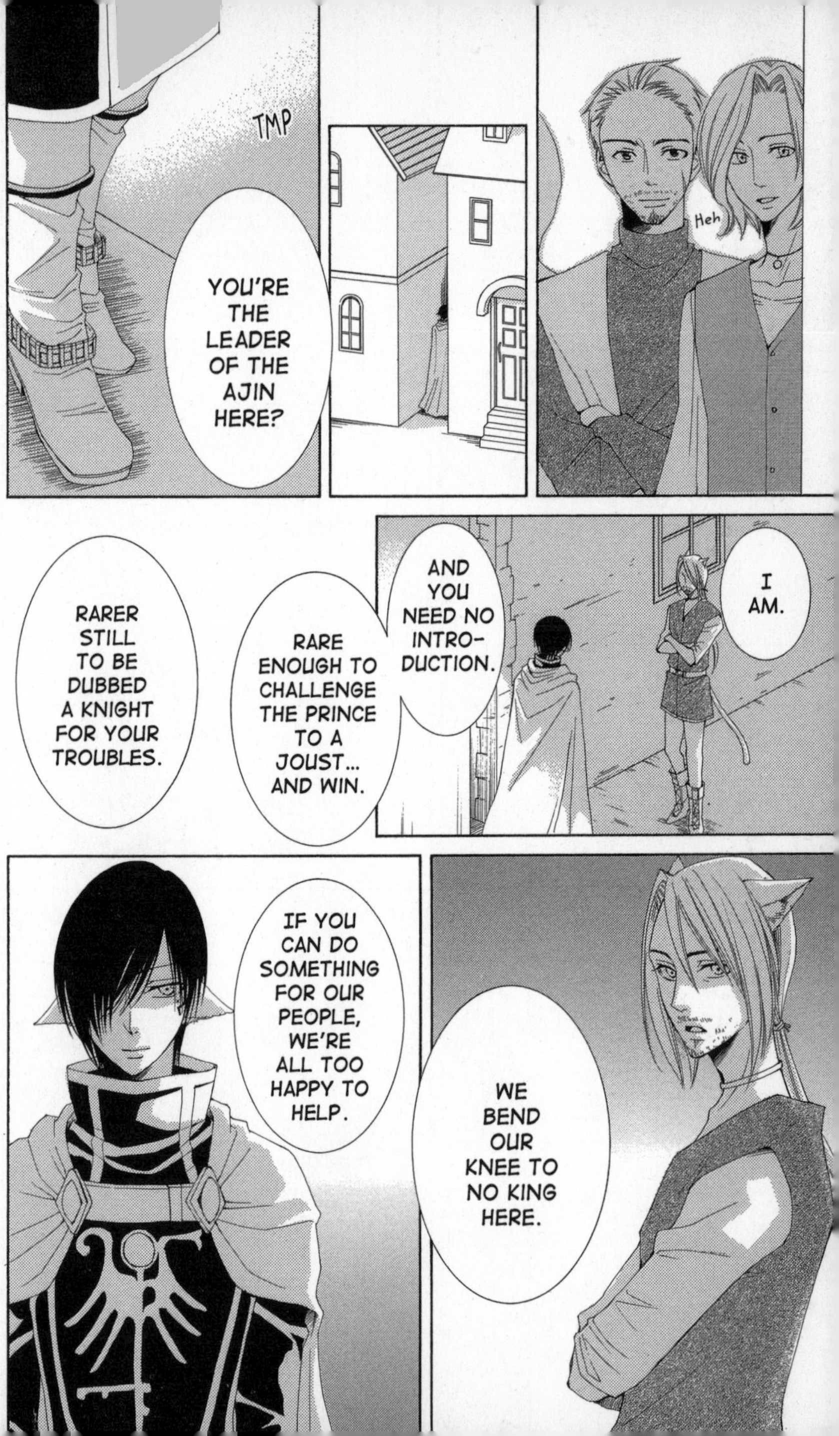
Heh
TMP
YOU'RE THE LEADER OF THE AJIN HERE?
I AM.
AND YOU NEED NO INTRODUCTION.
RARE ENOUGH TO CHALLENGE THE PRINCE TO A JOUST... AND WIN.
RARER STILL TO BE DUBBED A KNIGHT FOR YOUR TROUBLES.
WE BEND OUR KNEE TO NO KING HERE.
IF YOU CAN DO SOMETHING FOR OUR PEOPLE, WE'RE ALL TOO HAPPY TO HELP.

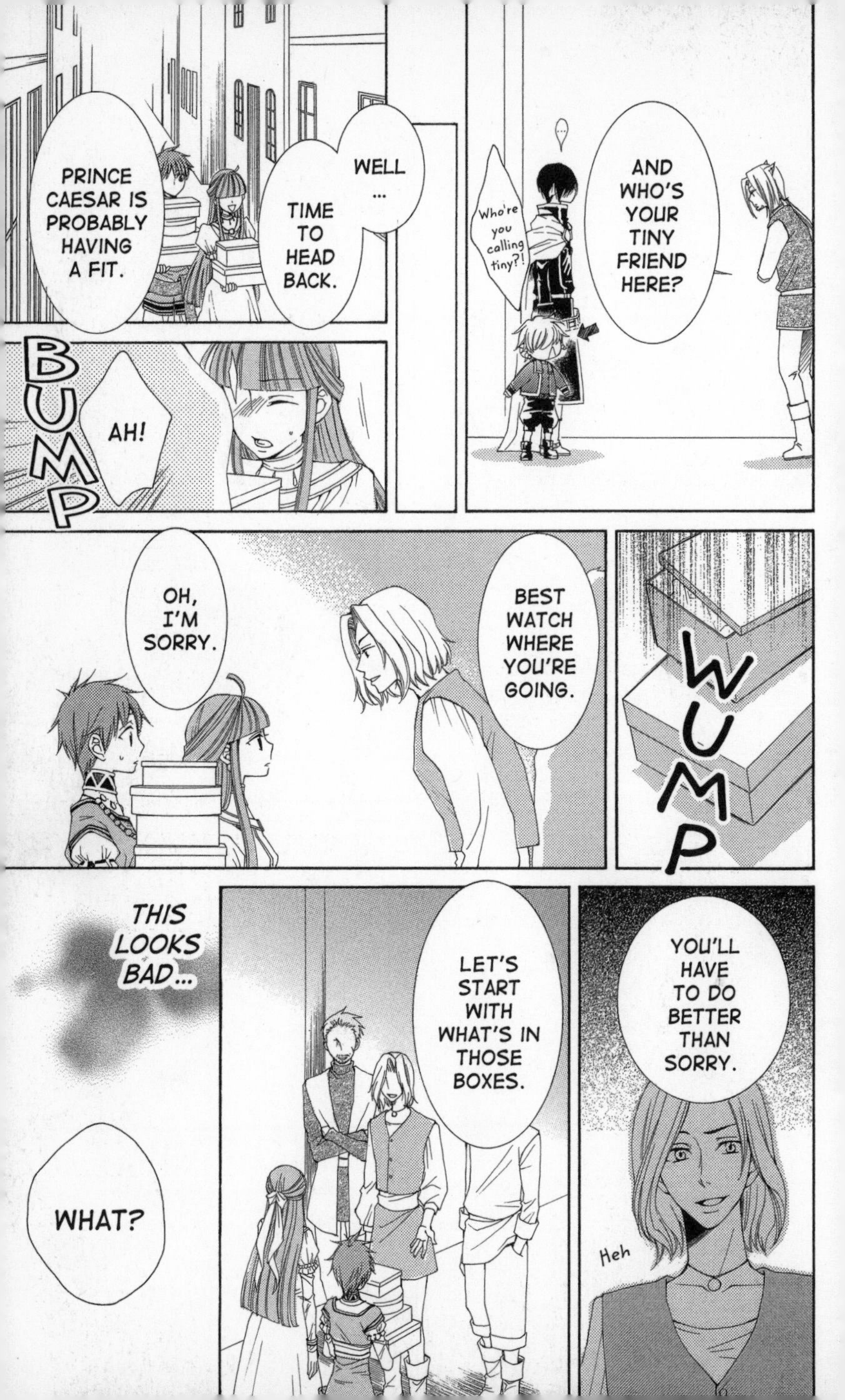
AND WHO'S YOUR TINY FRIEND HERE?
...
Who're you calling tiny?!
WELL ...
TIME TO HEAD BACK.
PRINCE CAESAR IS PROBABLY HAVING A FIT.
AH!
BUMP
WUMP
BEST WATCH WHERE YOU'RE GOING.
OH, I'M SORRY.
YOU'LL HAVE TO DO BETTER THAN SORRY.
Heh
LET'S START WITH WHAT'S IN THOSE BOXES.
THIS LOOKS BAD...
WHAT?

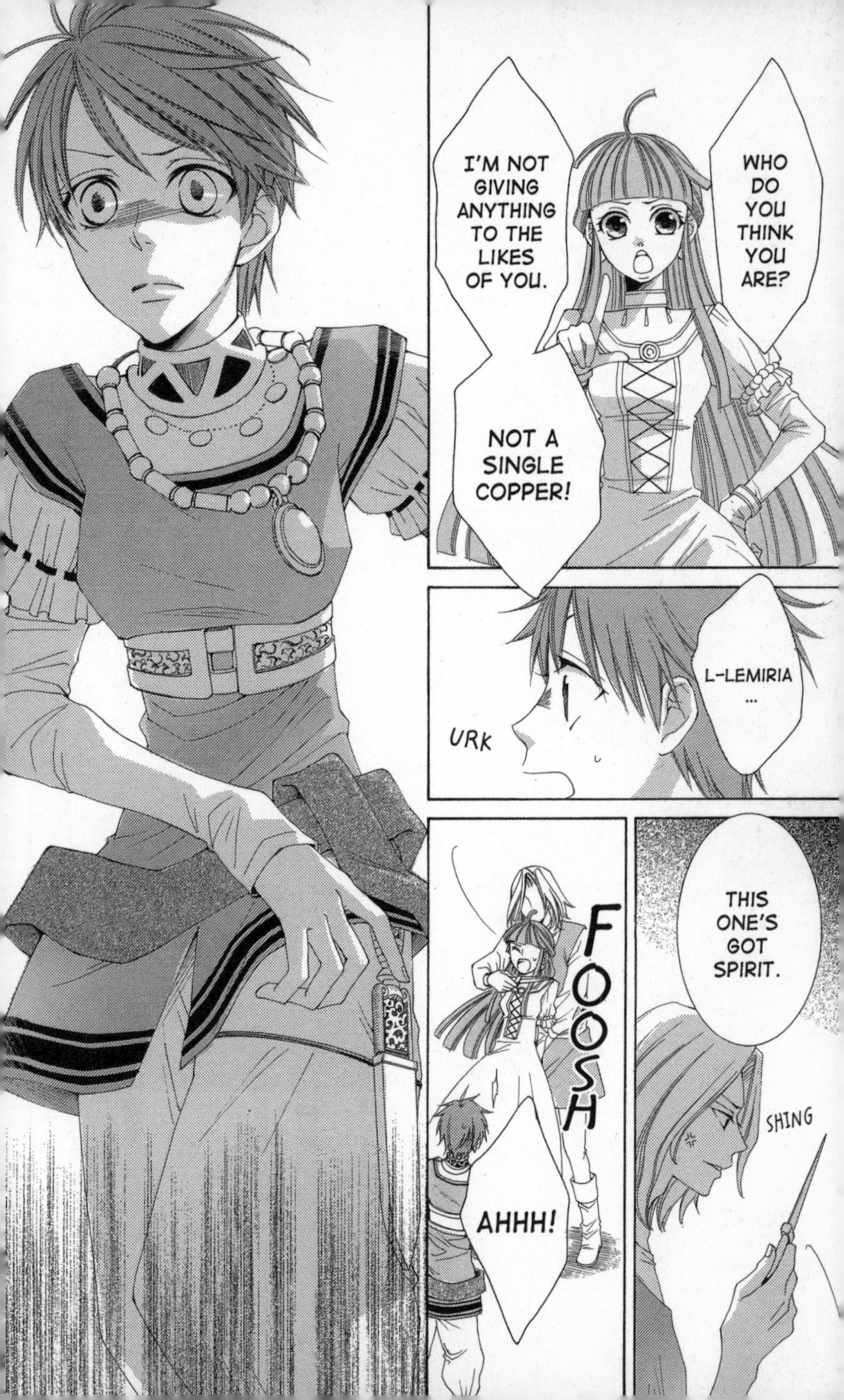
WHO DO YOU THINK YOU ARE?
I'M NOT GIVING ANYTHING TO THE LIKES OF YOU.
NOT A SINGLE COPPER!
L-LEMIRIA ...
URK
THIS ONE'S GOT SPIRIT.
SHING
FOOSH
AHHH!

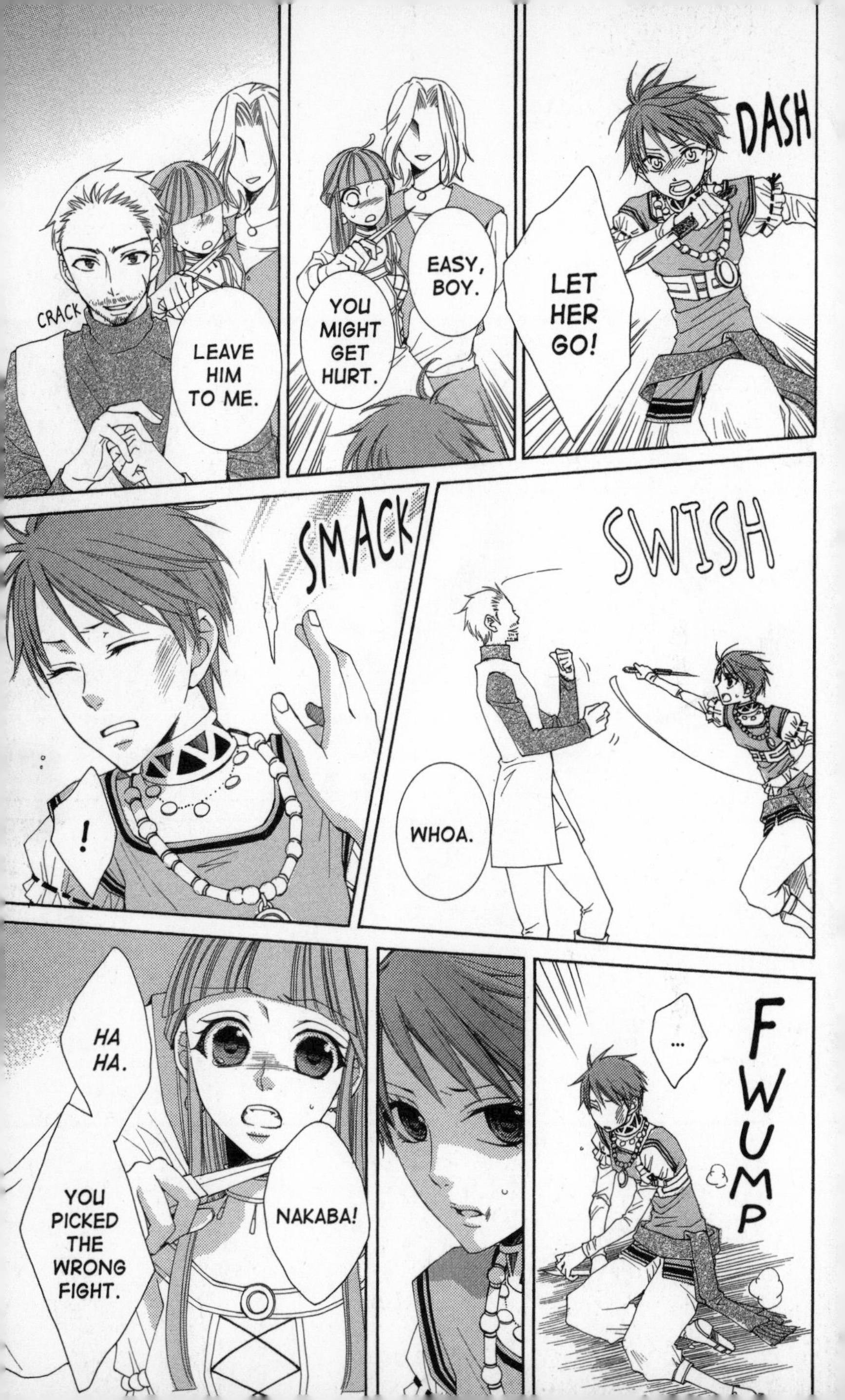
DASH
LET HER GO!
EASY, BOY.
YOU MIGHT GET HURT.
CRACK
LEAVE HIM TO ME.
SWISH
WHOA.
SMACK
!
...
FWUMP
HA HA.
NAKABA!
YOU PICKED THE WRONG FIGHT.

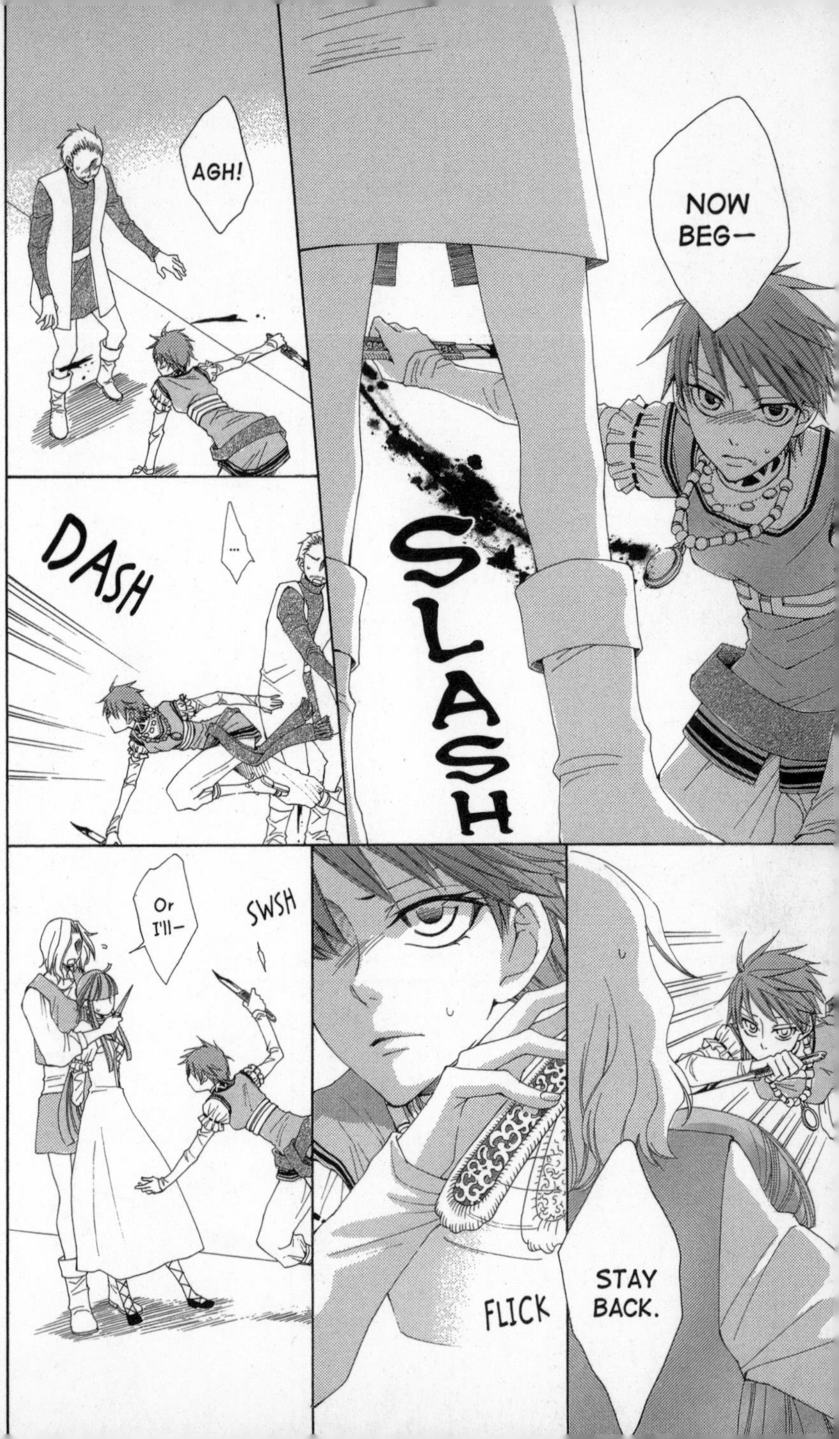
NOW BEG—
SLASH
AGH!
DASH
...
STAY BACK.
FLICK
Or I'll—
SWSH

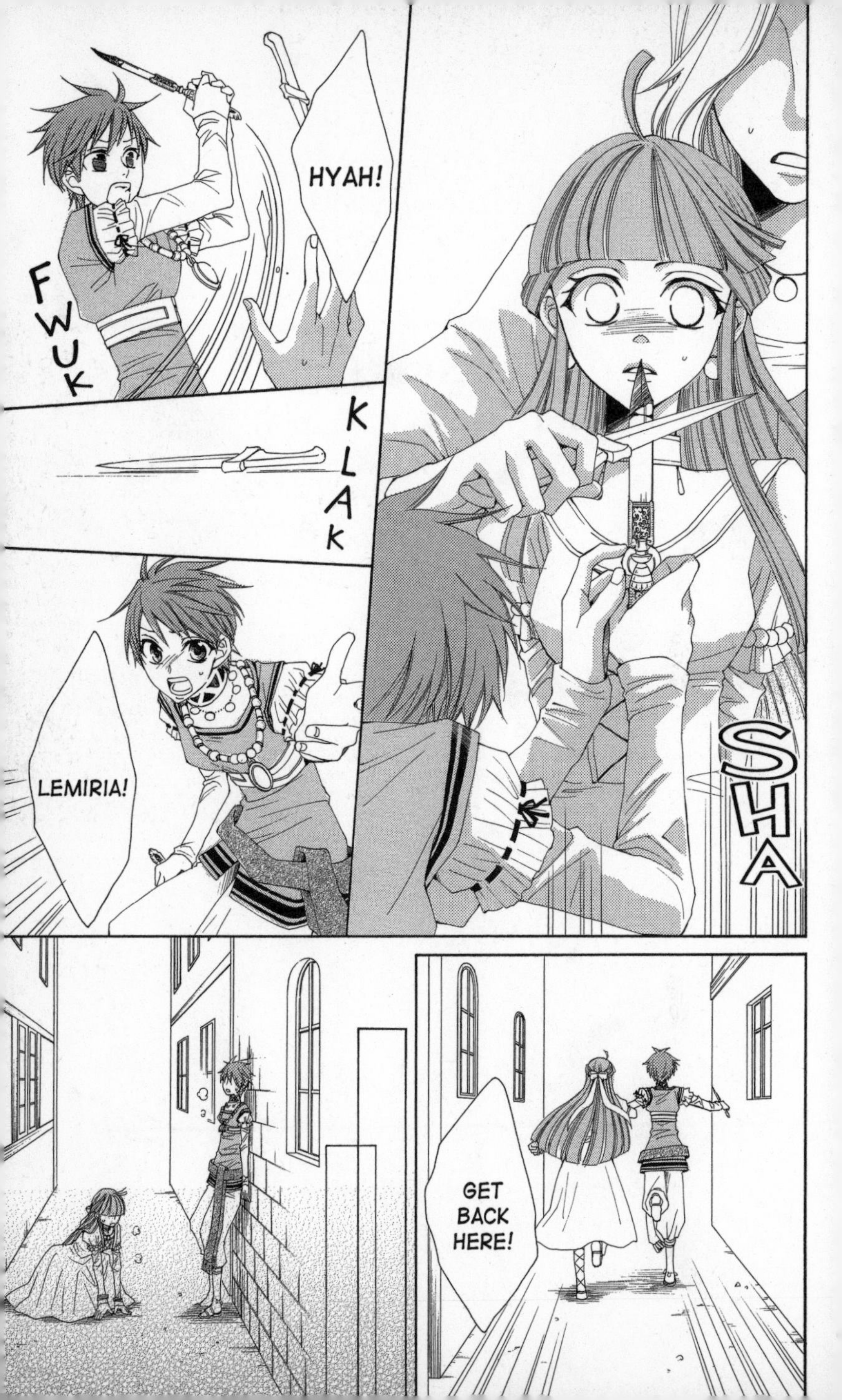
SHA
HYAH!
FWUK
KLAK
LEMIRIA!
GET BACK HERE!

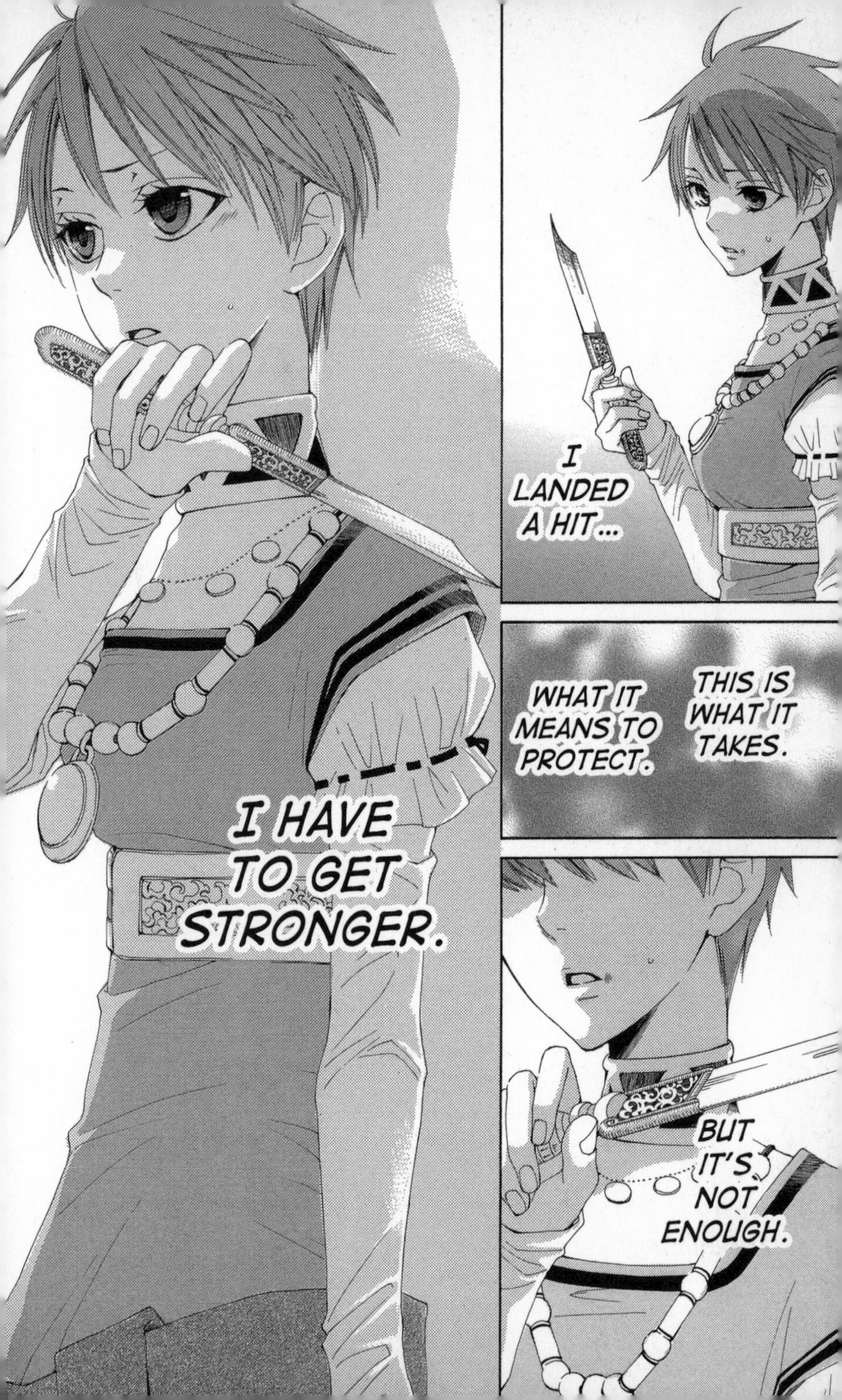
I LANDED A HIT...
THIS IS WHAT IT TAKES.
WHAT IT MEANS TO PROTECT.
BUT IT'S NOT ENOUGH.
I HAVE TO GET STRONGER.

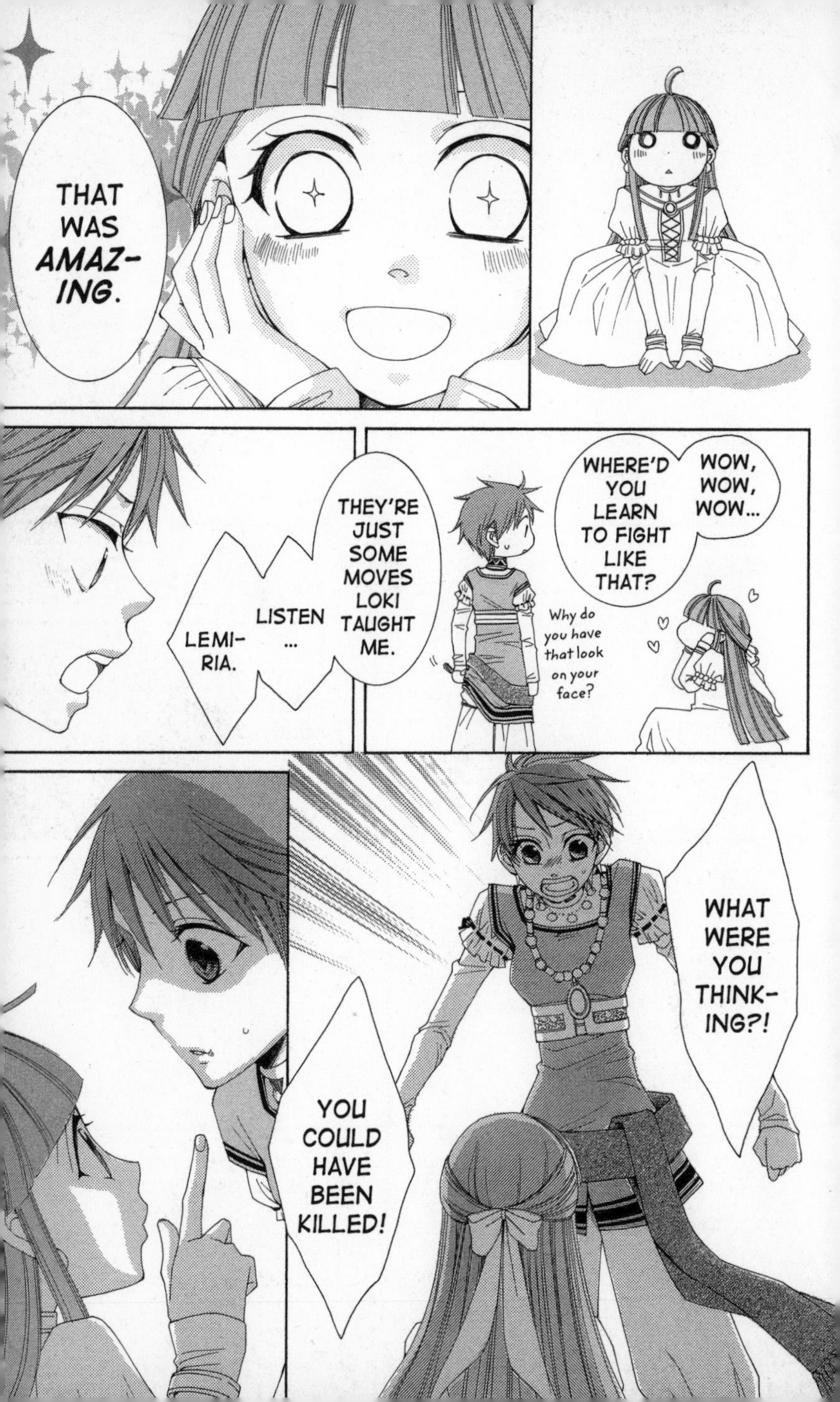
THAT WAS AMAZING.
WOW, WOW, WOW...
WHERE'D YOU LEARN TO FIGHT LIKE THAT?
Why do you have that look on your face?
THEY'RE JUST SOME MOVES LOKI TAUGHT ME.
LISTEN ...
LEMIRIA.
WHAT WERE YOU THINKING?!
YOU COULD HAVE BEEN KILLED!

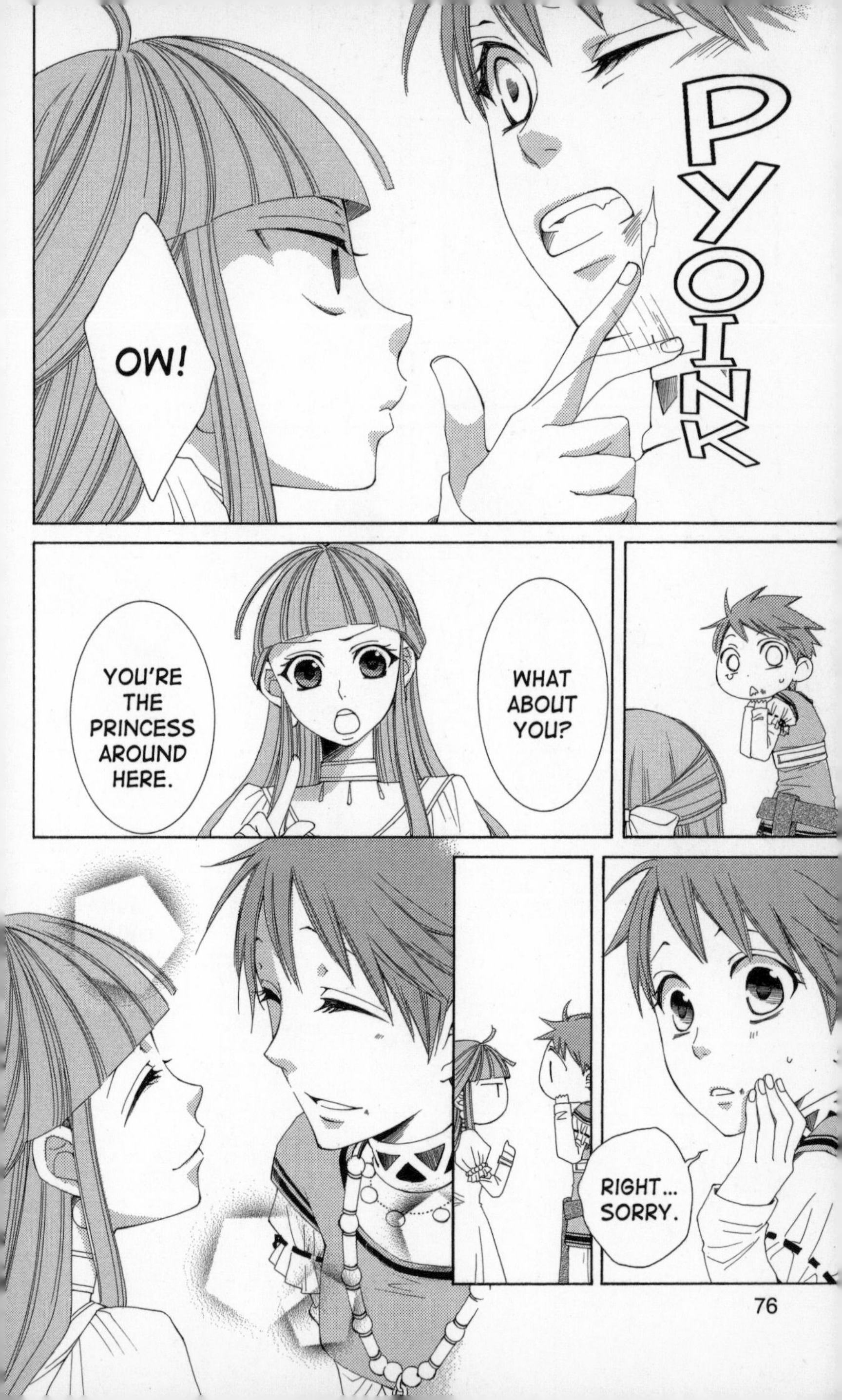
PYOINK
OW!
WHAT ABOUT YOU?
YOU'RE THE PRINCESS AROUND HERE.
RIGHT... SORRY.

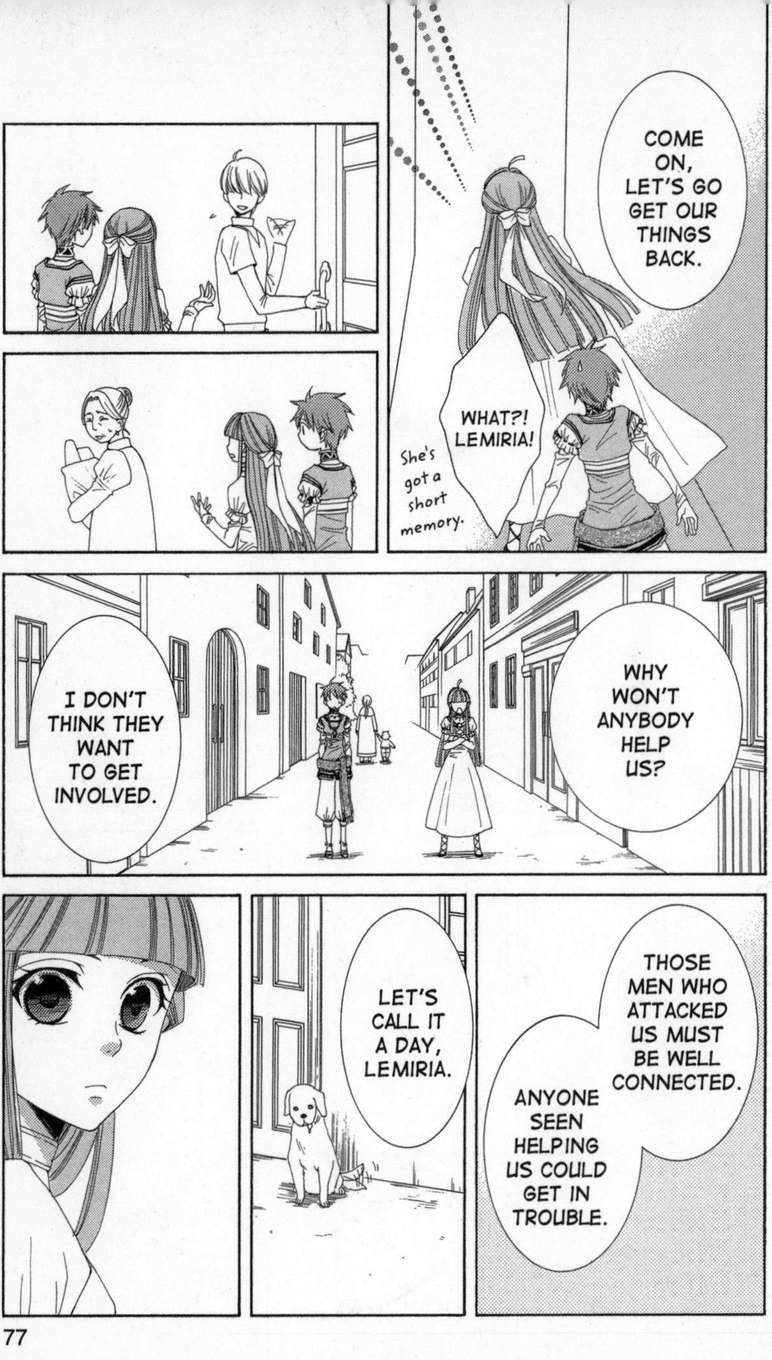
COME ON, LET'S GO GET OUR THINGS BACK.
WHAT?! LEMIRIA!
She's got a short memory.
WHY WON'T ANYBODY HELP US?
I DON'T THINK THEY WANT TO GET INVOLVED.
THOSE MEN WHO ATTACKED US MUST BE WELL CONNECTED.
ANYONE SEEN HELPING US COULD GET IN TROUBLE.
LET'S CALL IT A DAY, LEMIRIA.

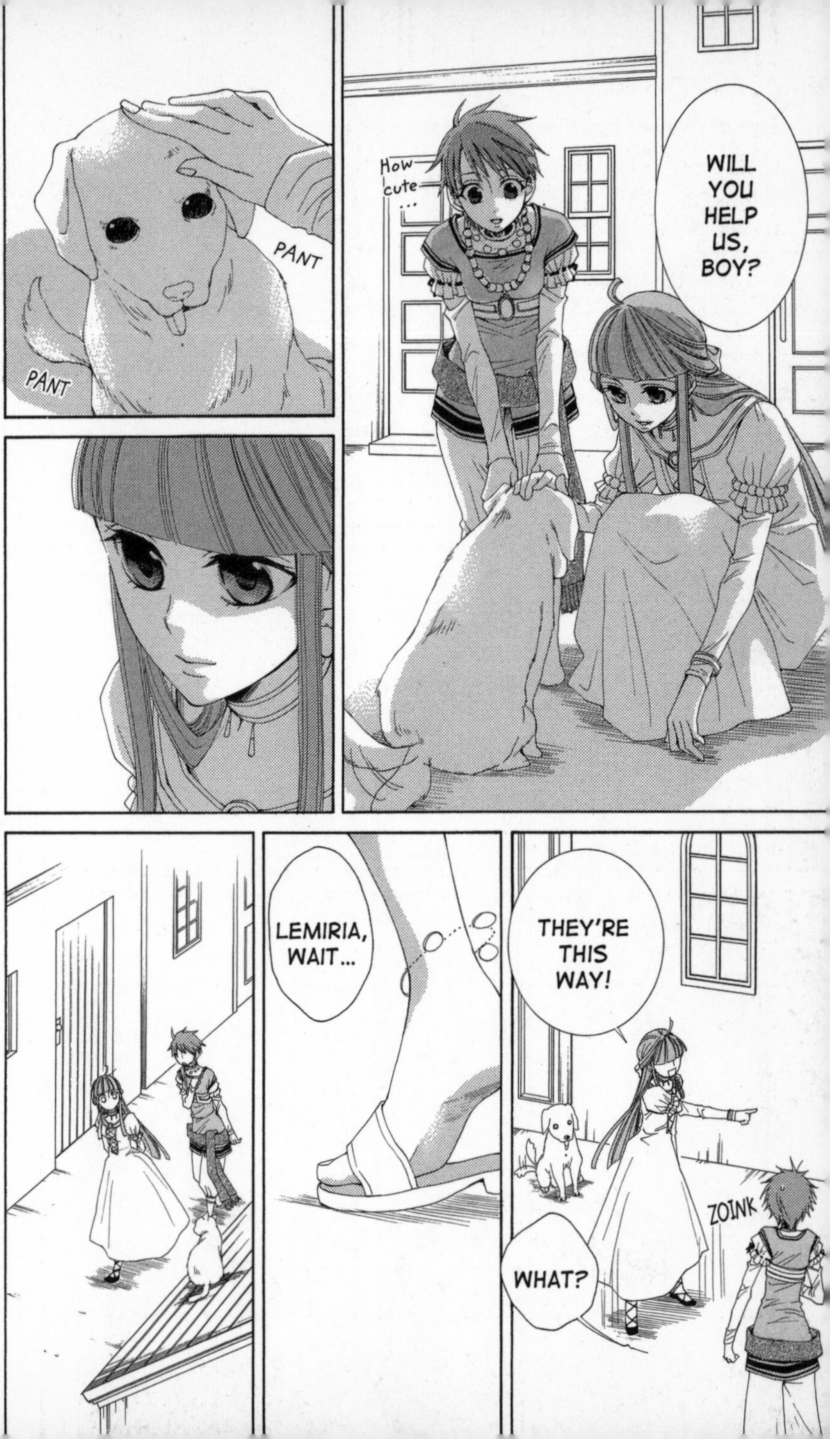
WILL YOU HELP US, BOY?
How cute...
PANT
PANT
THEY'RE THIS WAY!
ZOINK
WHAT?
LEMIRIA, WAIT...

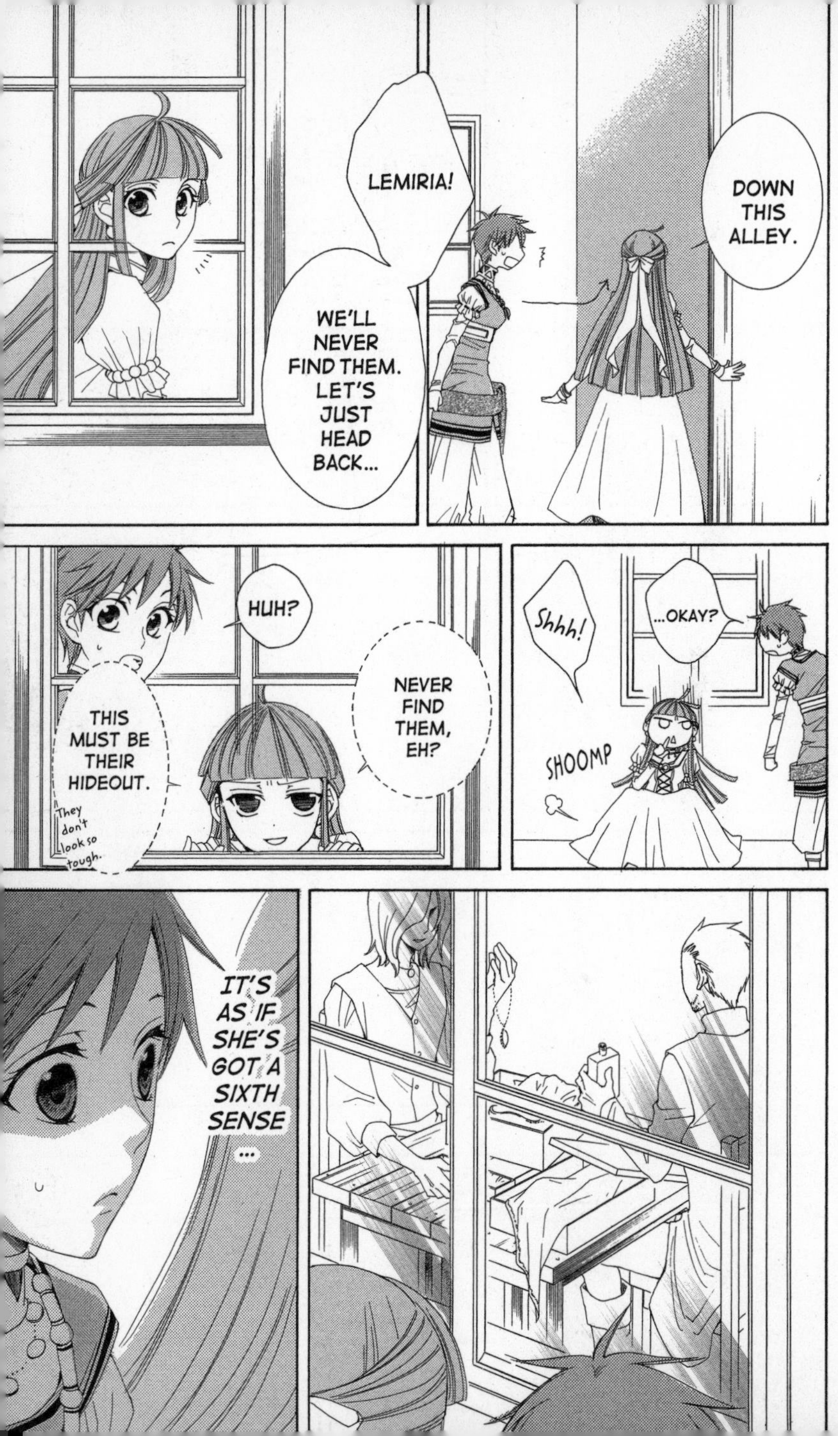
DOWN THIS ALLEY.
LEMIRIA!
WE'LL NEVER FIND THEM. LET'S JUST HEAD BACK...
...OKAY?
Shhh!
SHOOMP
HUH?
NEVER FIND THEM, EH?
THIS MUST BE THEIR HIDEOUT.
They don't look so tough.
IT'S AS IF SHE'S GOT A SIXTH SENSE...

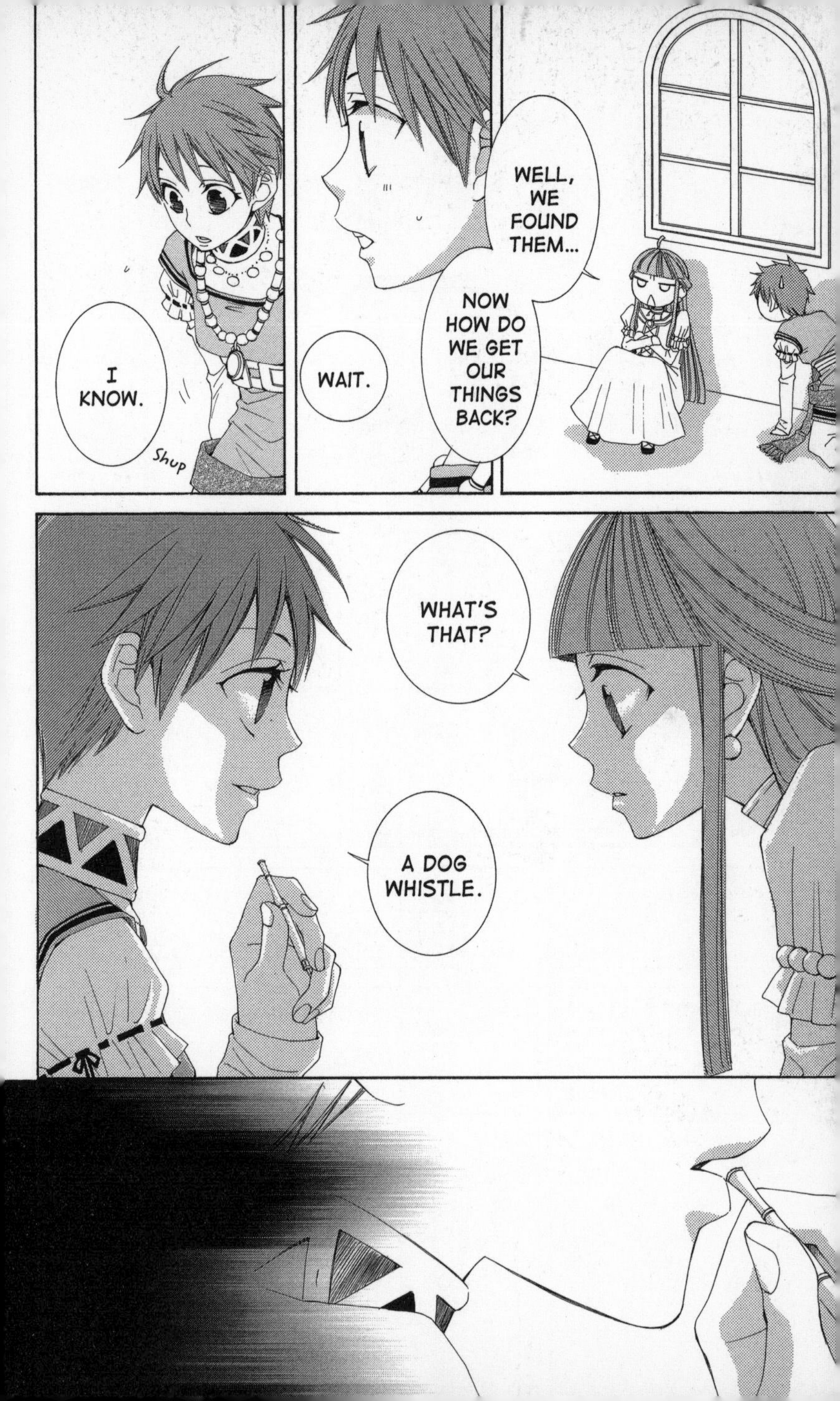
WELL, WE FOUND THEM...
NOW HOW DO WE GET OUR THINGS BACK?
WAIT.
I KNOW.
Shup
WHAT'S THAT?
A DOG WHISTLE.

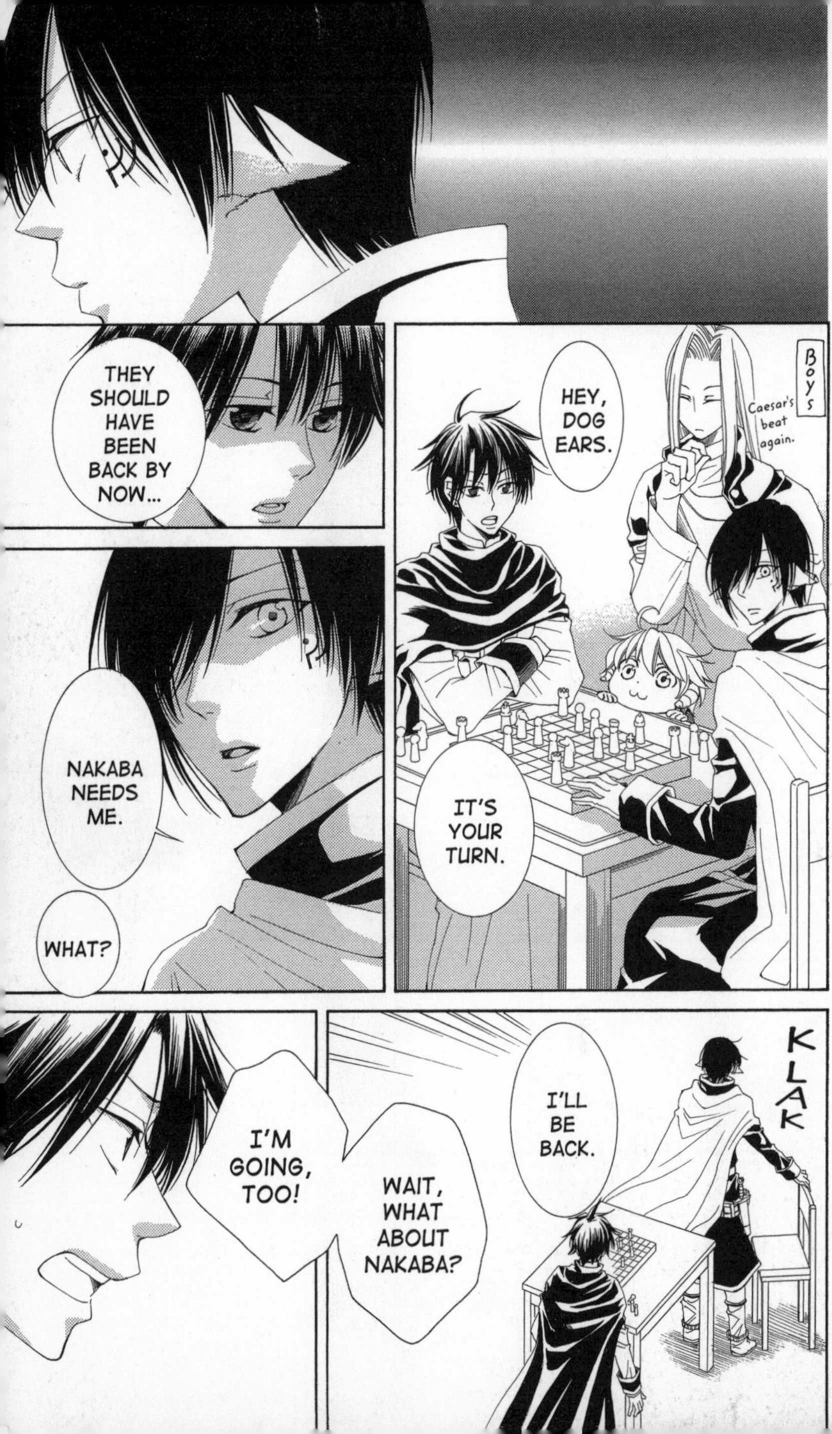
Boys
Caesar's beat again.
HEY, DOG EARS.
IT'S YOUR TURN.
THEY SHOULD HAVE BEEN BACK BY NOW...
NAKABA NEEDS ME.
WHAT?
KLAK
I'LL BE BACK.
WAIT, WHAT ABOUT NAKABA?
I'M GOING, TOO!

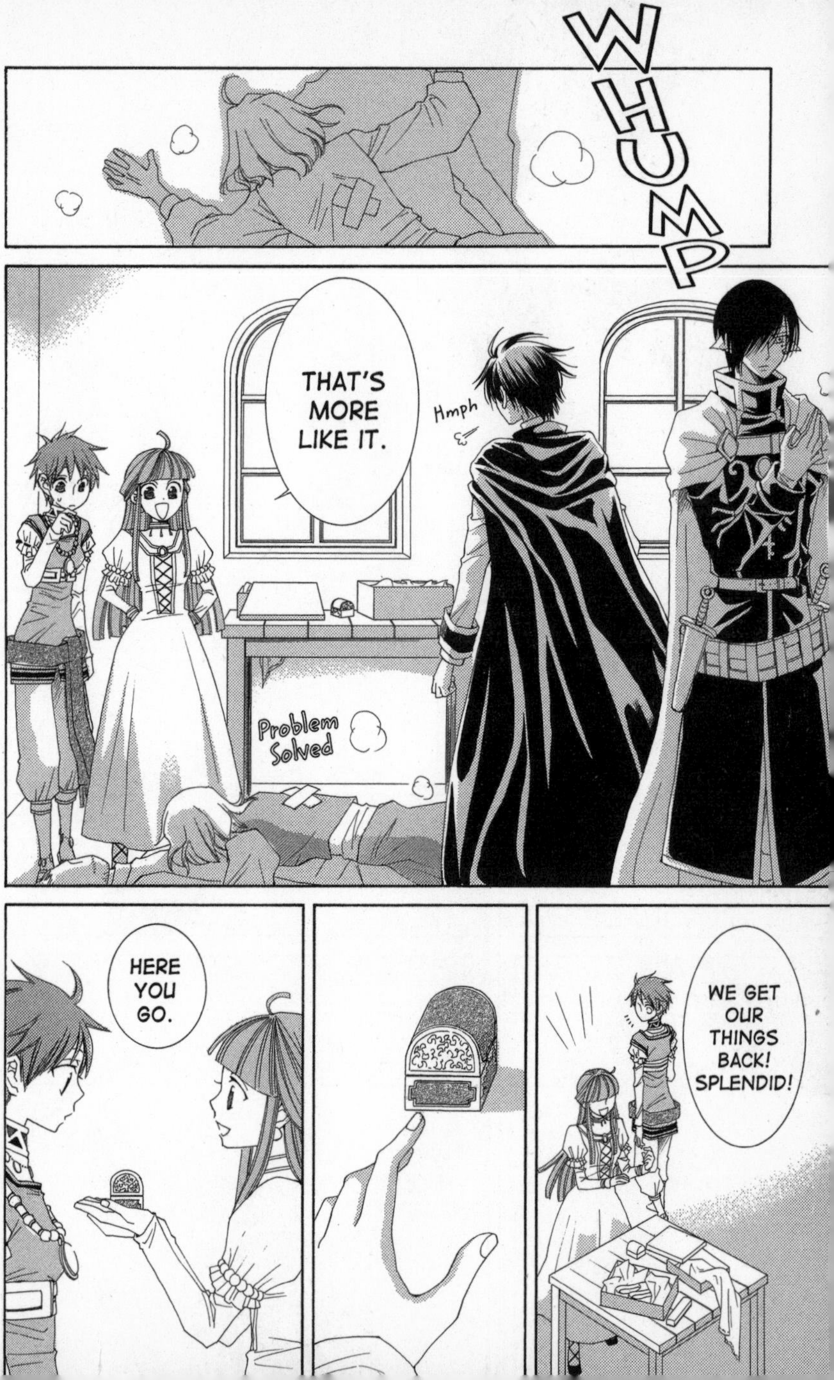
WHUMP
THAT'S MORE LIKE IT.
Hmph
Problem Solved
WE GET OUR THINGS BACK! SPLENDID!
HERE YOU GO.

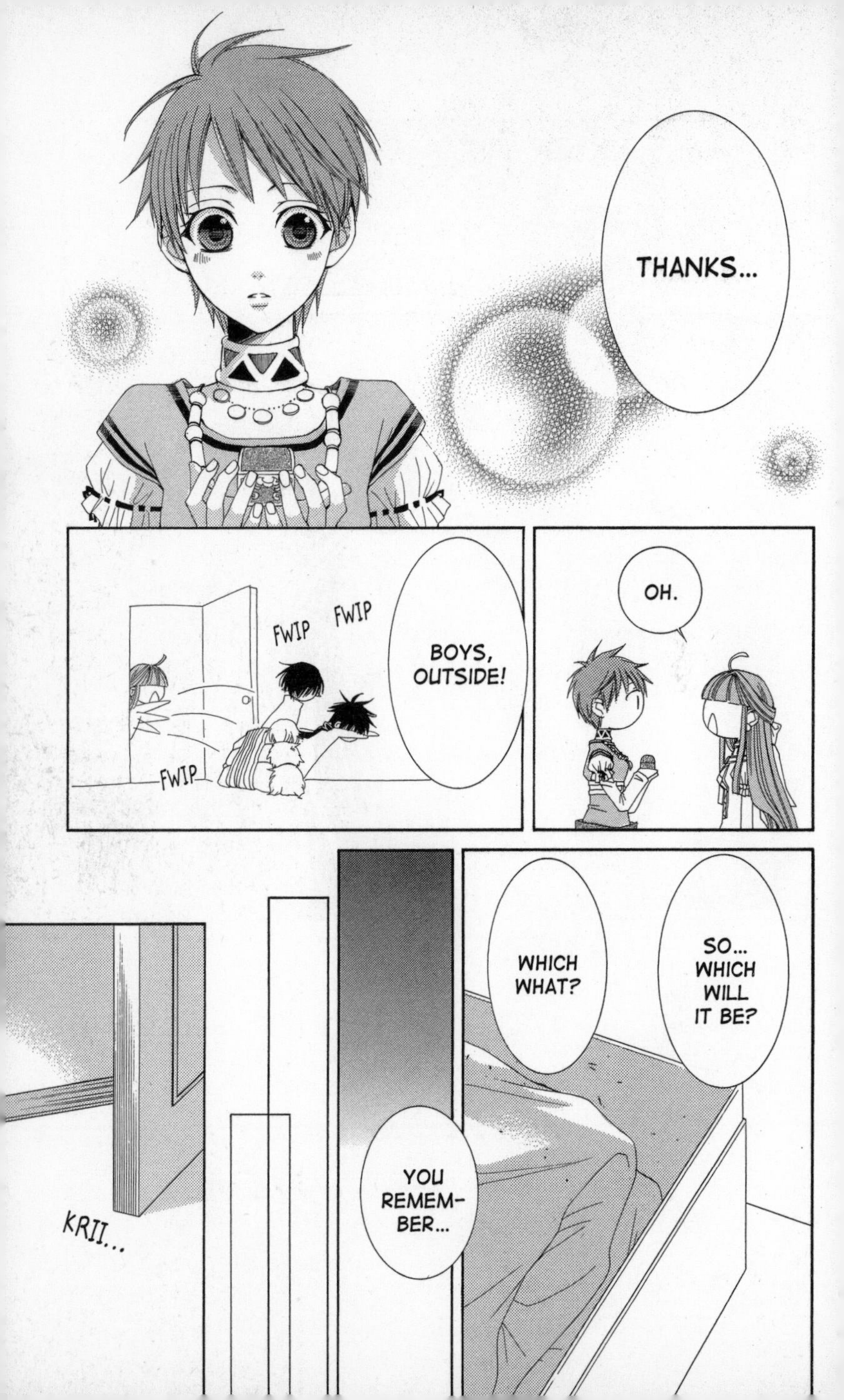
THANKS...
OH.
BOYS, OUTSIDE!
FWIP
FWIP
FWIP
SO... WHICH WILL IT BE?
WHICH WHAT?
YOU REMEM-BER...
KRII...

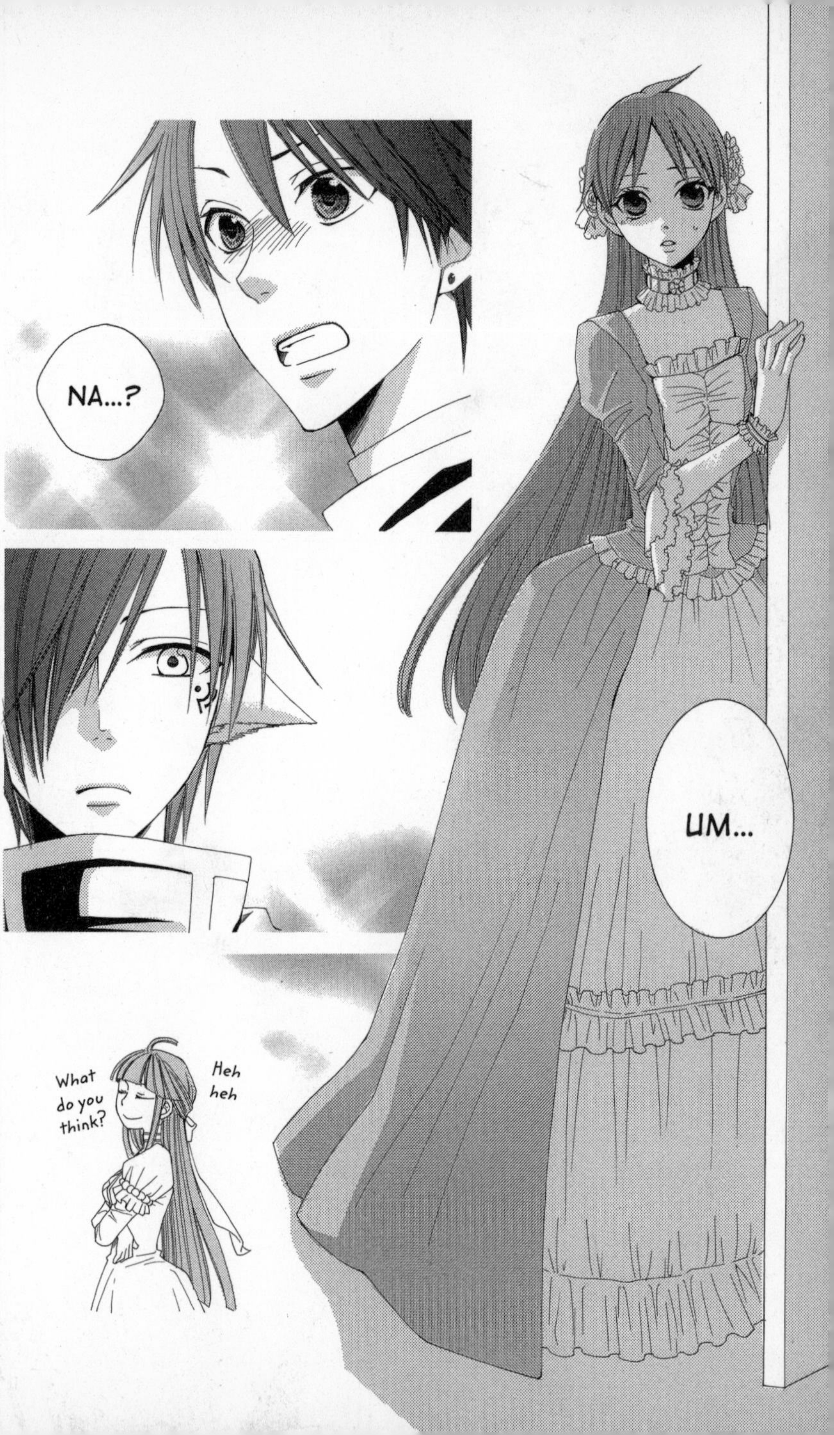
UM...
NA...?
Heh heh
What do you think?

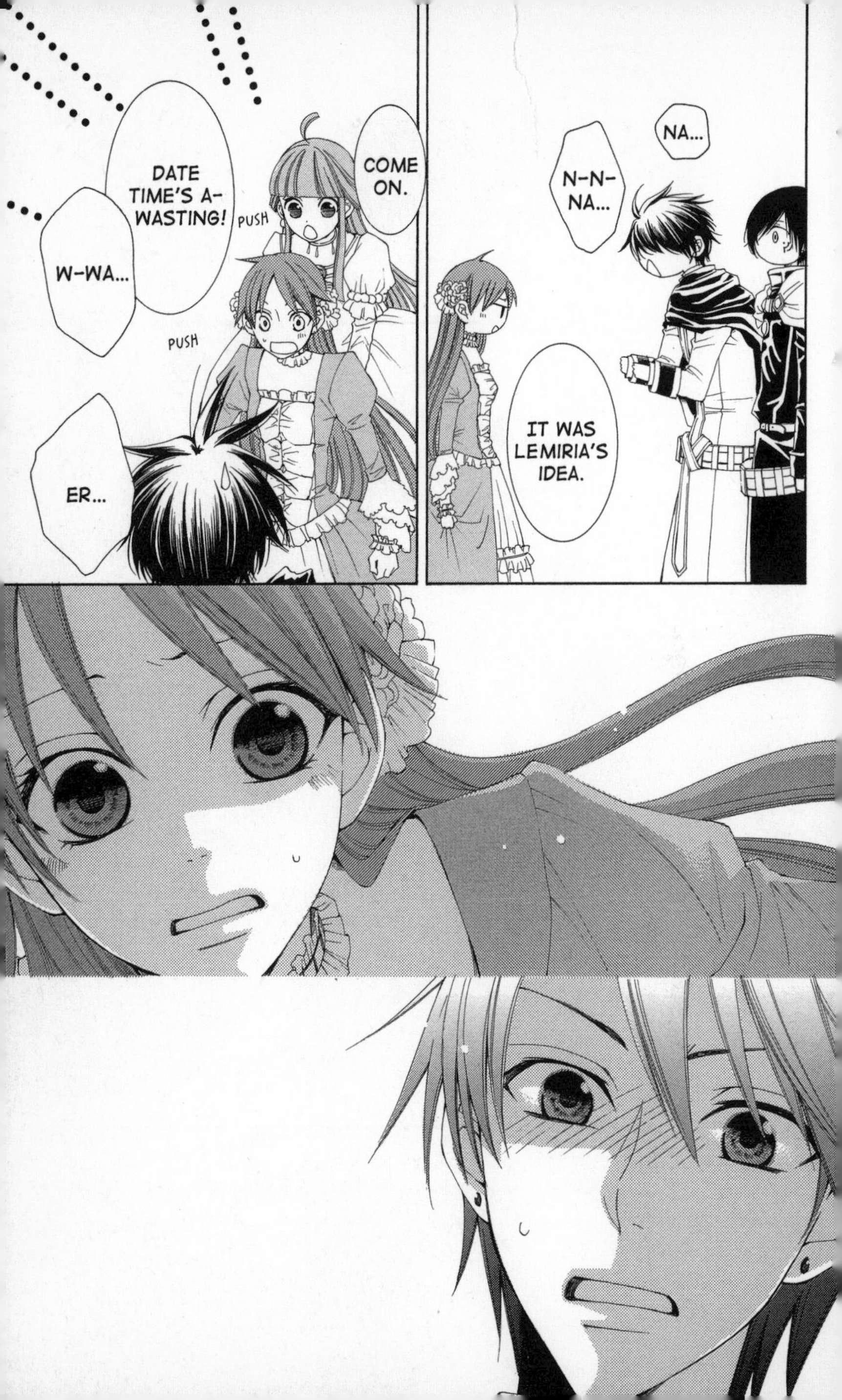
NA...
N-N-NA...
IT WAS LEMIRIA'S IDEA.
COME ON.
DATE TIME'S A-WASTING!
PUSH
W-WA...
PUSH
ER...

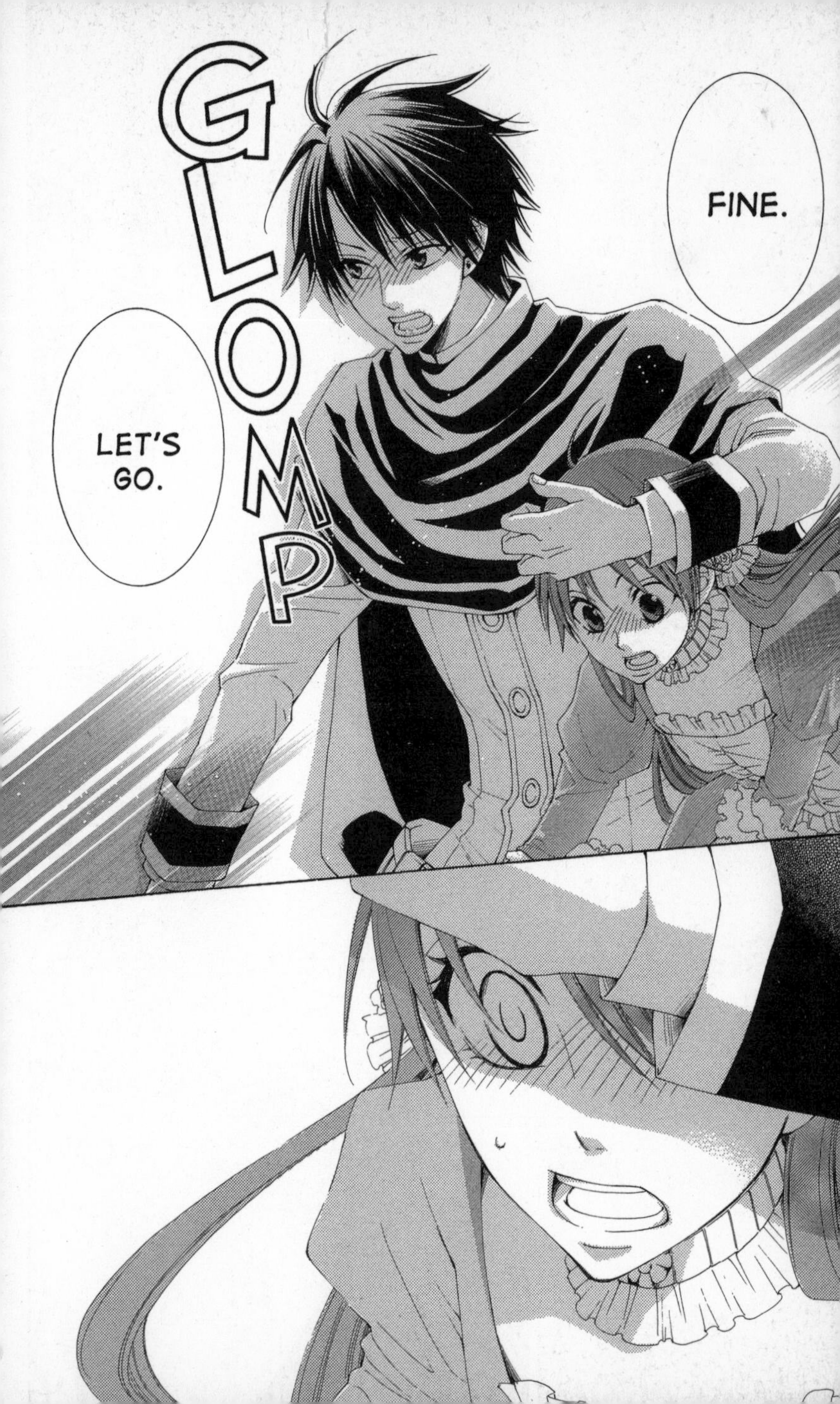
FINE.
GLOMP
LET'S GO.

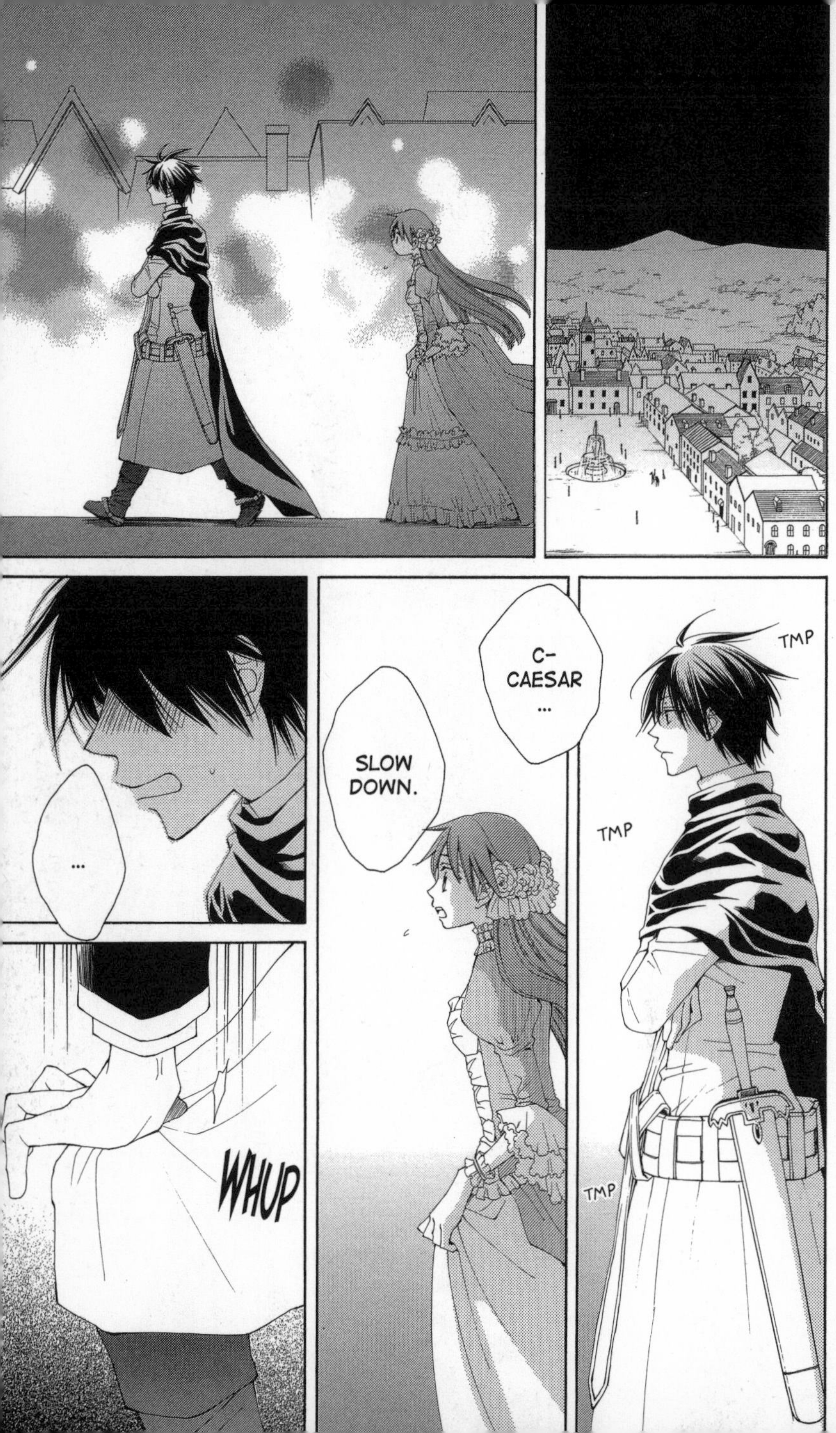
TMP
TMP
TMP
C-CAESAR...
SLOW DOWN.
...
WHUP

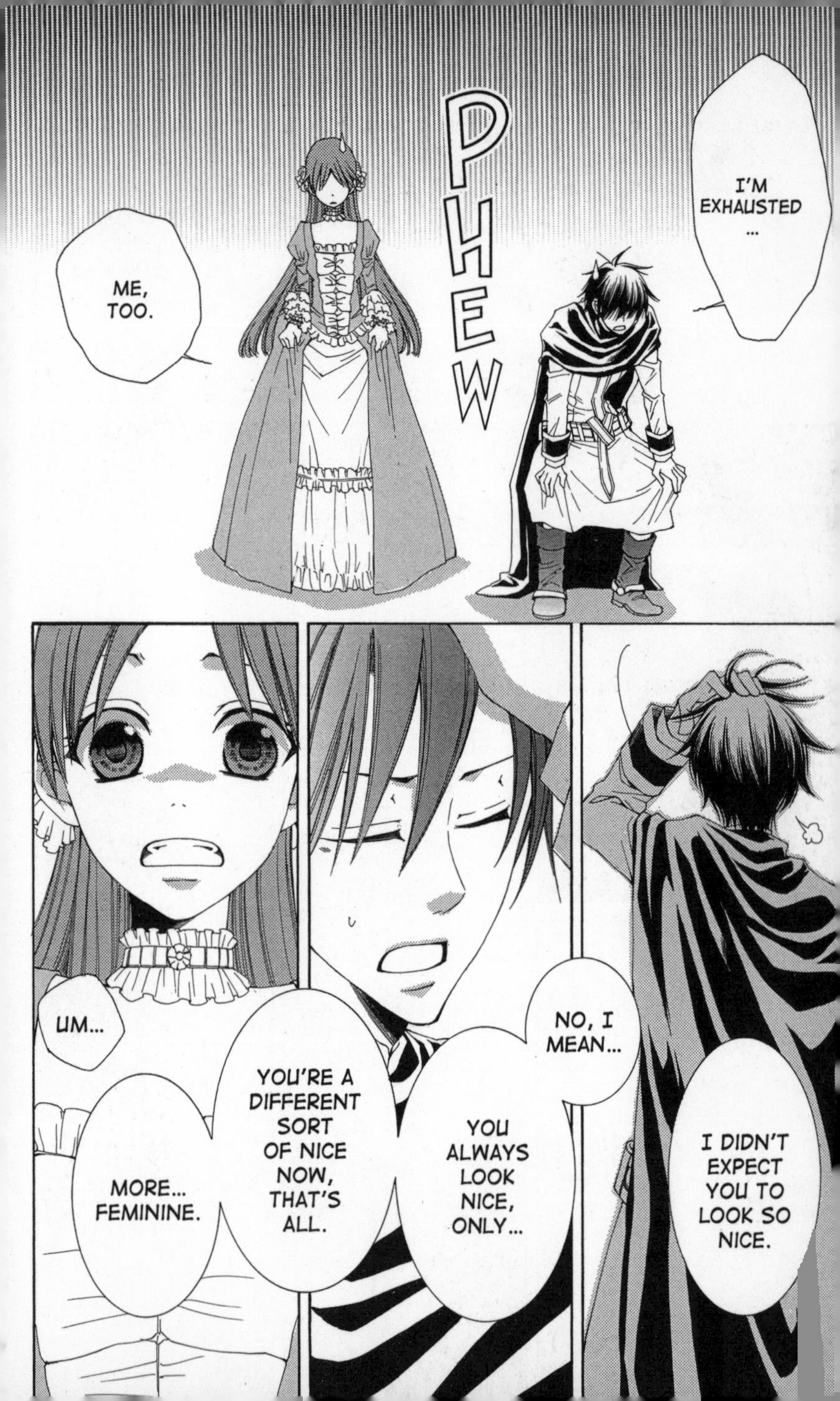
I'M EXHAUSTED ...
PHEW
ME, TOO.
I DIDN'T EXPECT YOU TO LOOK SO NICE.
NO, I MEAN...
YOU ALWAYS LOOK NICE, ONLY...
YOU'RE A DIFFERENT SORT OF NICE NOW, THAT'S ALL.
UM...
MORE... FEMININE.

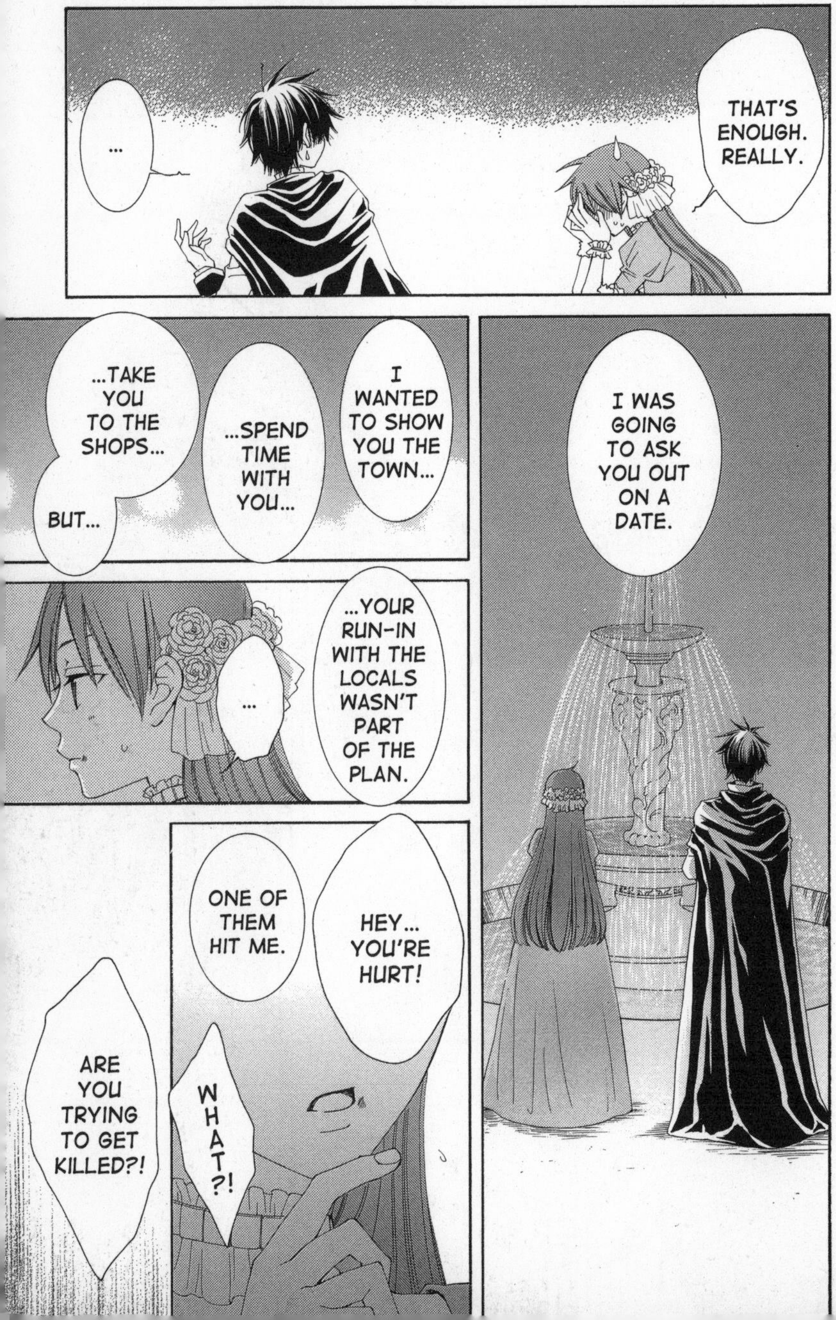
THAT'S ENOUGH. REALLY.
...
I WAS GOING TO ASK YOU OUT ON A DATE.
I WANTED TO SHOW YOU THE TOWN...
...SPEND TIME WITH YOU...
...TAKE YOU TO THE SHOPS...
BUT...
...YOUR RUN-IN WITH THE LOCALS WASN'T PART OF THE PLAN.
...
HEY... YOU'RE HURT!
ONE OF THEM HIT ME.
WHAT?!
ARE YOU TRYING TO GET KILLED?!

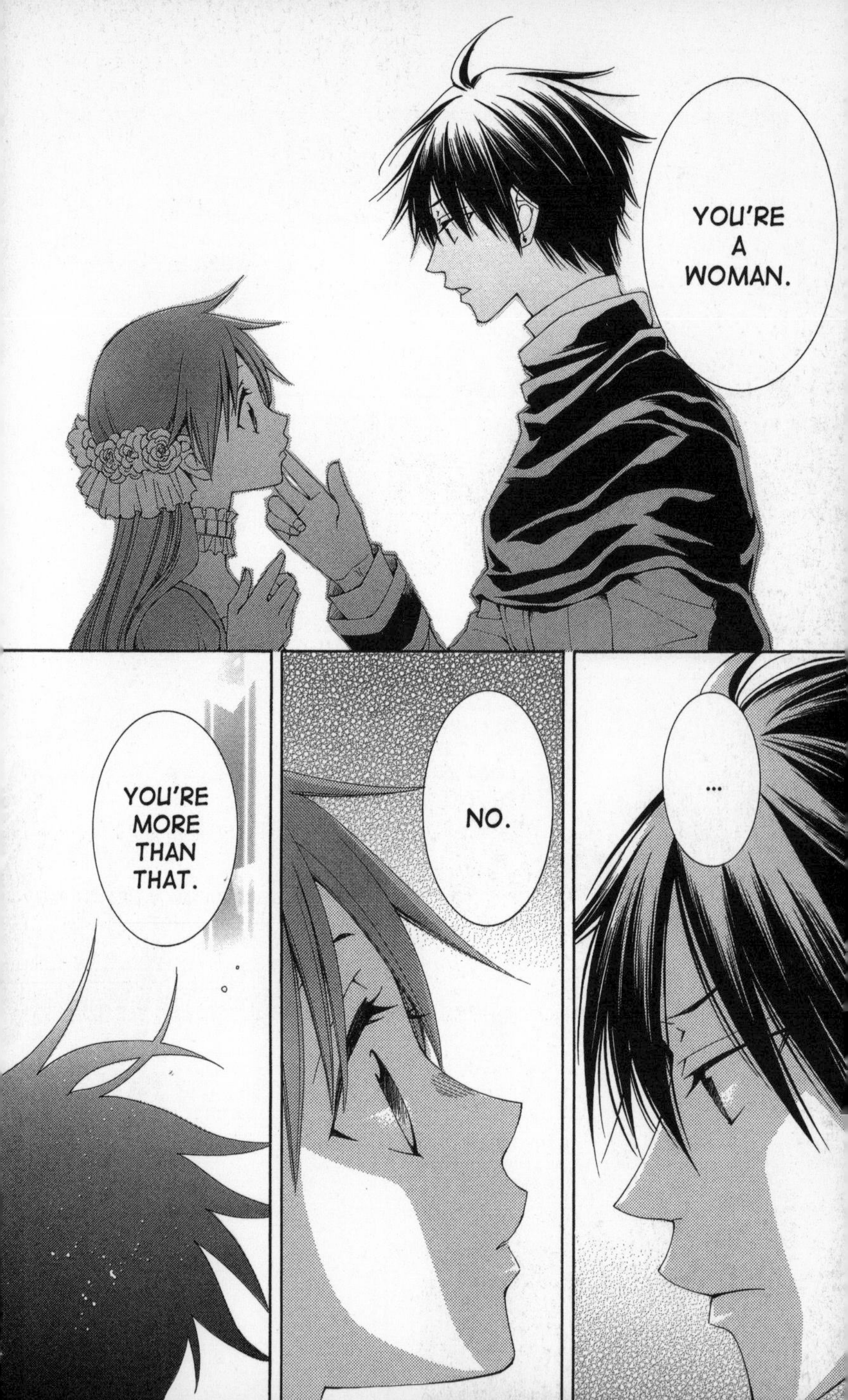
YOU'RE A WOMAN.
...
NO.
YOU'RE MORE THAN THAT.

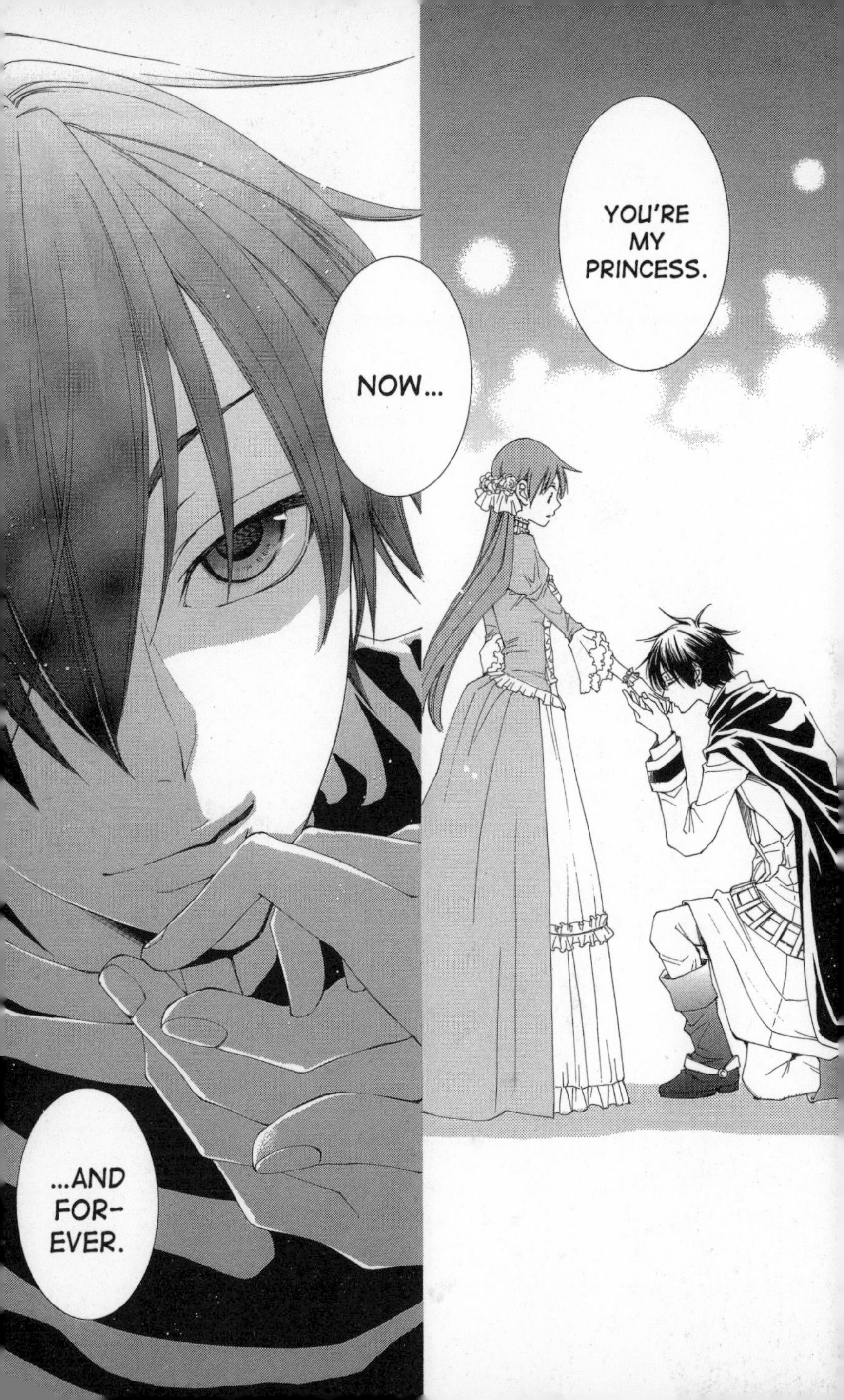
YOU'RE MY PRINCESS.
NOW...
...AND FOR-EVER.

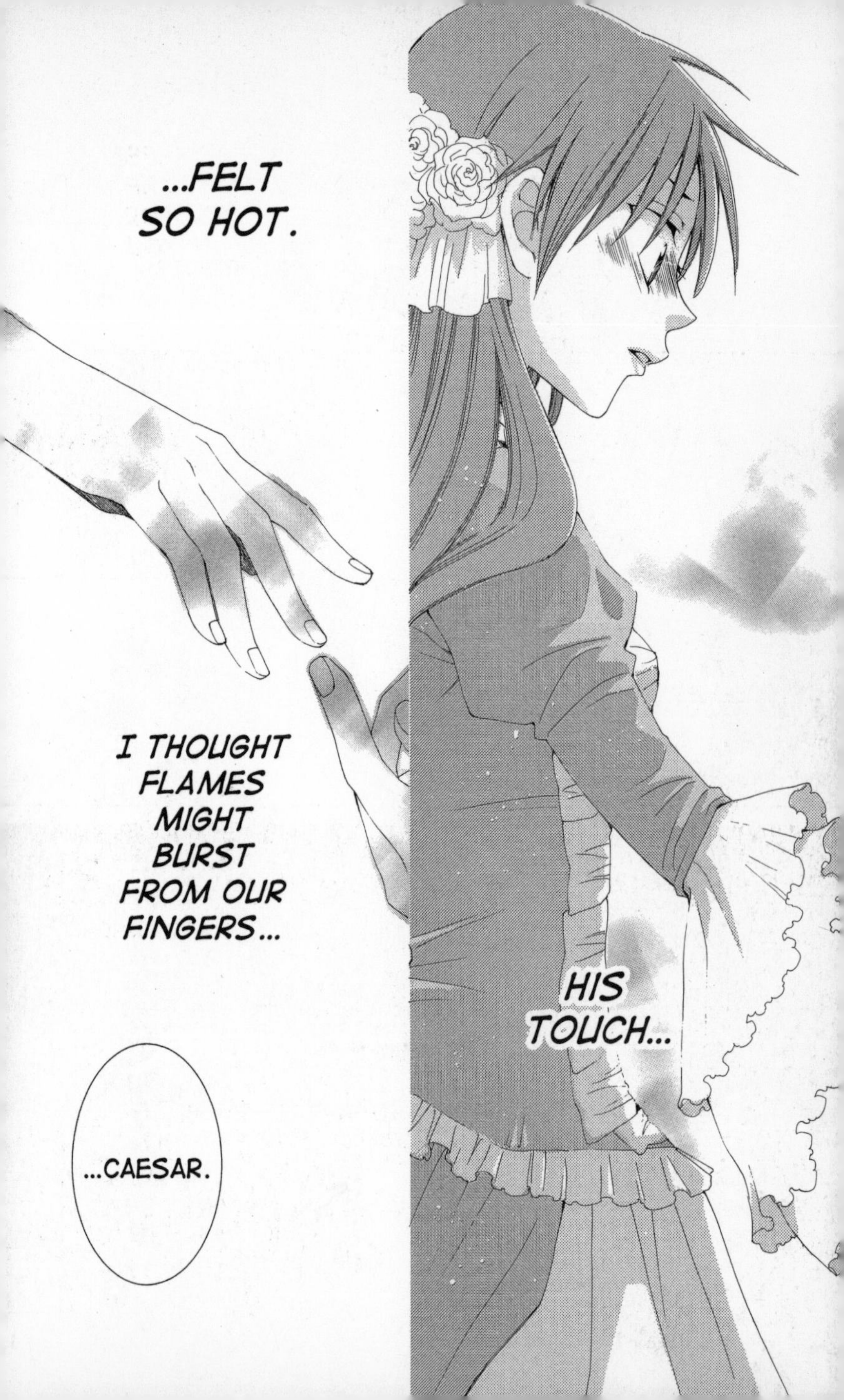
HIS TOUCH...
...FELT SO HOT.
I THOUGHT FLAMES MIGHT BURST FROM OUR FINGERS...
...CAESAR.

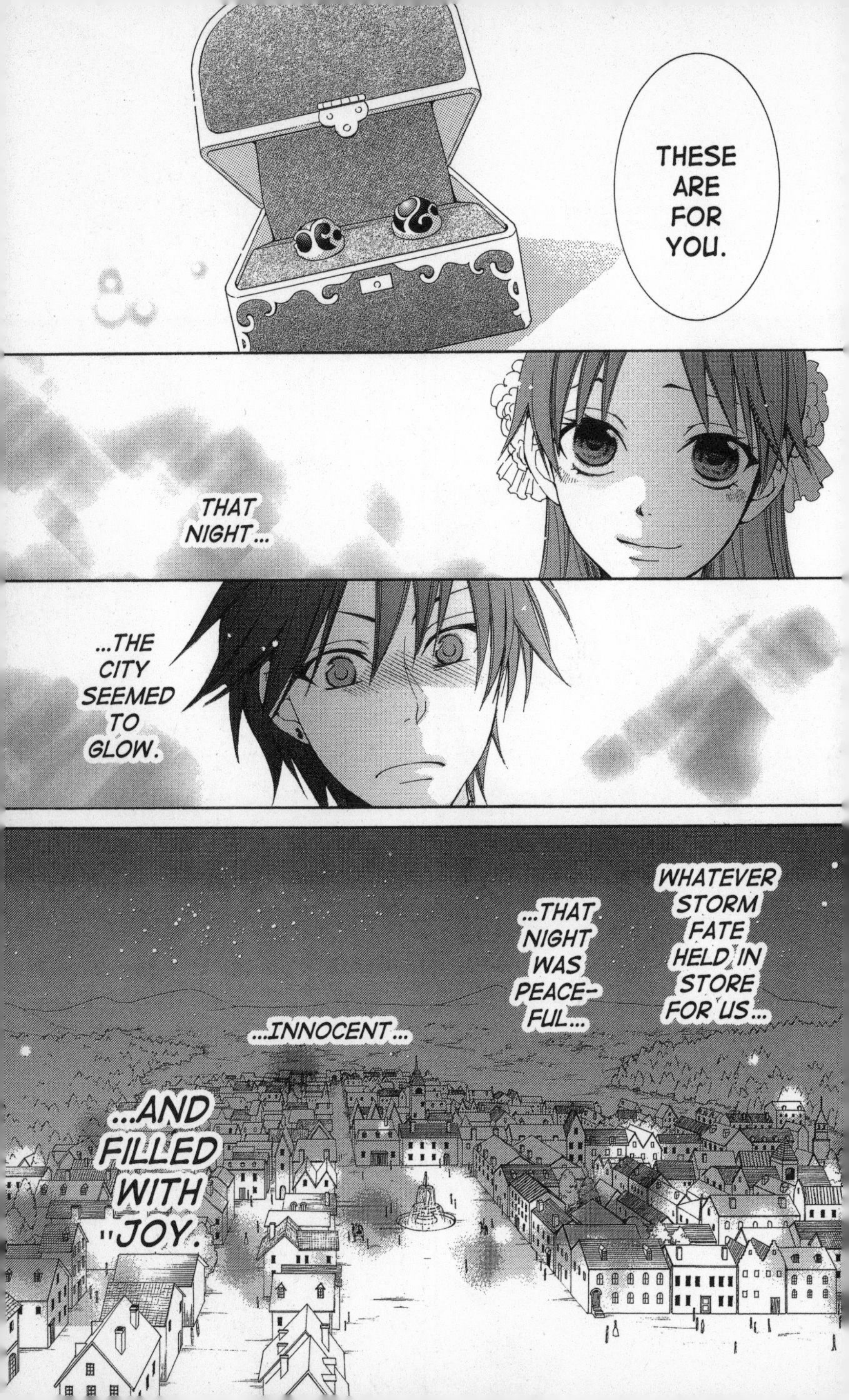
THESE ARE FOR YOU.
THAT NIGHT...
...THE CITY SEEMED TO GLOW.
WHATEVER STORM FATE HELD IN STORE FOR US...
...THAT NIGHT WAS PEACE-FUL...
...INNOCENT...
...AND FILLED WITH JOY.

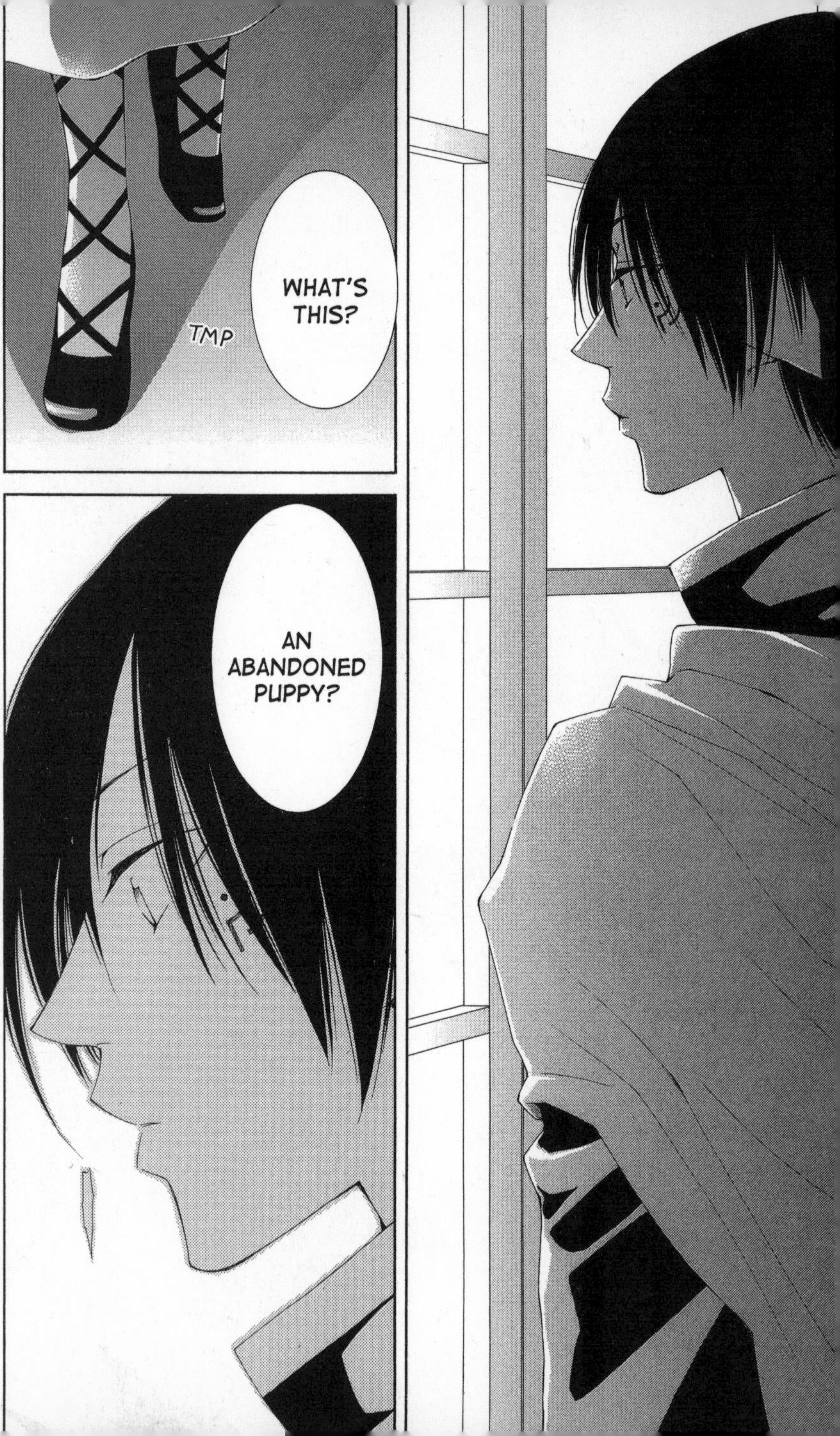
WHAT'S THIS?
TMP
AN ABANDONED PUPPY?

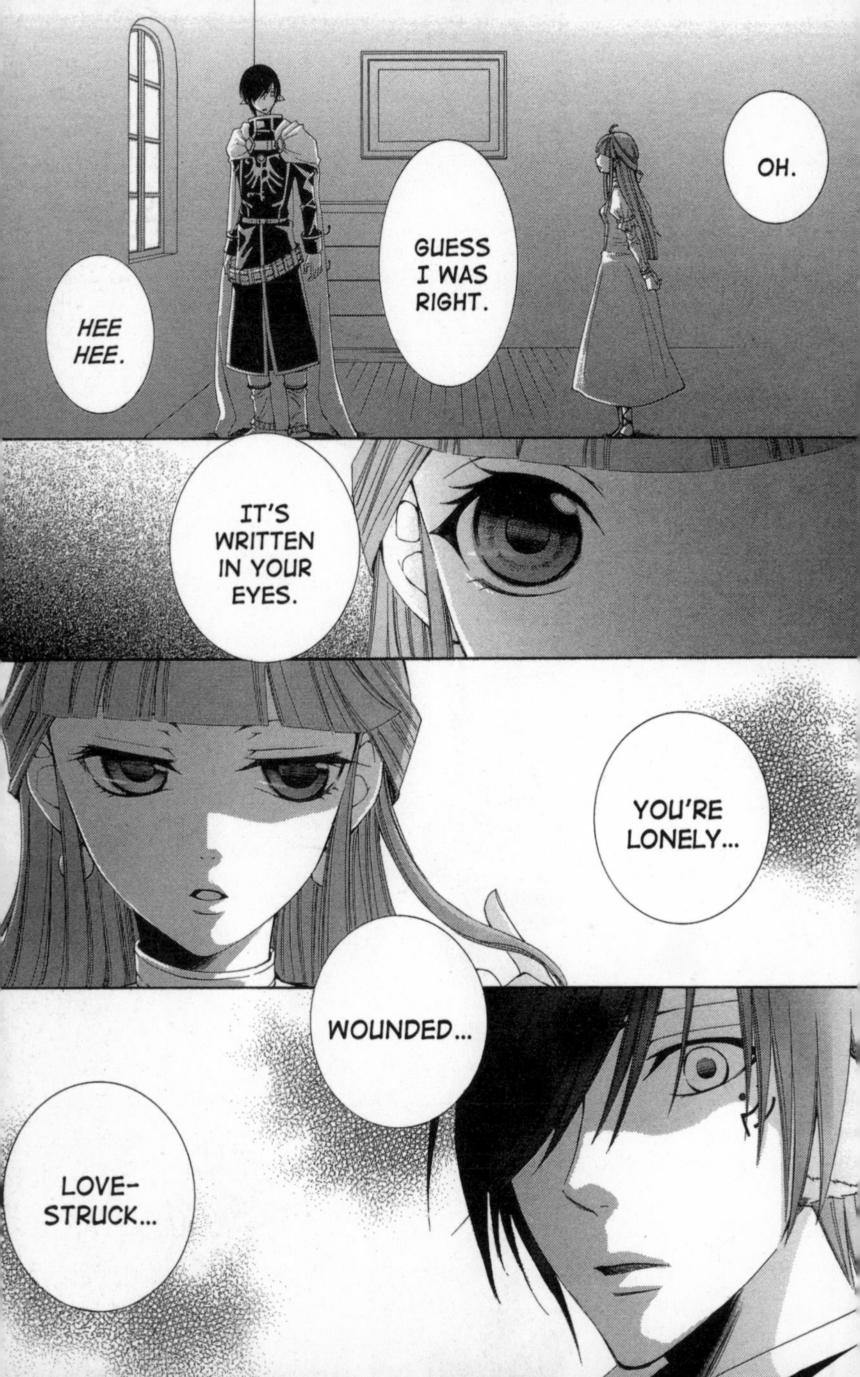
OH.
GUESS I WAS RIGHT.
HEE HEE.
IT'S WRITTEN IN YOUR EYES.
YOU'RE LONELY...
WOUNDED...
LOVE-STRUCK...

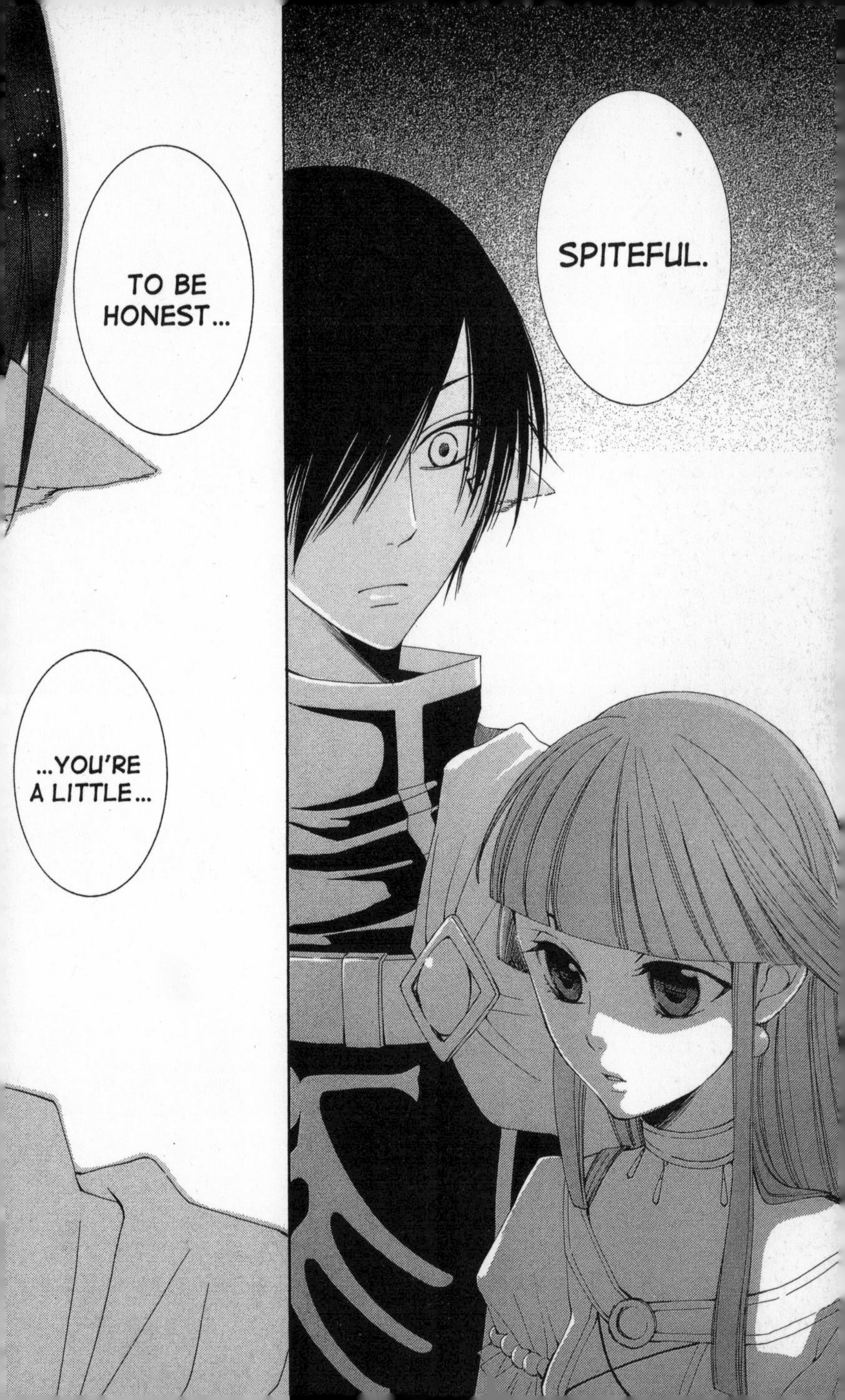
TO BE HONEST...
...YOU'RE A LITTLE...
SPITEFUL.

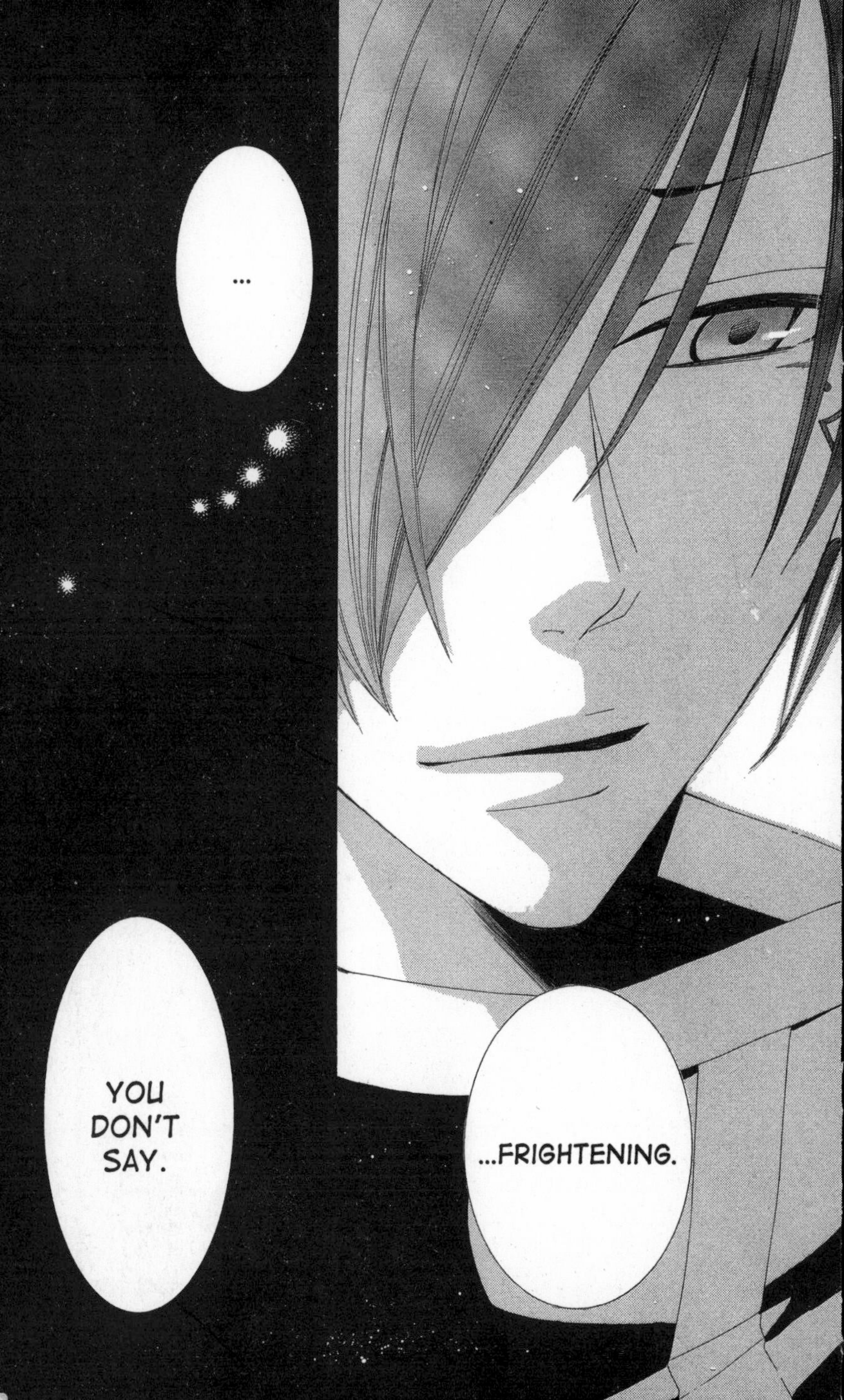
...FRIGHTENING.
...
YOU DON'T SAY.

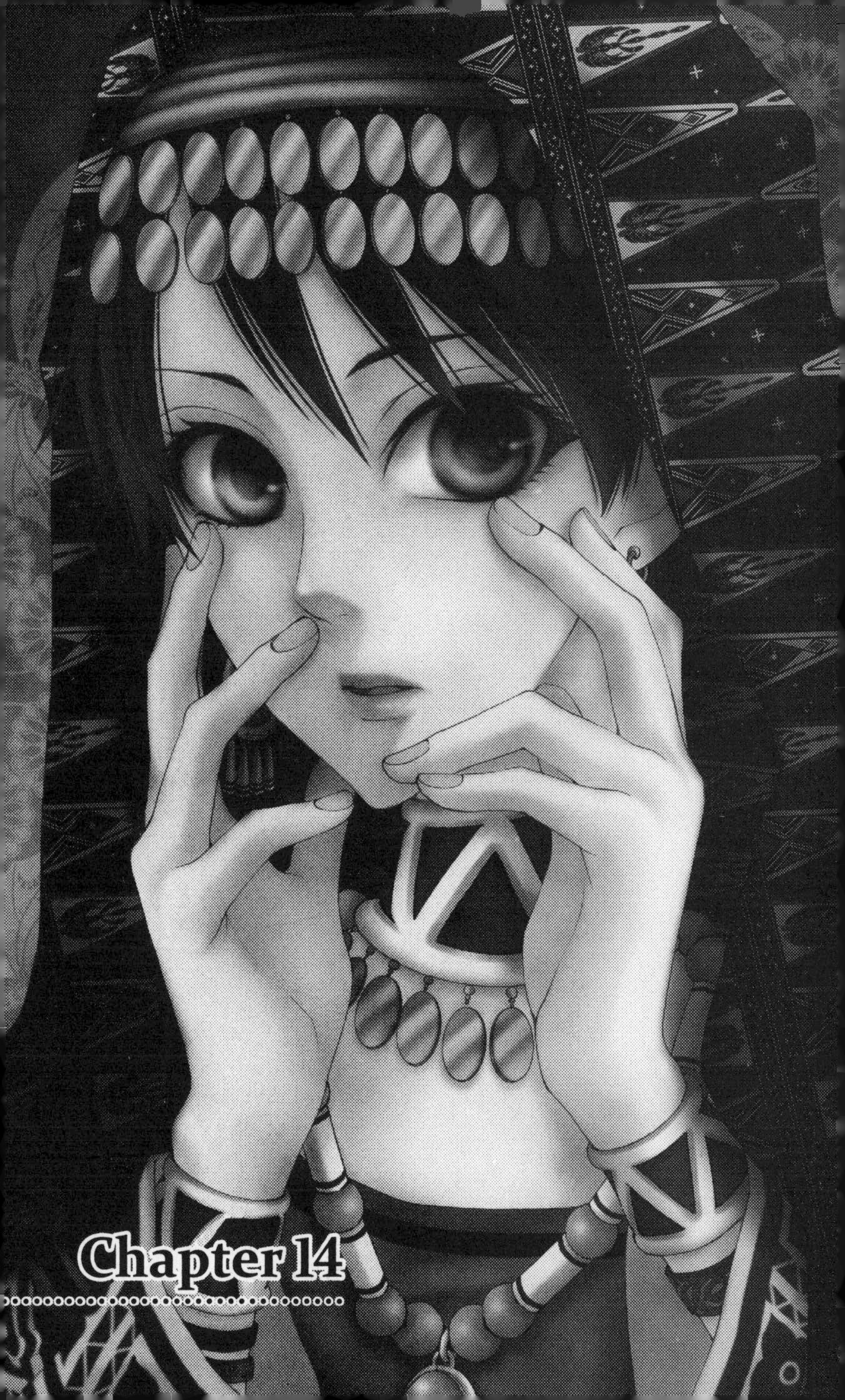
Chapter 14

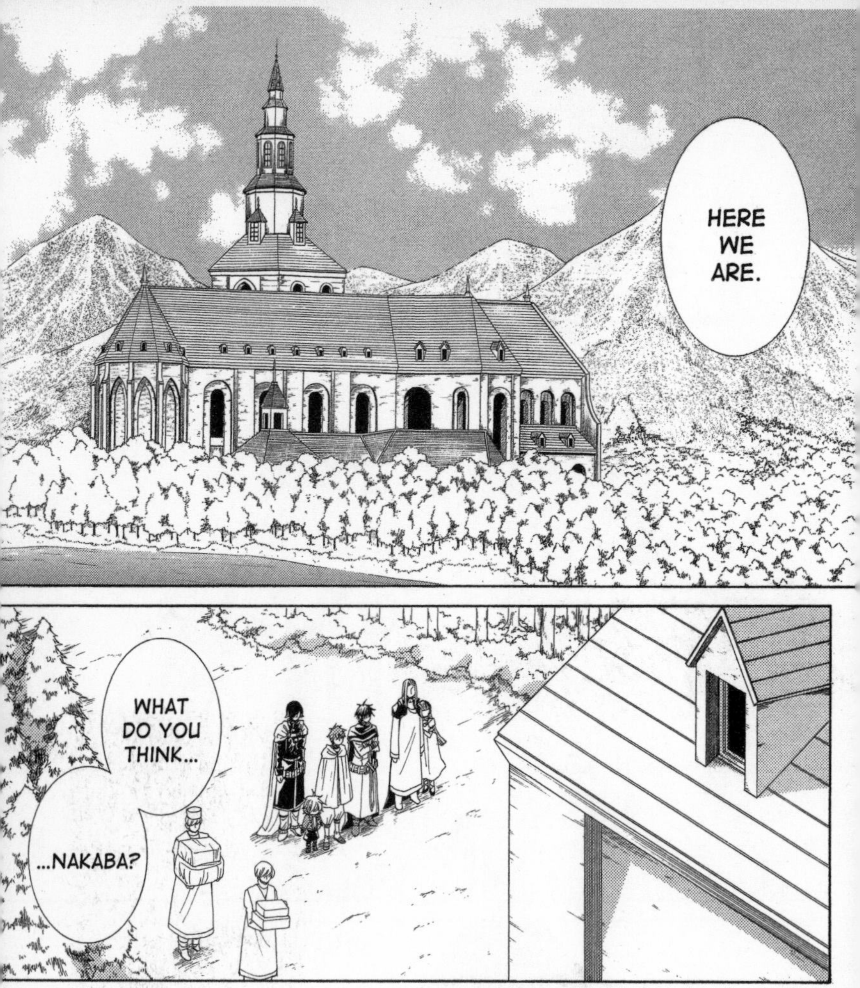
HERE WE ARE.
WHAT DO YOU THINK...
...NAKABA?

Dawn of the Arcana

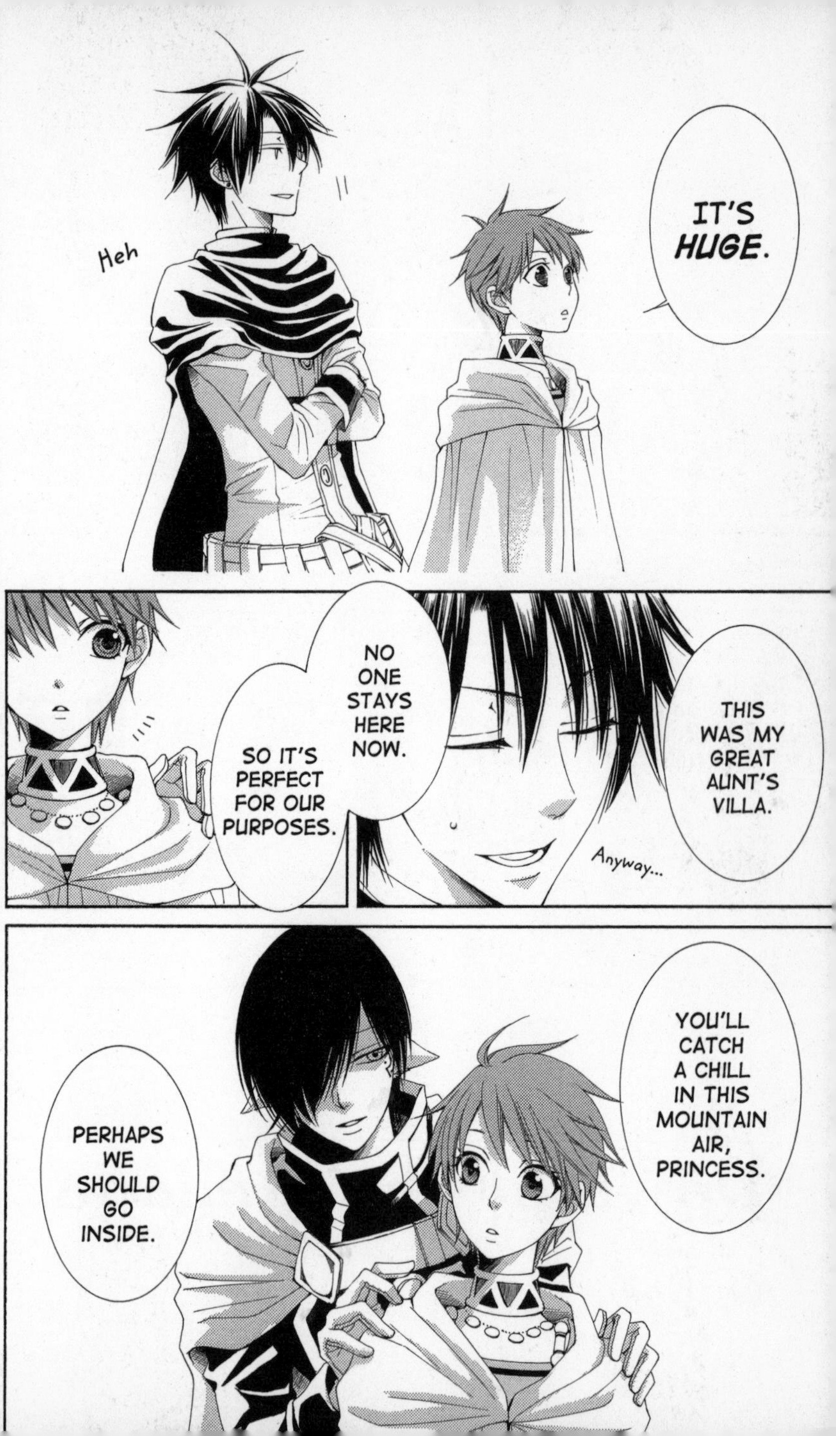
IT'S HUGE.
Heh
THIS WAS MY GREAT AUNT'S VILLA.
Anyway...
NO ONE STAYS HERE NOW.
SO IT'S PERFECT FOR OUR PURPOSES.
YOU'LL CATCH A CHILL IN THIS MOUNTAIN AIR, PRINCESS.
PERHAPS WE SHOULD GO INSIDE.

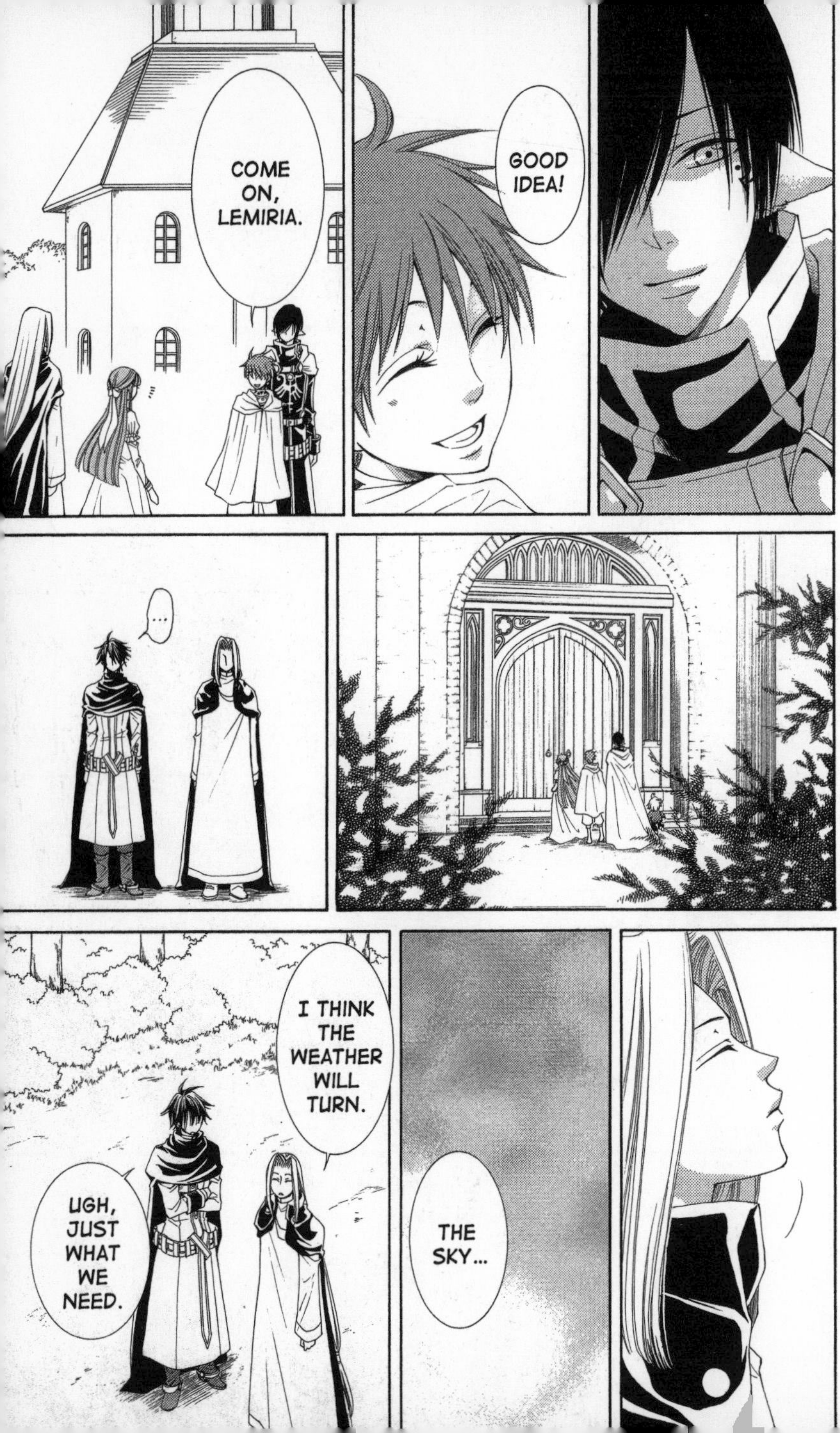
GOOD IDEA!
COME ON, LEMIRIA.
...
THE SKY...
I THINK THE WEATHER WILL TURN.
UGH, JUST WHAT WE NEED.

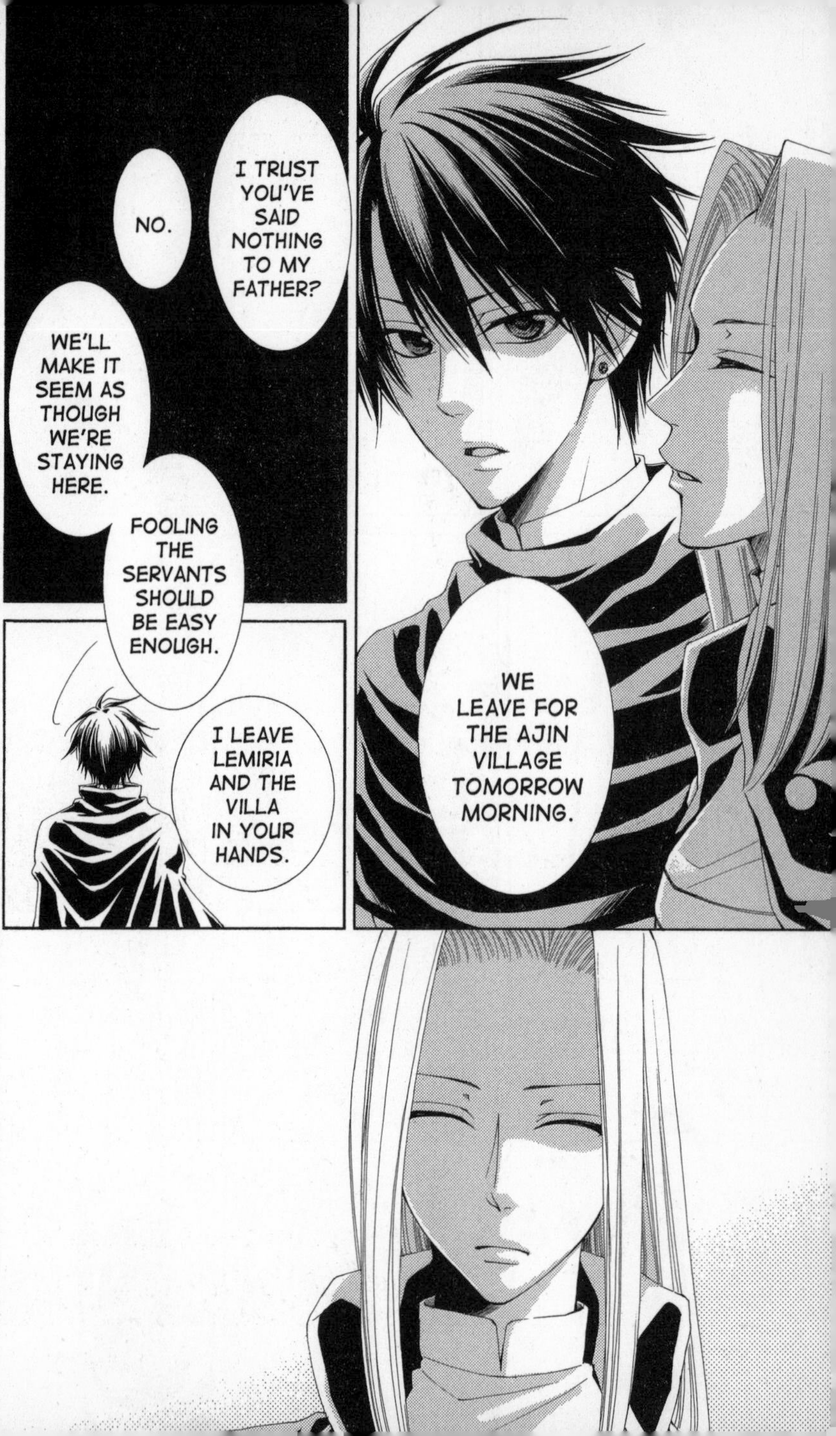
WE LEAVE FOR THE AJIN VILLAGE TOMORROW MORNING.
I TRUST YOU'VE SAID NOTHING TO MY FATHER?
NO.
WE'LL MAKE IT SEEM AS THOUGH WE'RE STAYING HERE.
FOOLING THE SERVANTS SHOULD BE EASY ENOUGH.
I LEAVE LEMIRIA AND THE VILLA IN YOUR HANDS.

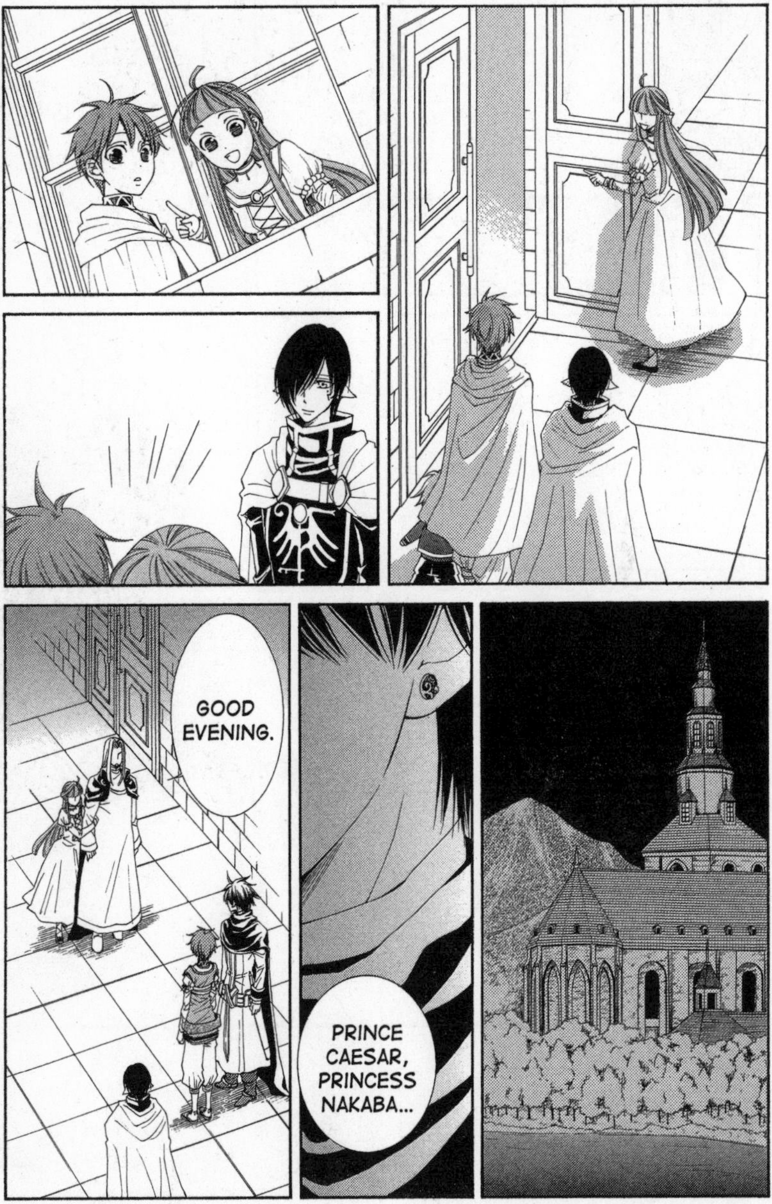
GOOD EVENING.
PRINCE CAESAR, PRINCESS NAKABA...

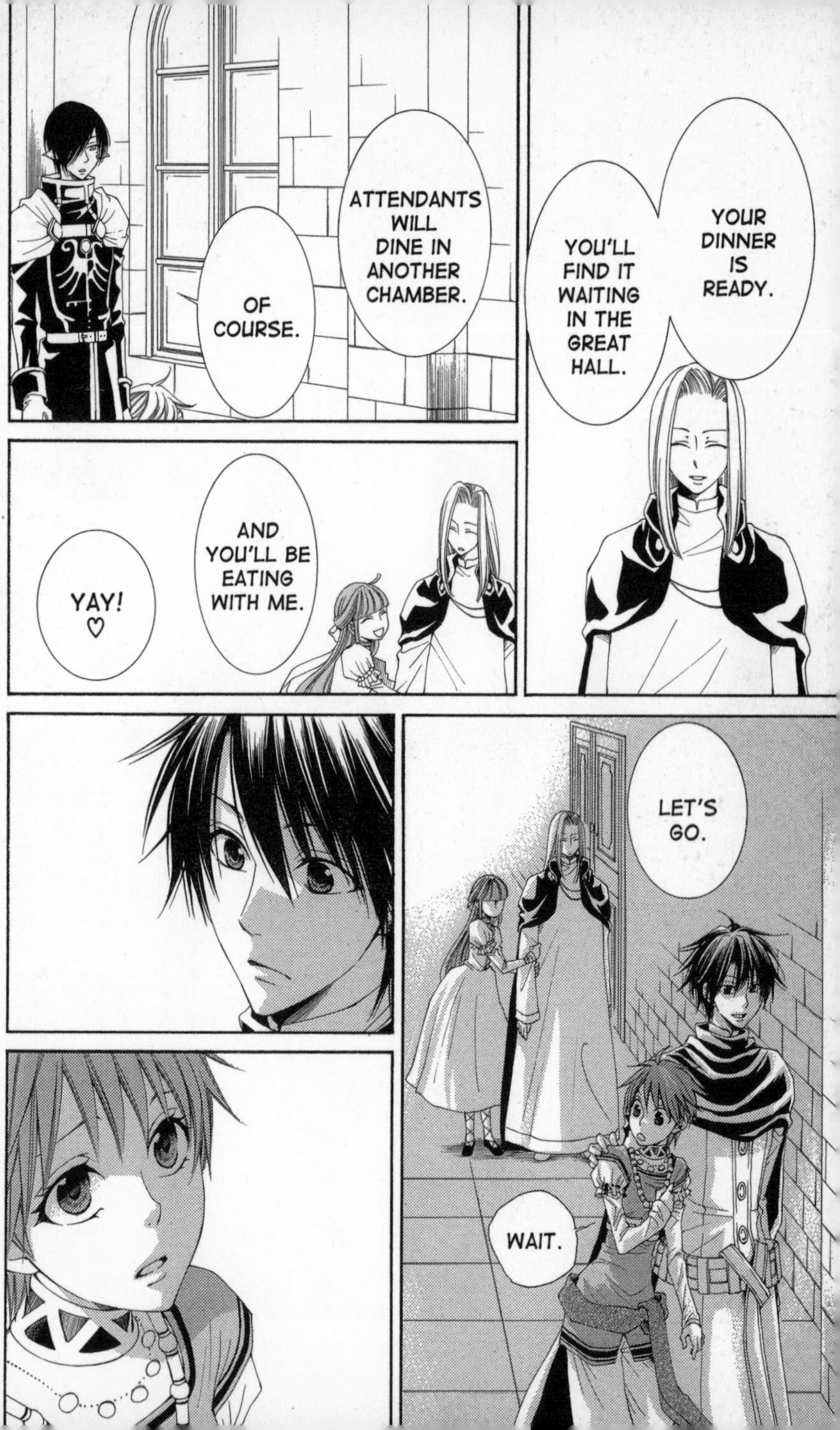
YOUR DINNER IS READY.
YOU'LL FIND IT WAITING IN THE GREAT HALL.
ATTENDANTS WILL DINE IN ANOTHER CHAMBER.
OF COURSE.
AND YOU'LL BE EATING WITH ME.
YAY! ♡
LET'S GO.
WAIT.

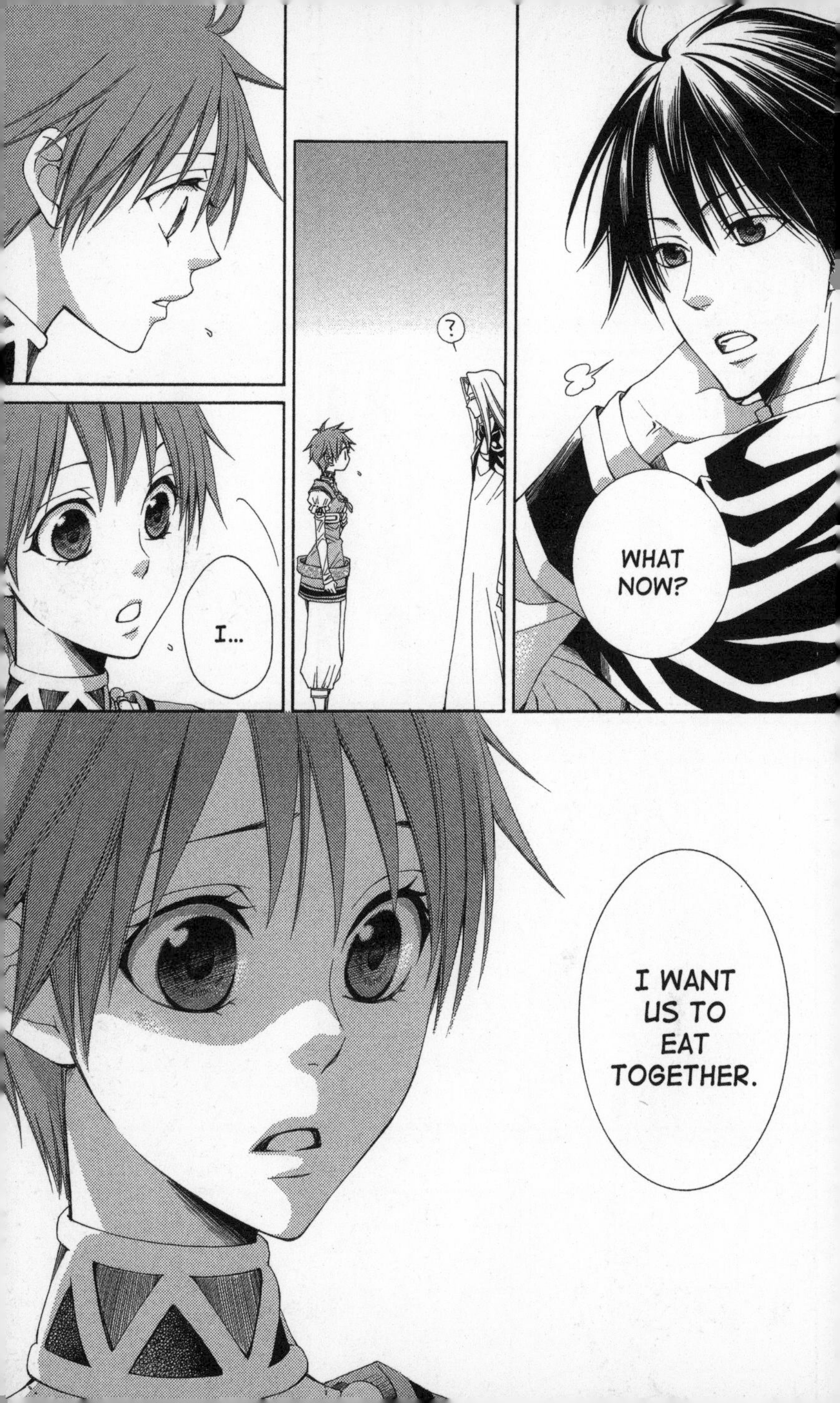
WHAT NOW?
?
I...
I WANT US TO EAT TOGETHER.

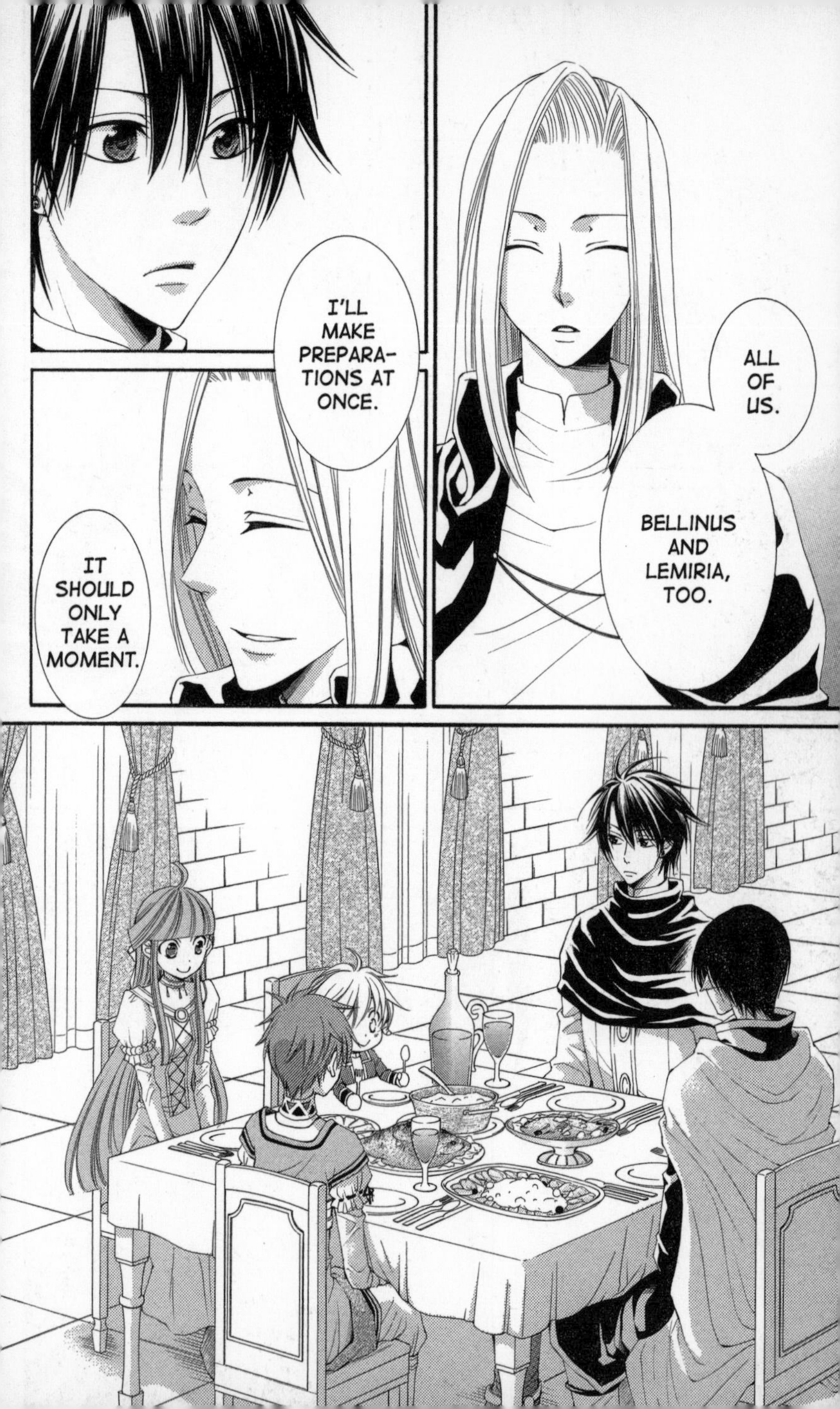
ALL OF US.
BELLINUS AND LEMIRIA, TOO.
I'LL MAKE PREPARATIONS AT ONCE.
IT SHOULD ONLY TAKE A MOMENT.

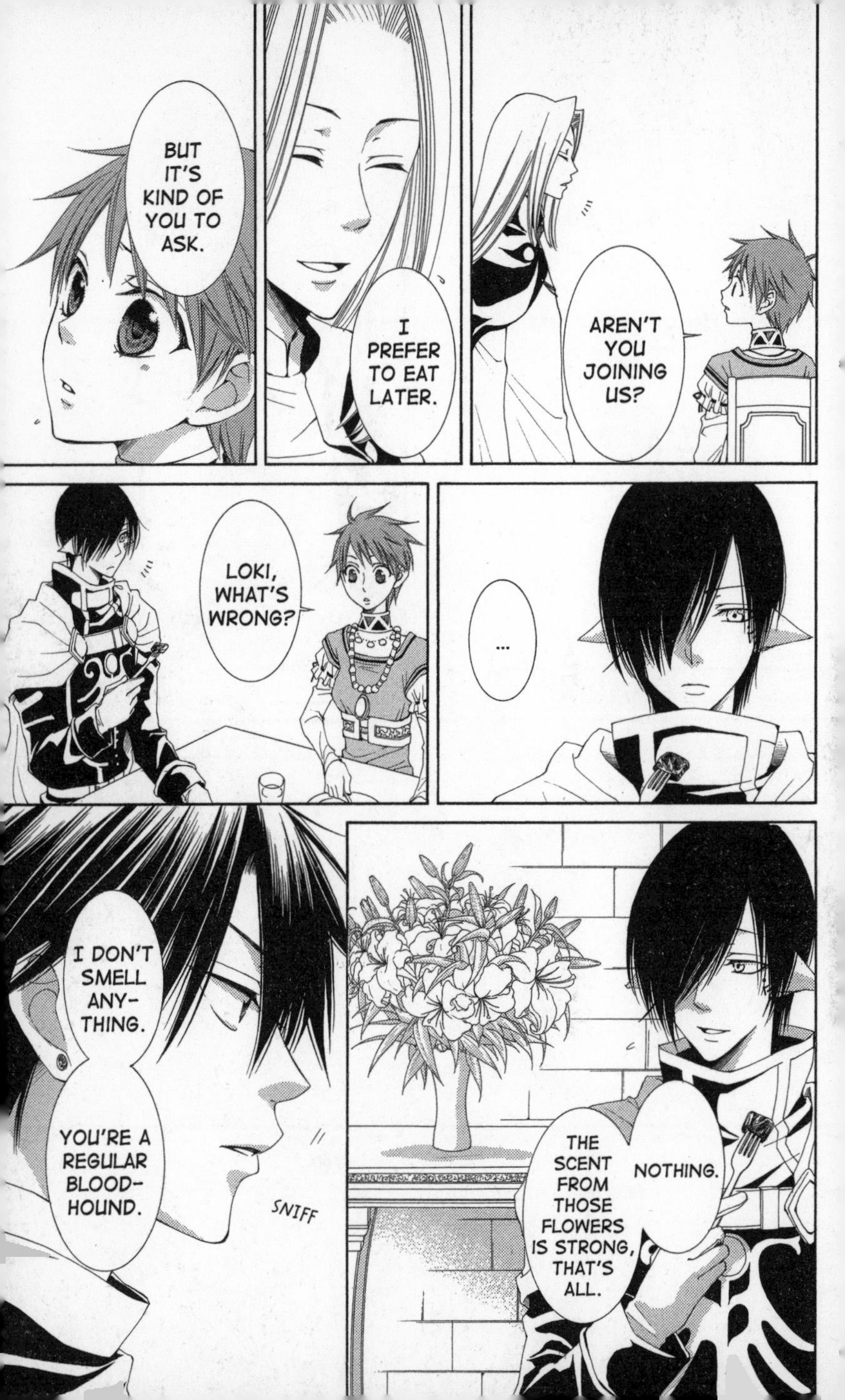
AREN'T YOU JOINING US?
I PREFER TO EAT LATER.
BUT IT'S KIND OF YOU TO ASK.
...
LOKI, WHAT'S WRONG?
NOTHING.
THE SCENT FROM THOSE FLOWERS IS STRONG, THAT'S ALL.
I DON'T SMELL ANYTHING.
SNIFF
YOU'RE A REGULAR BLOODHOUND.

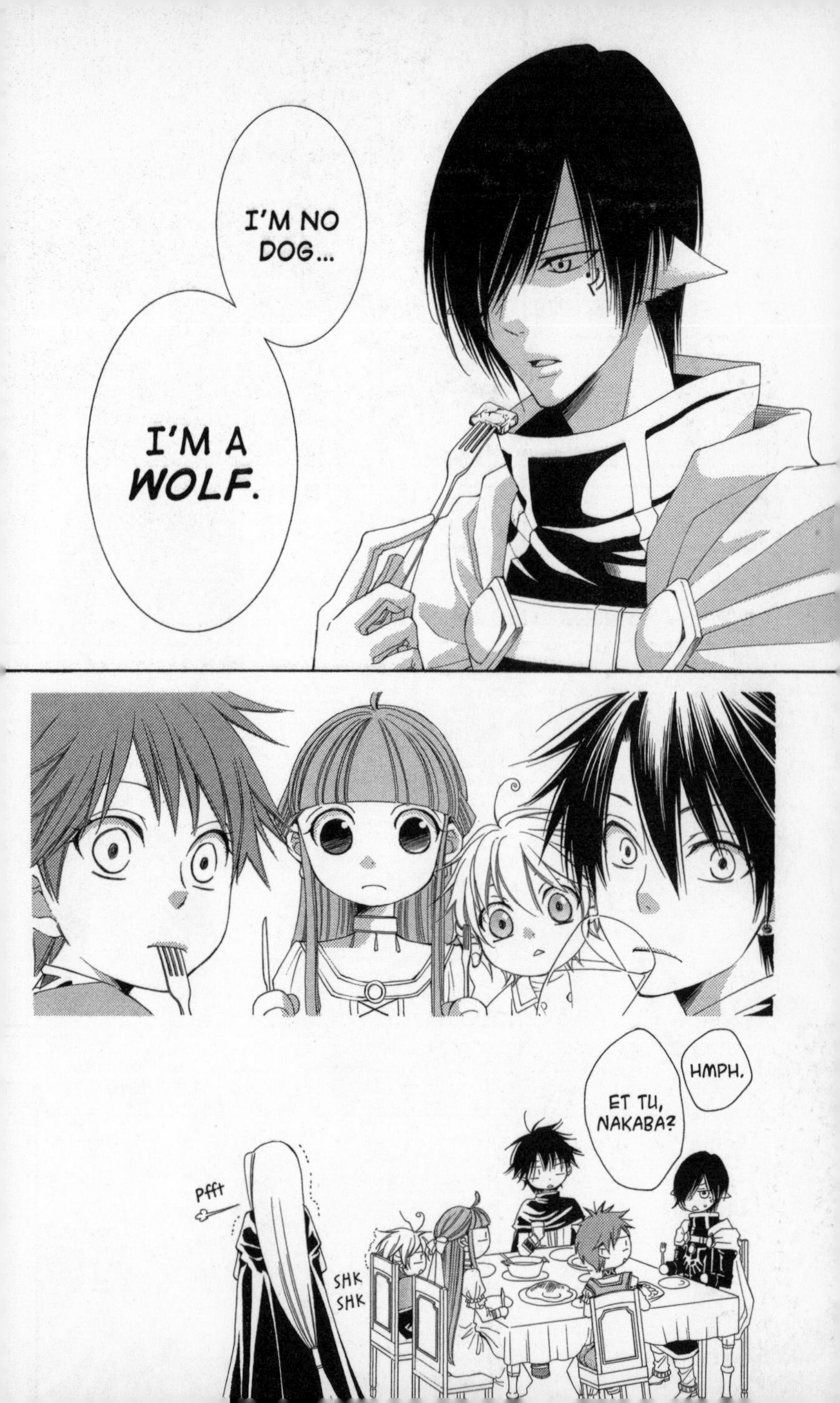
I'M NO DOG...
I'M A WOLF.
HMPH.
ET TU, NAKABA?
SHK SHK
Pfft

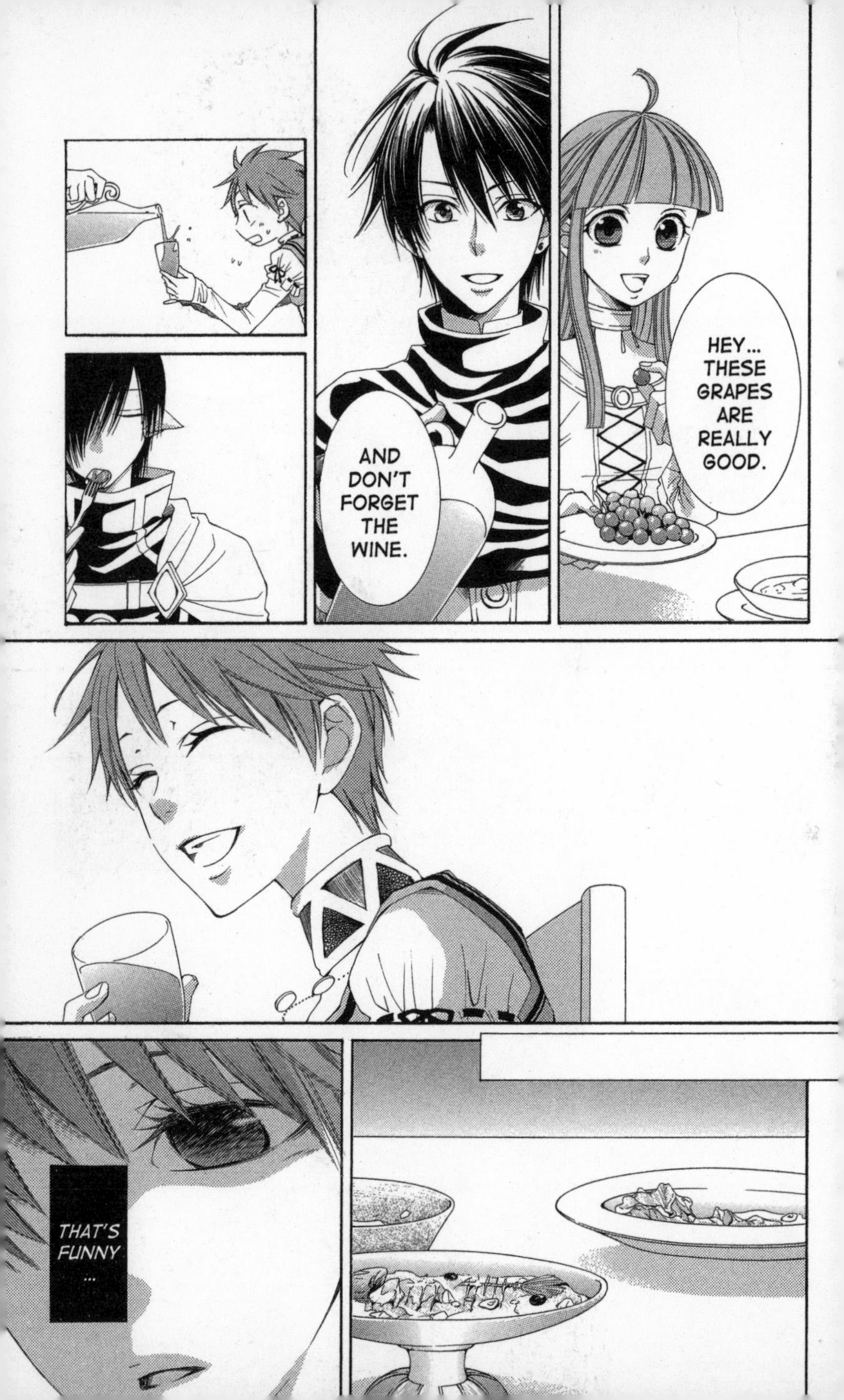
HEY... THESE GRAPES ARE REALLY GOOD.
AND DON'T FORGET THE WINE.
THAT'S FUNNY ...

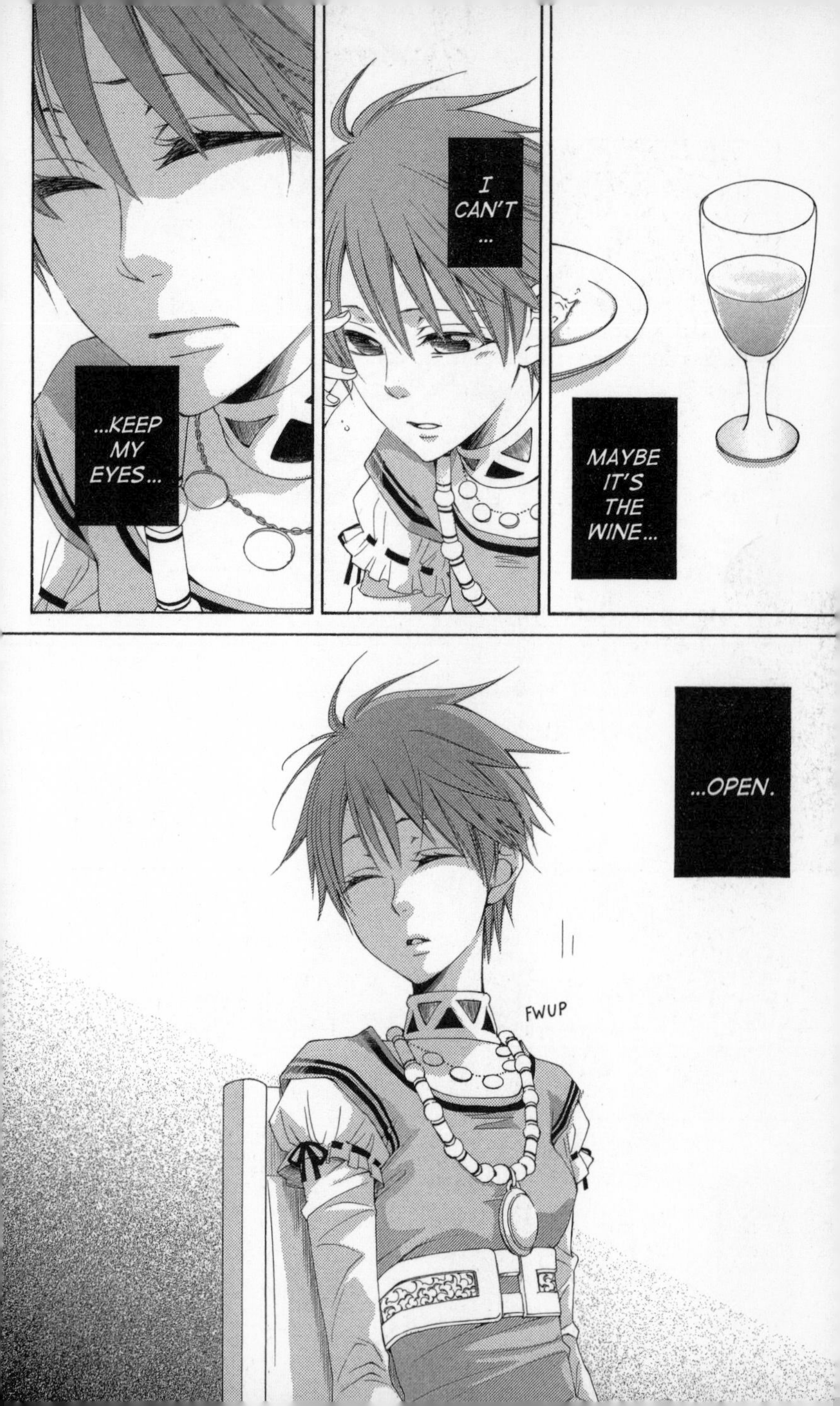
MAYBE IT'S THE WINE...
I CAN'T ...
...KEEP MY EYES...
...OPEN.
FWUP

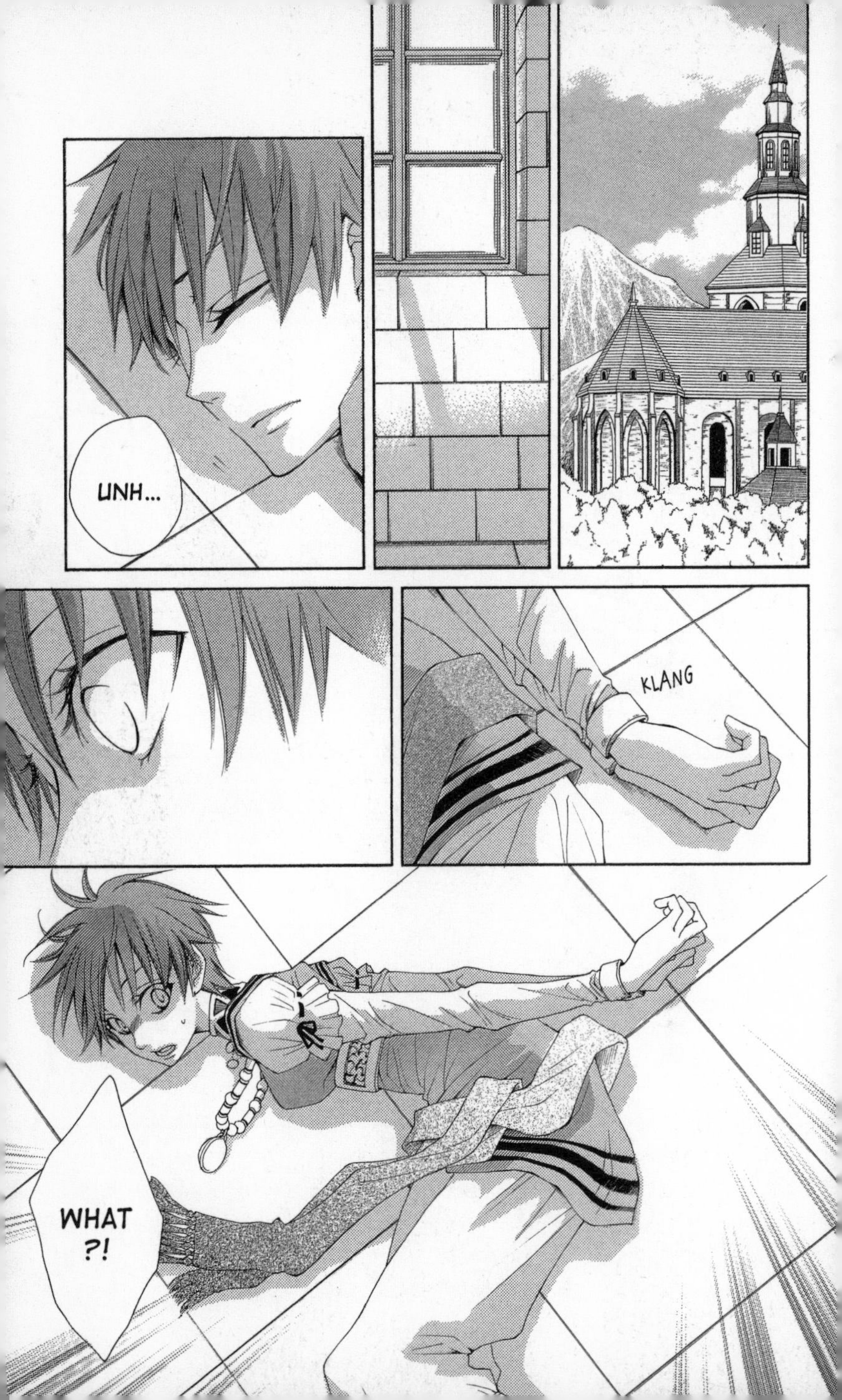
UNH...
KLANG
WHAT ?!

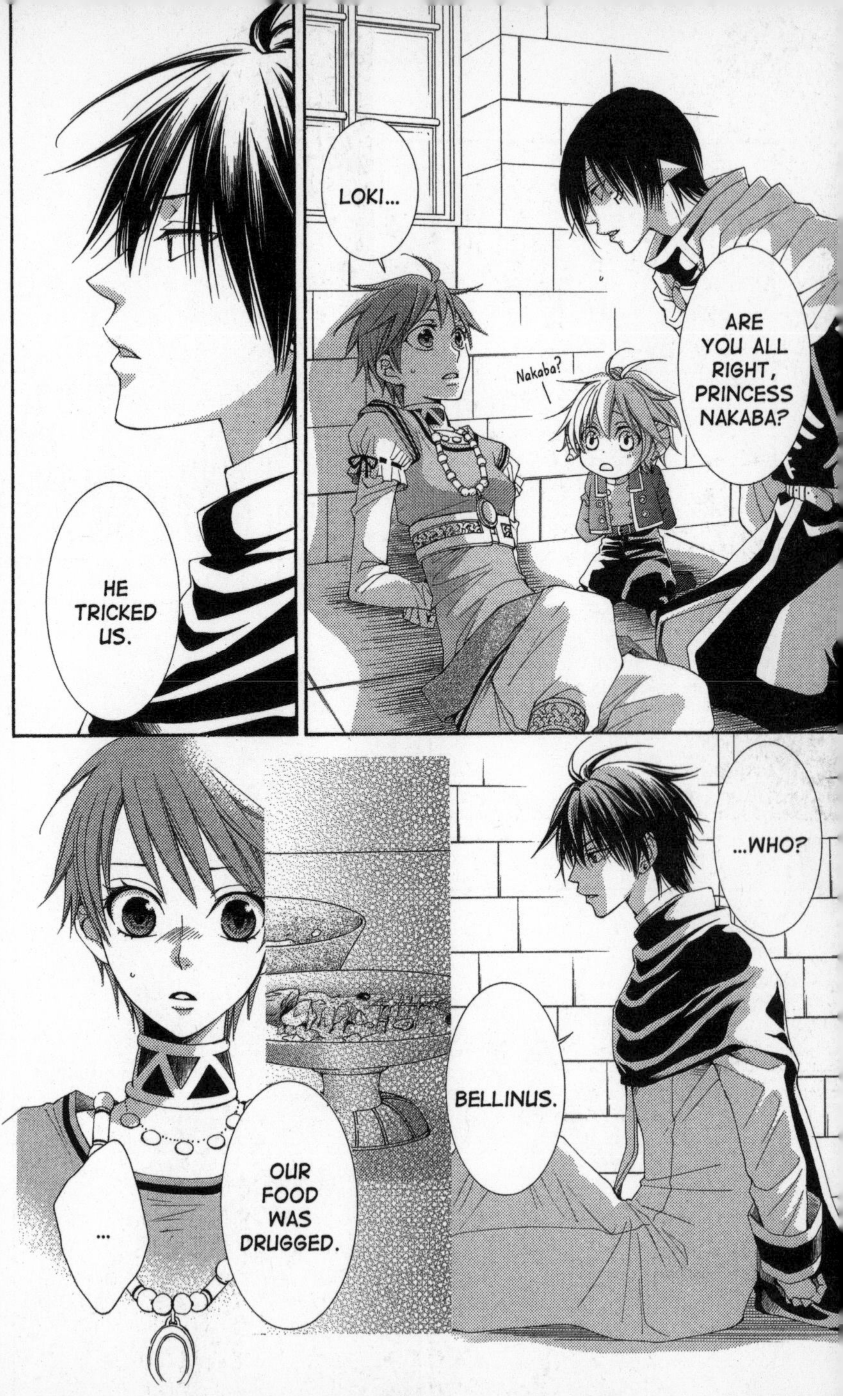
LOKI...
ARE YOU ALL RIGHT, PRINCESS NAKABA?
Nakaba?
HE TRICKED US.
...WHO?
BELLINUS.
OUR FOOD WAS DRUGGED.
...

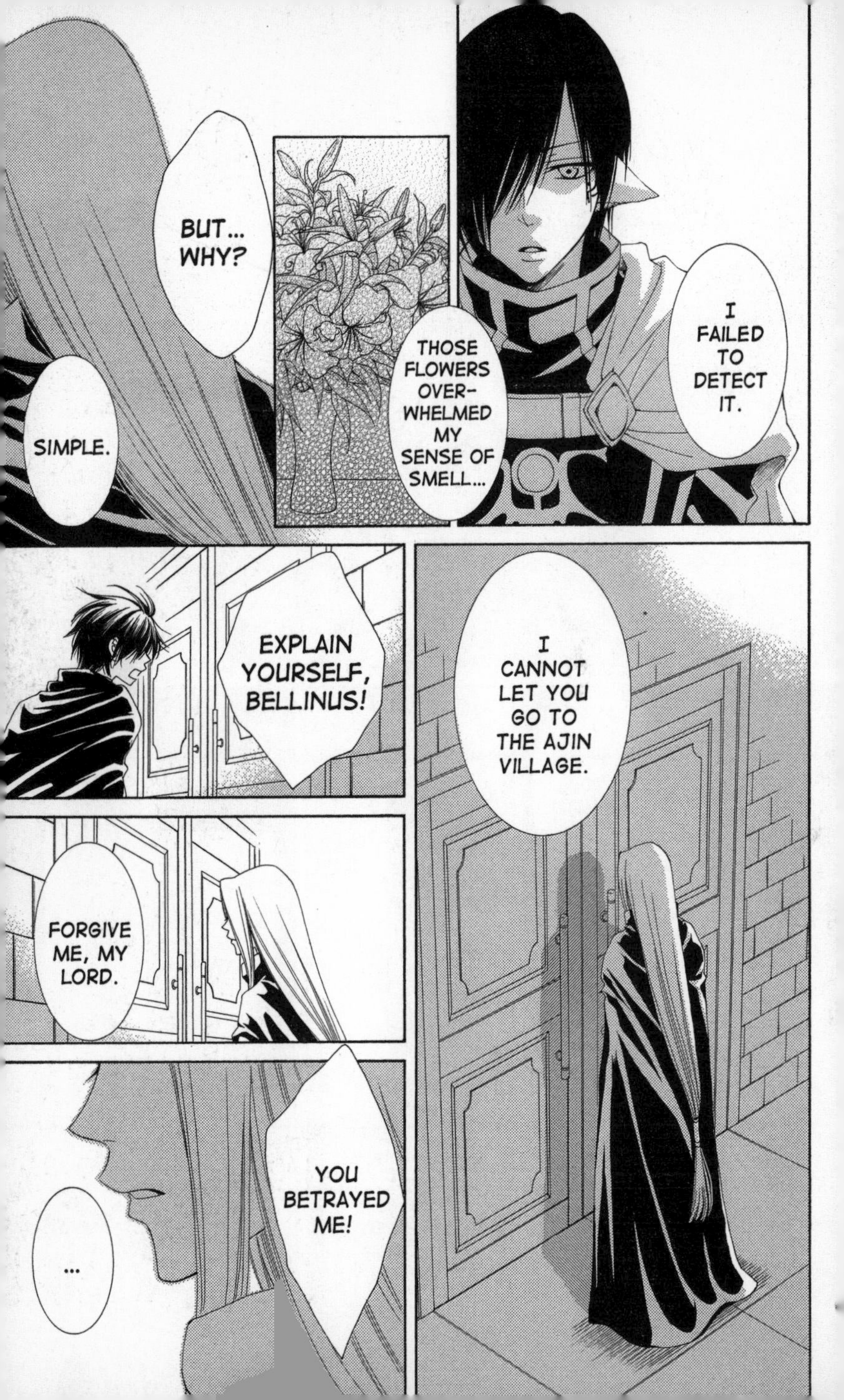
I FAILED TO DETECT IT.
THOSE FLOWERS OVER-WHELMED MY SENSE OF SMELL...
BUT... WHY?
SIMPLE.
I CANNOT LET YOU GO TO THE AJIN VILLAGE.
EXPLAIN YOURSELF, BELLINUS!
FORGIVE ME, MY LORD.
YOU BETRAYED ME!
...

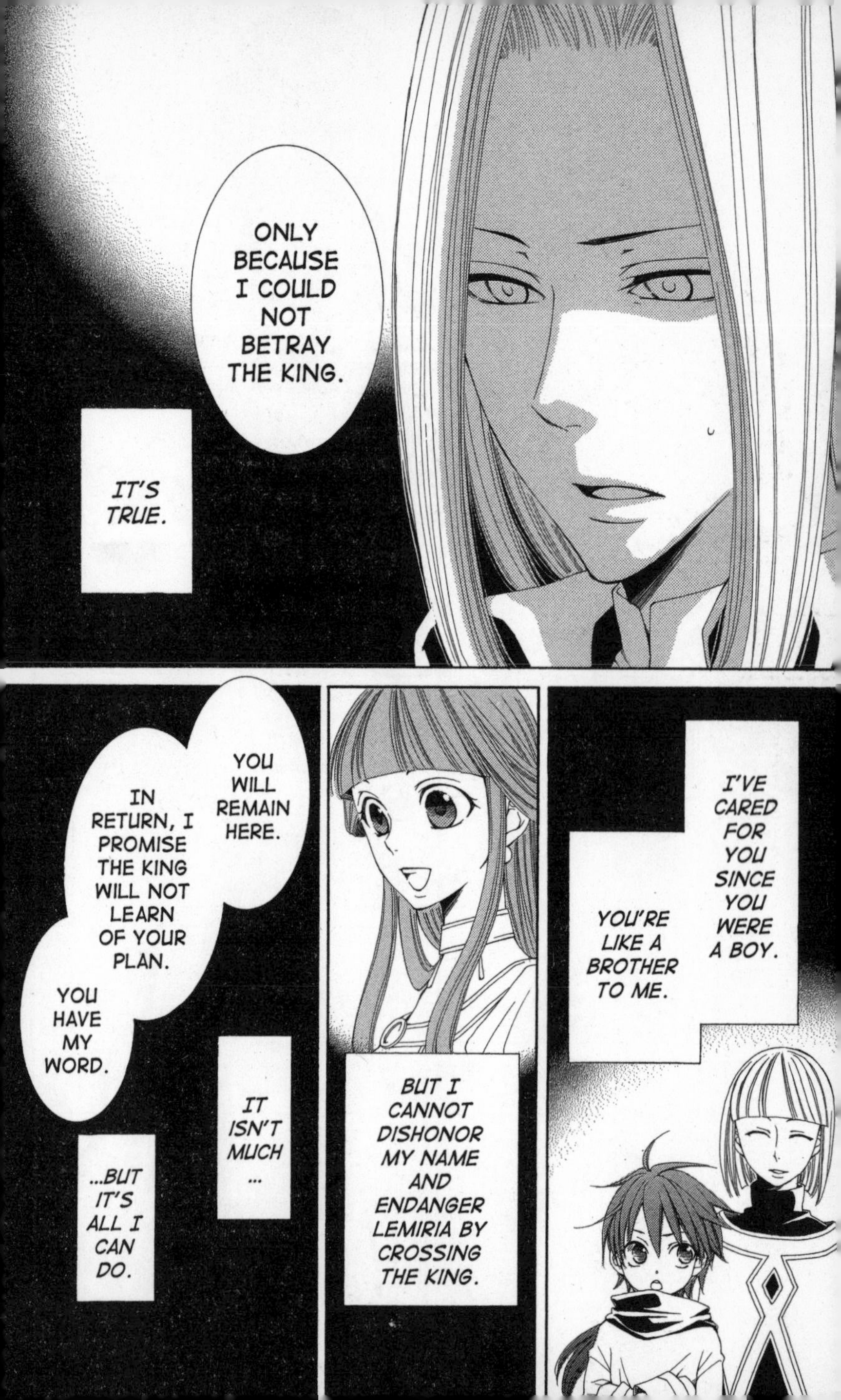
ONLY BECAUSE I COULD NOT BETRAY THE KING.
IT'S TRUE.
I'VE CARED FOR YOU SINCE YOU WERE A BOY.
YOU'RE LIKE A BROTHER TO ME.
BUT I CANNOT DISHONOR MY NAME AND ENDANGER LEMIRIA BY CROSSING THE KING.
YOU WILL REMAIN HERE.
IN RETURN, I PROMISE THE KING WILL NOT LEARN OF YOUR PLAN.
YOU HAVE MY WORD.
IT ISN'T MUCH ...
...BUT IT'S ALL I CAN DO.

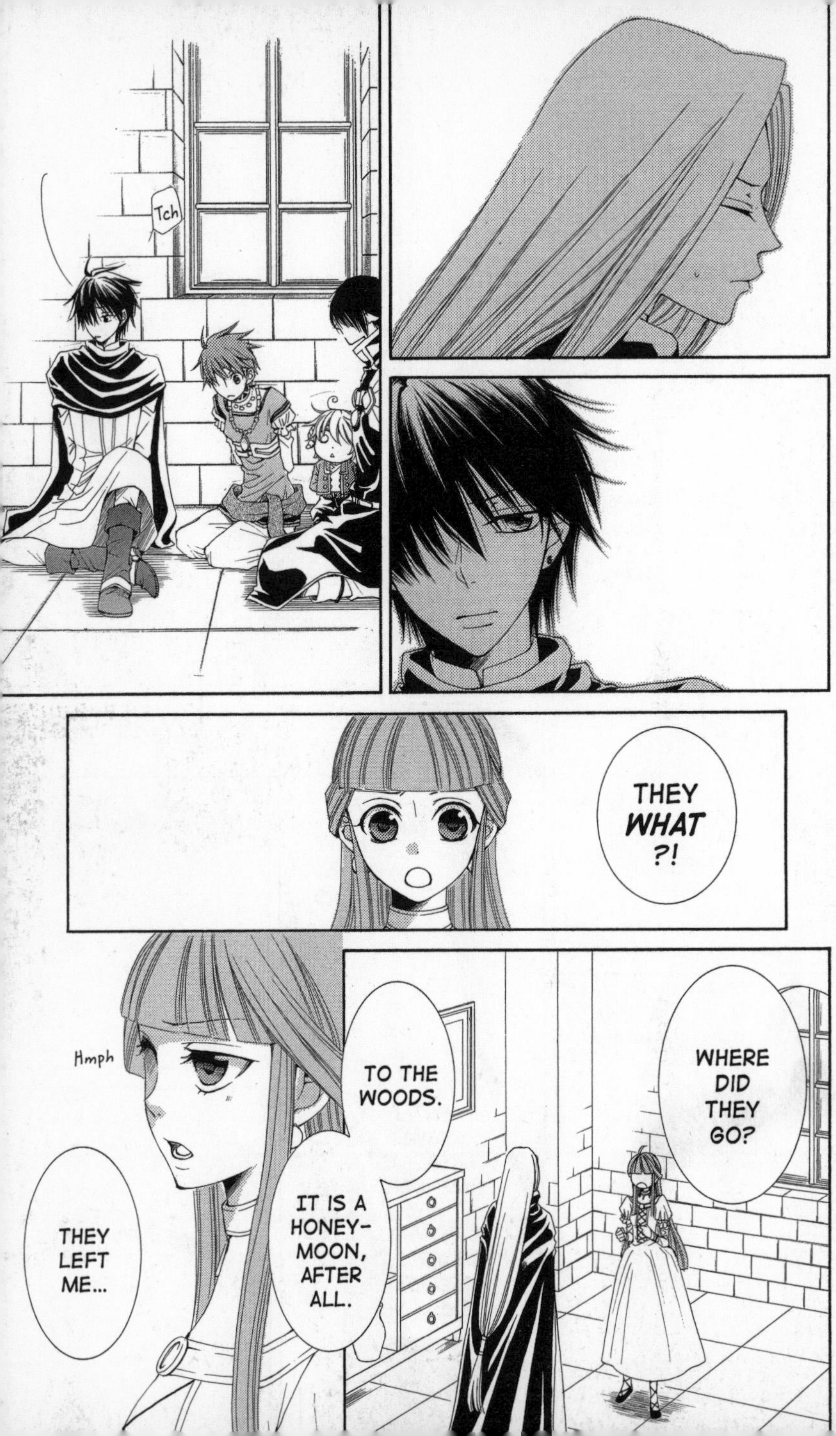
Tch
THEY *WHAT* ?!
WHERE DID THEY GO?
TO THE WOODS.
IT IS A HONEY-MOON, AFTER ALL.
Hmph
THEY LEFT ME...

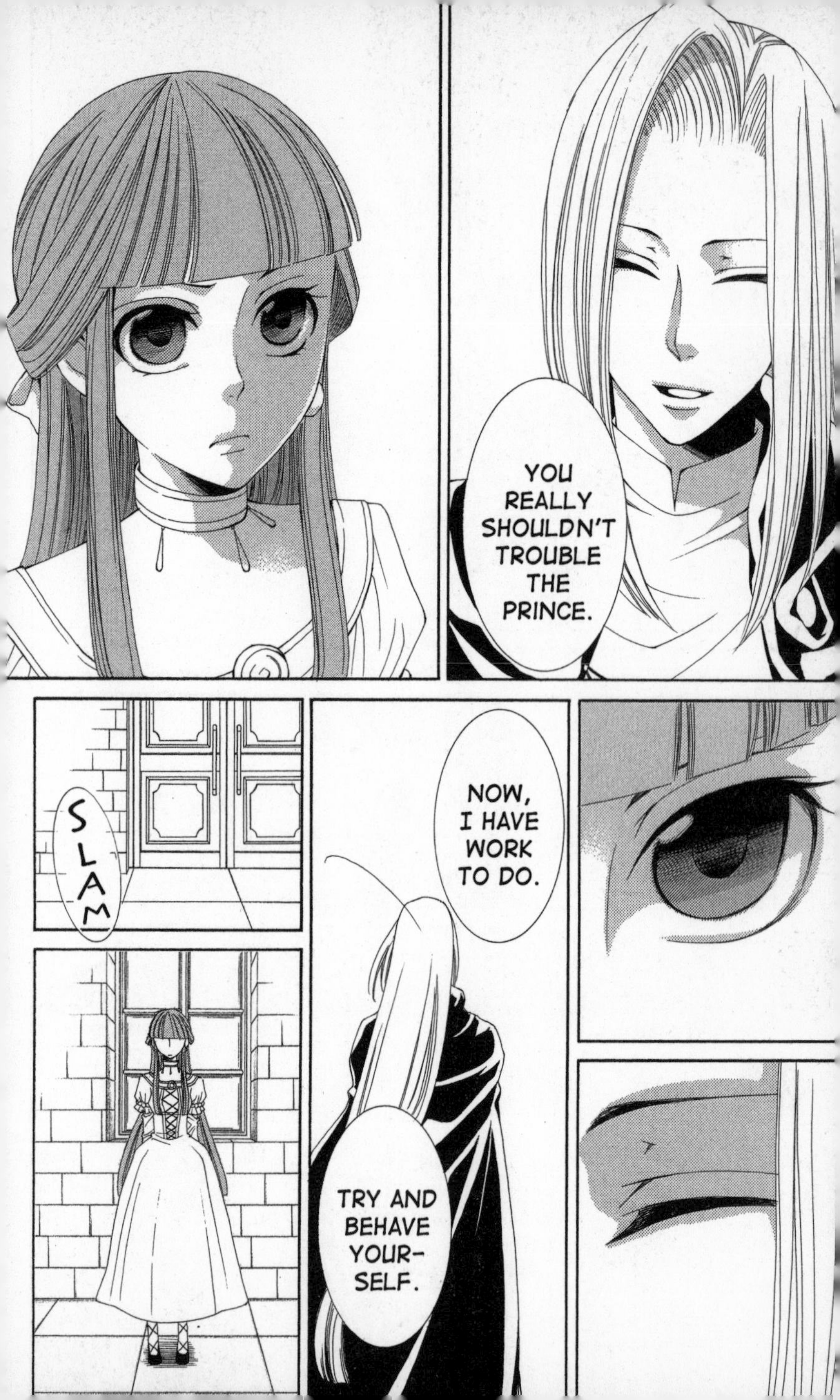
YOU REALLY SHOULDN'T TROUBLE THE PRINCE.
NOW, I HAVE WORK TO DO.
TRY AND BEHAVE YOUR-SELF.
SLAM

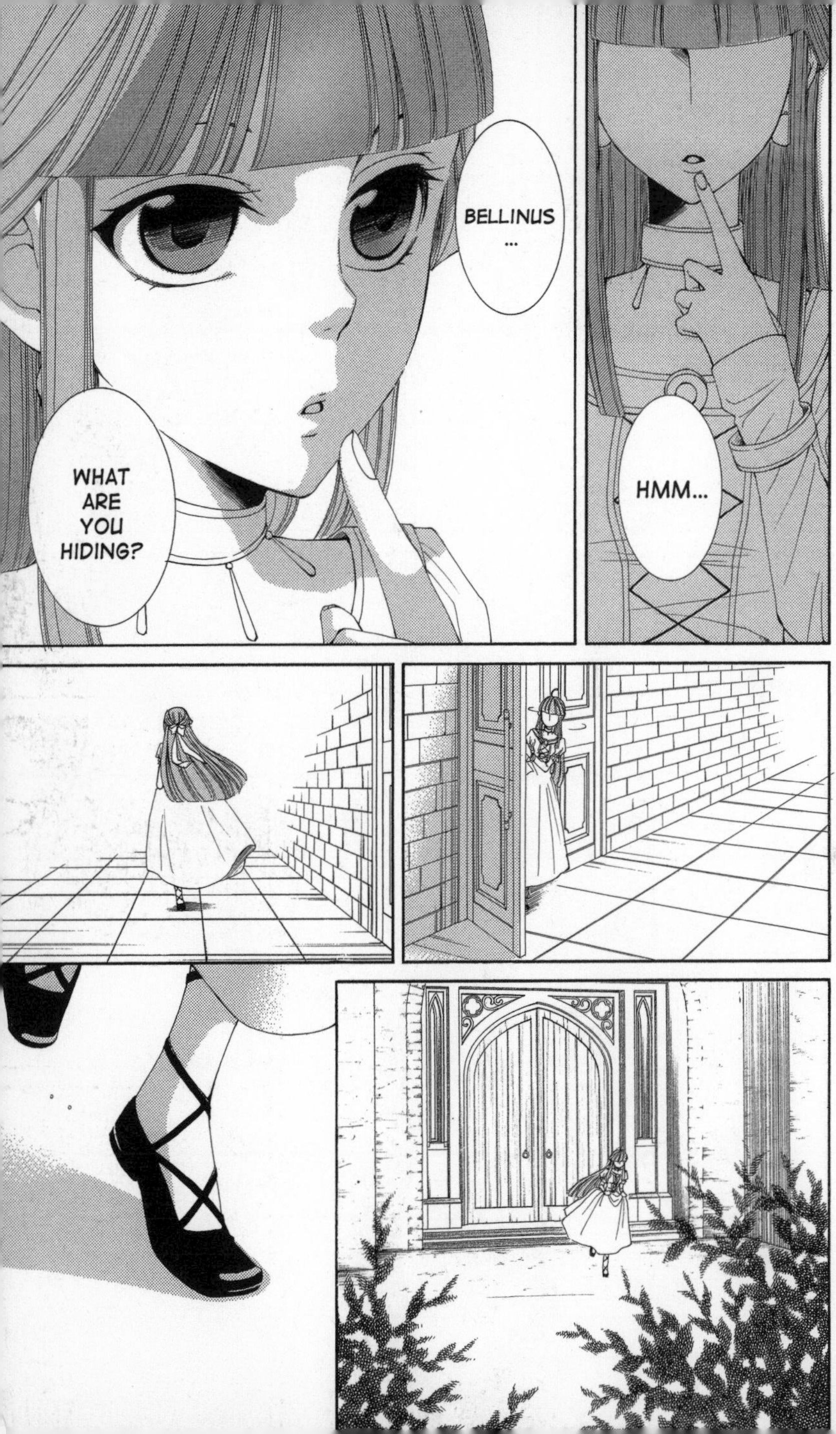
HMM...
BELLINUS ...
WHAT ARE YOU HIDING?

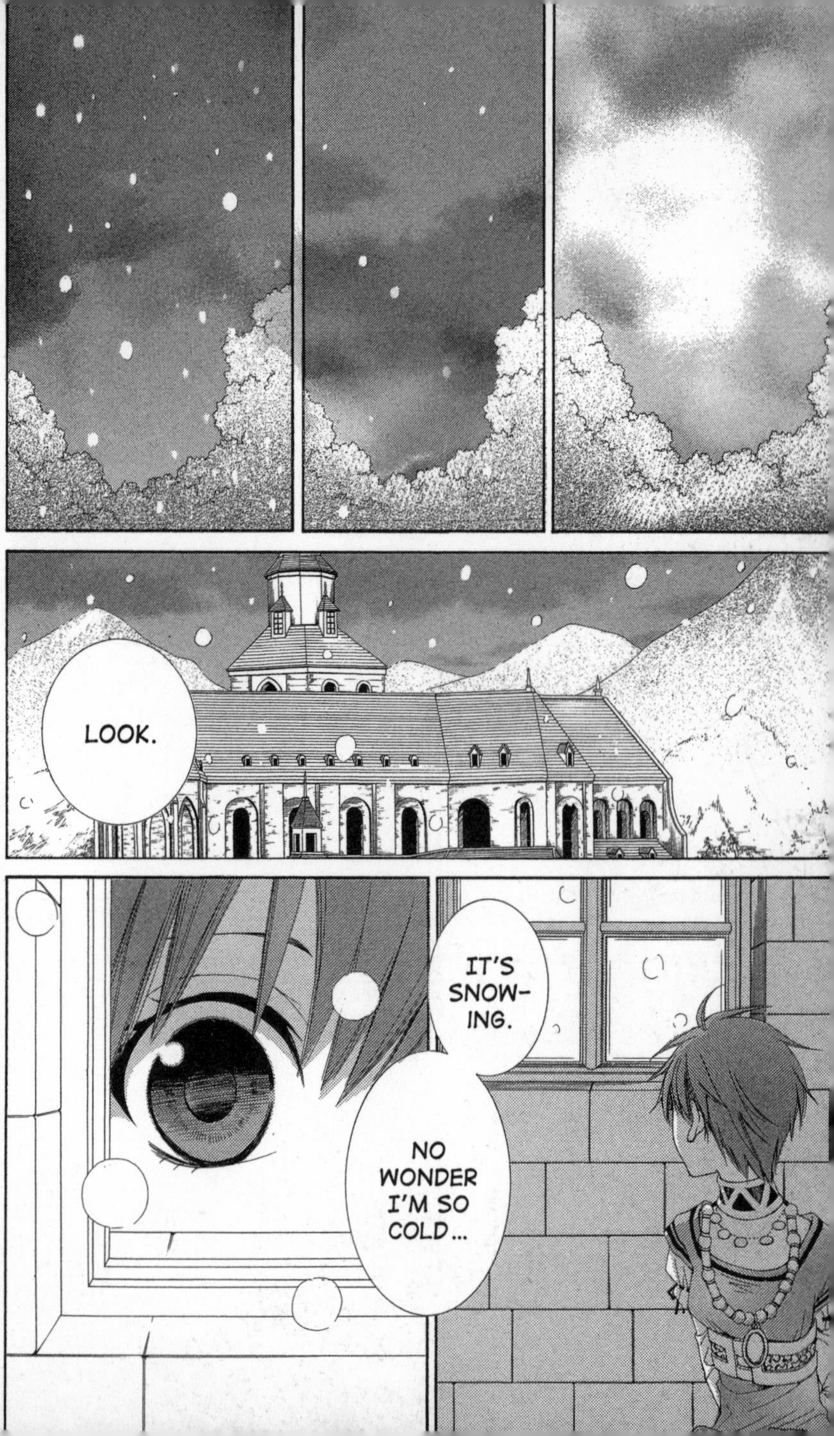
LOOK.
IT'S SNOW-ING.
NO WONDER I'M SO COLD...

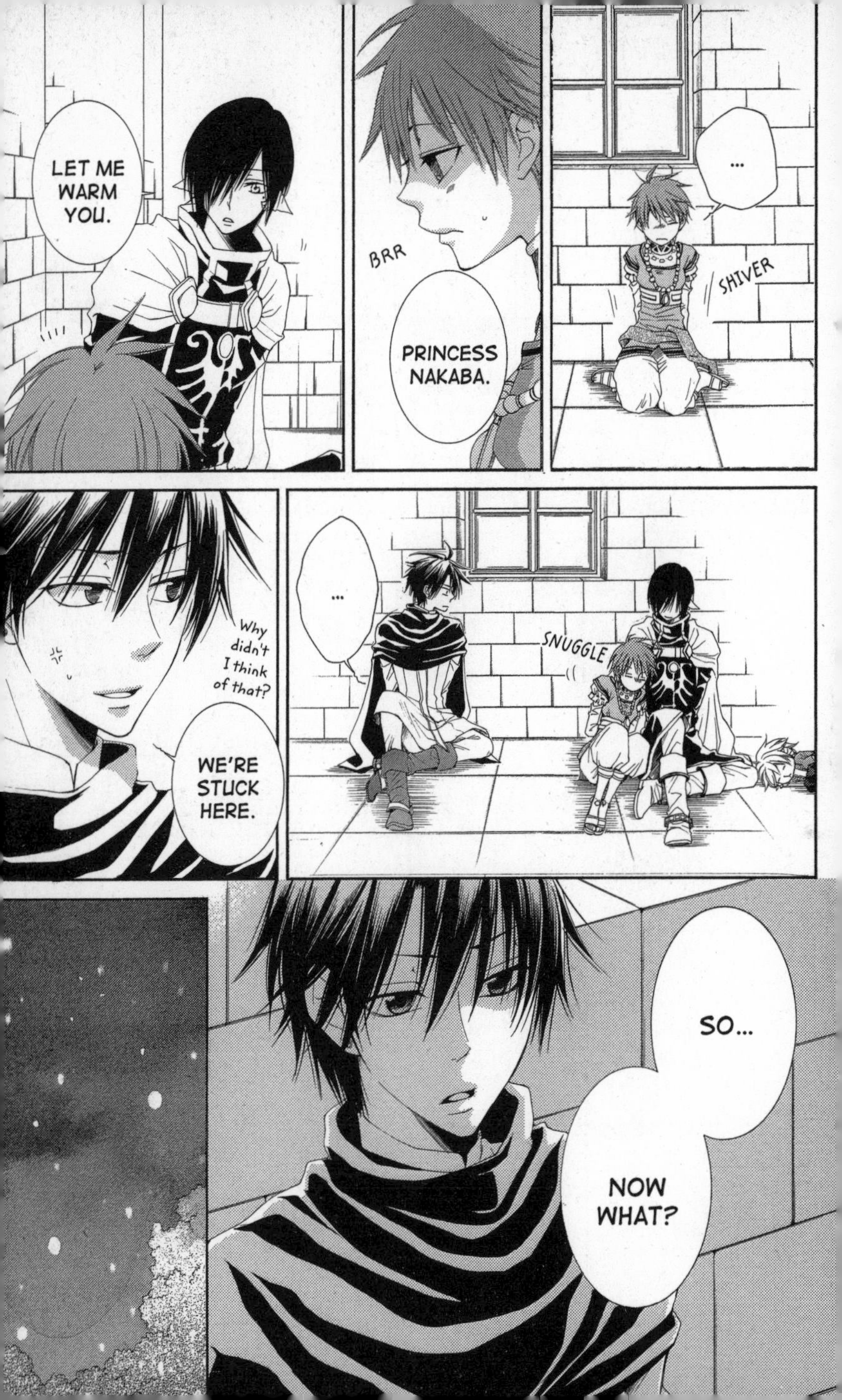
...
SHIVER
BRR
PRINCESS NAKABA.
LET ME WARM YOU.
...
SNUGGLE
Why didn't I think of that?
WE'RE STUCK HERE.
SO...
NOW WHAT?

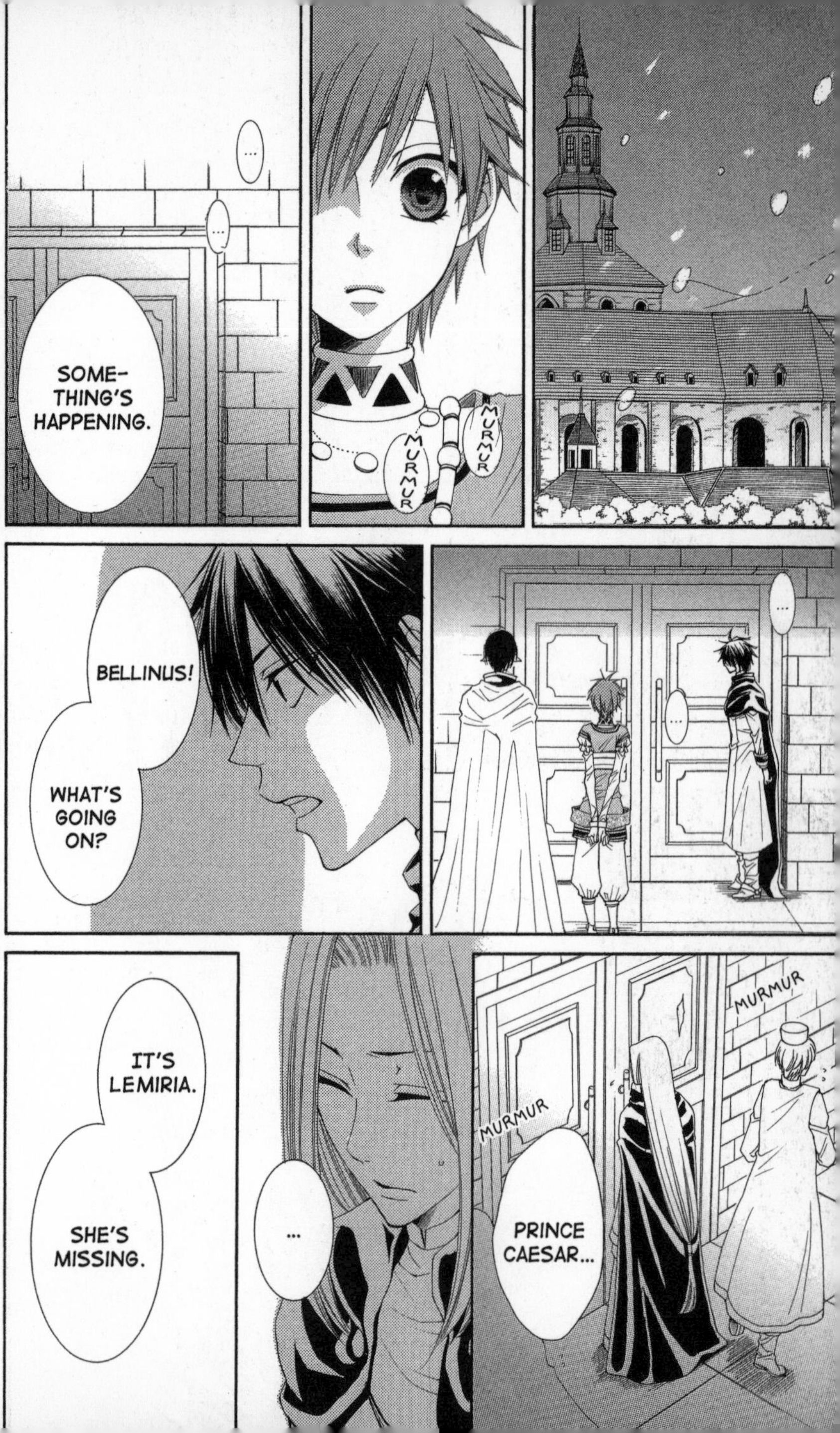

MURMUR
MURMUR
...
...
SOME-THING'S HAPPENING.
...
...
BELLINUS!
WHAT'S GOING ON?
MURMUR
MURMUR
PRINCE CAESAR...
...
IT'S LEMIRIA.
SHE'S MISSING.

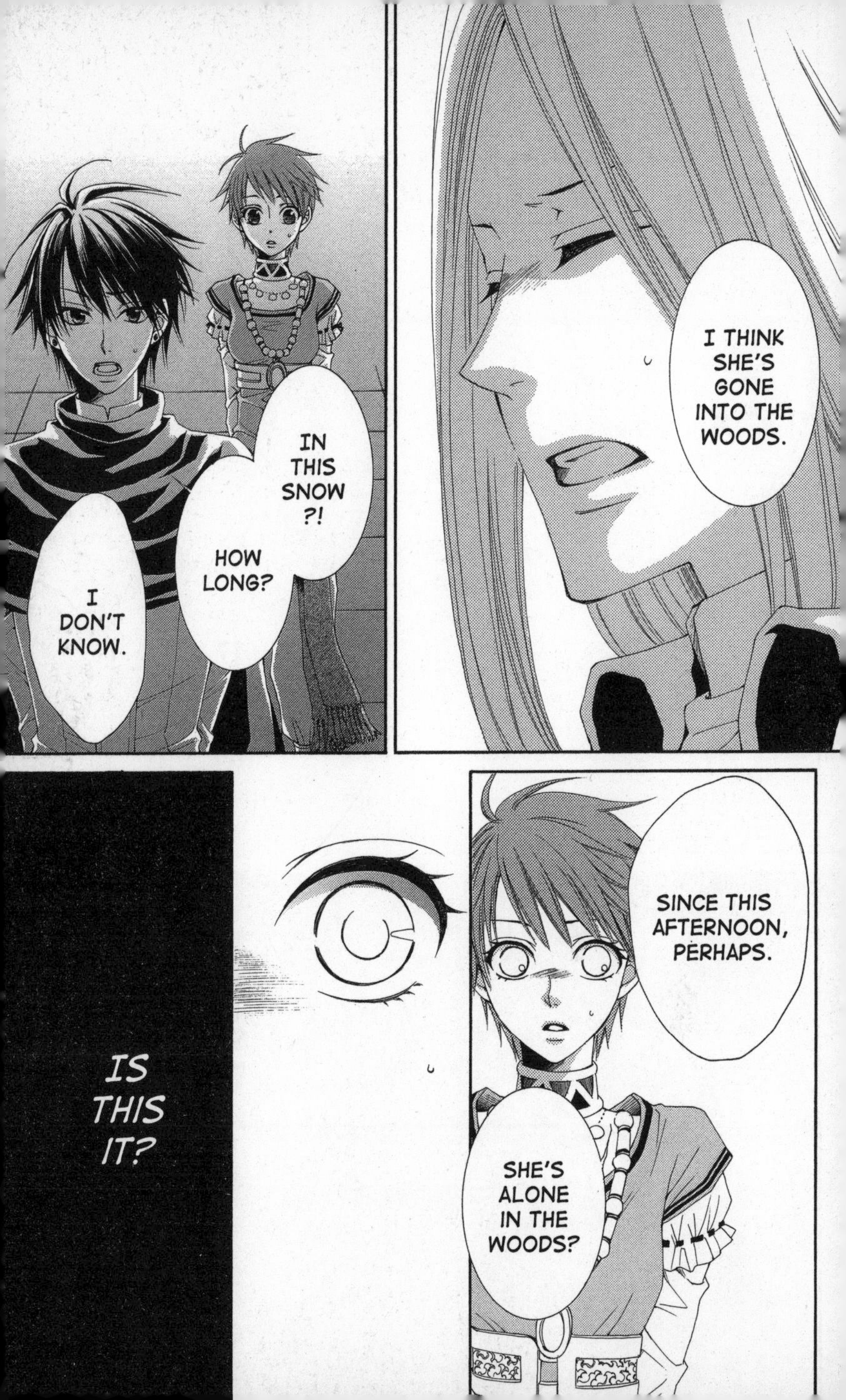
I THINK SHE'S GONE INTO THE WOODS.
IN THIS SNOW ?!
HOW LONG?
I DON'T KNOW.
SINCE THIS AFTERNOON, PERHAPS.
SHE'S ALONE IN THE WOODS?
IS THIS IT?

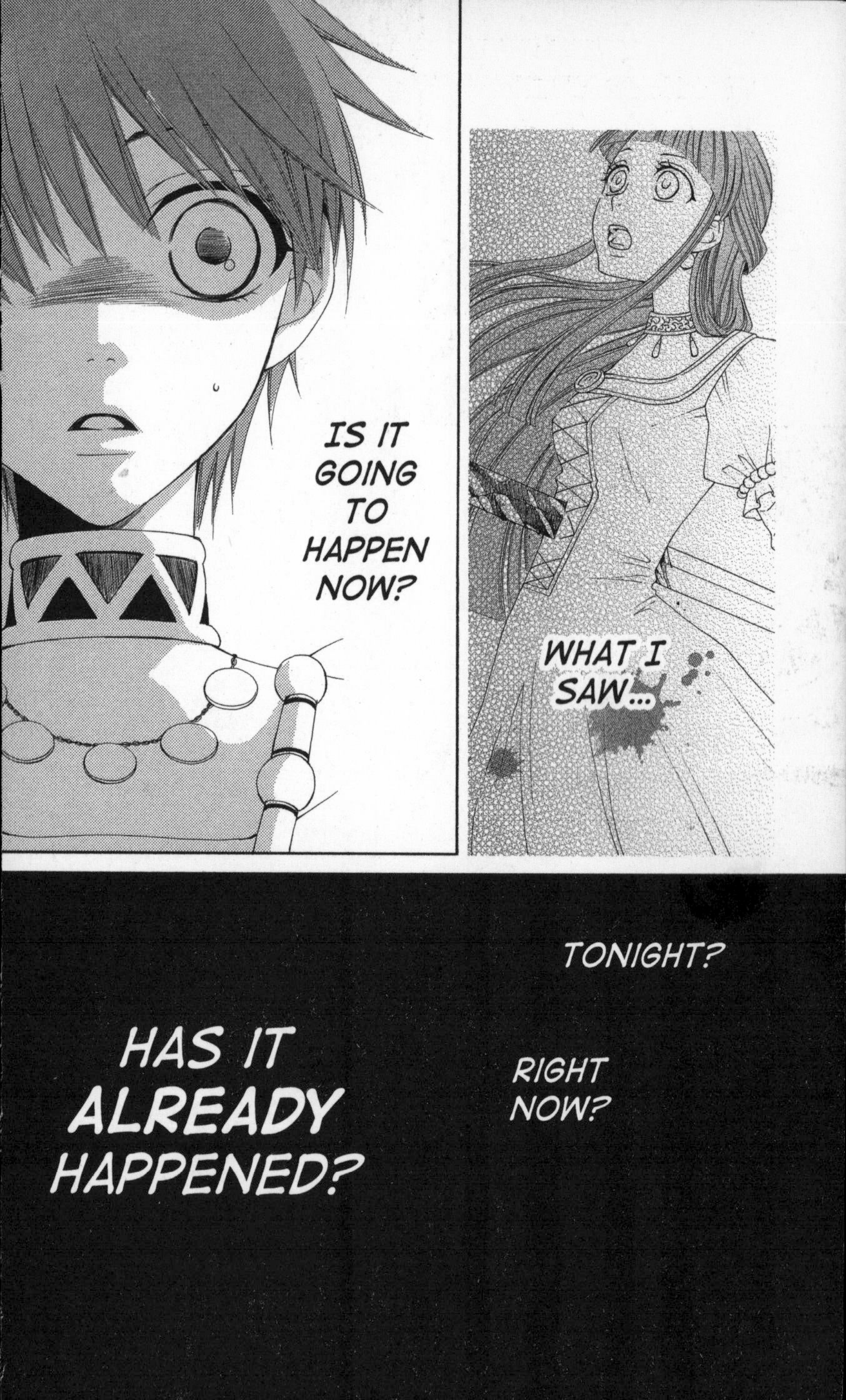
WHAT I SAW...
IS IT GOING TO HAPPEN NOW?
TONIGHT?
RIGHT NOW?
HAS IT ALREADY HAPPENED?

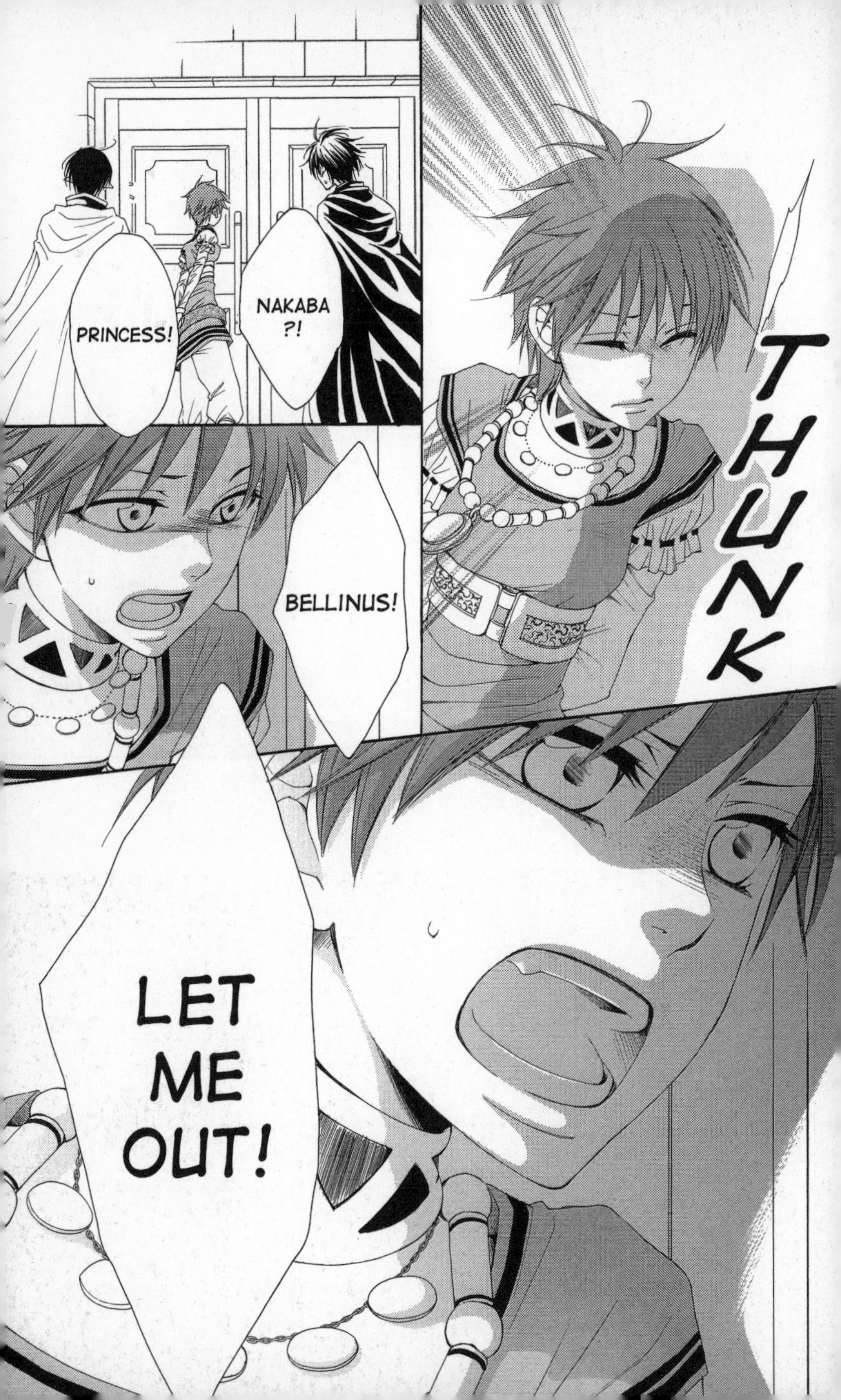
THUNK
NAKABA ?!
PRINCESS!
BELLINUS!
LET ME OUT!

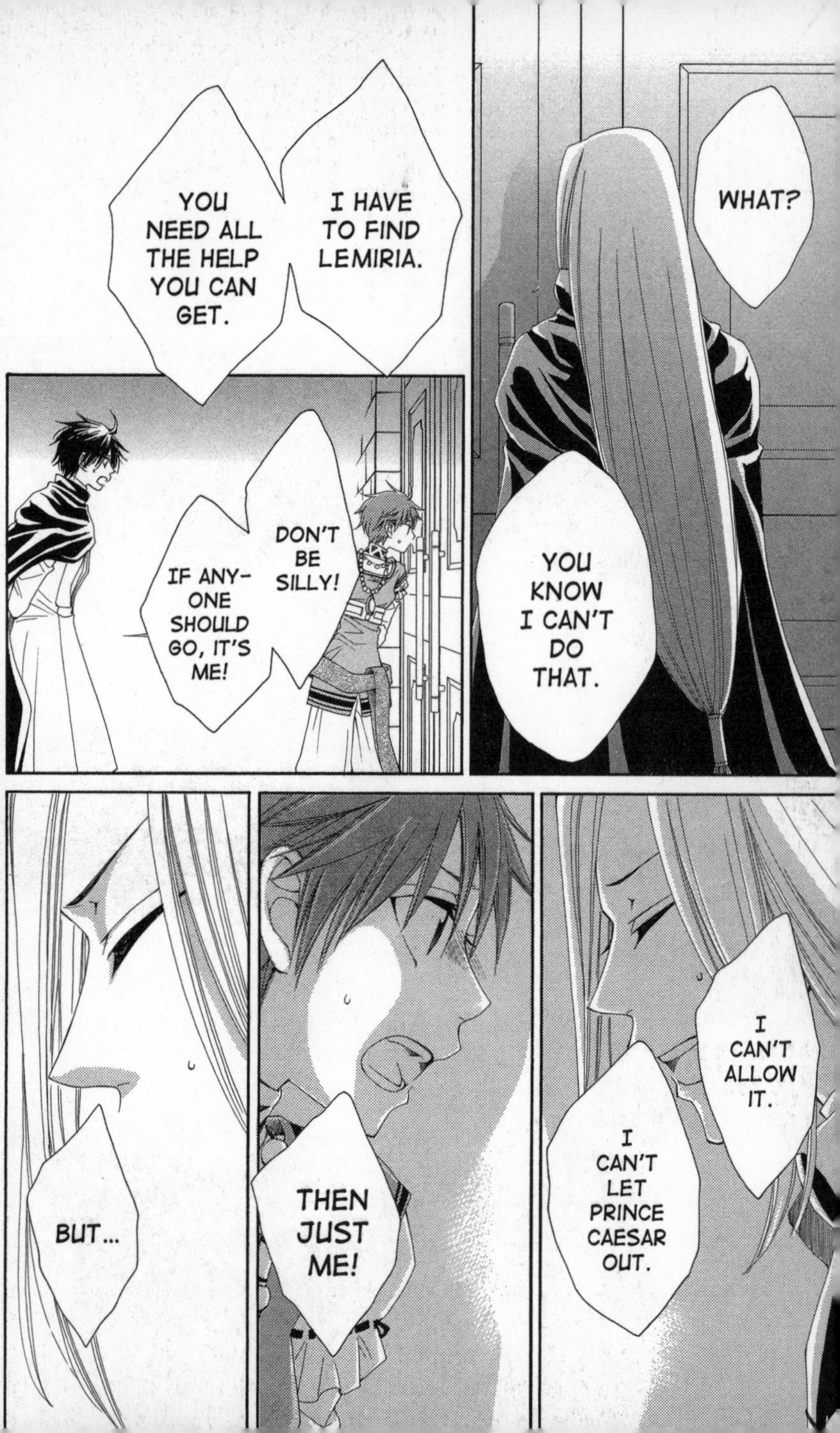

WHAT?
YOU KNOW I CAN'T DO THAT.
I HAVE TO FIND LEMIRIA.
YOU NEED ALL THE HELP YOU CAN GET.
DON'T BE SILLY!
IF ANY-ONE SHOULD GO, IT'S ME!
I CAN'T ALLOW IT.
I CAN'T LET PRINCE CAESAR OUT.
THEN JUST ME!
BUT...

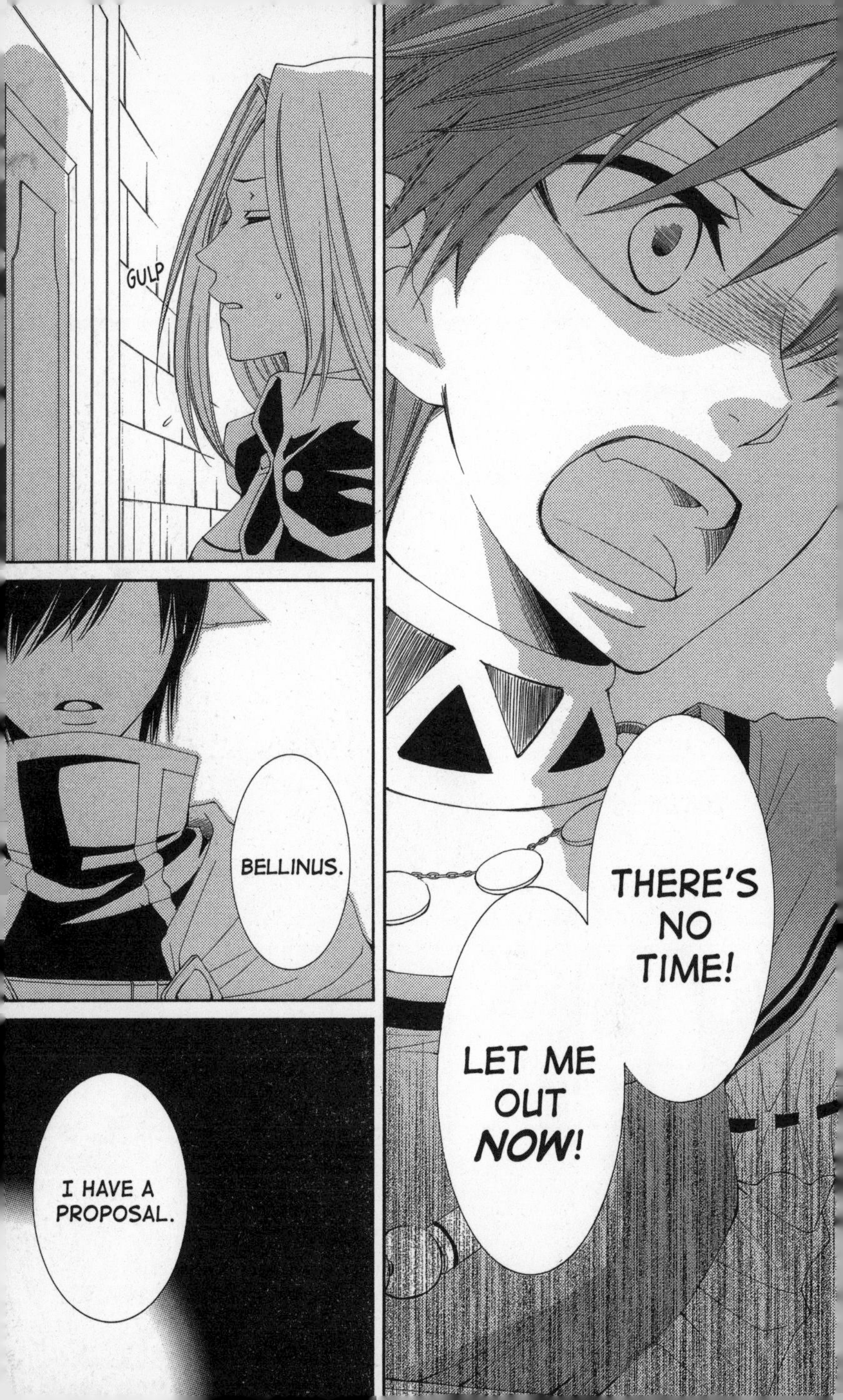
THERE'S NO TIME!
LET ME OUT NOW!
GULP
BELLINUS.
I HAVE A PROPOSAL.

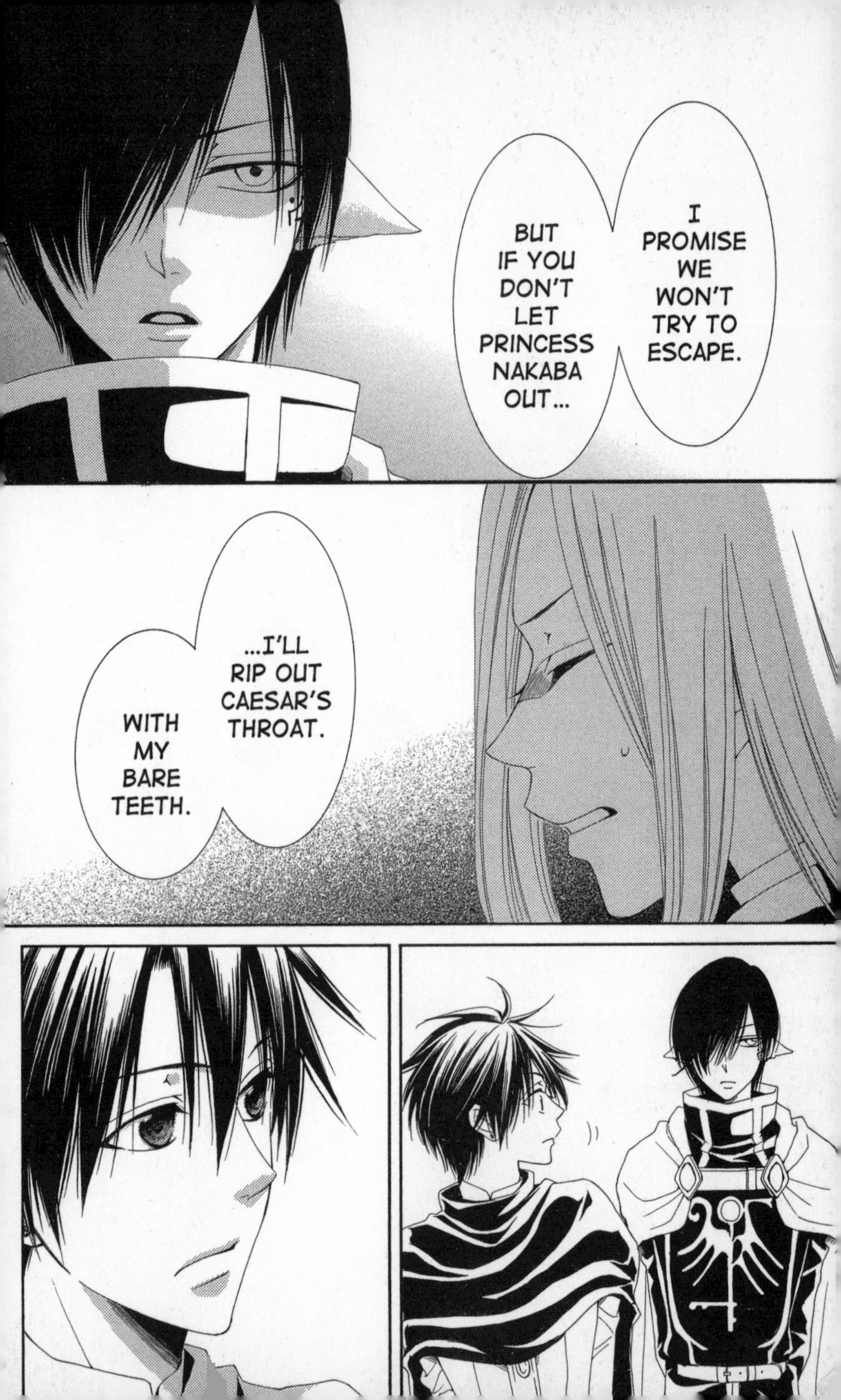
I PROMISE WE WON'T TRY TO ESCAPE.
BUT IF YOU DON'T LET PRINCESS NAKABA OUT...
...I'LL RIP OUT CAESAR'S THROAT.
WITH MY BARE TEETH.

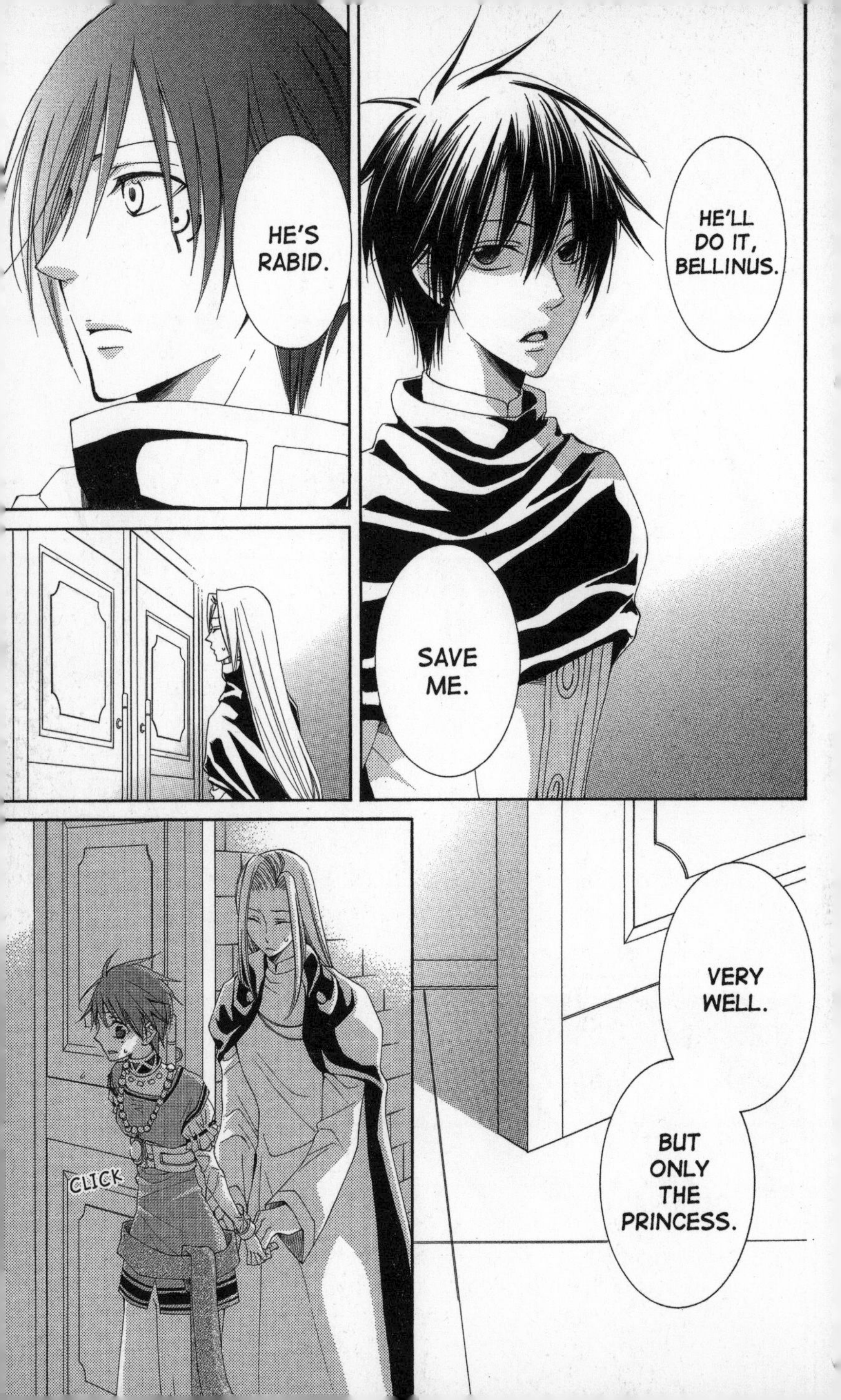
HE'LL DO IT, BELLINUS.
SAVE ME.
HE'S RABID.
VERY WELL.
BUT ONLY THE PRINCESS.
CLICK

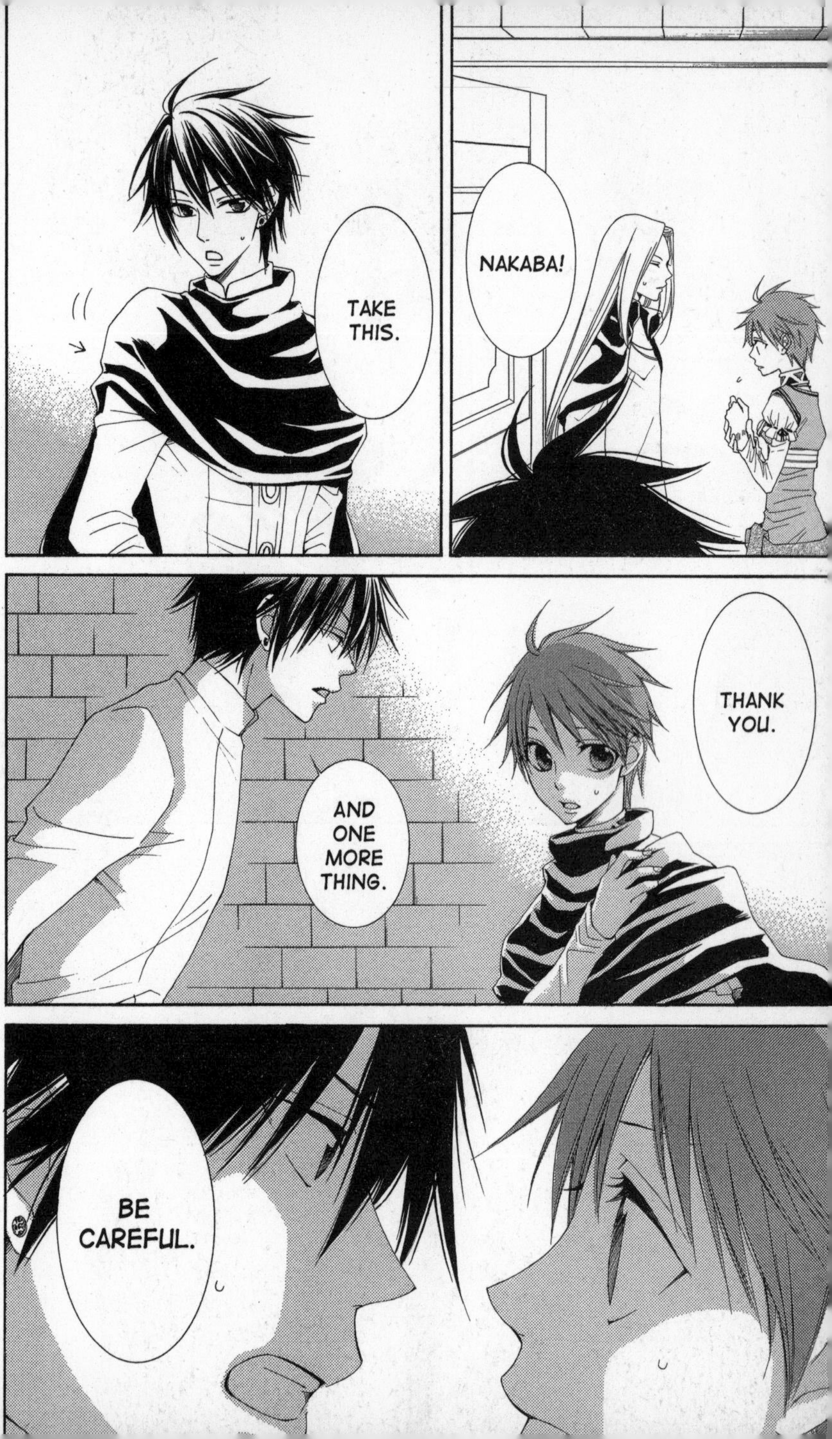
NAKABA!
TAKE THIS.
THANK YOU.
AND ONE MORE THING.
BE CAREFUL.

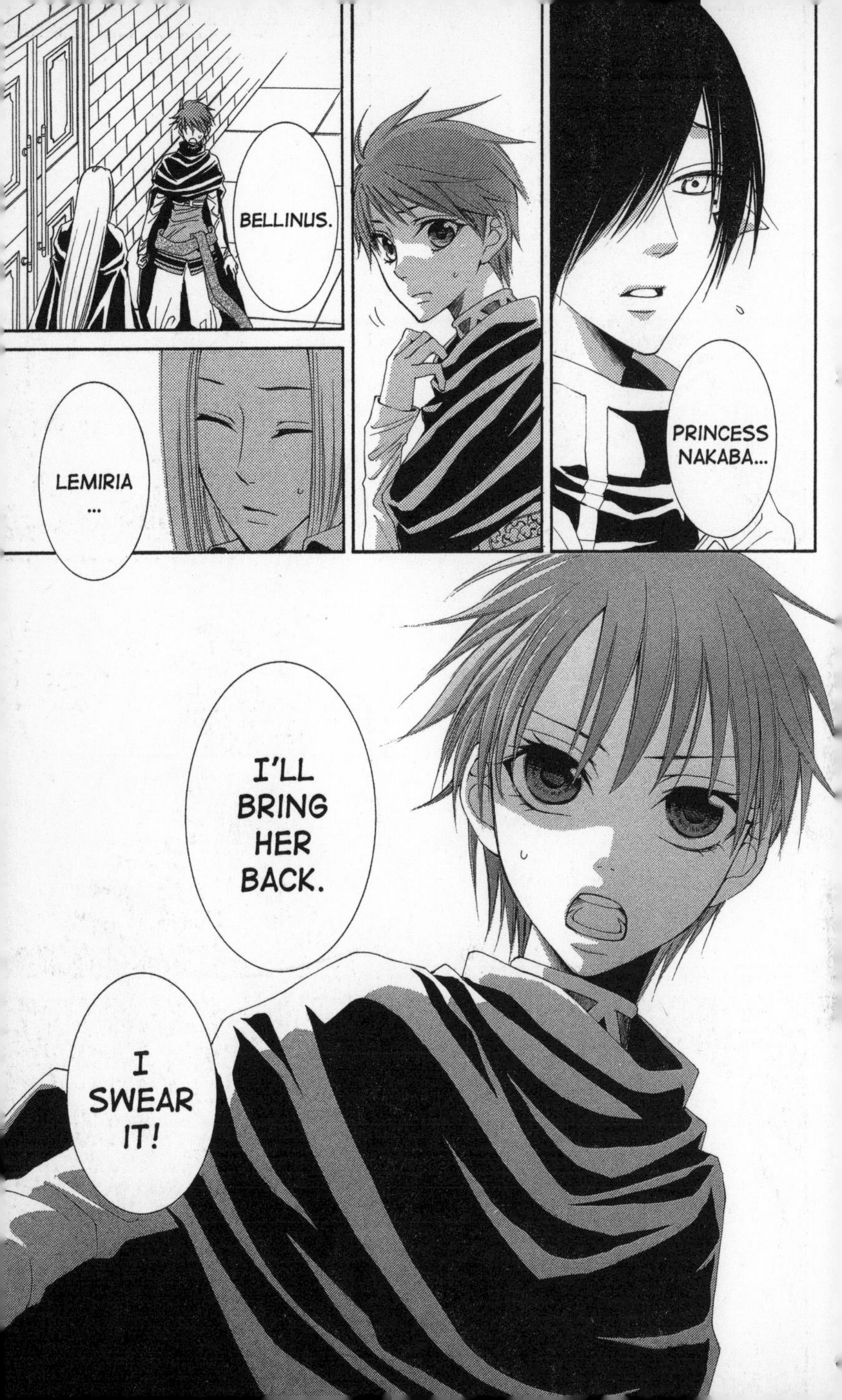
PRINCESS NAKABA...
BELLINUS.
LEMIRIA ...
I'LL BRING HER BACK.
I SWEAR IT!

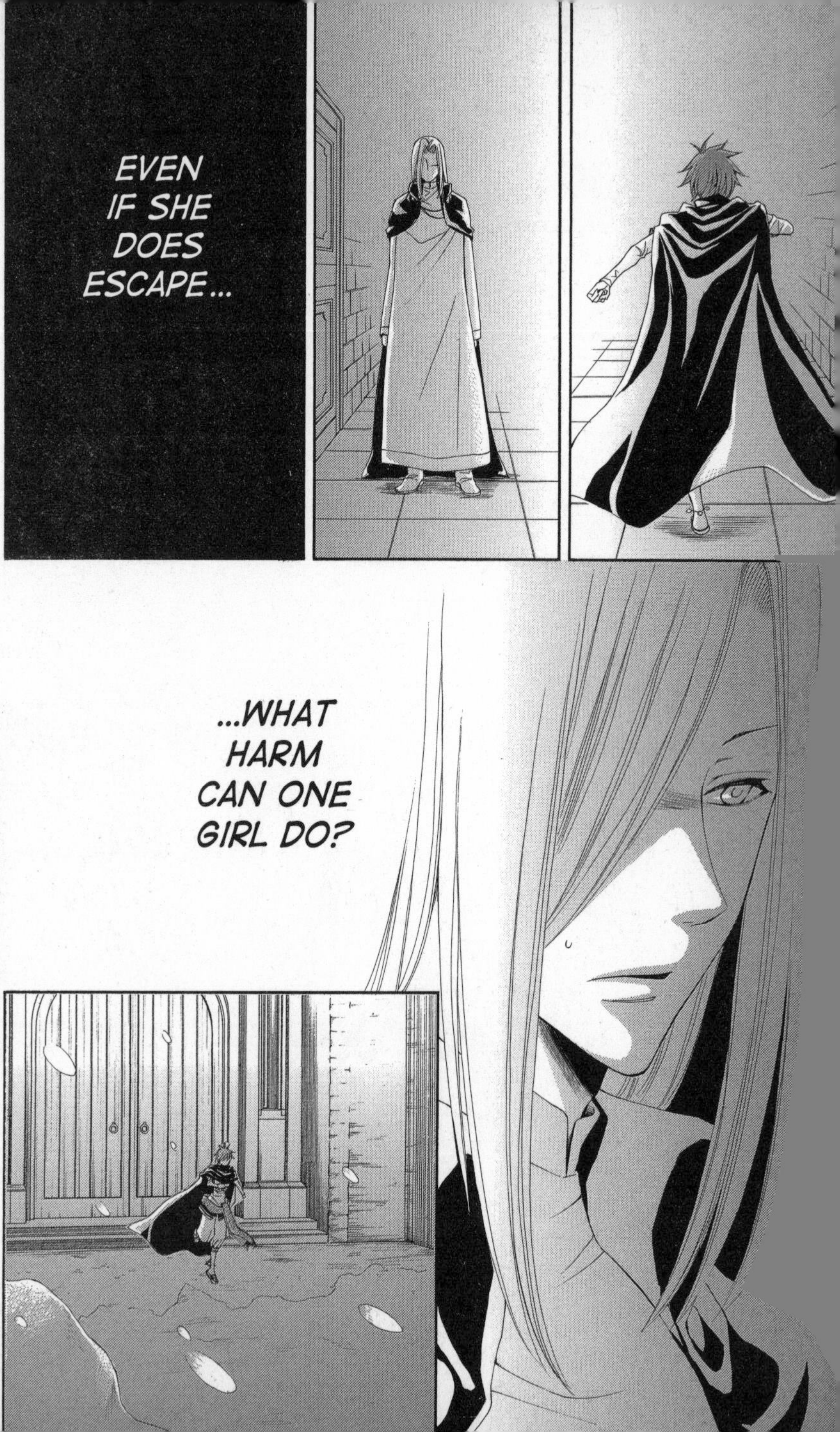
EVEN IF SHE DOES ESCAPE...
...WHAT HARM CAN ONE GIRL DO?

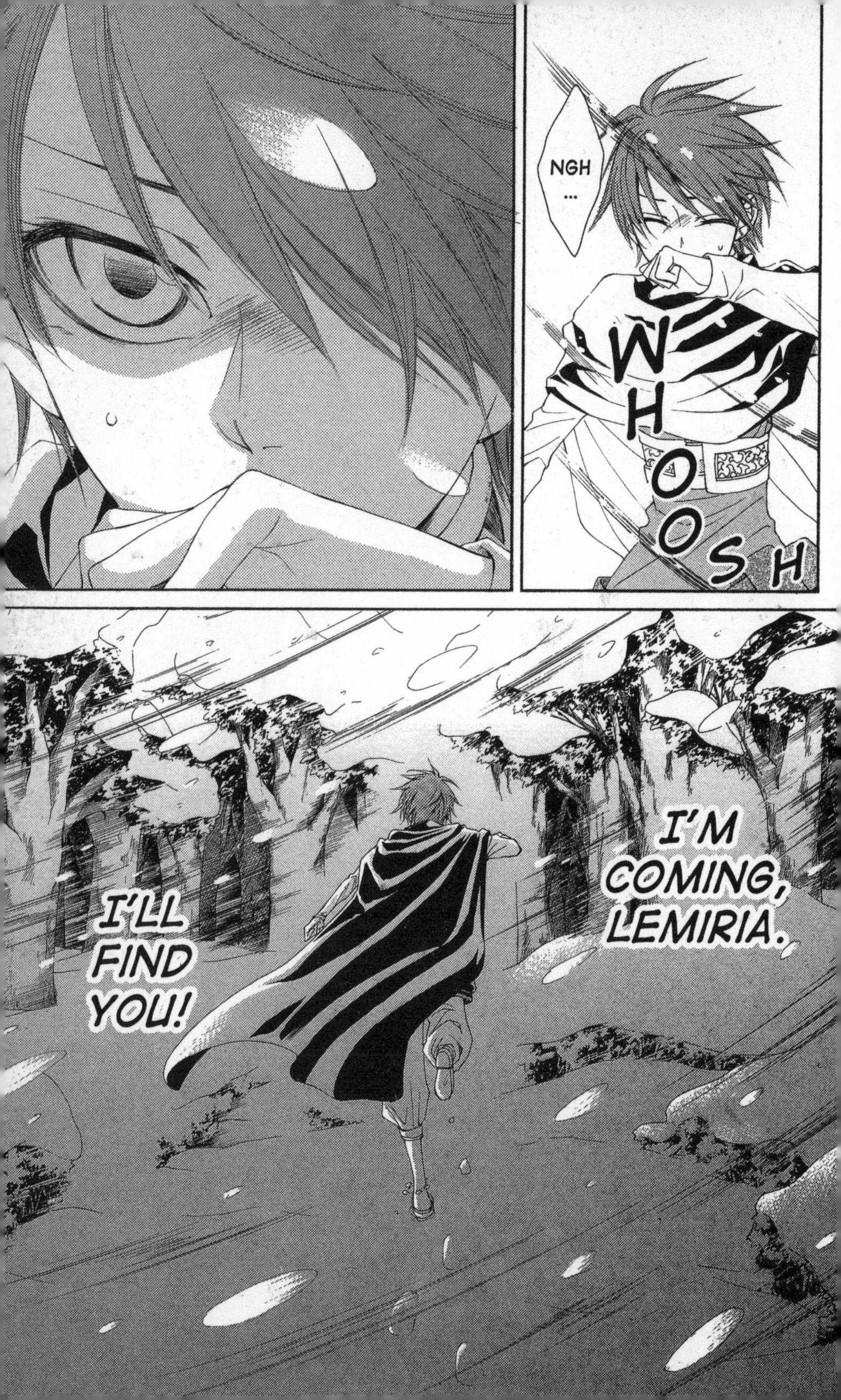
NGH ...
WHOOSH
I'M COMING, LEMIRIA.
I'LL FIND YOU!

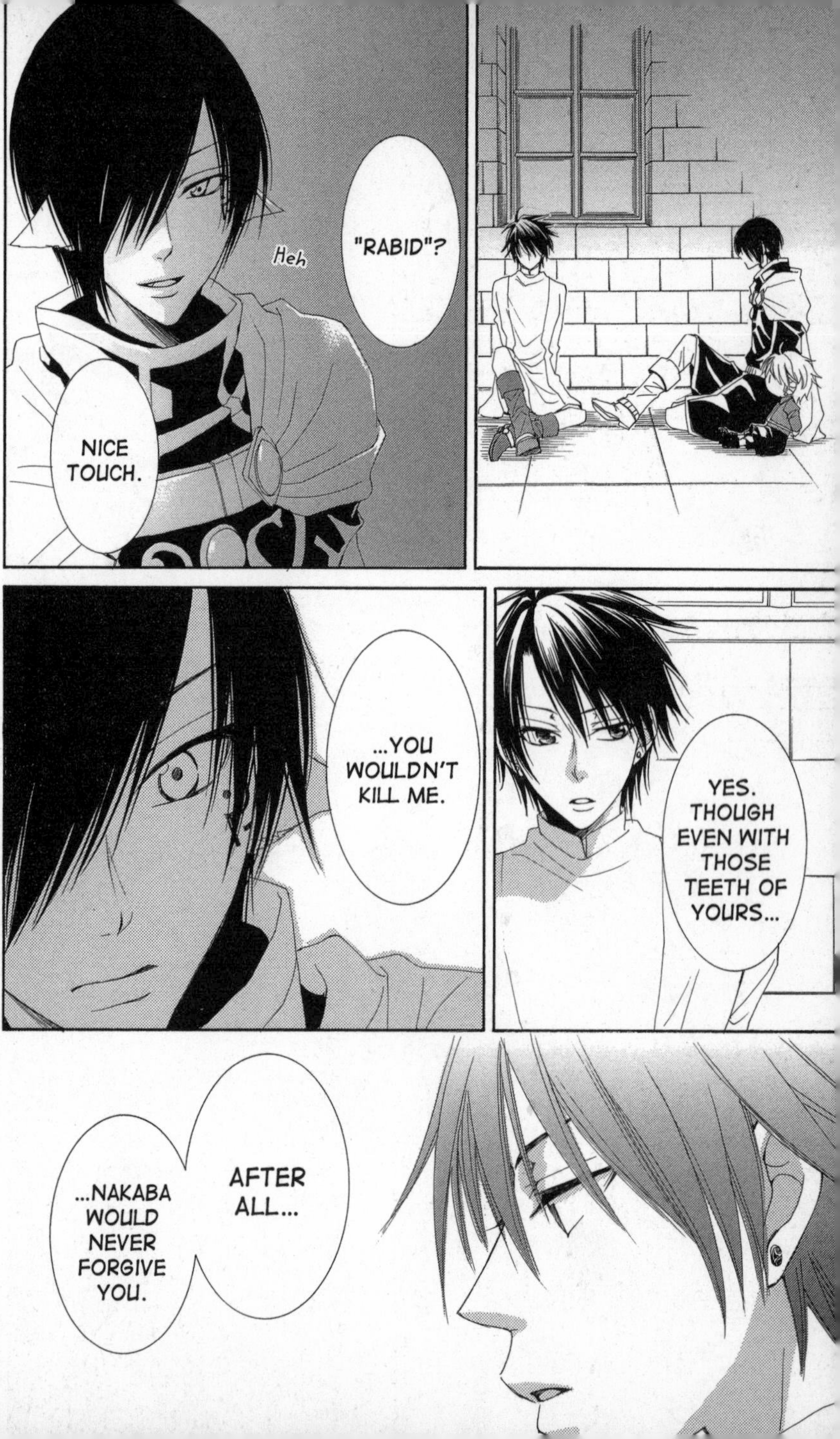
"RABID"?
Heh
NICE TOUCH.
YES. THOUGH EVEN WITH THOSE TEETH OF YOURS...
...YOU WOULDN'T KILL ME.
AFTER ALL...
...NAKABA WOULD NEVER FORGIVE YOU.

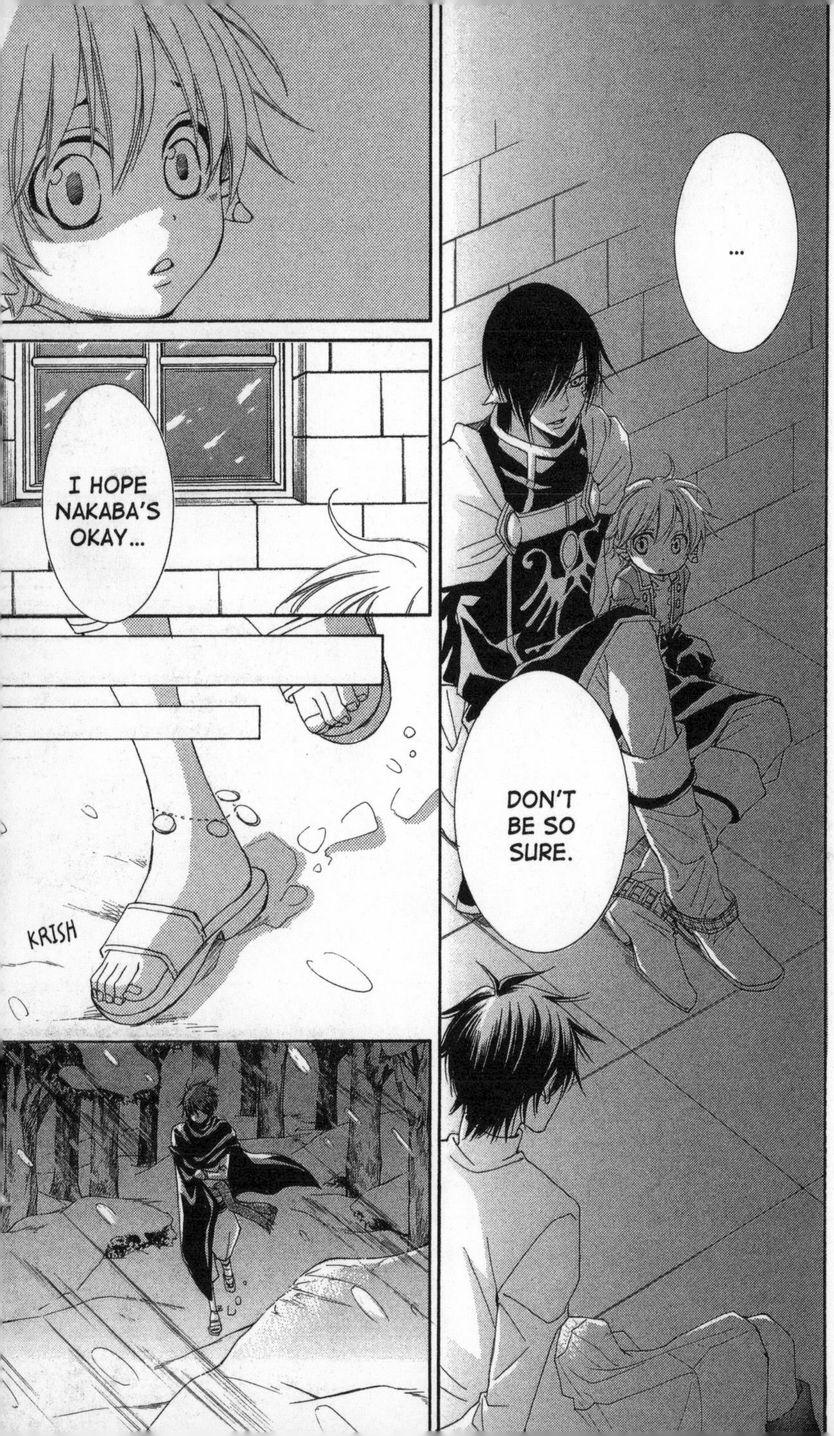
...
DON'T BE SO SURE.
I HOPE NAKABA'S OKAY...
KRISH

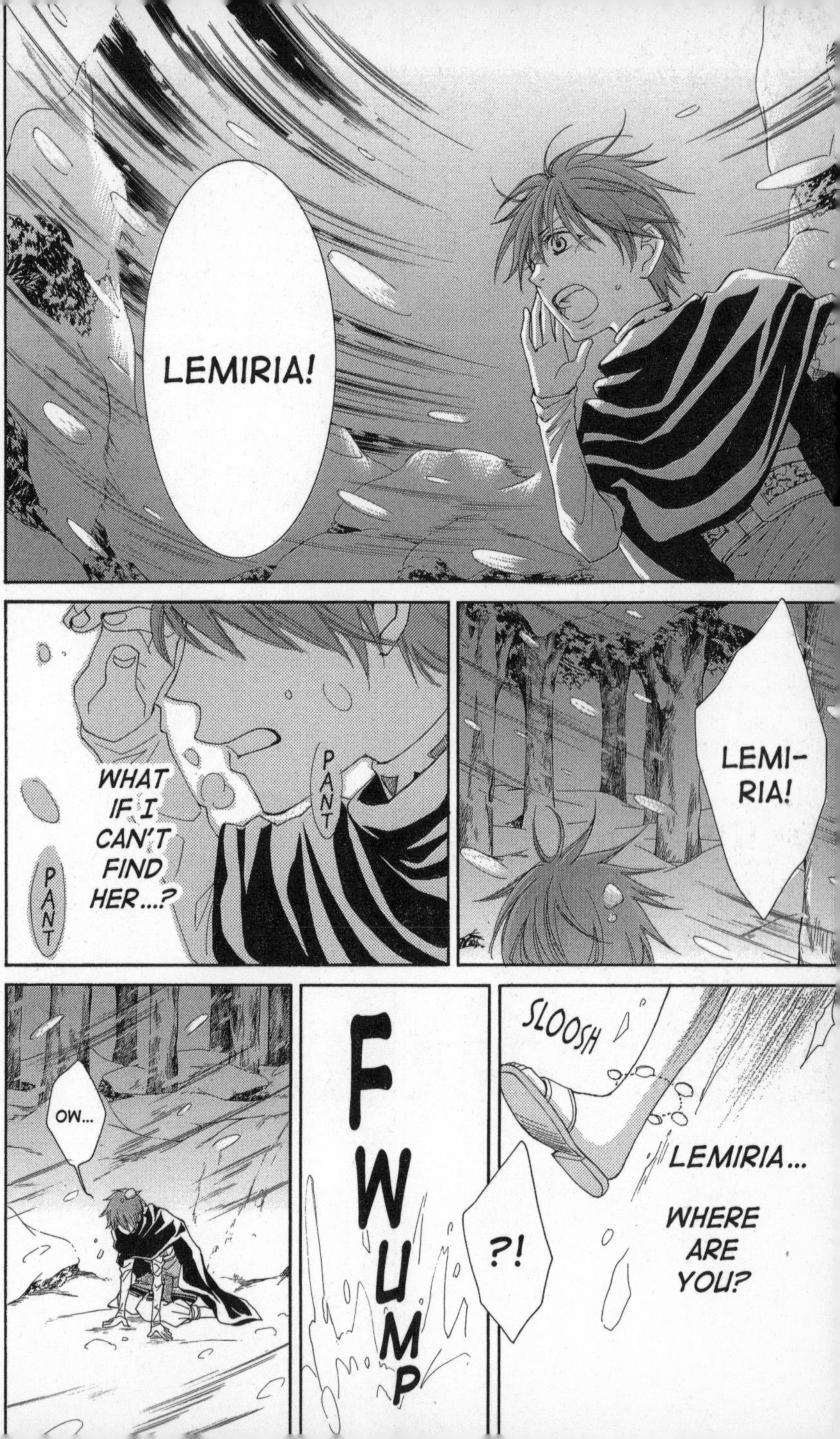
LEMIRIA!
LEMI-RIA!
PANT
WHAT IF I CAN'T FIND HER...?
PANT
SLOOSH
LEMIRIA...
WHERE ARE YOU?
?!
FWUMP
OW...

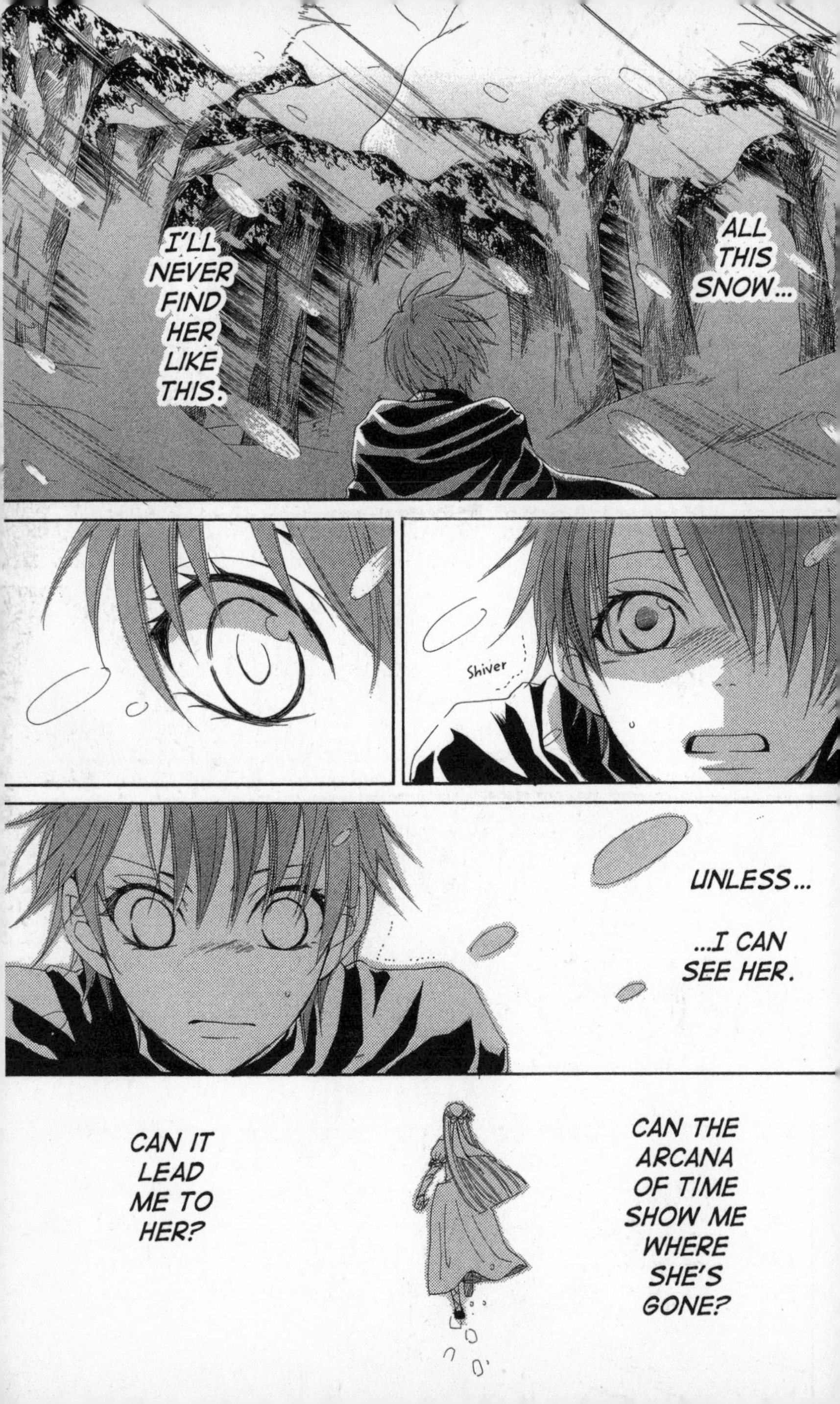
ALL THIS SNOW...
I'LL NEVER FIND HER LIKE THIS.
Shiver
UNLESS...
...I CAN SEE HER.
CAN THE ARCANA OF TIME SHOW ME WHERE SHE'S GONE?
CAN IT LEAD ME TO HER?

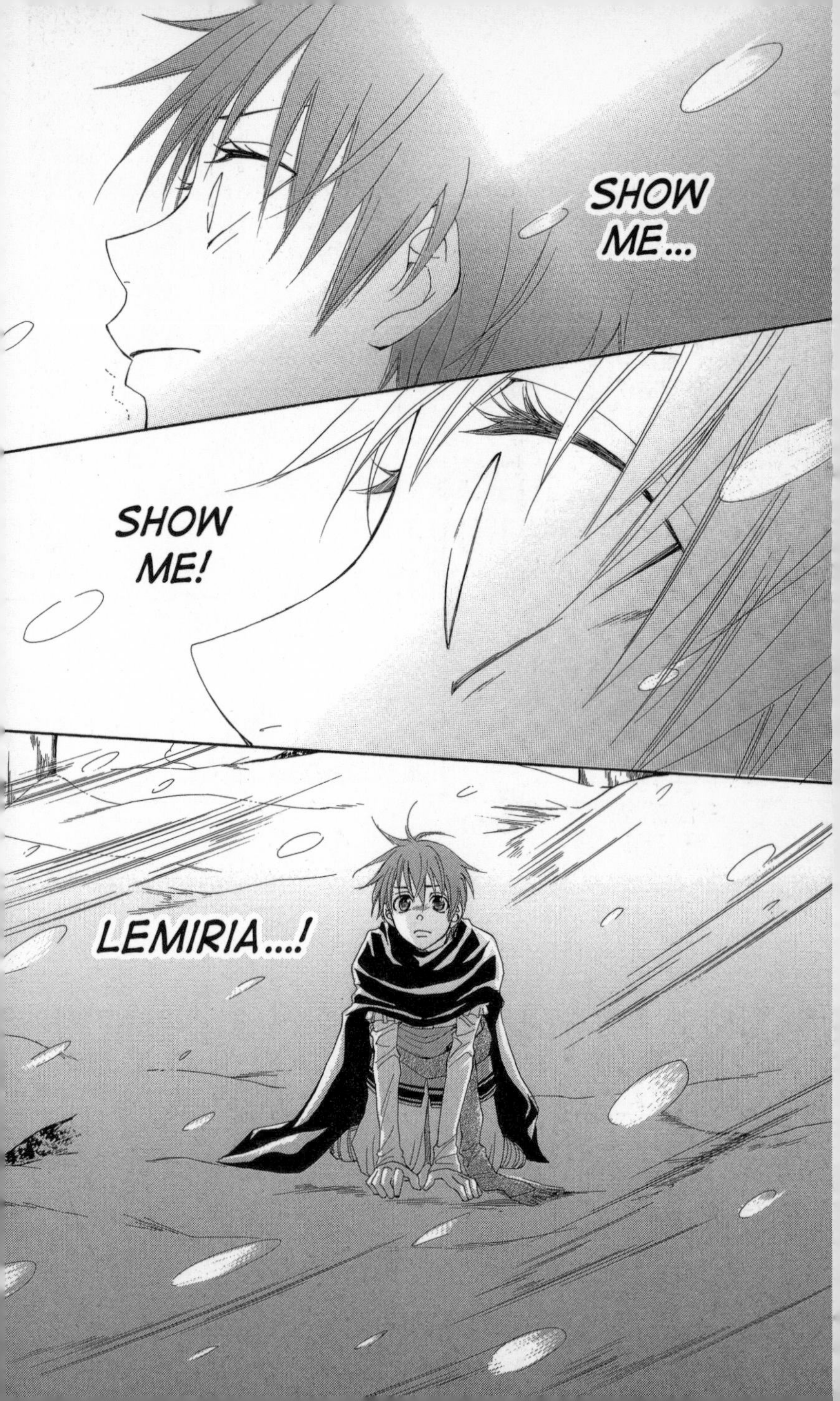
SHOW ME...
SHOW ME!
LEMIRIA...!

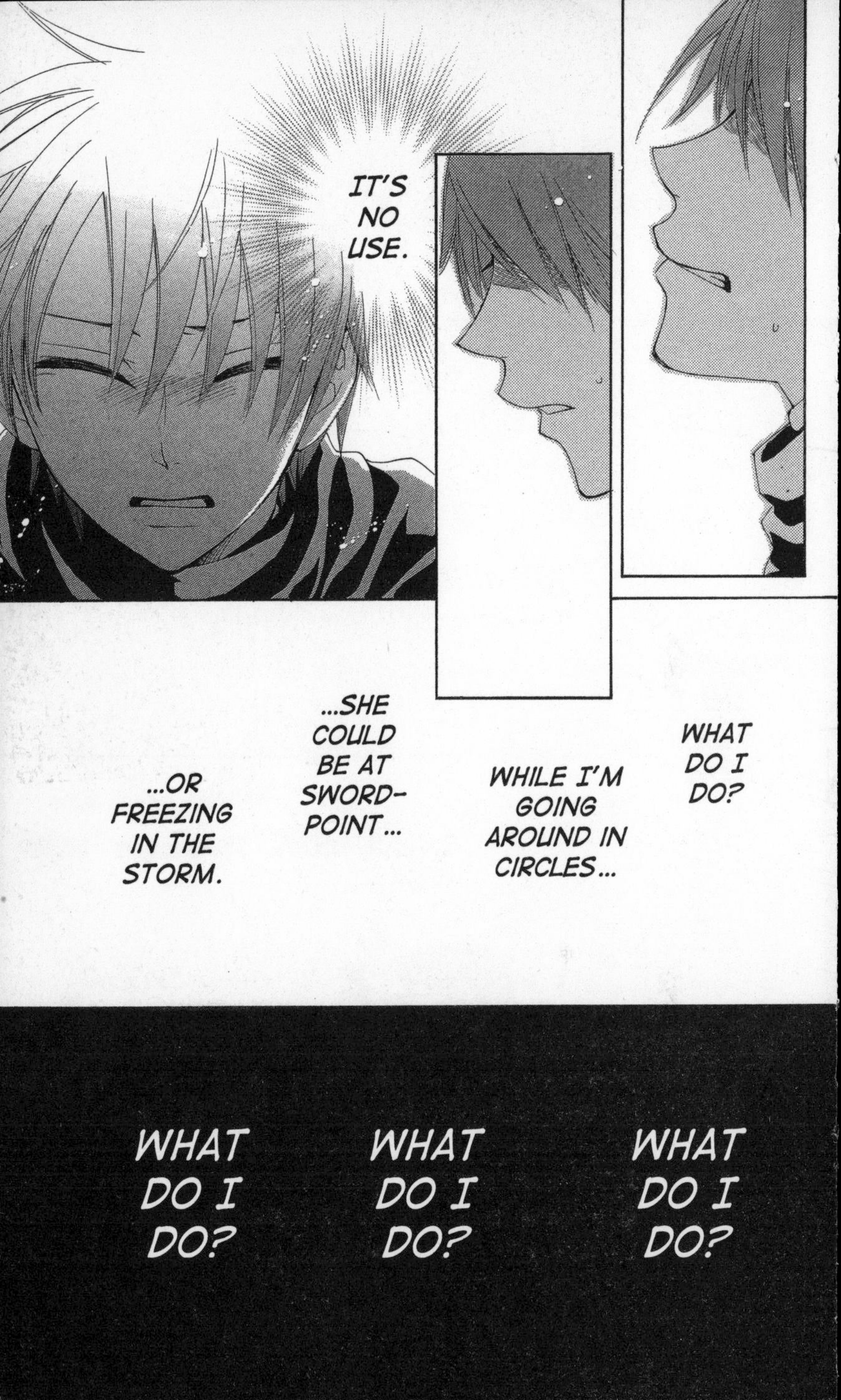
IT'S NO USE.
WHAT DO I DO?
WHILE I'M GOING AROUND IN CIRCLES...
...SHE COULD BE AT SWORD-POINT...
...OR FREEZING IN THE STORM.
WHAT DO I DO?
WHAT DO I DO?
WHAT DO I DO?

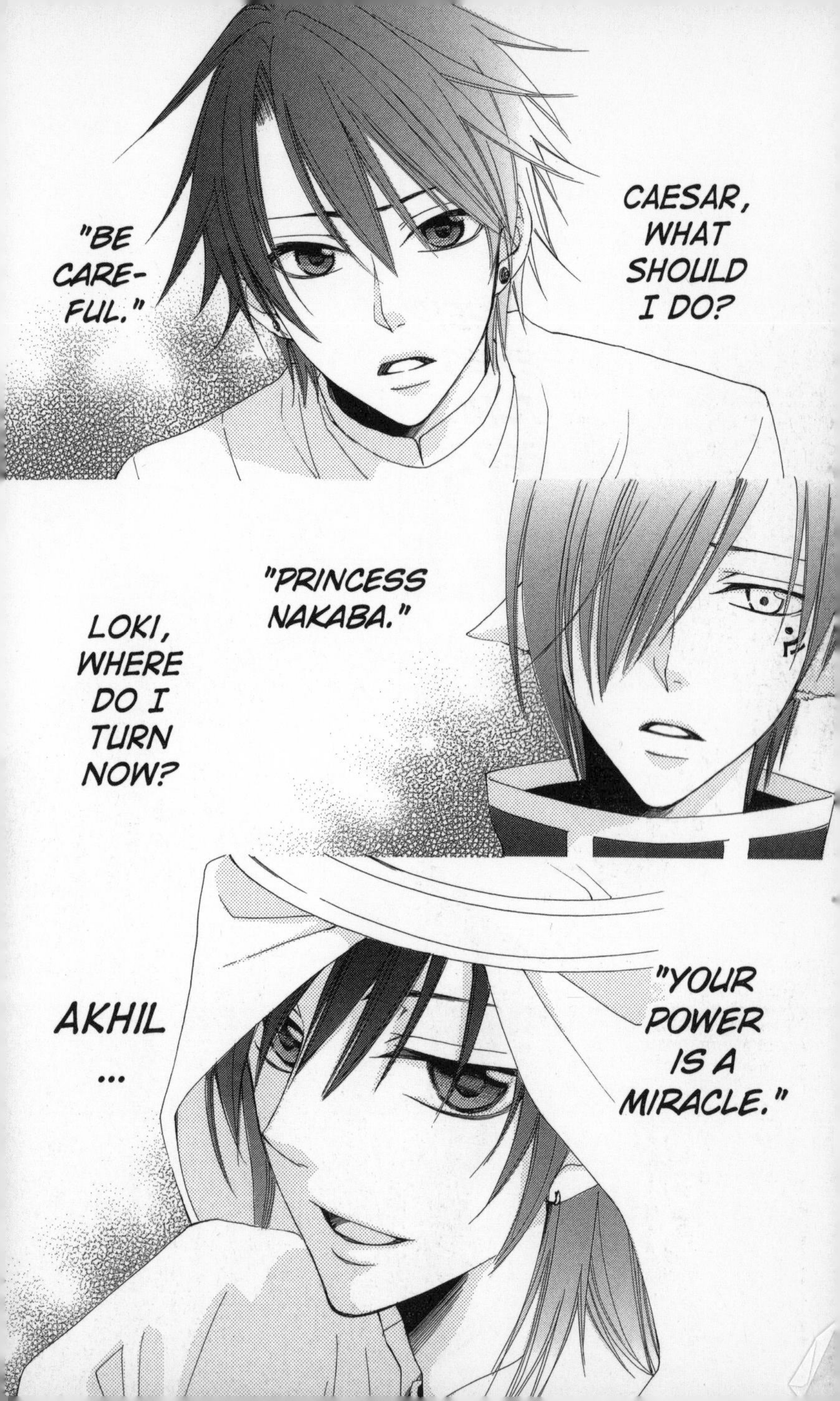
CAESAR, WHAT SHOULD I DO?
"BE CAREFUL."
"PRINCESS NAKABA."
LOKI, WHERE DO I TURN NOW?
"YOUR POWER IS A MIRACLE."
AKHIL ...

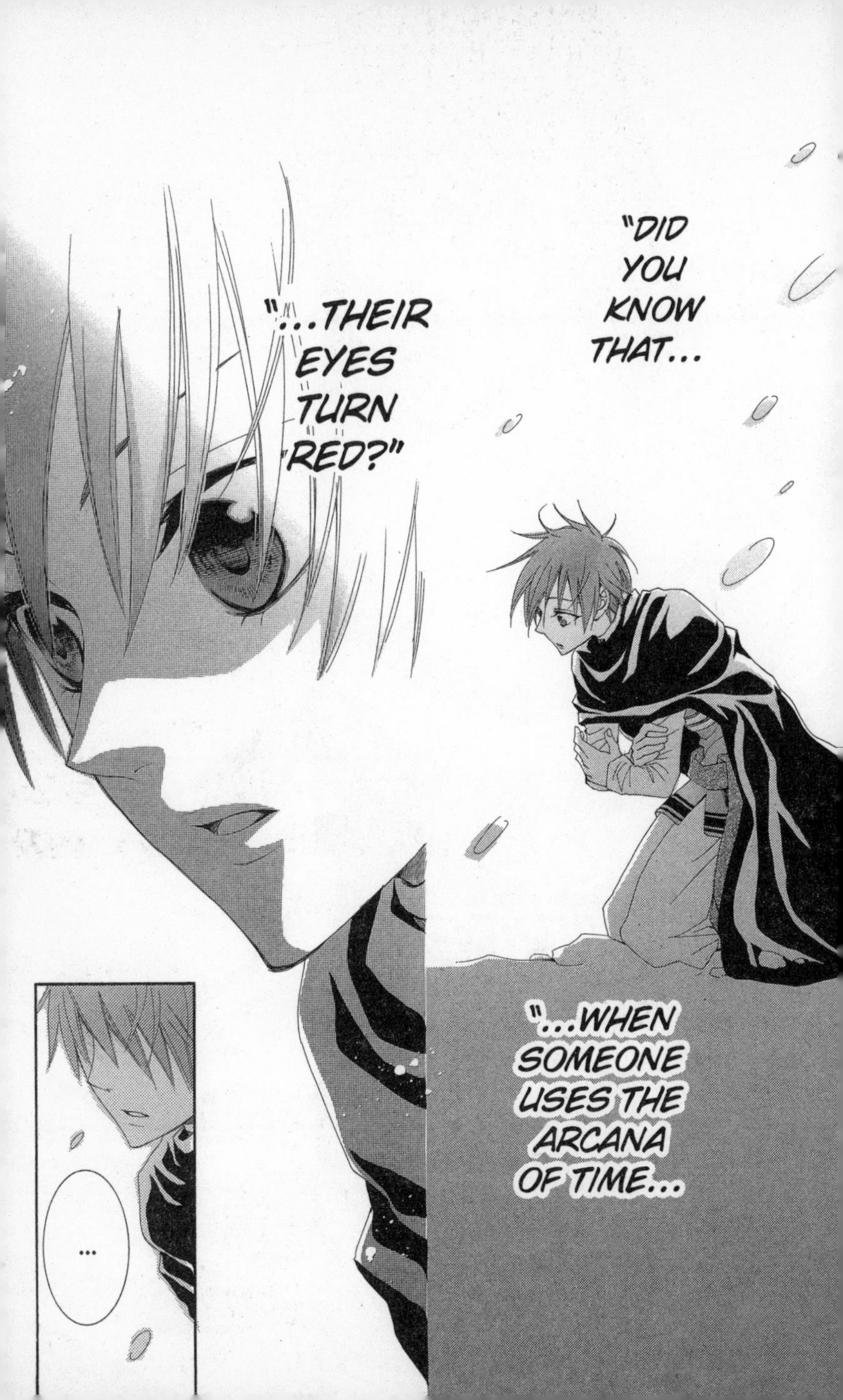
"DID YOU KNOW THAT...
"...WHEN SOMEONE USES THE ARCANA OF TIME...
"...THEIR EYES TURN RED?"
...

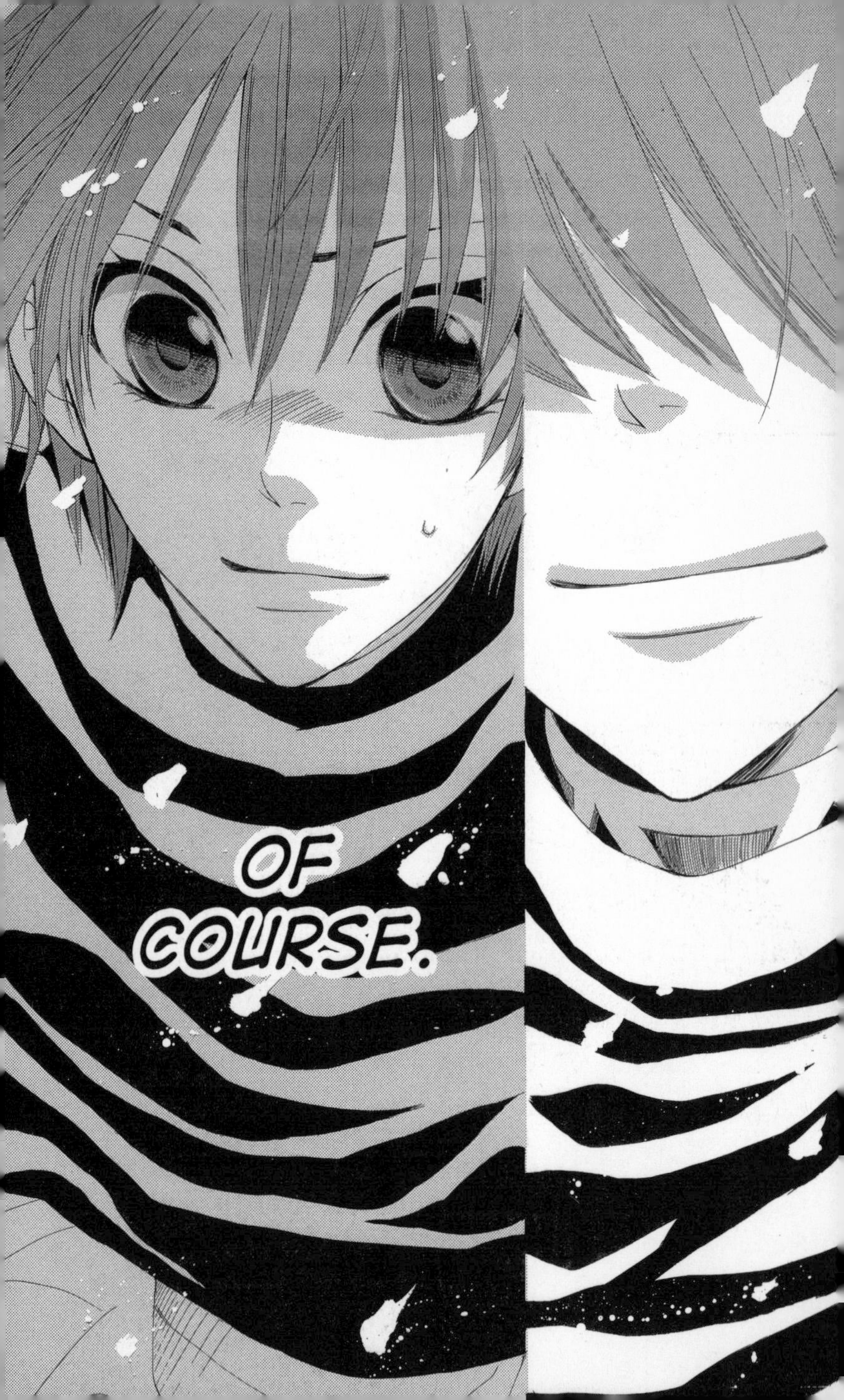
OF COURSE.

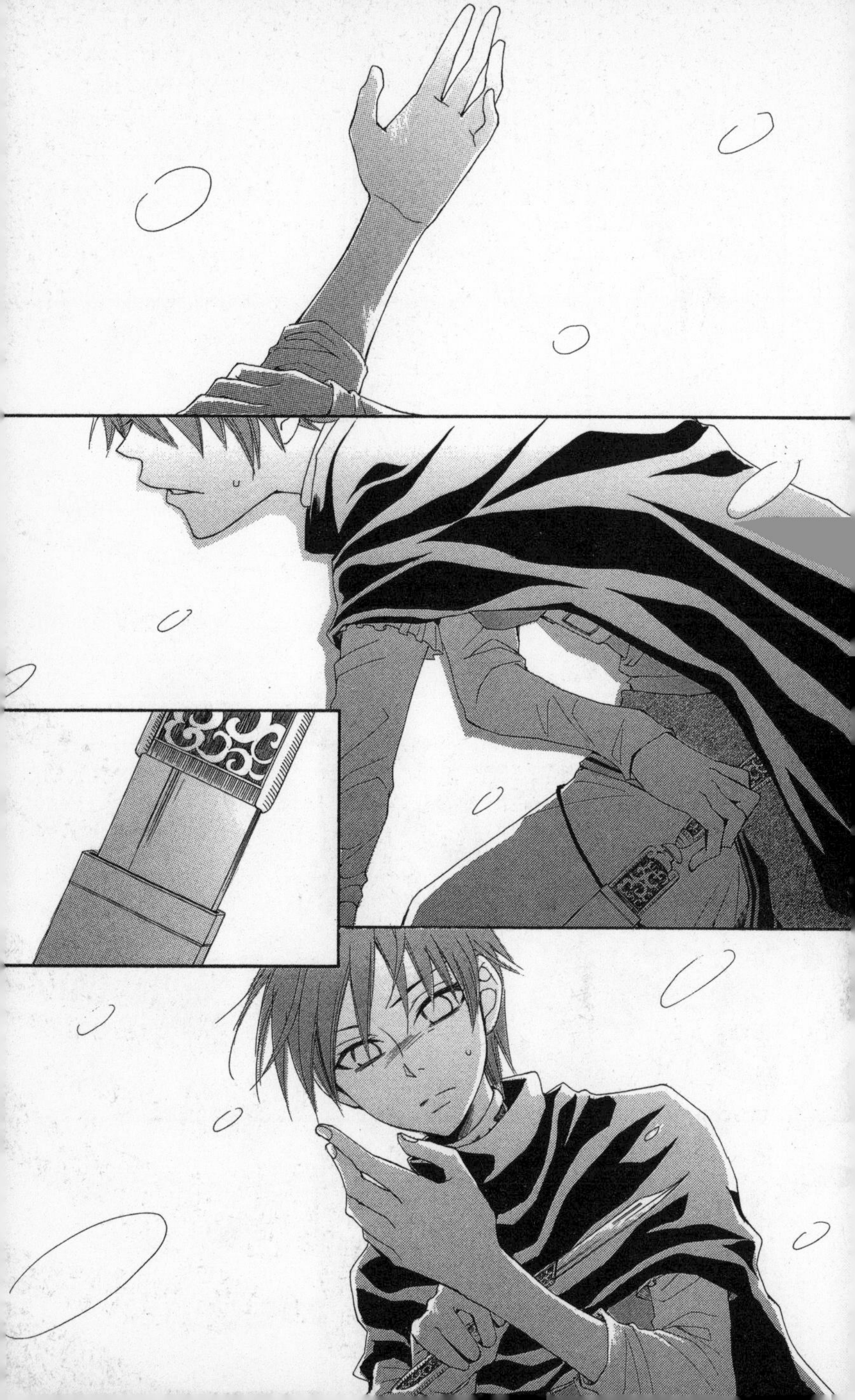

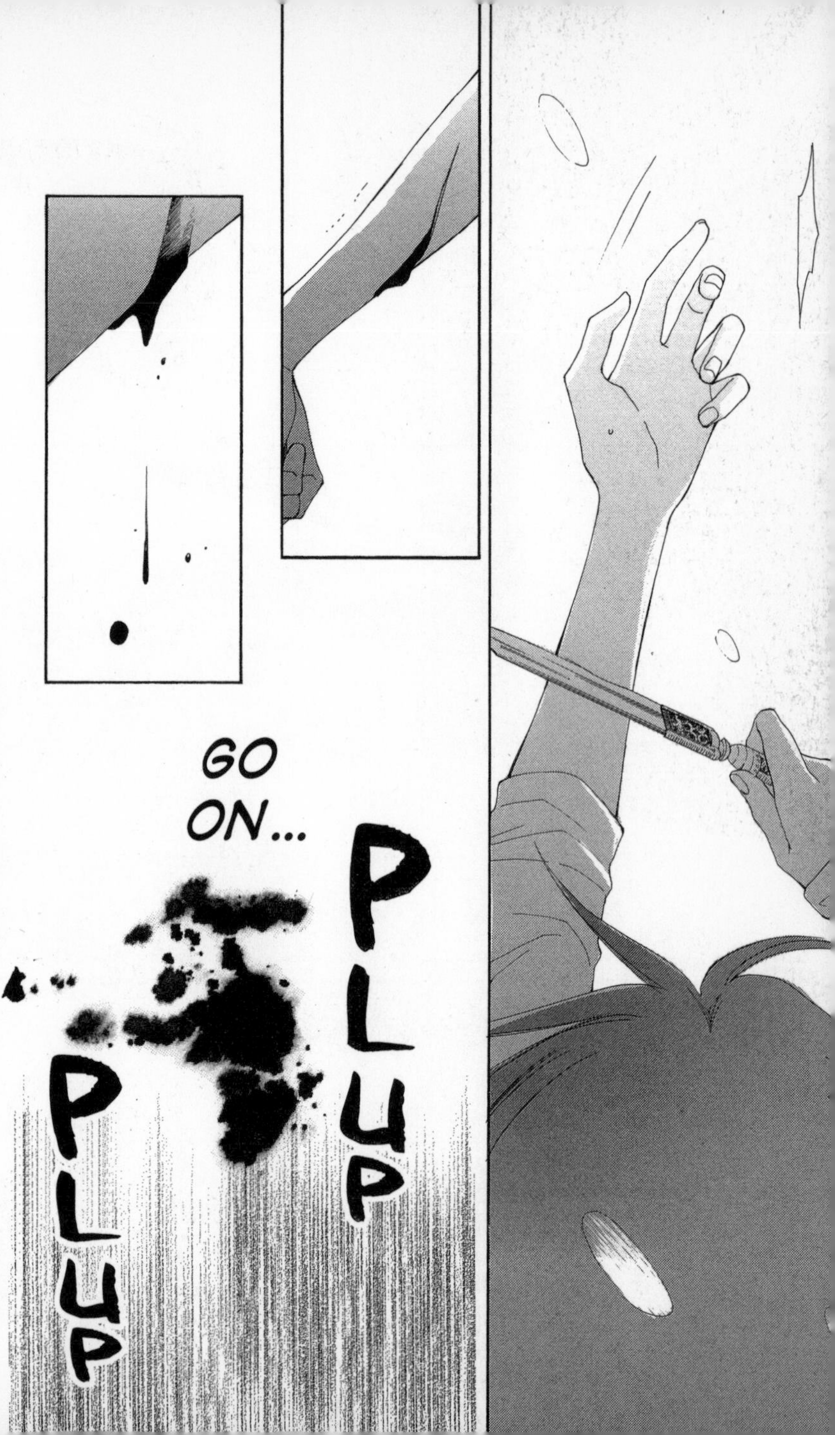
GO ON...
PLUP
PLUP

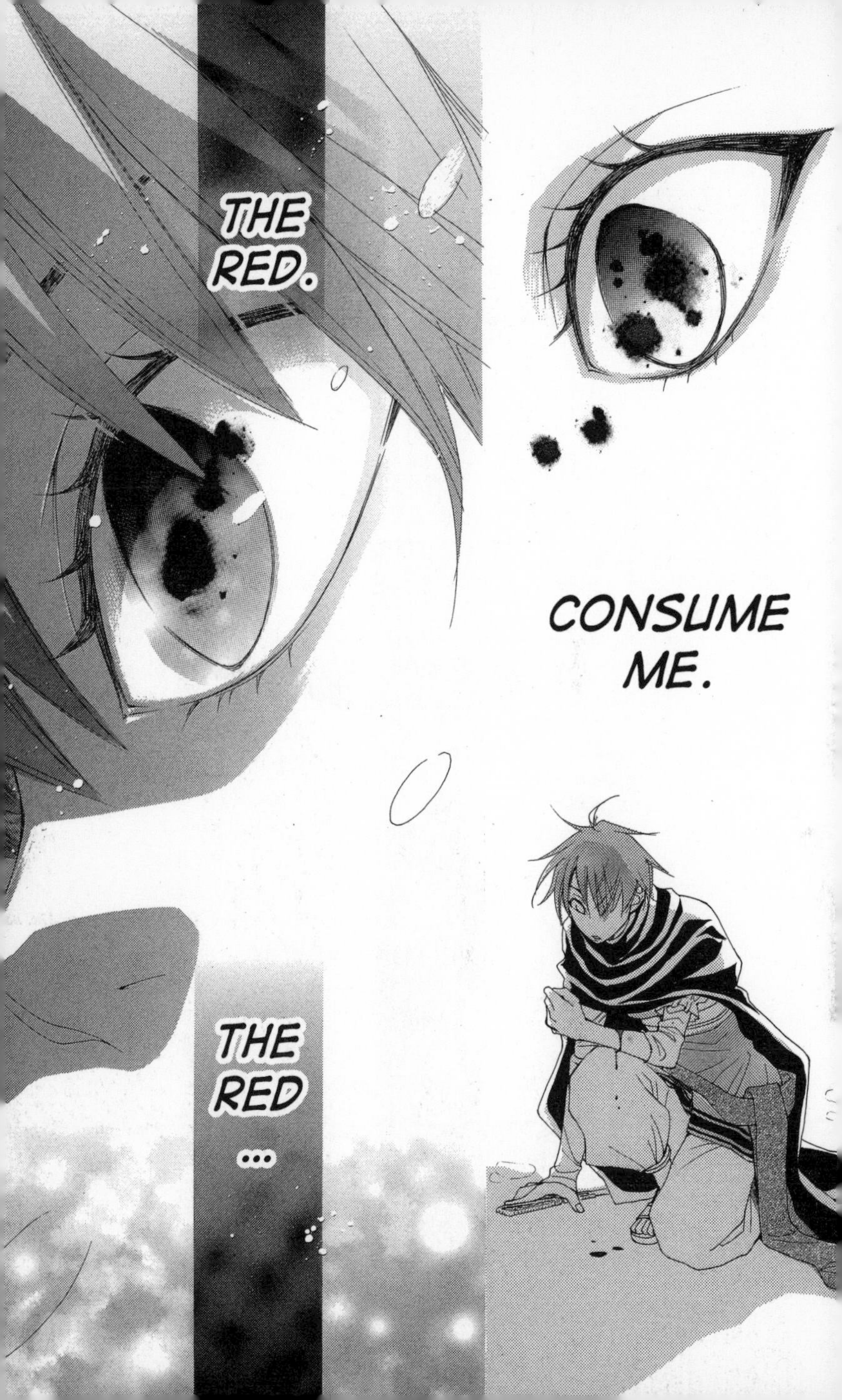
CONSUME ME.
THE RED.
THE RED ...

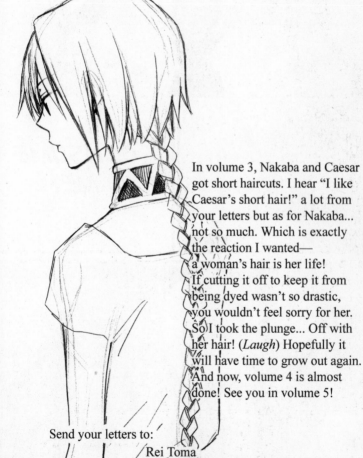

In volume 3, Nakaba and Caesar got short haircuts. I hear "I like Caesar's short hair!" a lot from your letters but as for Nakaba... not so much. Which is exactly the reaction I wanted— a woman's hair is her life! If cutting it off to keep it from being dyed wasn't so drastic, you wouldn't feel sorry for her. So I took the plunge... Off with her hair! (*Laugh*) Hopefully it will have time to grow out again. And now, volume 4 is almost done! See you in volume 5!

Send your letters to:

Rei Toma
c/o Dawn of the Arcana Editor
Viz Media
P.O. Box 77010
San Francisco, CA 94107

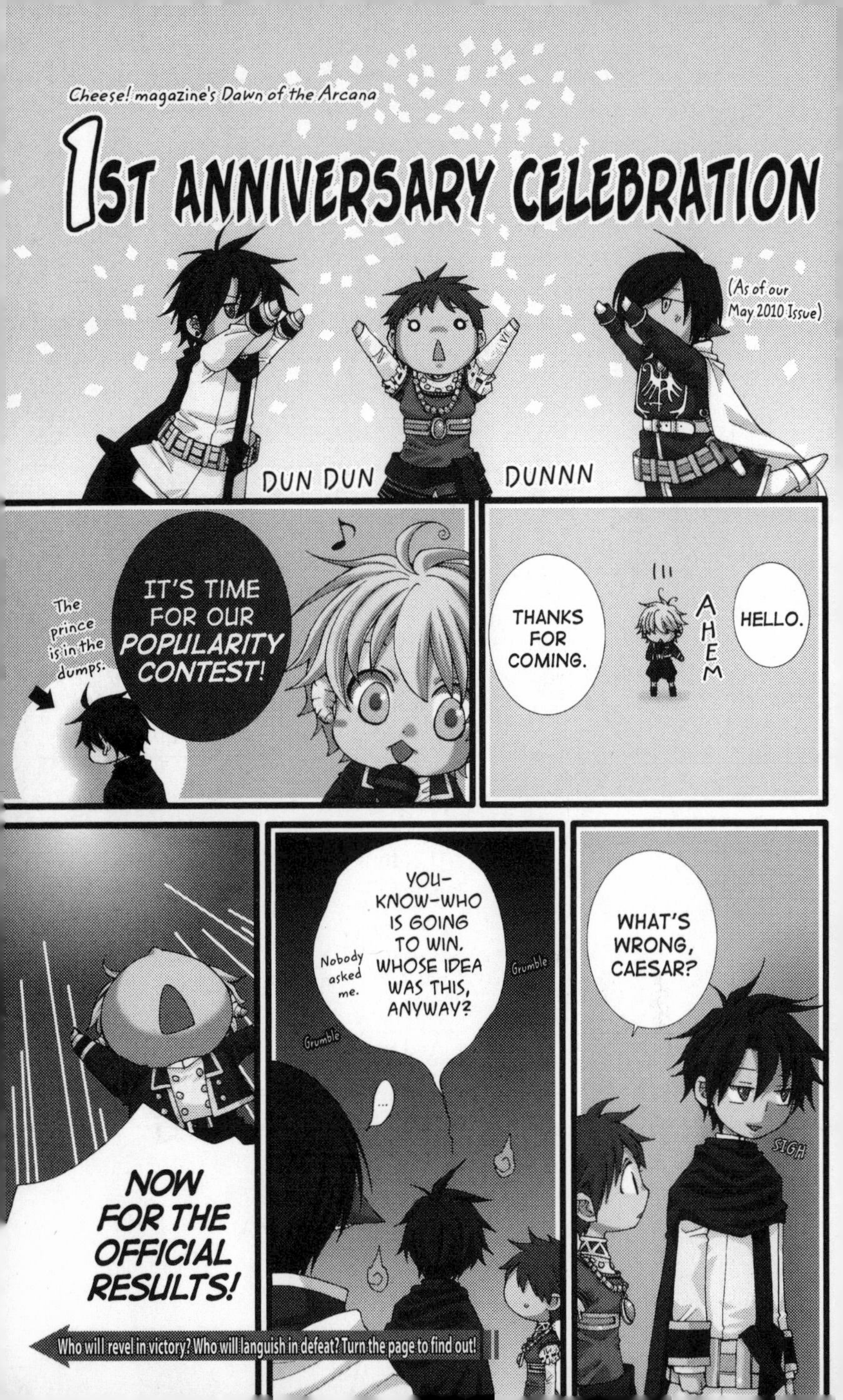

Cheese! magazine's Dawn of the Arcana
1ST ANNIVERSARY CELEBRATION
(As of our May 2010 Issue)
DUN DUN DUNNN
HELLO.
AHEM
THANKS FOR COMING.
IT'S TIME FOR OUR POPULARITY CONTEST!
The prince is in the dumps.
WHAT'S WRONG, CAESAR?
SIGH
YOU-KNOW-WHO IS GOING TO WIN. WHOSE IDEA WAS THIS, ANYWAY?
Grumble
Nobody asked me.
Grumble
...
NOW FOR THE OFFICIAL RESULTS!
Who will revel in victory? Who will languish in defeat? Turn the page to find out!

Chapter 15

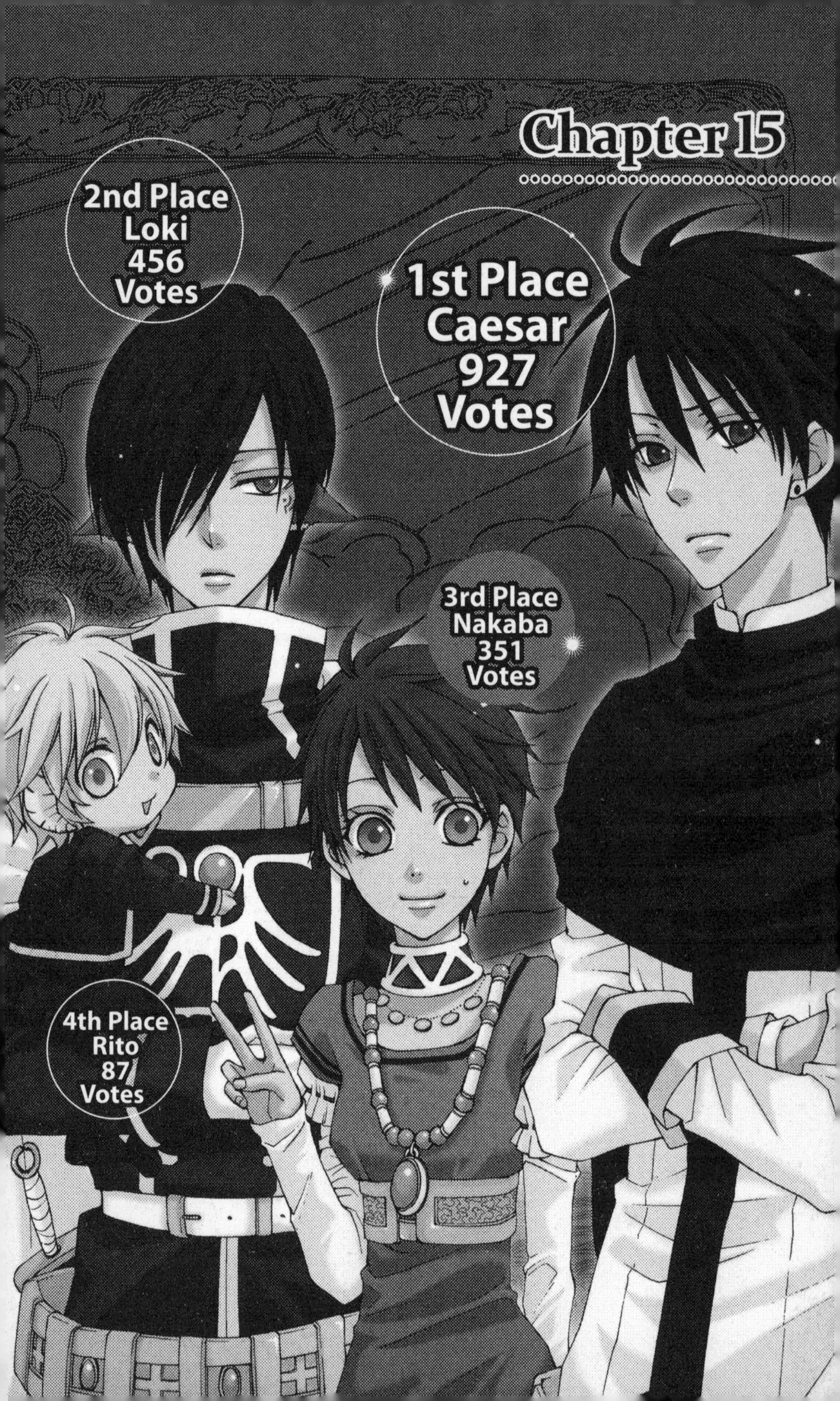
1st Place
Caesar
927
Votes
2nd Place
Loki
456
Votes
3rd Place
Nakaba
351
Votes
4th Place
Rito
87
Votes

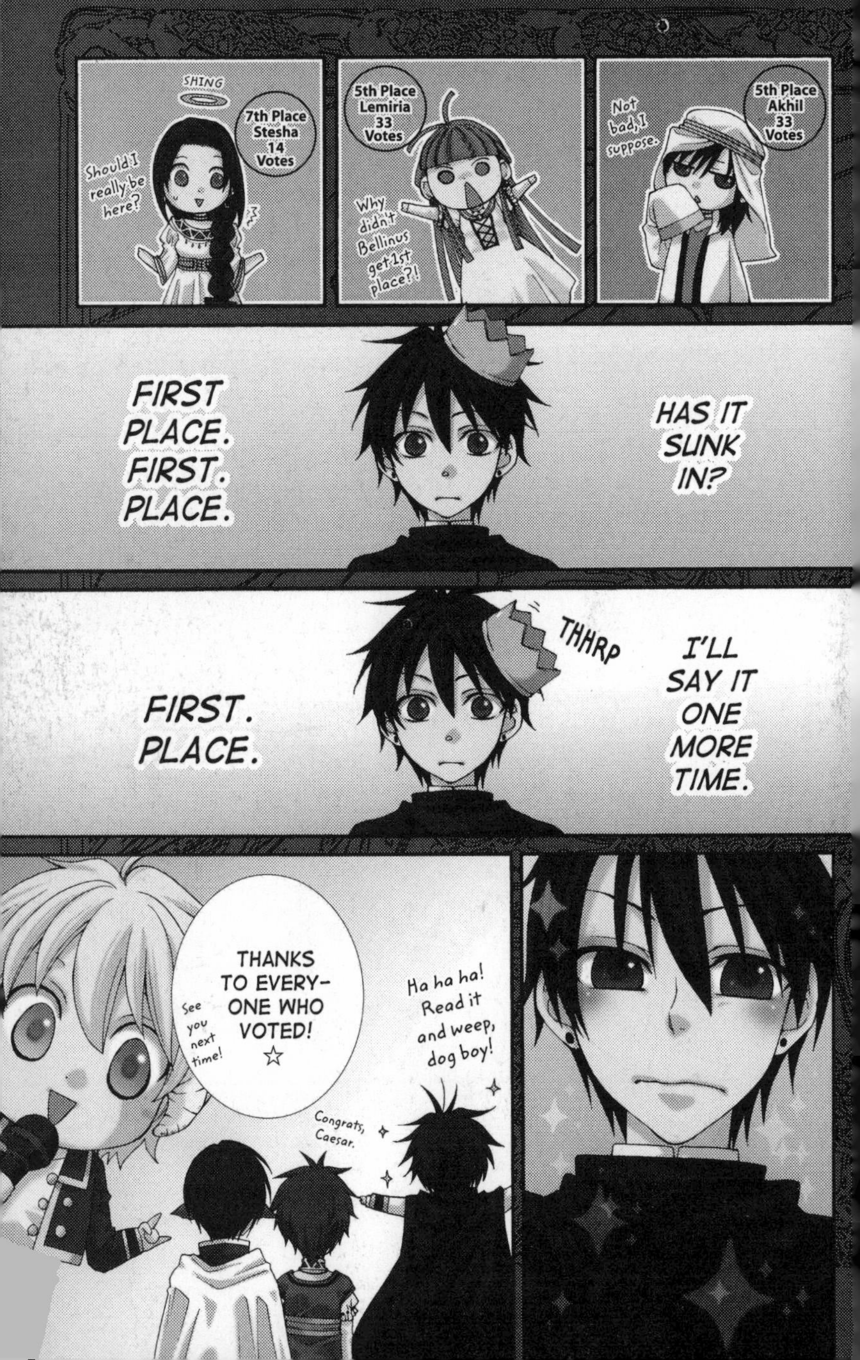
5th Place Akhil 33 Votes
Not bad, I suppose.
5th Place Lemiria 33 Votes
Why didn't Bellinus get 1st place?!
SHING
7th Place Stesha 14 Votes
Should I really be here?
HAS IT SUNK IN?
FIRST PLACE. FIRST. PLACE.
THHRP
I'LL SAY IT ONE MORE TIME.
FIRST. PLACE.
Ha ha ha! Read it and weep, dog boy!
Congrats, Caesar.
THANKS TO EVERY-ONE WHO VOTED! ☆
See you next time!

Dawn of the Arcana

Unscheduled News Bulletin

ARCANA FAN PAGE

Our fair prince makes first place with room to spare!

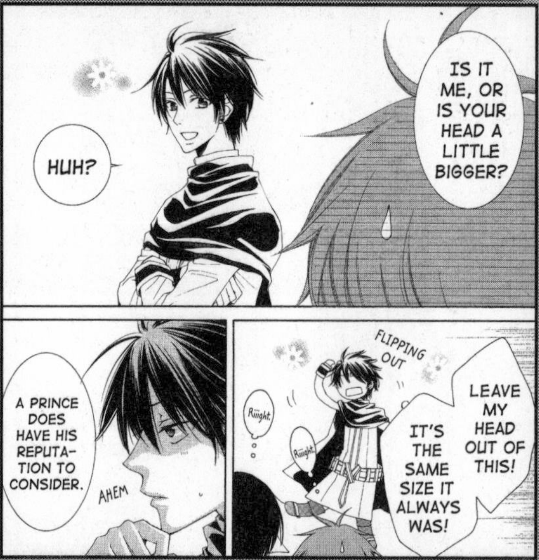
IS IT ME, OR IS YOUR HEAD A LITTLE BIGGER?
HUH?
FLIPPING OUT
LEAVE MY HEAD OUT OF THIS!
IT'S THE SAME SIZE IT ALWAYS WAS!
Riiight.
Riiight.
A PRINCE DOES HAVE HIS REPUTATION TO CONSIDER.
AHEM

↓ Here's how everyone else placed ↓

- **7th** Cain, First Prince of Belquat ......14 Votes
- **9th** Bellinus, Caesar's Attendant ......8 Votes
- **10th** Louise, Cain's Fiancée ......7 Votes
- **11th** Guran, King of Belquat ......5 Votes
- **12th** Nathalie, Queen of Senan ......2 Votes
- **13th** Douglas, Louise's Father ......1 Vote
- **13th** Morris, King of Senan ......1 Vote
- **13th** Rei Toma ......1 Vote

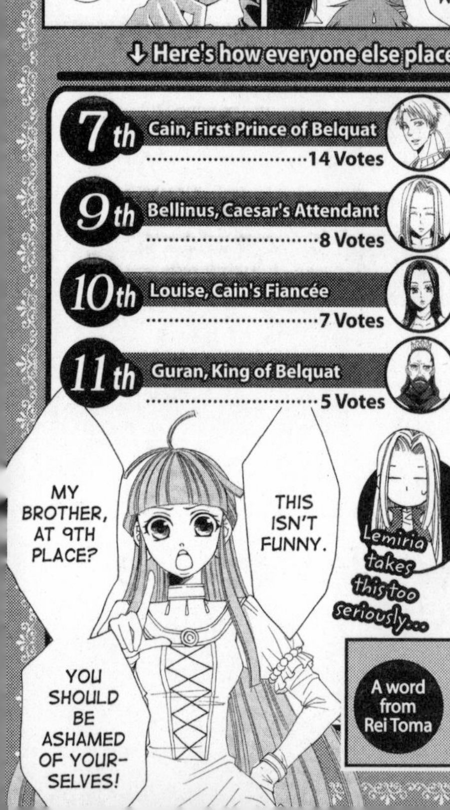
THIS ISN'T FUNNY.
MY BROTHER, AT 9TH PLACE?
YOU SHOULD BE ASHAMED OF YOURSELVES!
Lemiria takes this too seriously...

Even Rei Toma pulled in a vote! There were some other off-ballot votes. Who knows? Maybe those names will show up on future characters!

A word from Rei Toma

I thought Loki would win, so no one was more surprised than me. Way to go, Caesar! A sincere thanks to everyone who voted. Especially whoever casted a vote for me!

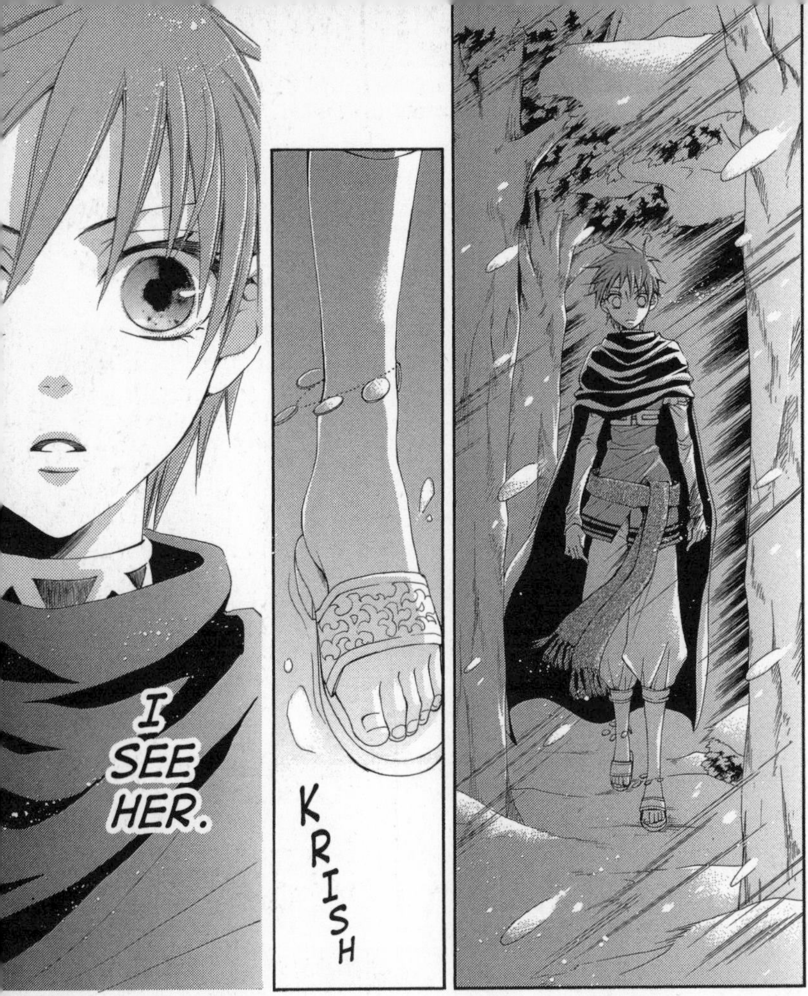
KRISH
I SEE HER.

Dawn of the Arcana

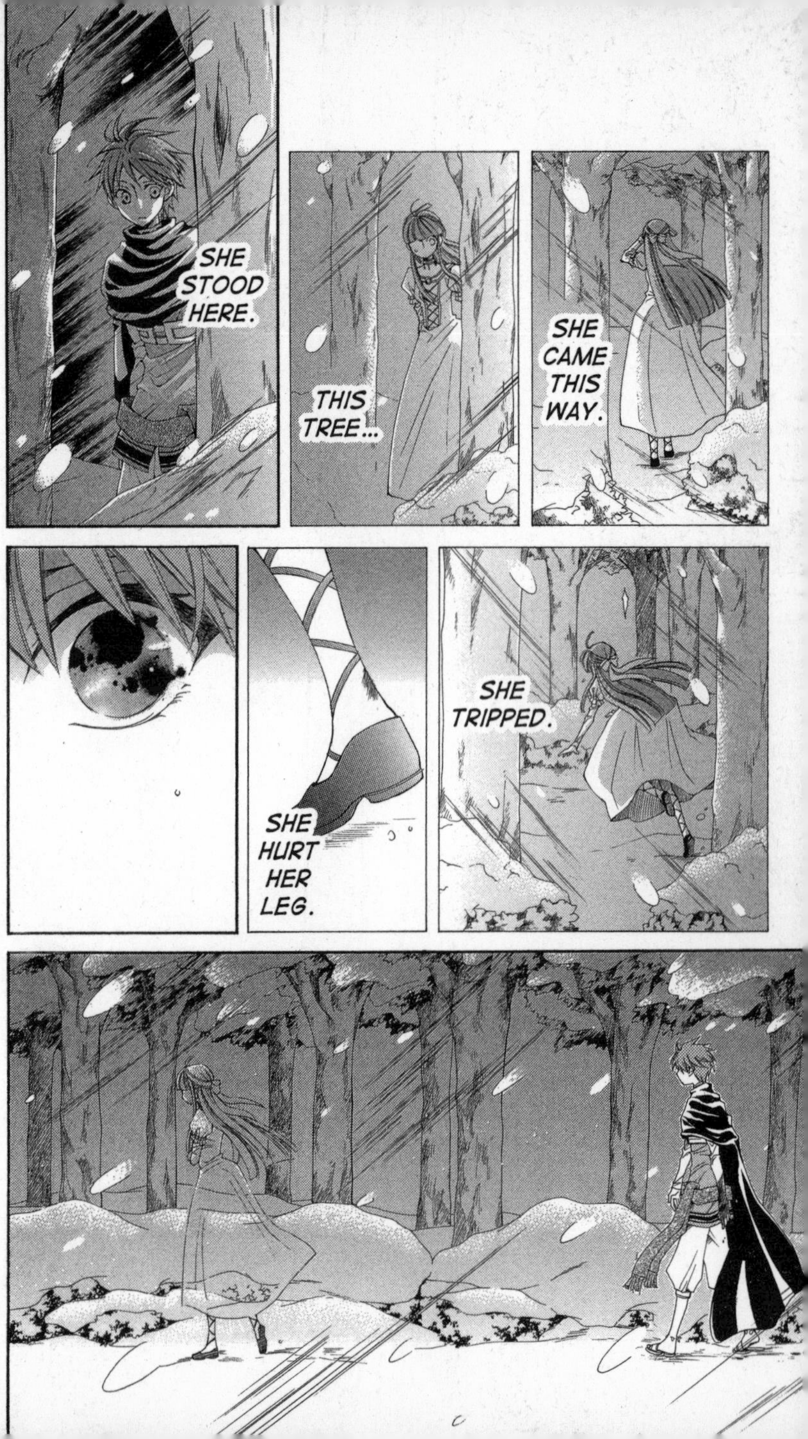
SHE CAME THIS WAY.
THIS TREE...
SHE STOOD HERE.
SHE TRIPPED.
SHE HURT HER LEG.

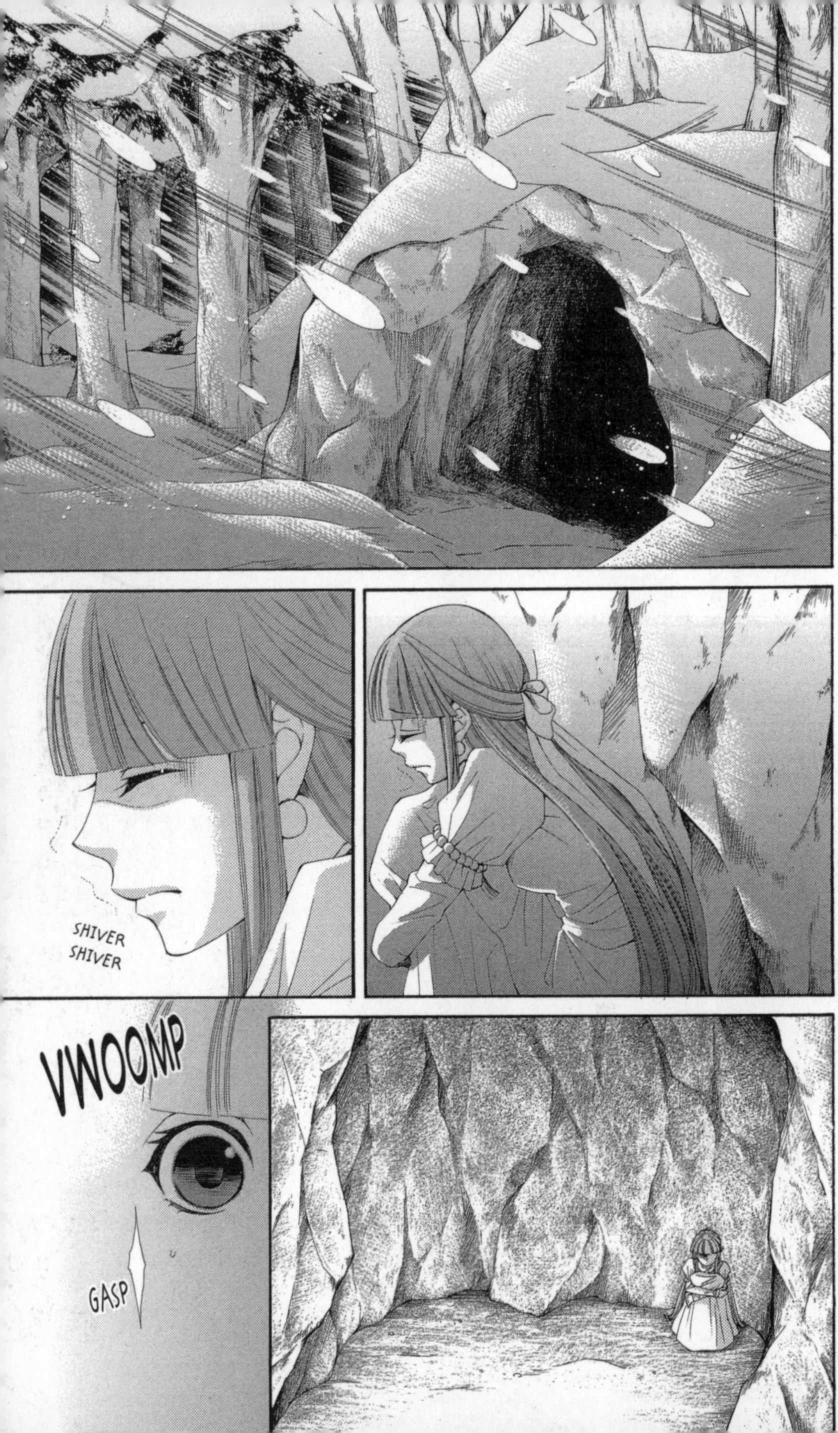
SHIVER
SHIVER
VWOOMP
GASP

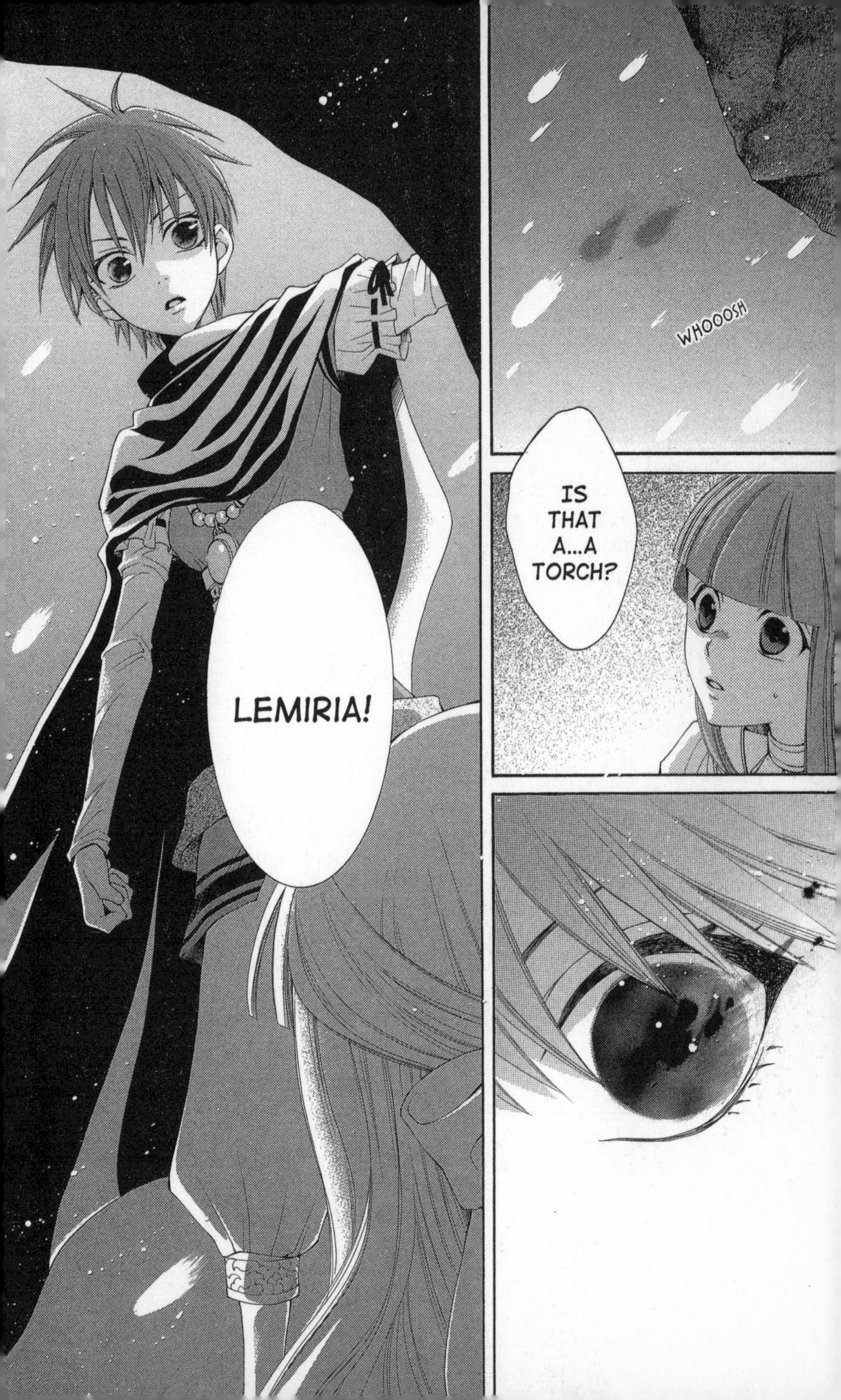
WHOOOSH
IS THAT A...A TORCH?
LEMIRIA!

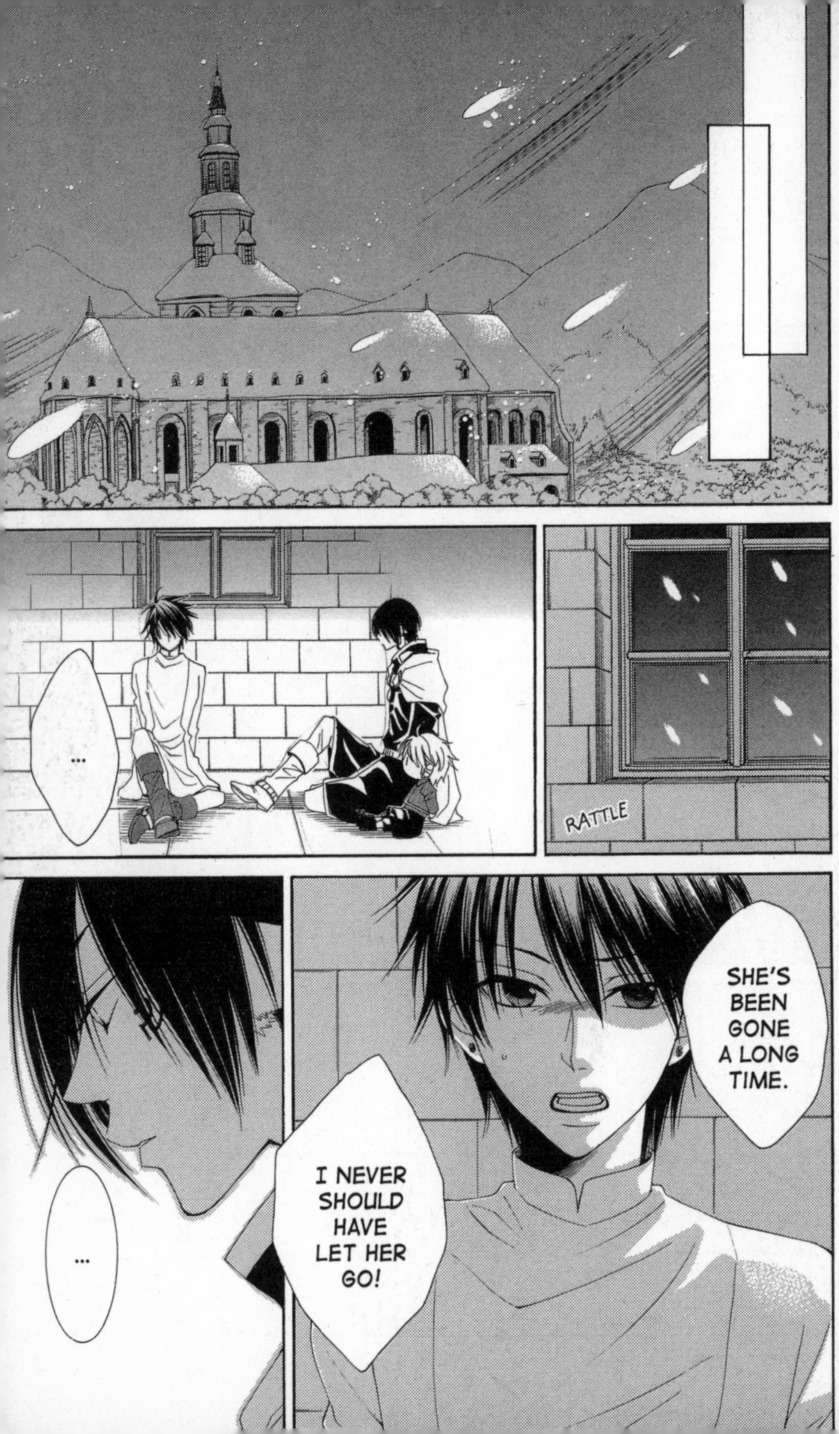
RATTLE
...
SHE'S BEEN GONE A LONG TIME.
I NEVER SHOULD HAVE LET HER GO!
...

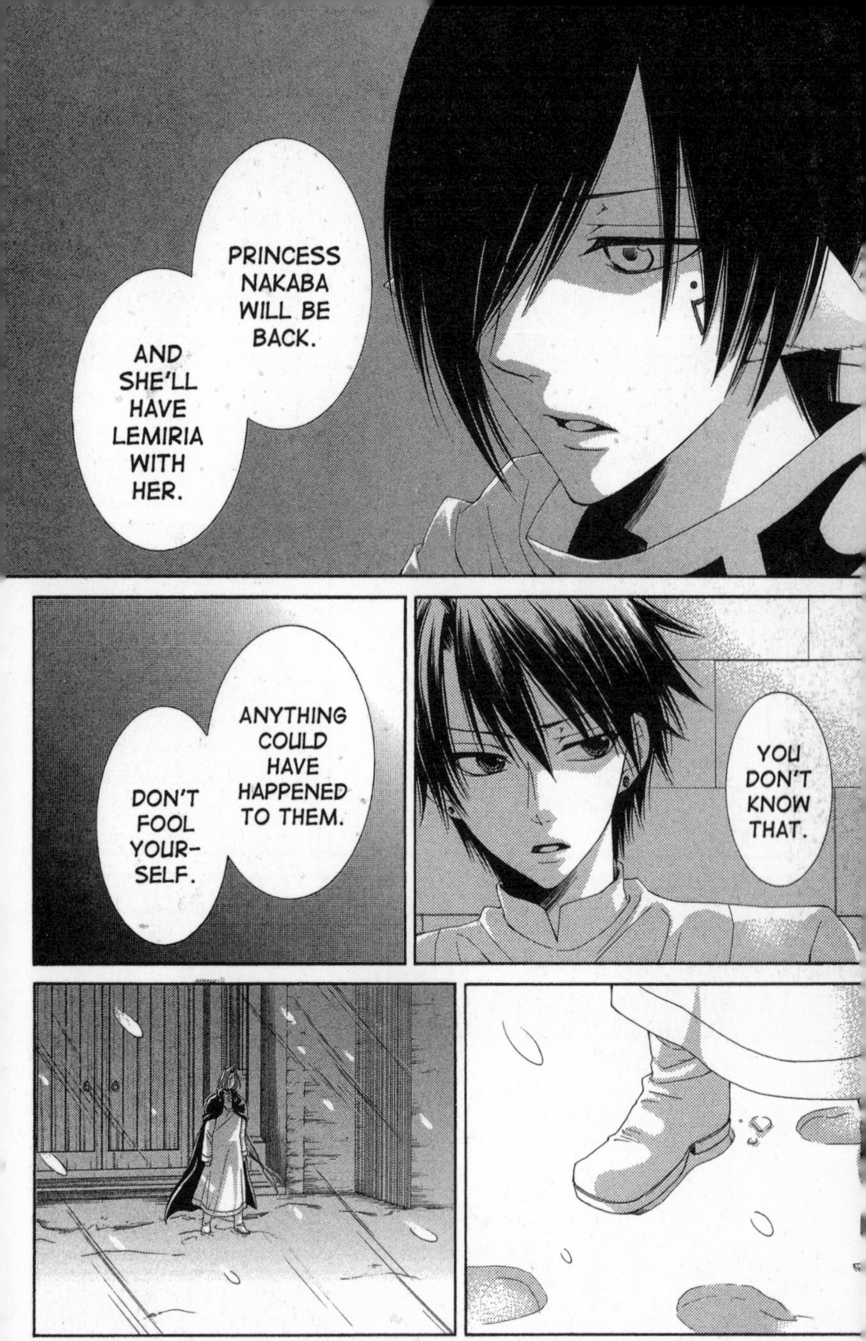
PRINCESS NAKABA WILL BE BACK.
AND SHE'LL HAVE LEMIRIA WITH HER.
YOU DON'T KNOW THAT.
ANYTHING COULD HAVE HAPPENED TO THEM.
DON'T FOOL YOUR-SELF.

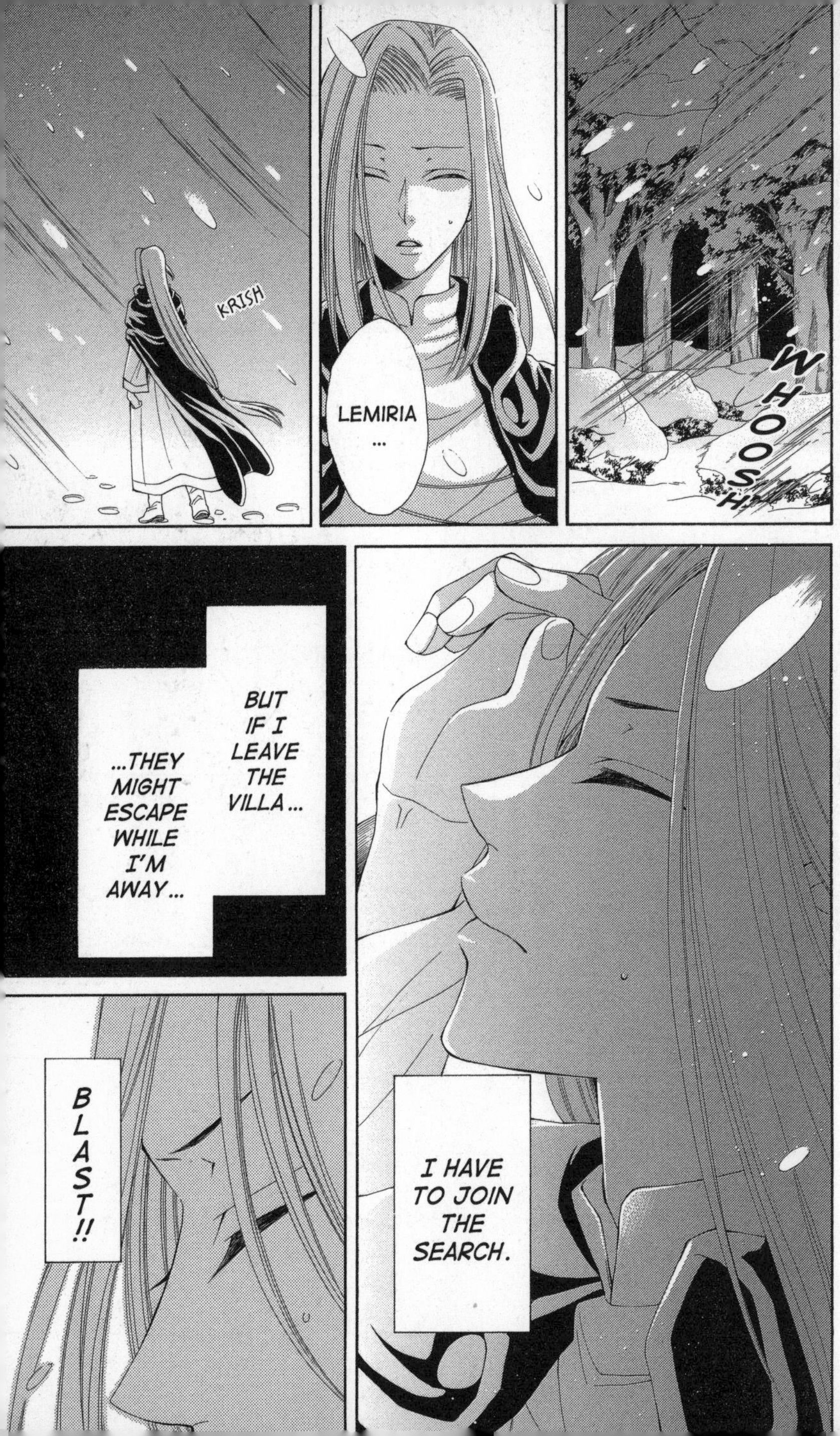
WHOOSH
LEMIRIA ...
KRISH
I HAVE TO JOIN THE SEARCH.
BUT IF I LEAVE THE VILLA ...
...THEY MIGHT ESCAPE WHILE I'M AWAY ...
BLAST!!

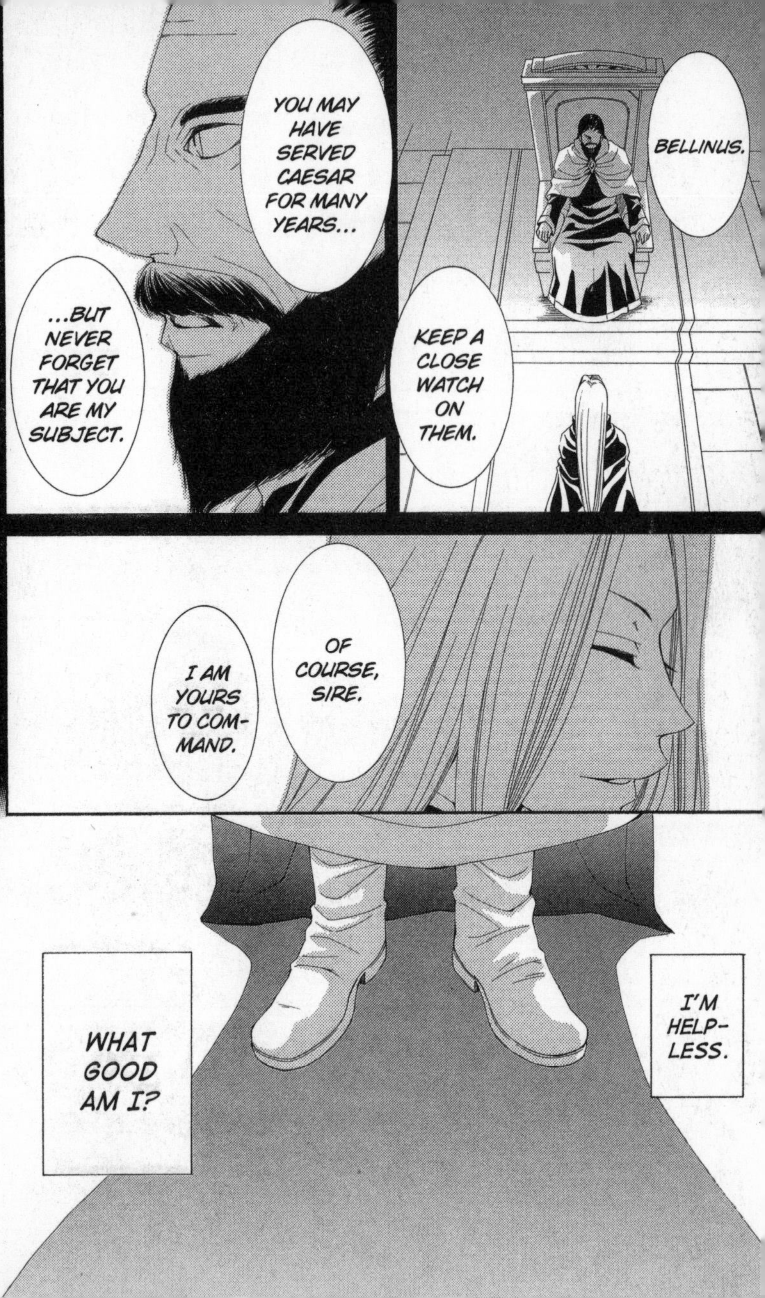
BELLINUS.
KEEP A CLOSE WATCH ON THEM.
YOU MAY HAVE SERVED CAESAR FOR MANY YEARS...
...BUT NEVER FORGET THAT YOU ARE MY SUBJECT.
OF COURSE, SIRE.
I AM YOURS TO COM-MAND.
I'M HELP-LESS.
WHAT GOOD AM I?

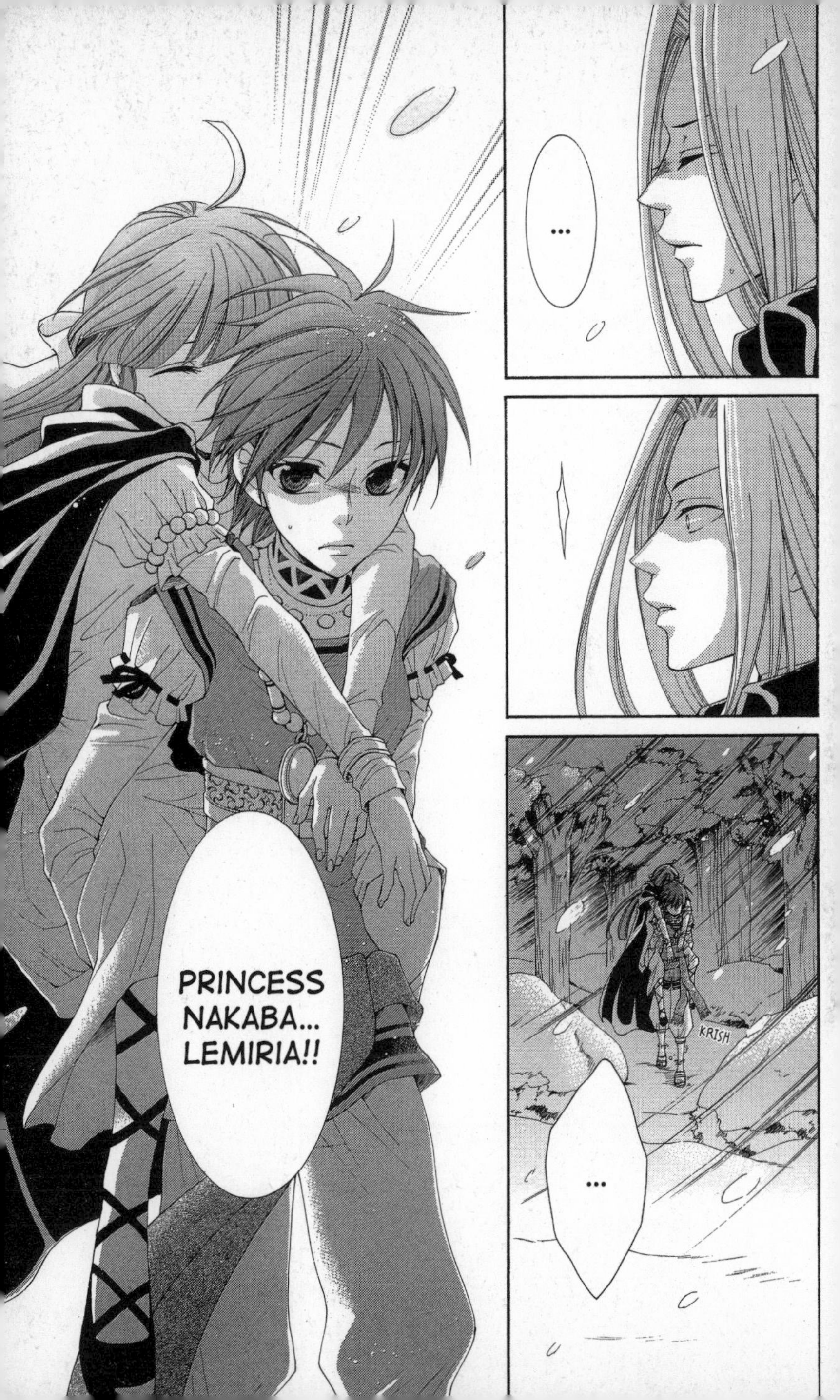
...
KRISH
...
PRINCESS NAKABA... LEMIRIA!!

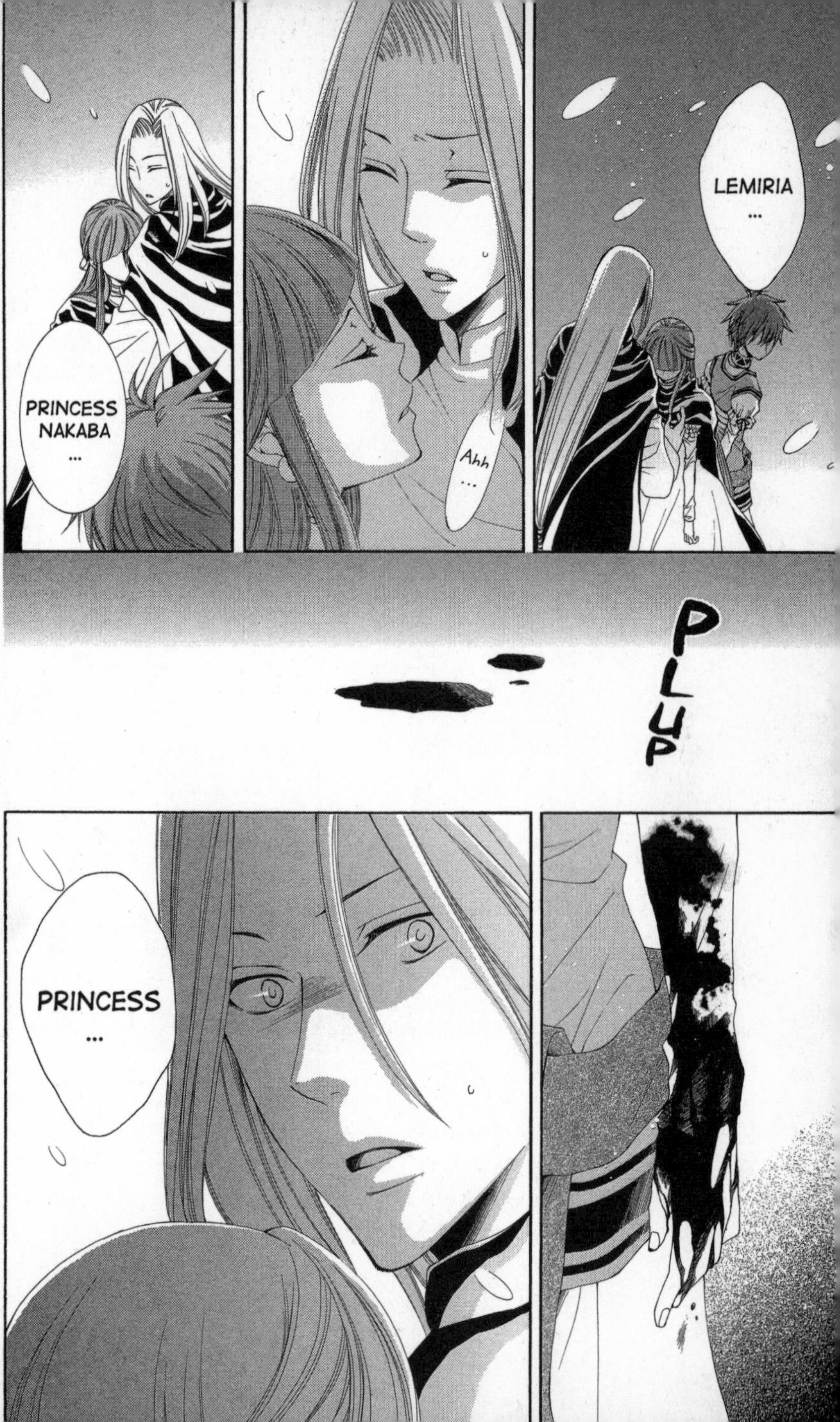
LEMIRIA ...
Ahh ...
PRINCESS NAKABA ...
PLUP
PRINCESS ...

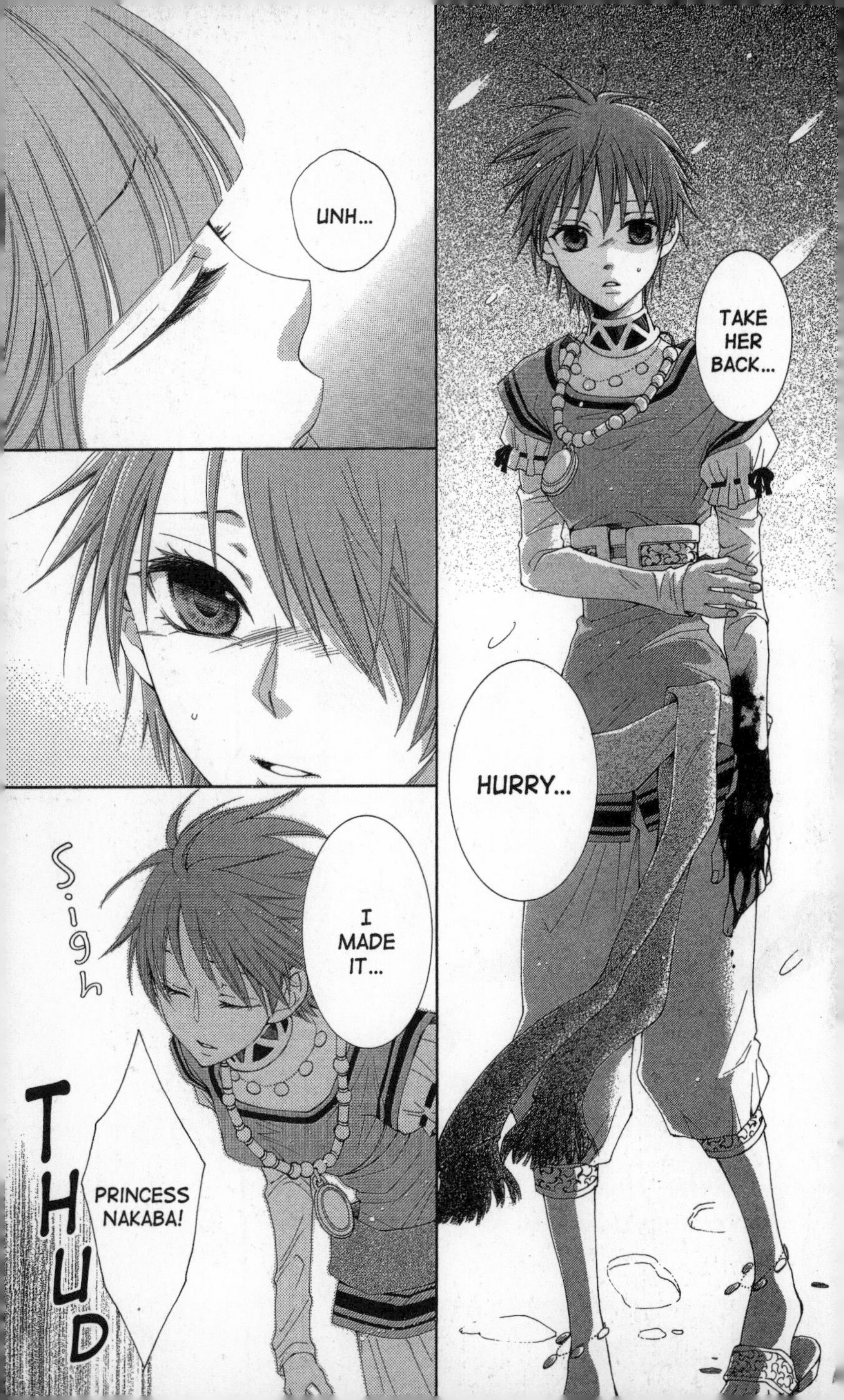
TAKE HER BACK...
HURRY...
UNH...
I MADE IT...
Sigh
PRINCESS NAKABA!
THUD

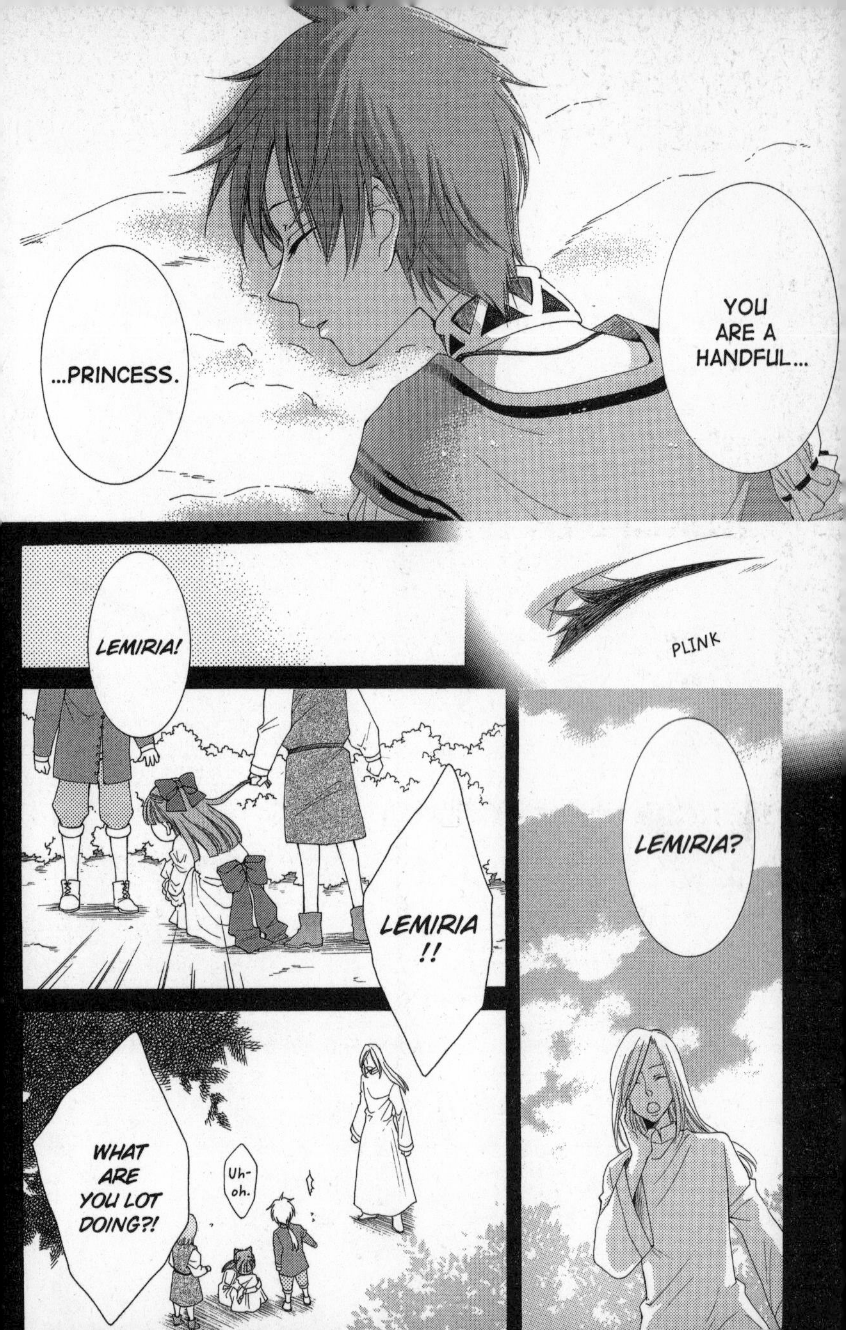
YOU ARE A HANDFUL...
...PRINCESS.
PLINK
LEMIRIA!
LEMIRIA?
LEMIRIA !!
WHAT ARE YOU LOT DOING?!
Uh-oh.

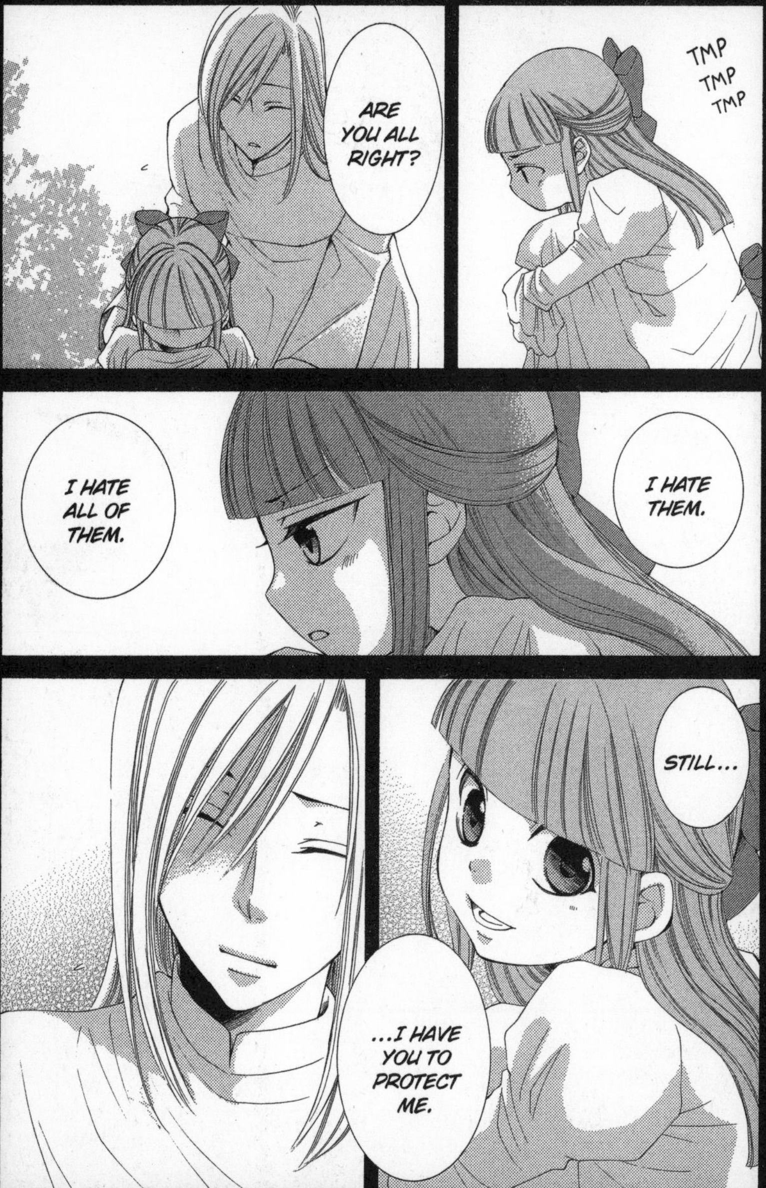
TMP TMP TMP
ARE YOU ALL RIGHT?
I HATE THEM.
I HATE ALL OF THEM.
STILL...
...I HAVE YOU TO PROTECT ME.

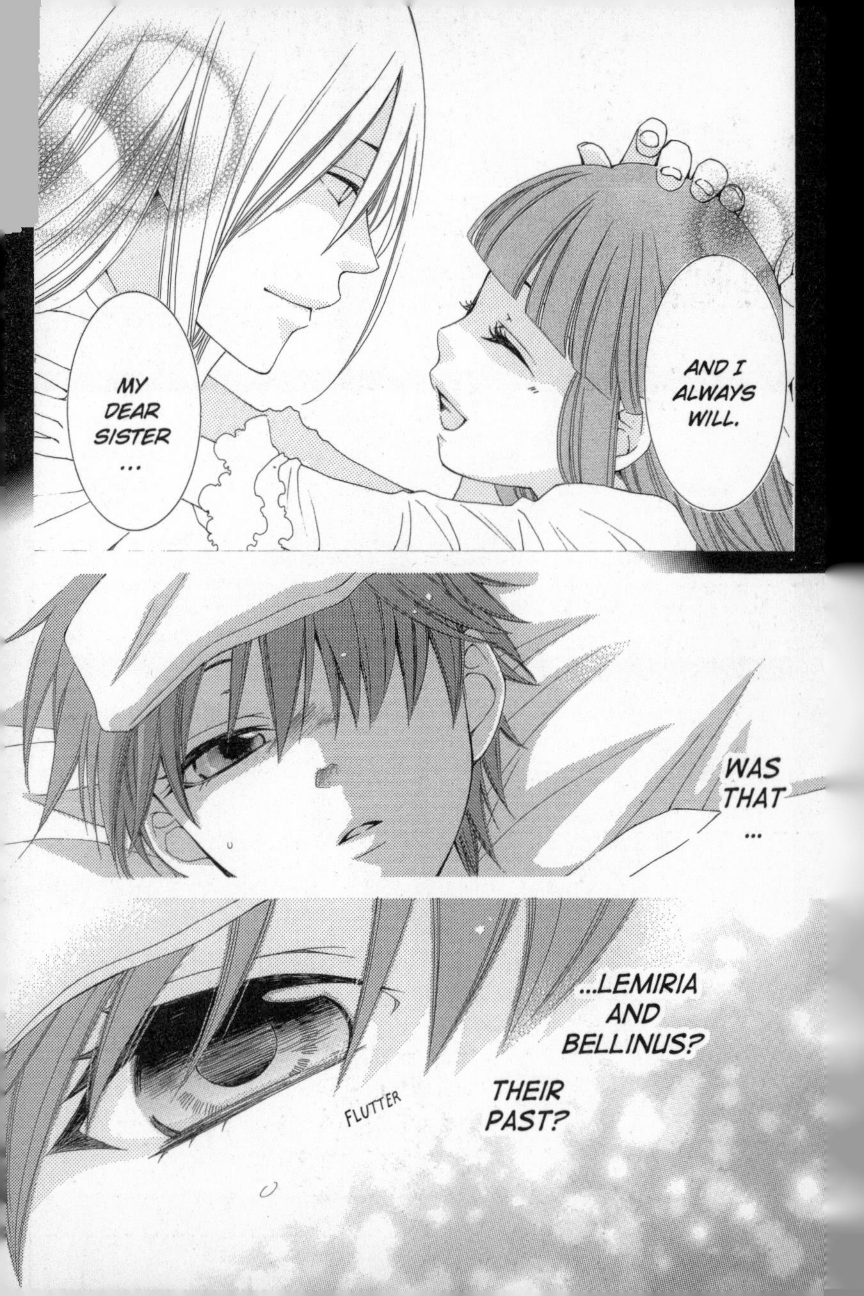
AND I ALWAYS WILL.
MY DEAR SISTER ...
WAS THAT ...
...LEMIRIA AND BELLINUS?
THEIR PAST?
FLUTTER

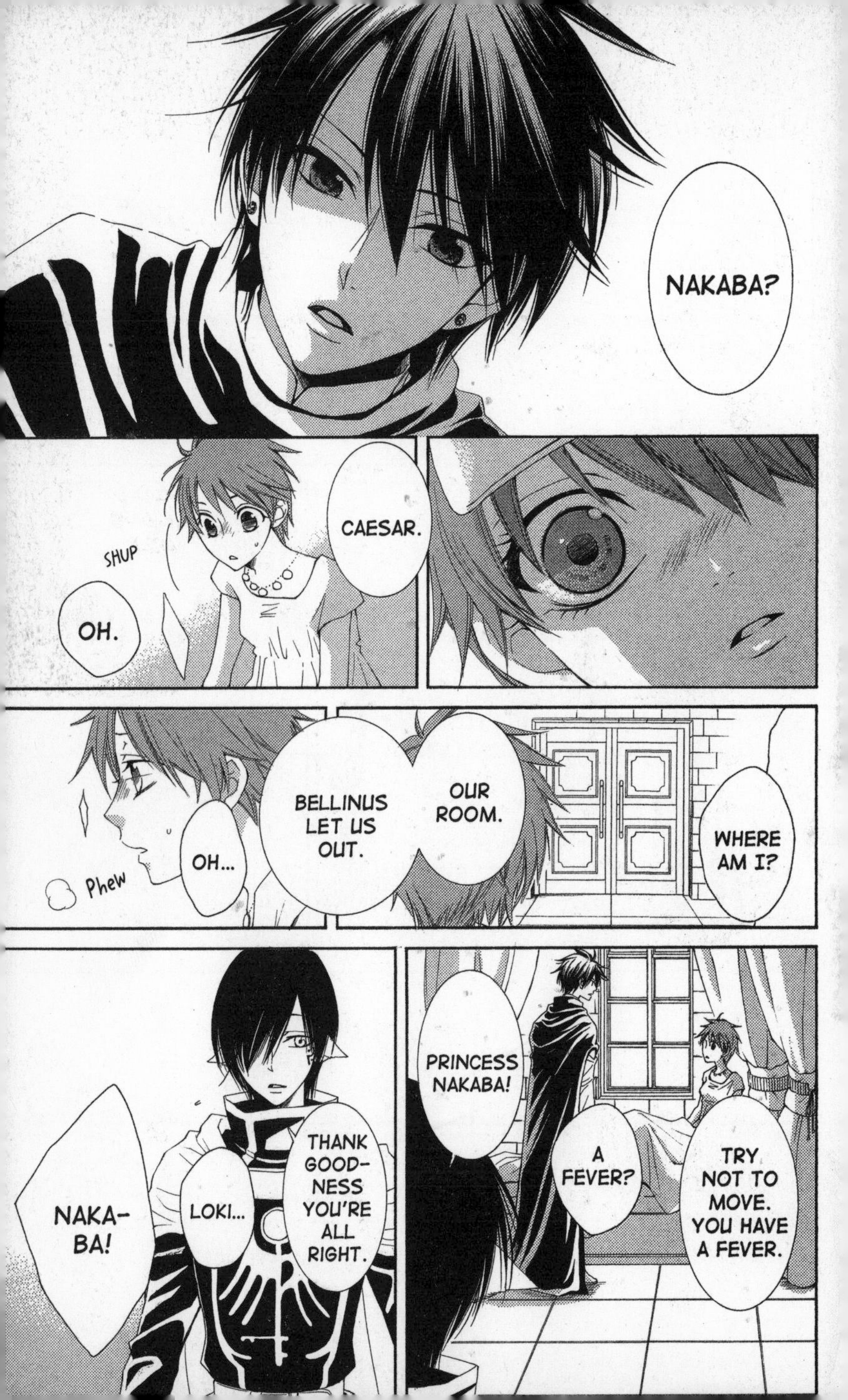
NAKABA?
CAESAR.
SHUP
OH.
WHERE AM I?
OUR ROOM.
BELLINUS LET US OUT.
OH...
Phew
TRY NOT TO MOVE. YOU HAVE A FEVER.
A FEVER?
PRINCESS NAKABA!
THANK GOODNESS YOU'RE ALL RIGHT.
LOKI...
NAKA-BA!

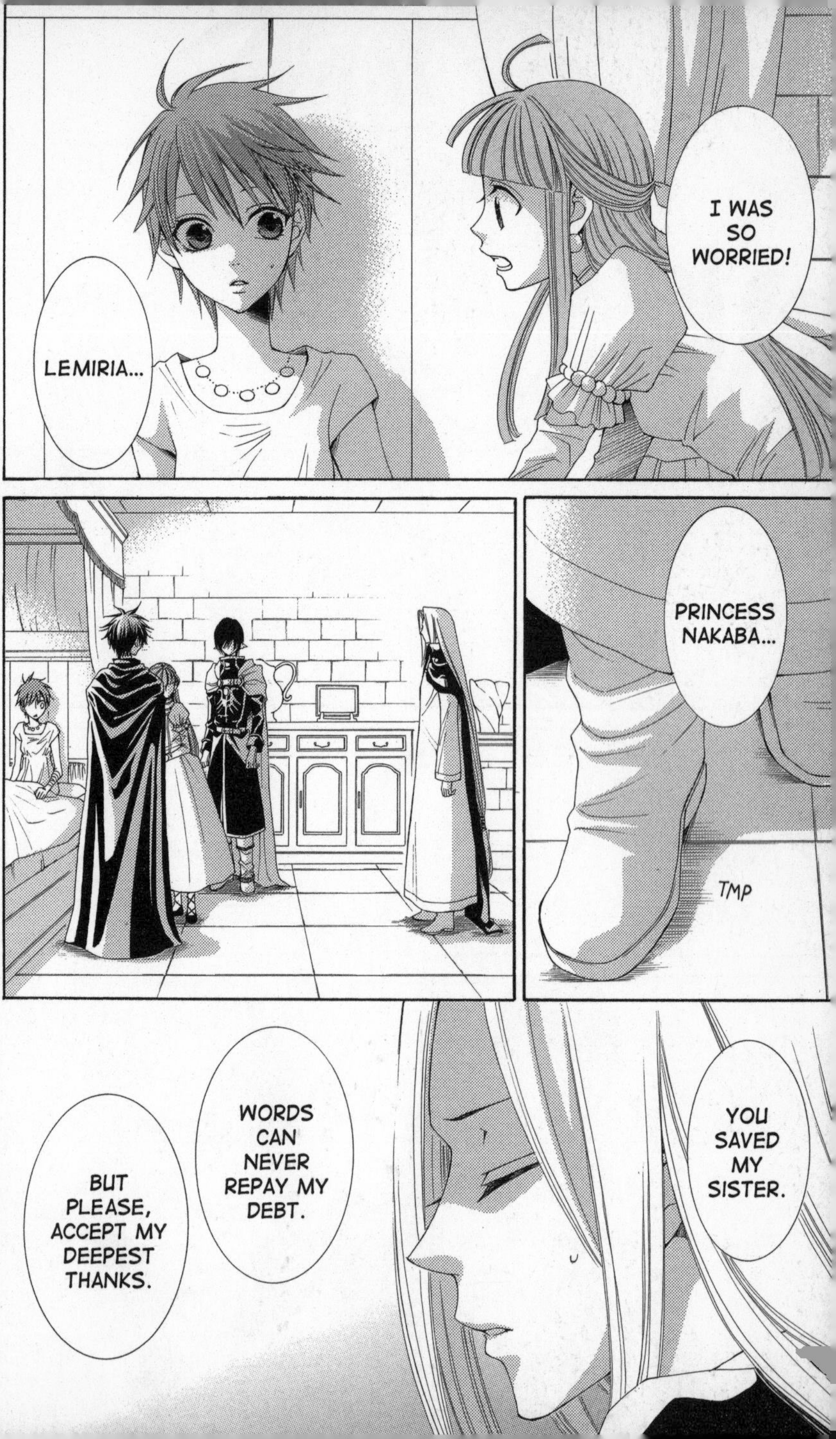
I WAS SO WORRIED!
LEMIRIA...
PRINCESS NAKABA...
TMP
YOU SAVED MY SISTER.
WORDS CAN NEVER REPAY MY DEBT.
BUT PLEASE, ACCEPT MY DEEPEST THANKS.

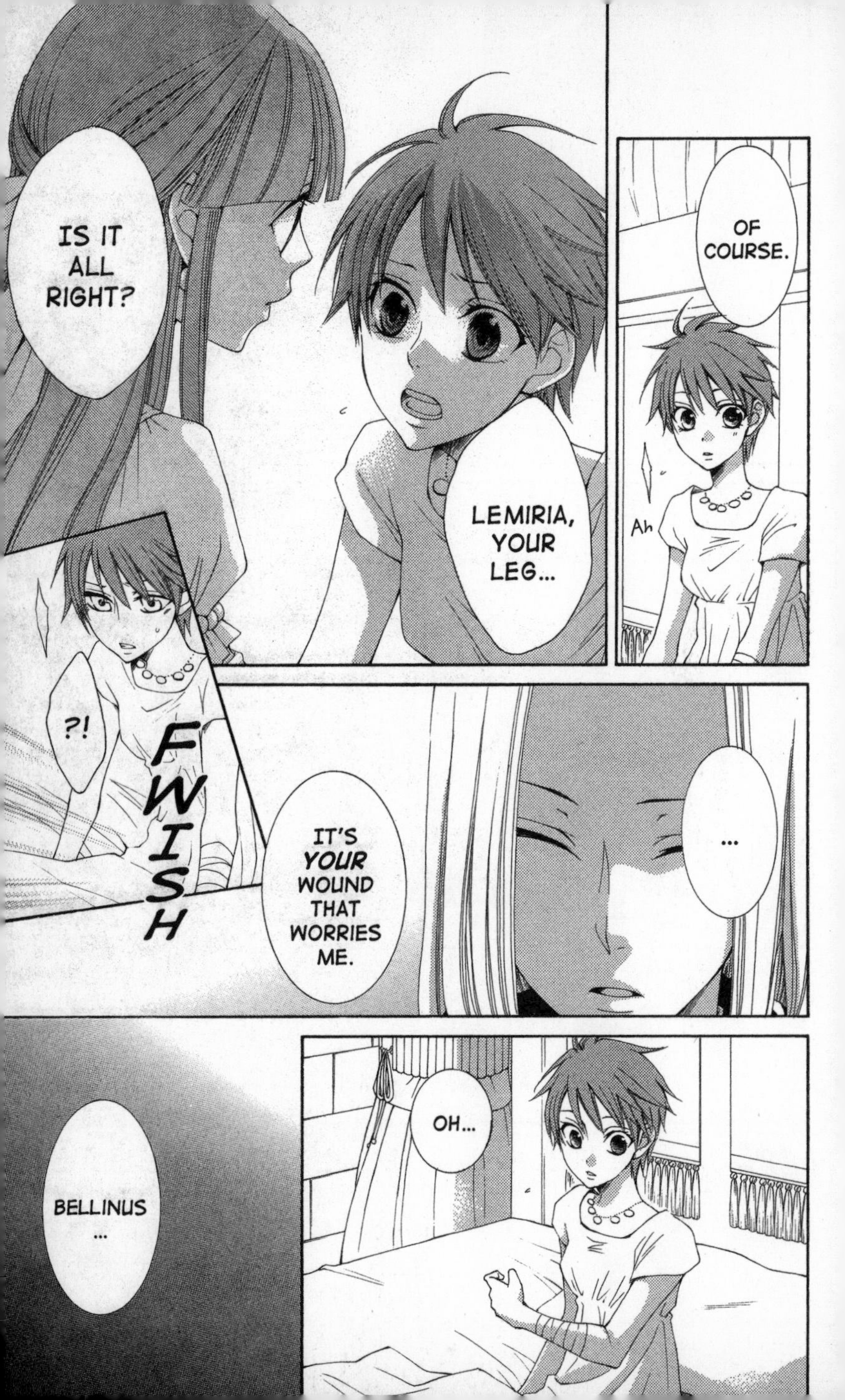
OF COURSE.
Ah
LEMIRIA, YOUR LEG...
IS IT ALL RIGHT?
...
IT'S *YOUR* WOUND THAT WORRIES ME.
?!
FWISH
OH...
BELLINUS ...

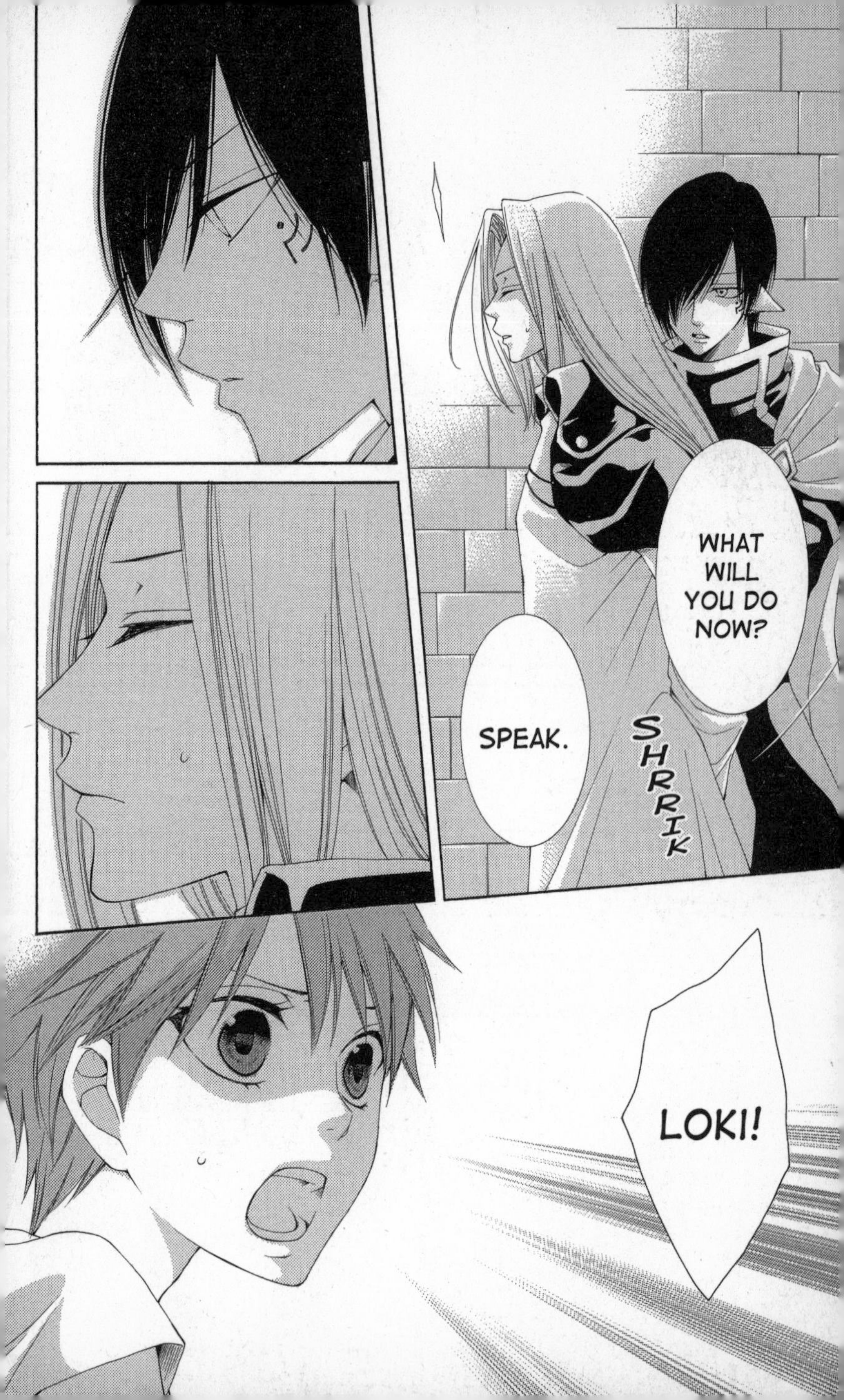
WHAT WILL YOU DO NOW?
SPEAK.
SHRRIK
LOKI!

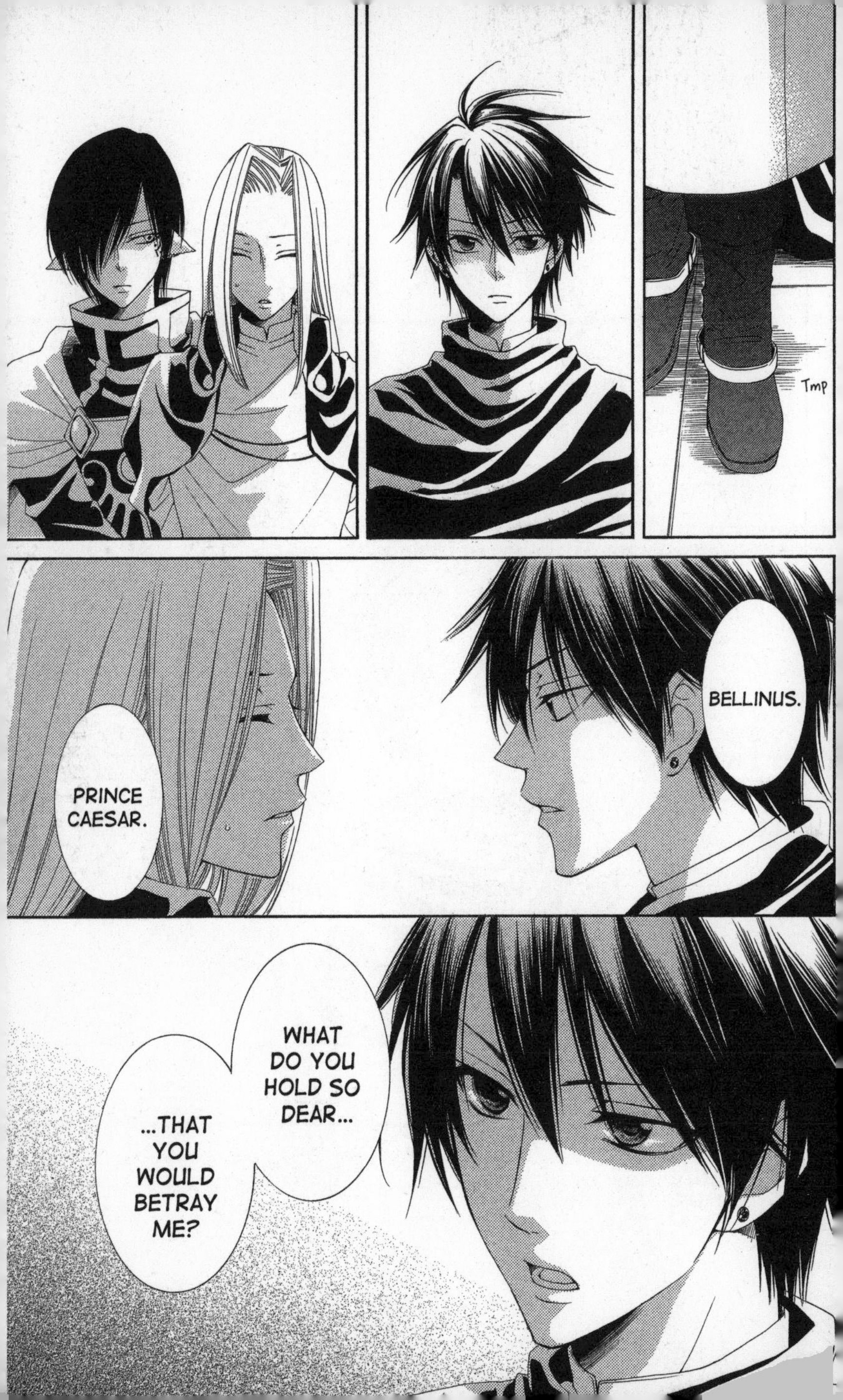
Tmp
BELLINUS.
PRINCE CAESAR.
WHAT DO YOU HOLD SO DEAR...
...THAT YOU WOULD BETRAY ME?

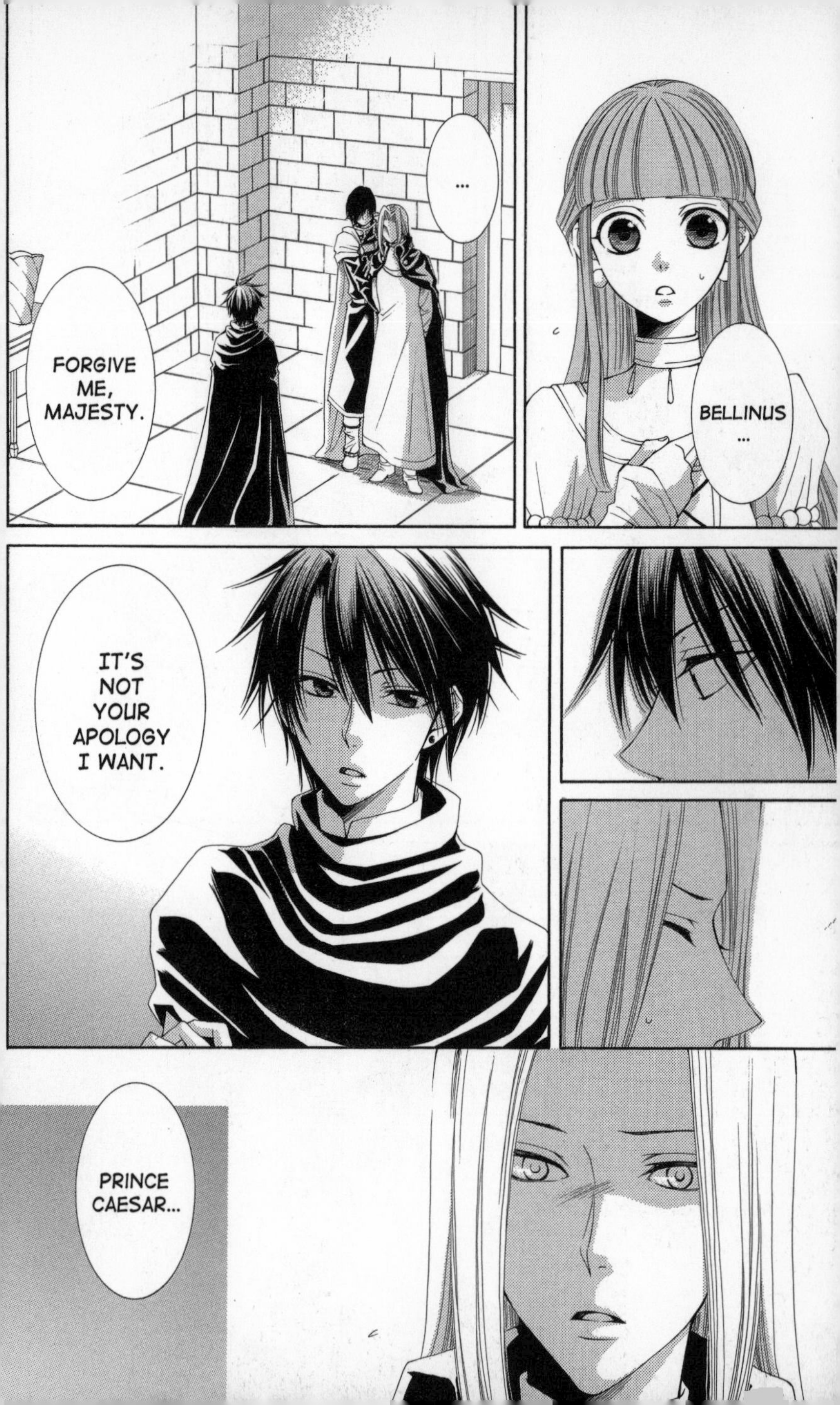
BELLINUS ...
...
FORGIVE ME, MAJESTY.
IT'S NOT YOUR APOLOGY I WANT.
PRINCE CAESAR...

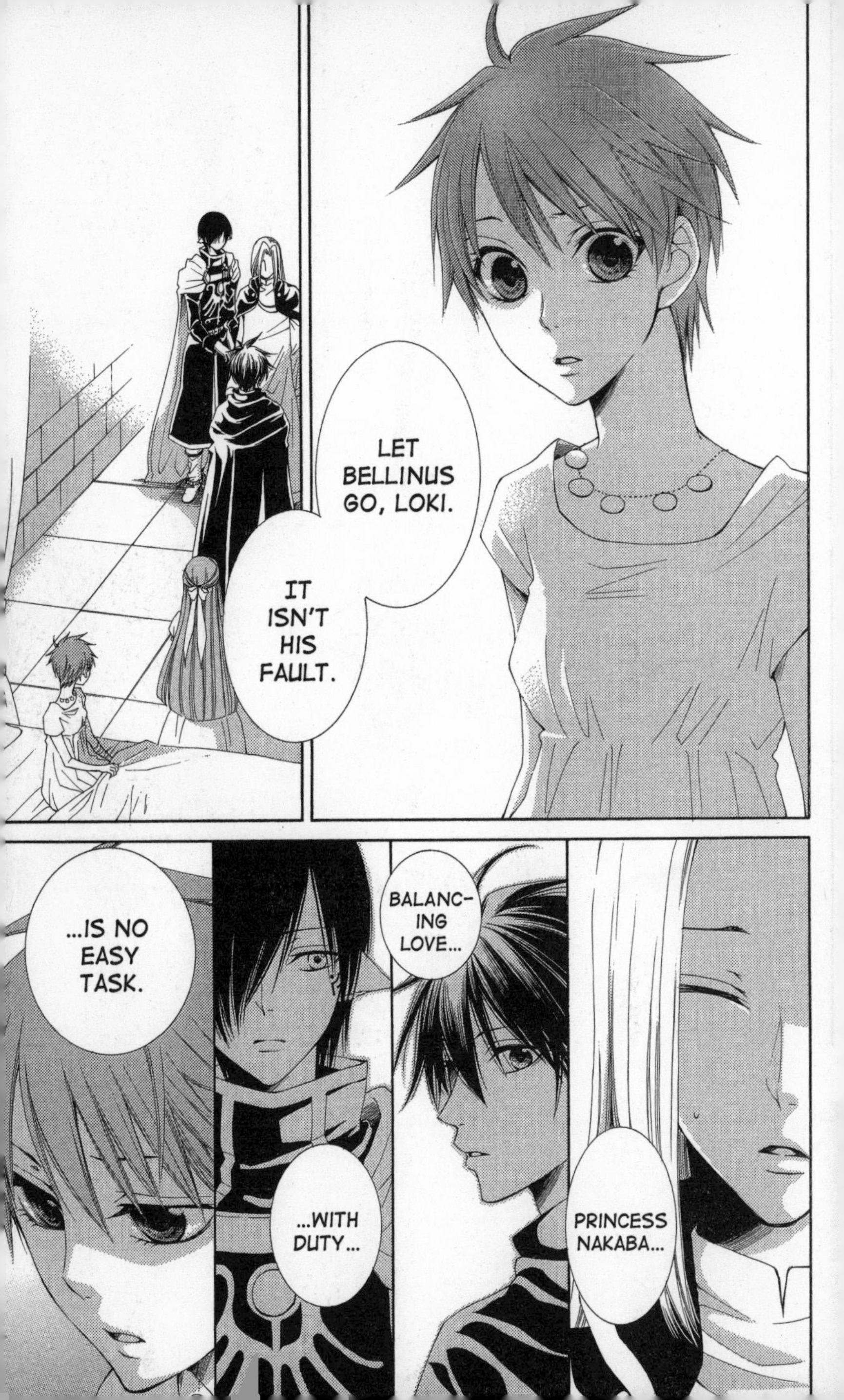
LET BELLINUS GO, LOKI.
IT ISN'T HIS FAULT.
PRINCESS NAKABA...
BALANC-ING LOVE...
...WITH DUTY...
...IS NO EASY TASK.

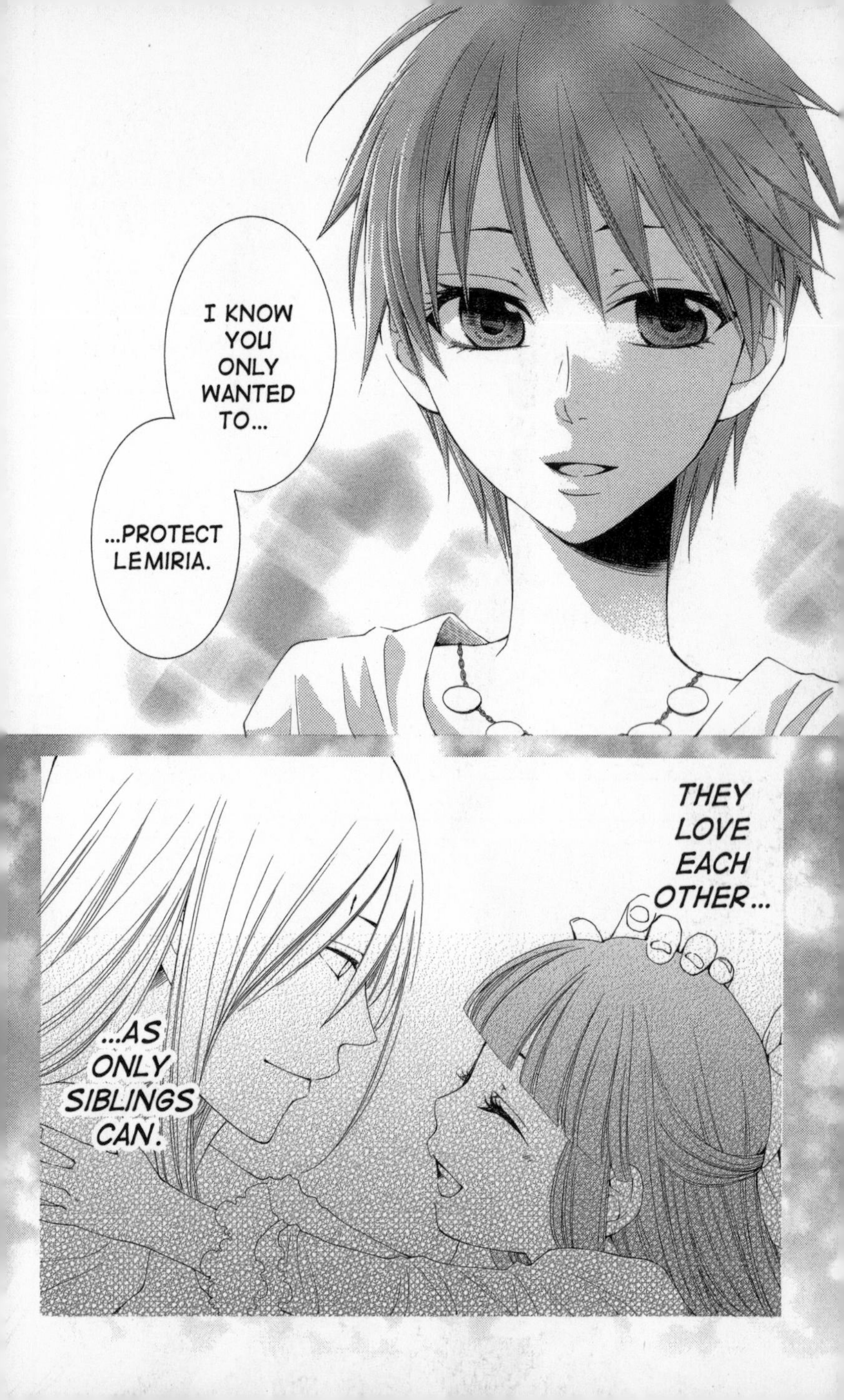
I KNOW YOU ONLY WANTED TO...
...PROTECT LEMIRIA.
THEY LOVE EACH OTHER...
...AS ONLY SIBLINGS CAN.

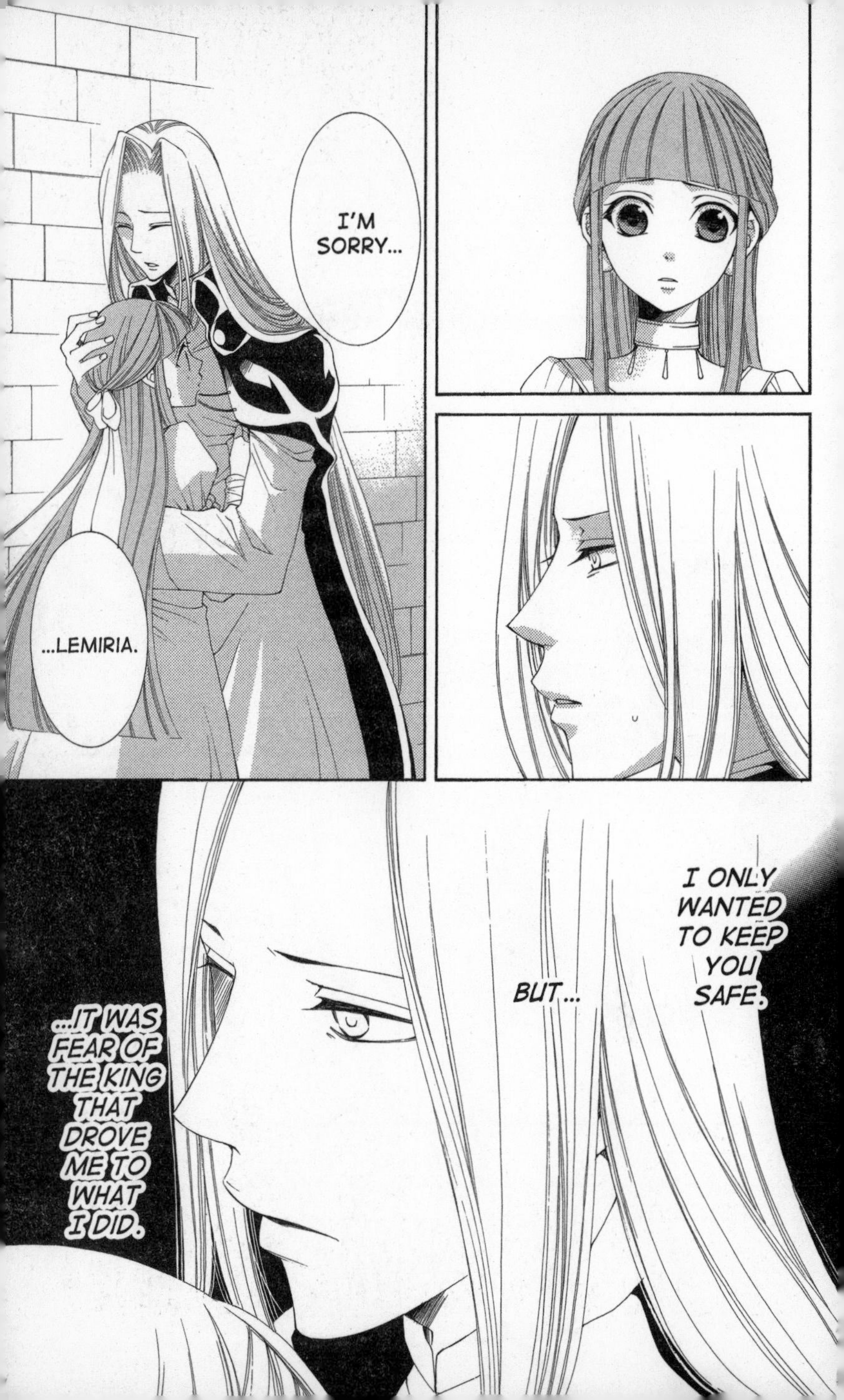
I'M SORRY...
...LEMIRIA.
I ONLY WANTED TO KEEP YOU SAFE.
BUT...
...IT WAS FEAR OF THE KING THAT DROVE ME TO WHAT I DID.

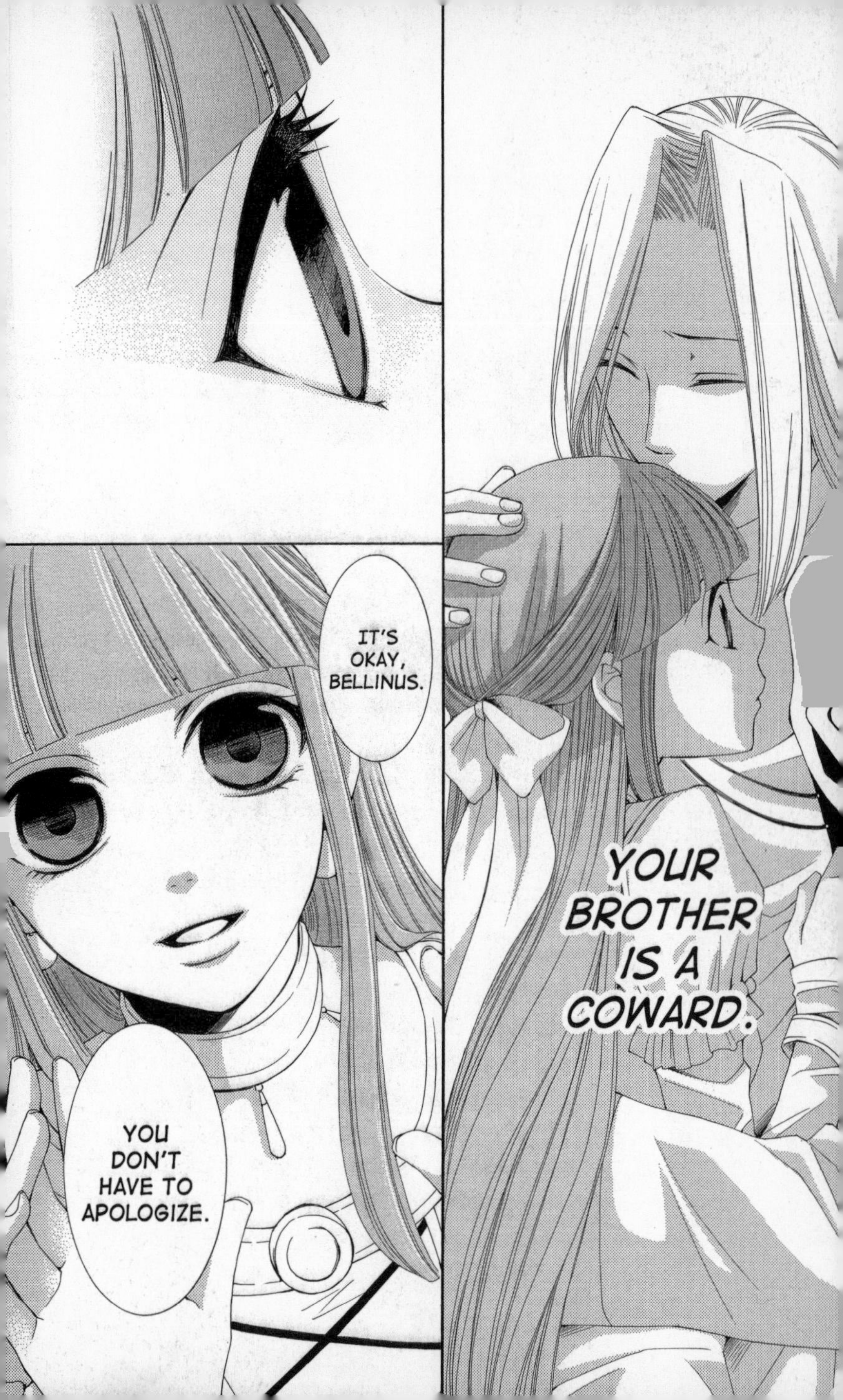
YOUR BROTHER IS A COWARD.
IT'S OKAY, BELLINUS.
YOU DON'T HAVE TO APOLOGIZE.

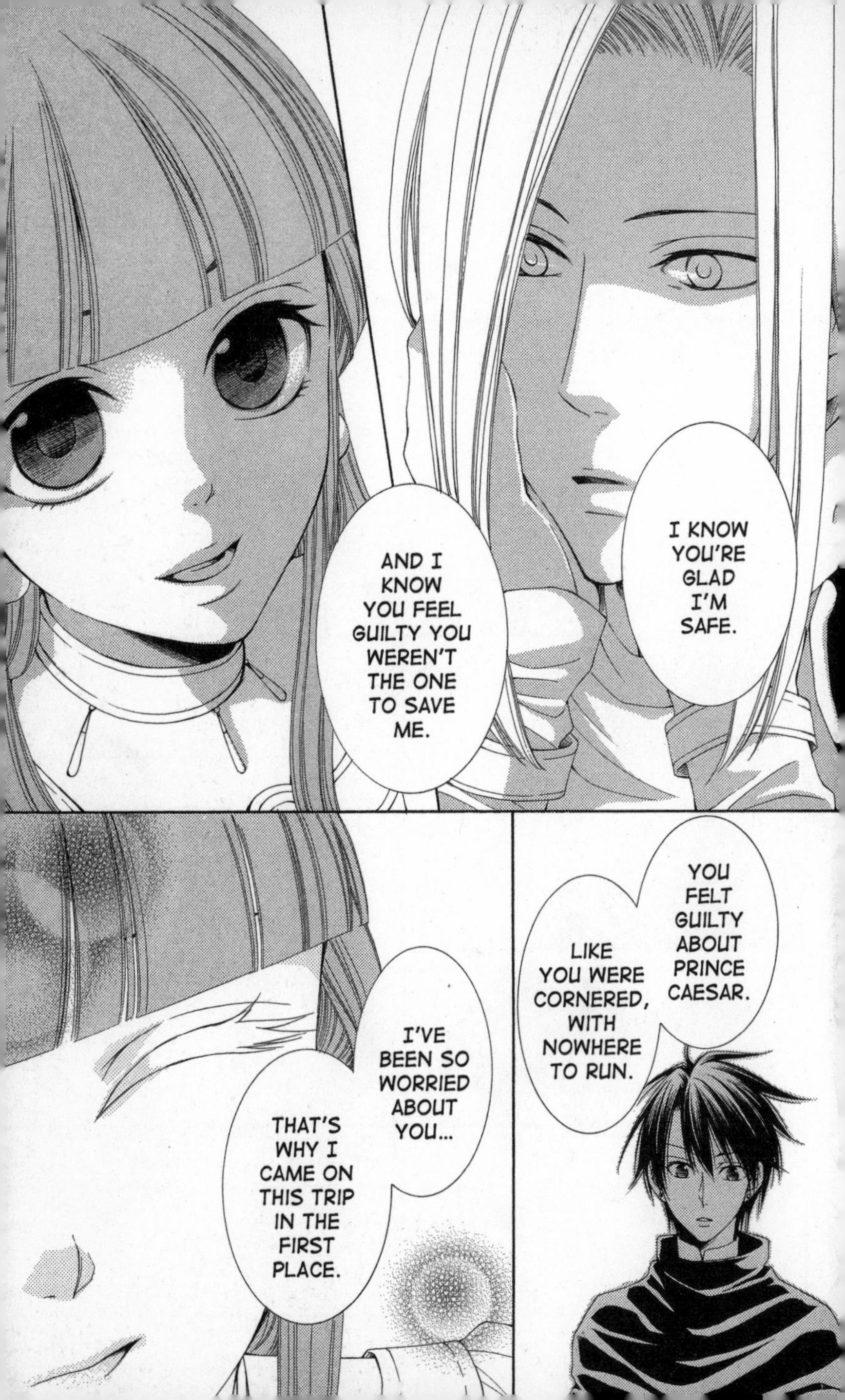
I KNOW YOU'RE GLAD I'M SAFE.
AND I KNOW YOU FEEL GUILTY YOU WEREN'T THE ONE TO SAVE ME.
YOU FELT GUILTY ABOUT PRINCE CAESAR.
LIKE YOU WERE CORNERED, WITH NOWHERE TO RUN.
I'VE BEEN SO WORRIED ABOUT YOU...
THAT'S WHY I CAME ON THIS TRIP IN THE FIRST PLACE.

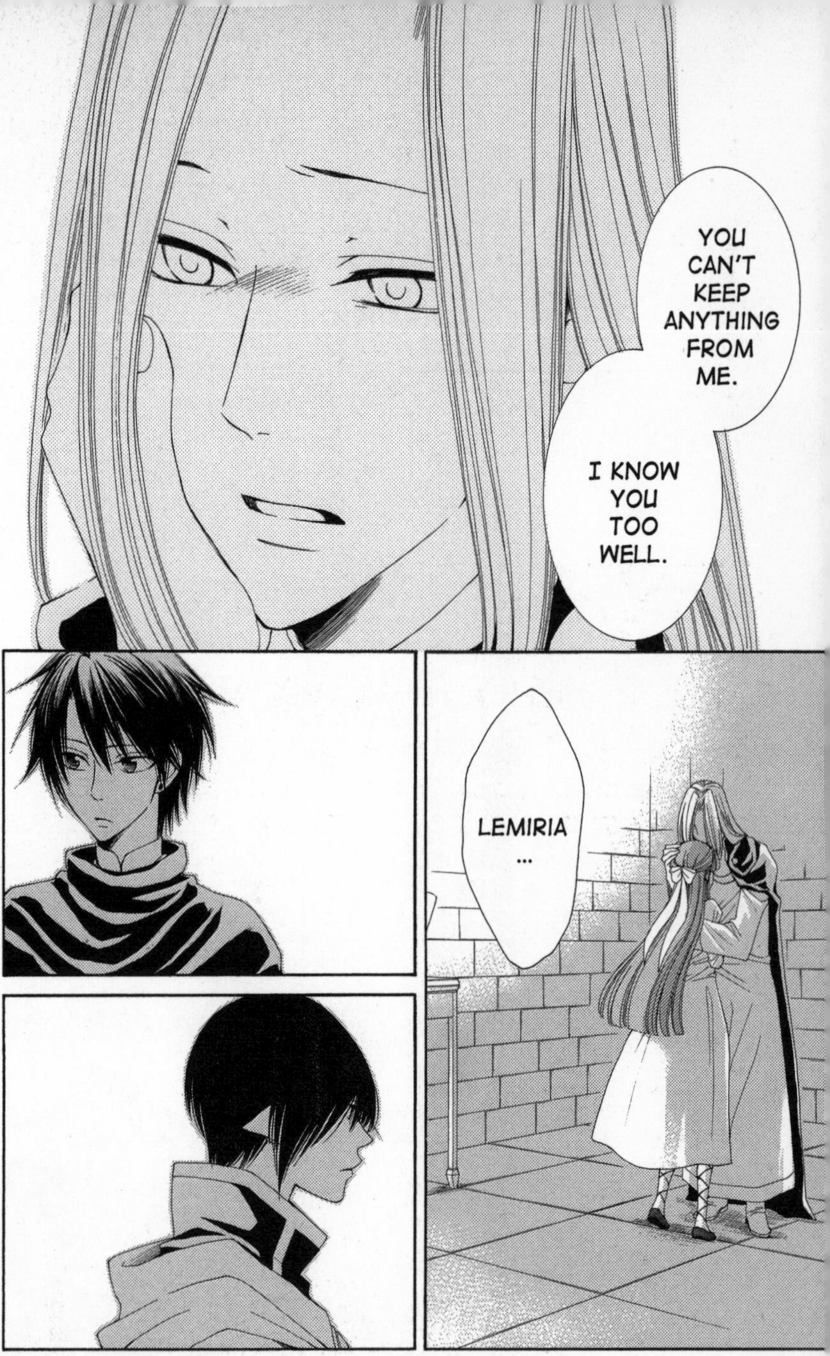
YOU CAN'T KEEP ANYTHING FROM ME.
I KNOW YOU TOO WELL.
LEMIRIA ...

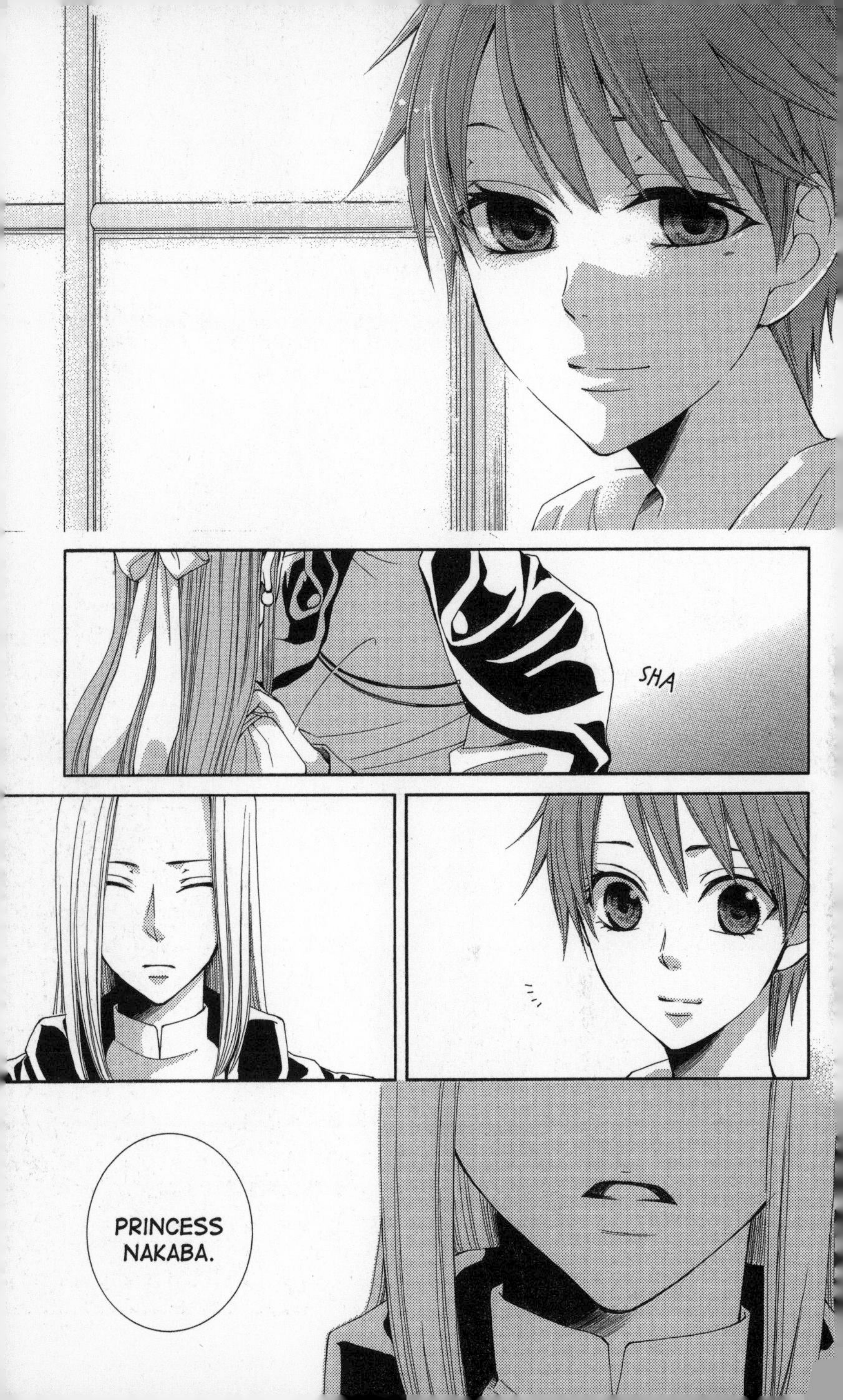
SHA
PRINCESS NAKABA.

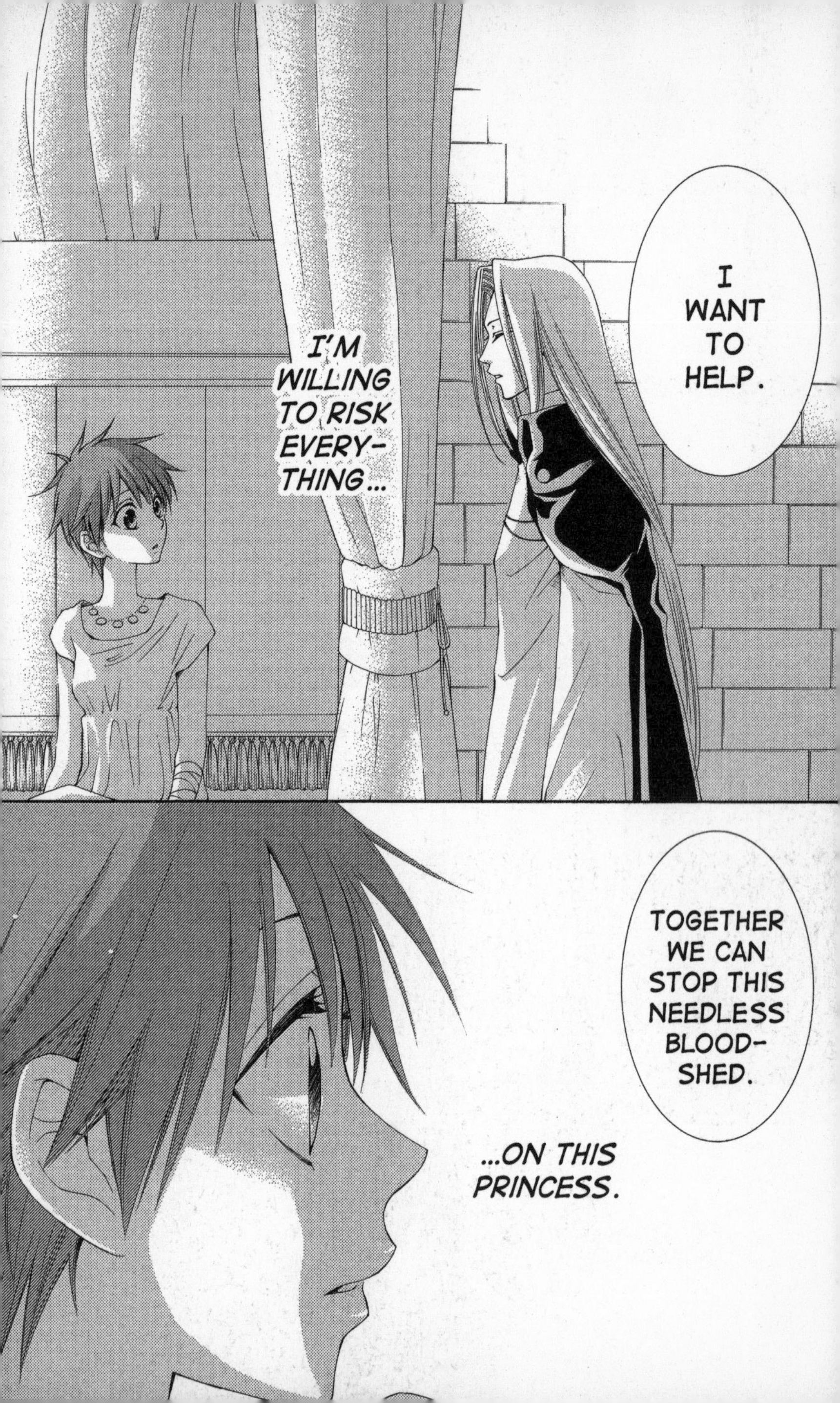
I WANT TO HELP.
I'M WILLING TO RISK EVERYTHING...
TOGETHER WE CAN STOP THIS NEEDLESS BLOODSHED.
...ON THIS PRINCESS.

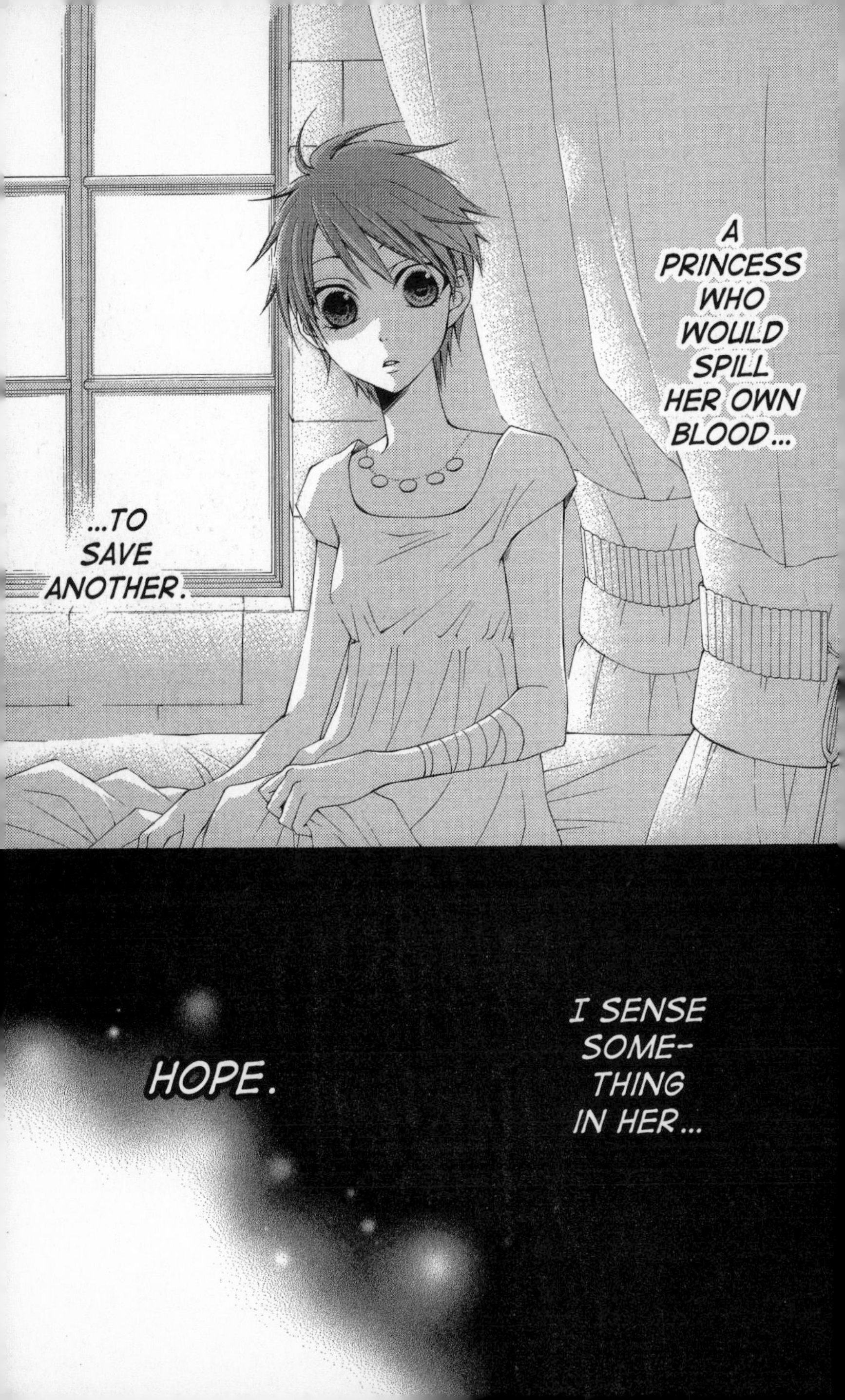
A PRINCESS WHO WOULD SPILL HER OWN BLOOD...
...TO SAVE ANOTHER.
I SENSE SOME-THING IN HER...
HOPE.

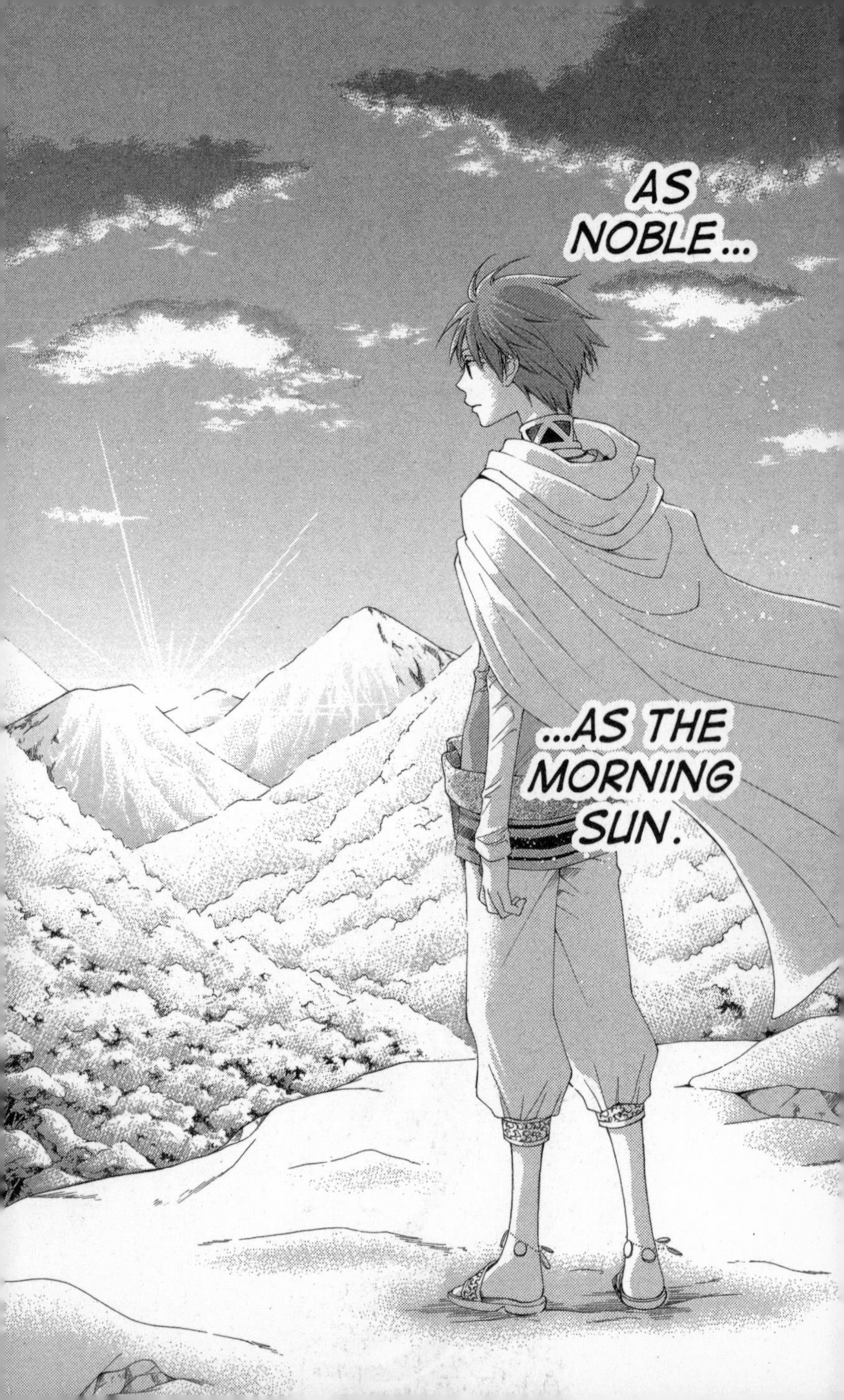
AS NOBLE...
...AS THE MORNING SUN.

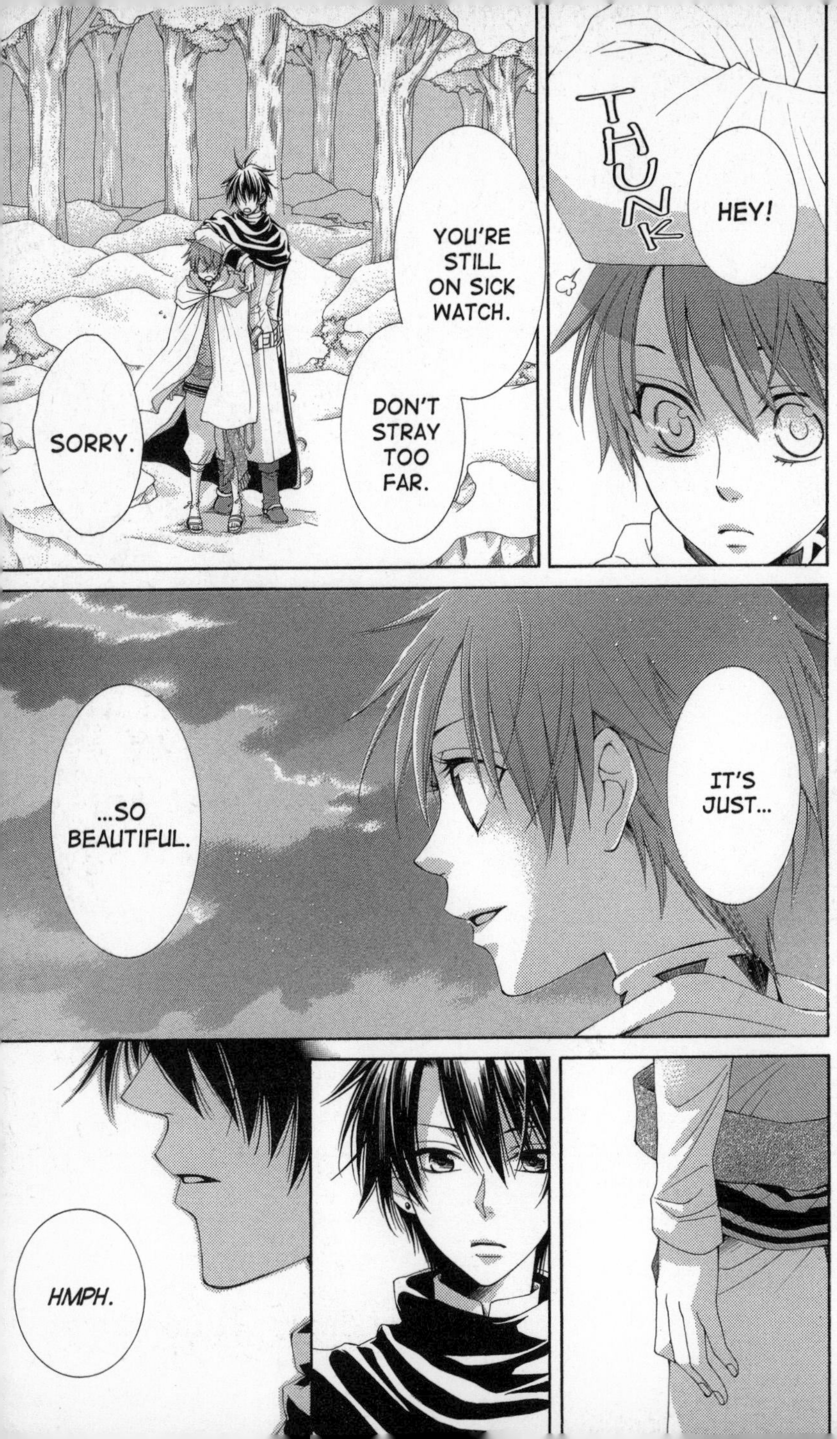
THUNK
HEY!
YOU'RE STILL ON SICK WATCH.
DON'T STRAY TOO FAR.
SORRY.
IT'S JUST...
...SO BEAUTIFUL.
HMPH.

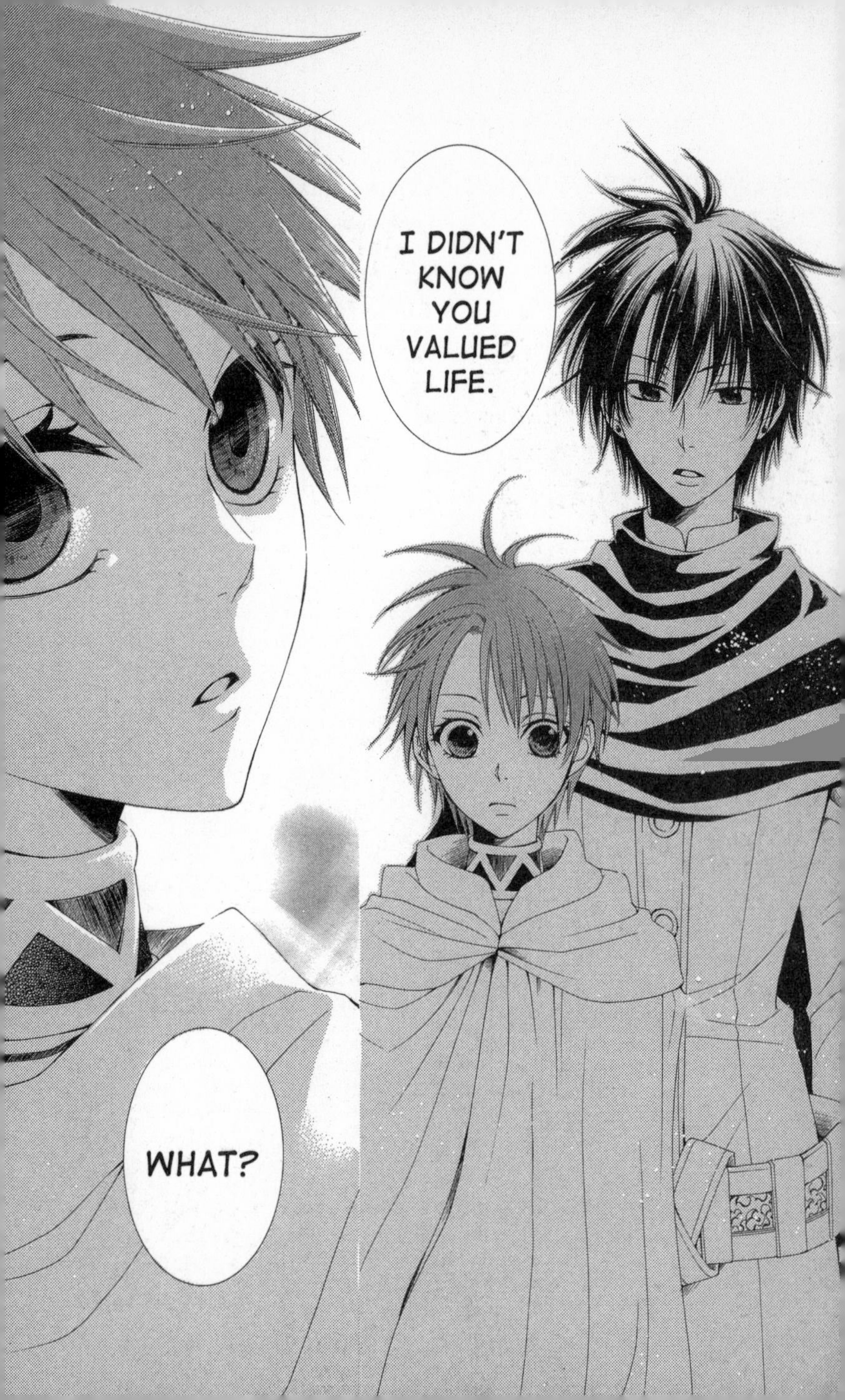
I DIDN'T KNOW YOU VALUED LIFE.
WHAT?

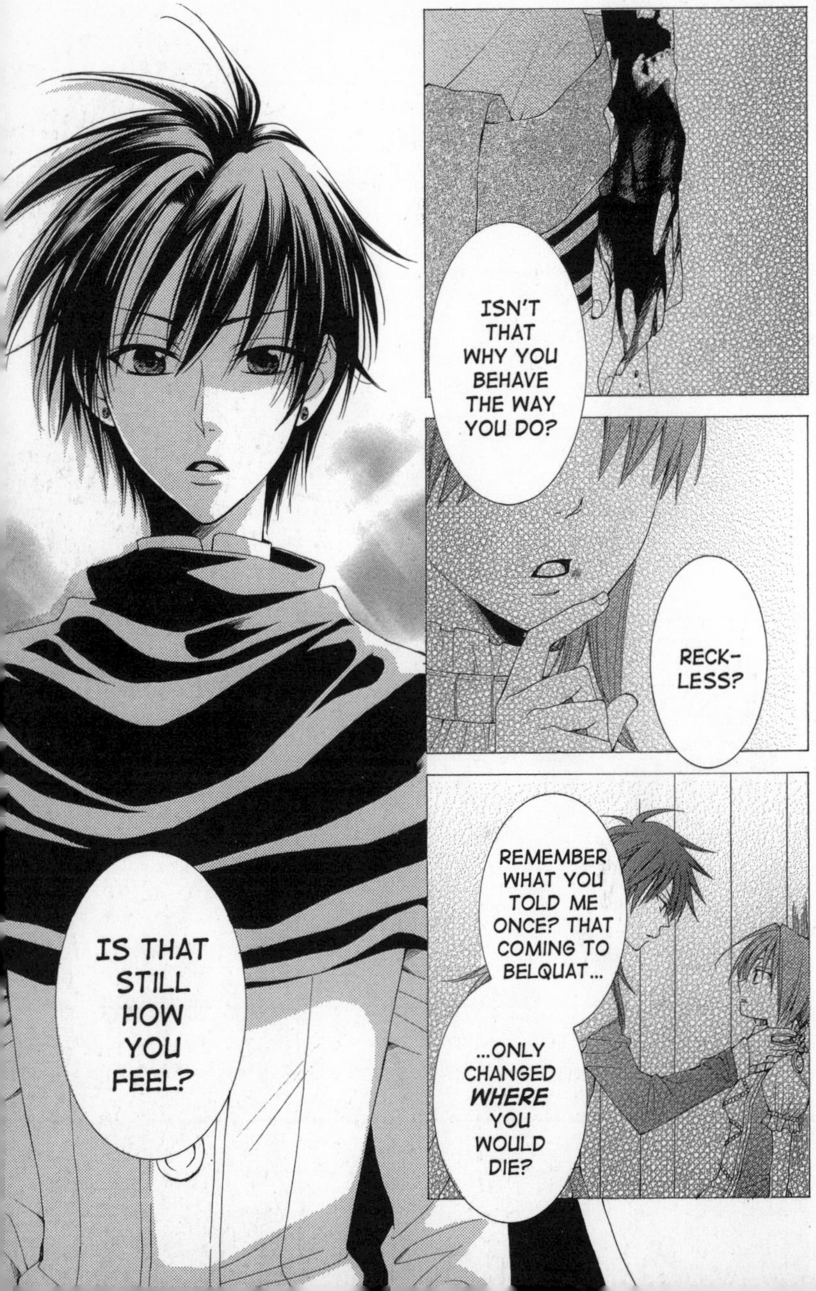
ISN'T THAT WHY YOU BEHAVE THE WAY YOU DO?
RECK-LESS?
REMEMBER WHAT YOU TOLD ME ONCE? THAT COMING TO BELQUAT...
...ONLY CHANGED *WHERE* YOU WOULD DIE?
IS THAT STILL HOW YOU FEEL?

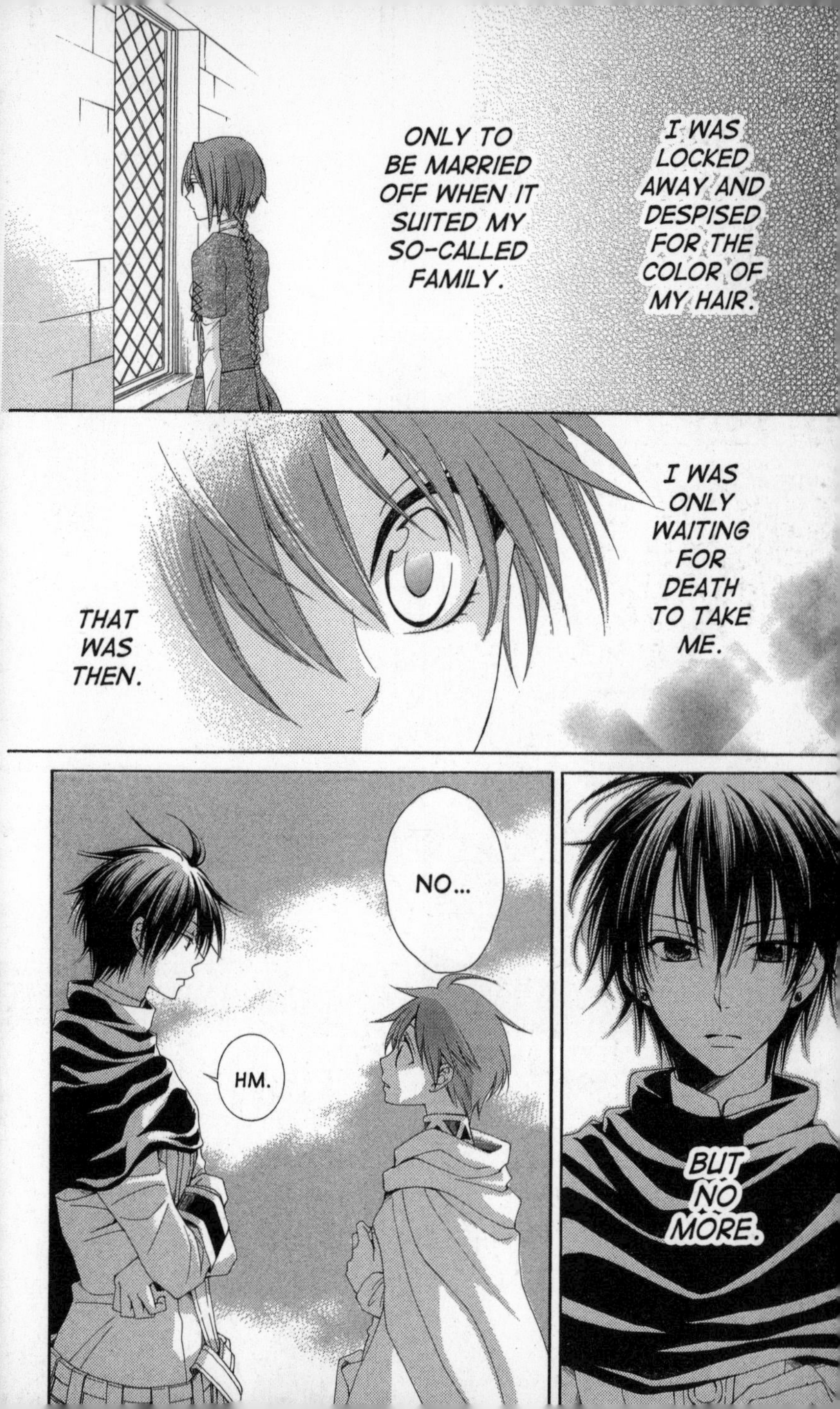
I WAS LOCKED AWAY AND DESPISED FOR THE COLOR OF MY HAIR.
ONLY TO BE MARRIED OFF WHEN IT SUITED MY SO-CALLED FAMILY.
I WAS ONLY WAITING FOR DEATH TO TAKE ME.
THAT WAS THEN.
BUT NO MORE.
NO...
HM.

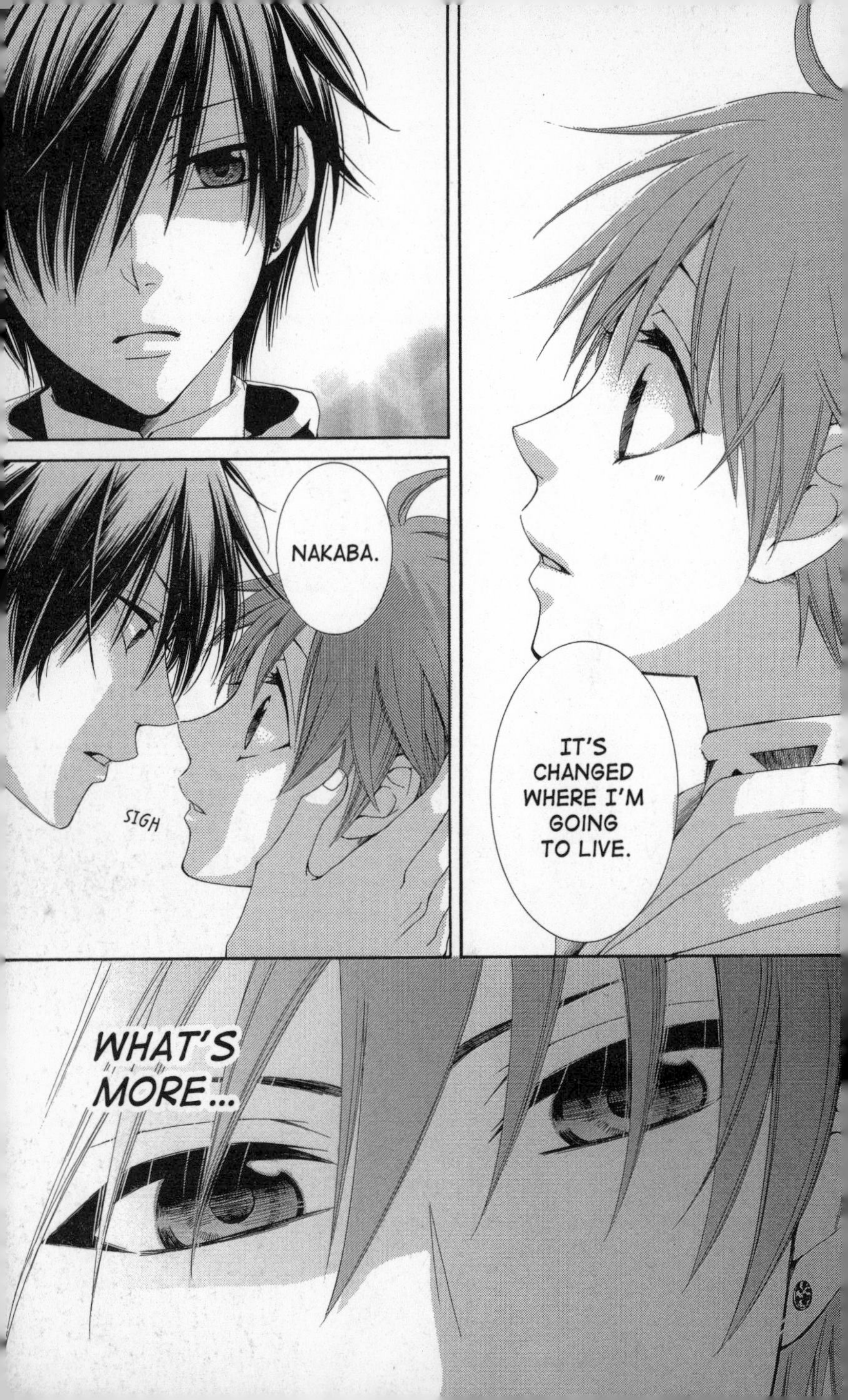
IT'S CHANGED WHERE I'M GOING TO LIVE.
NAKABA.
SIGH
WHAT'S MORE...

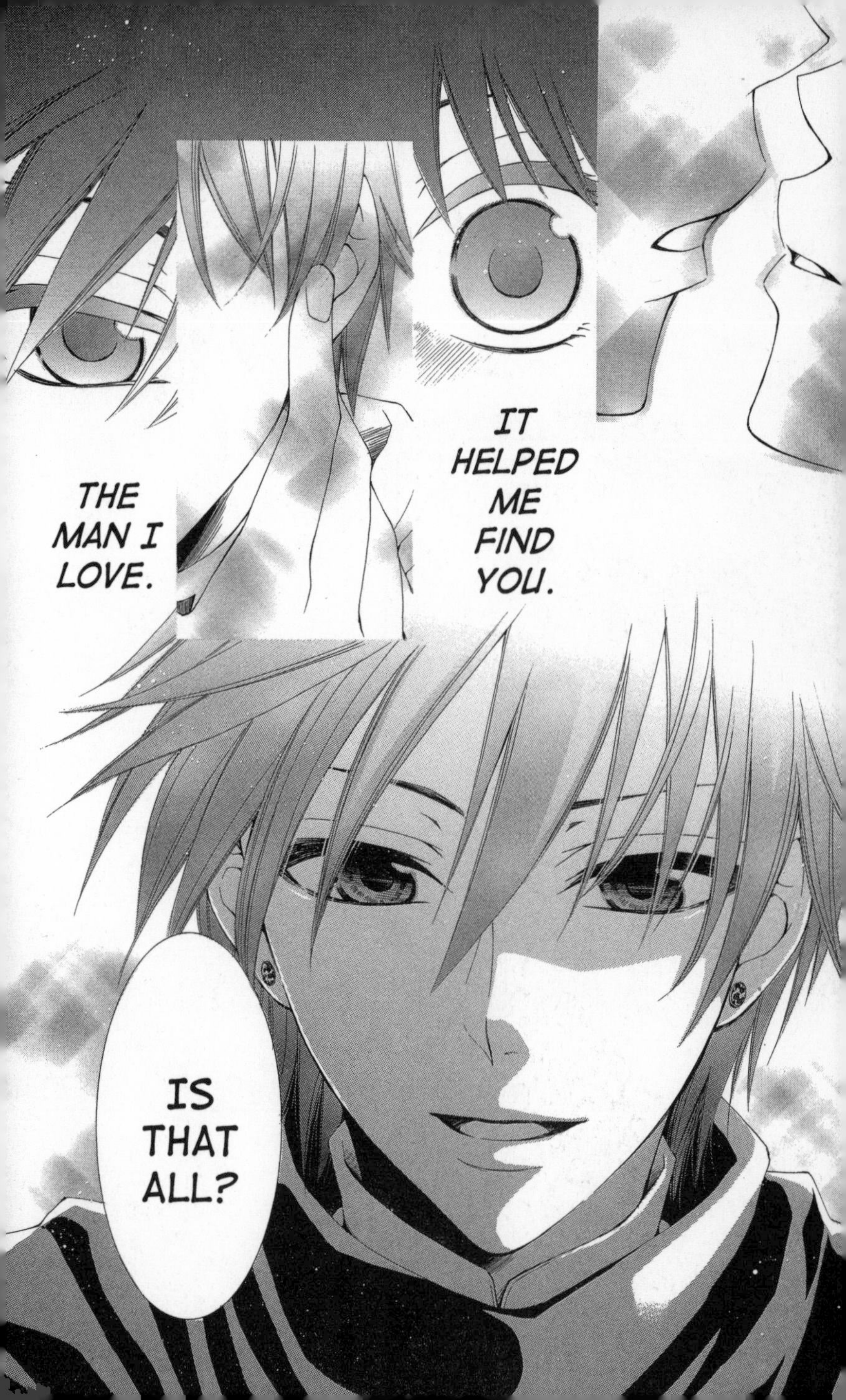
IT HELPED ME FIND YOU.
THE MAN I LOVE.
IS THAT ALL?

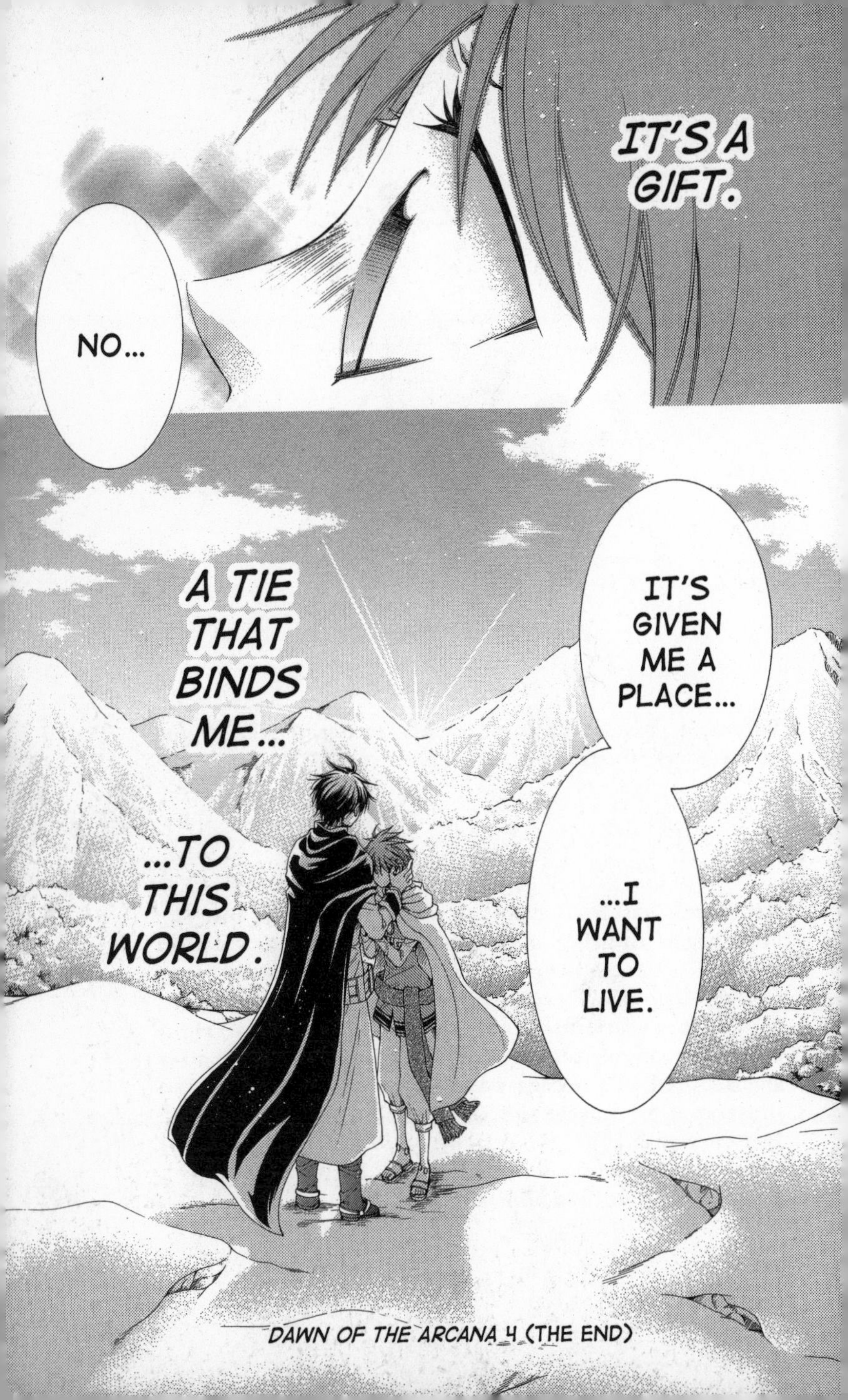
IT'S A GIFT.
NO...
IT'S GIVEN ME A PLACE...
...I WANT TO LIVE.
A TIE THAT BINDS ME...
...TO THIS WORLD.
DAWN OF THE ARCANA 4 (THE END)

Volume 4 already! Took me a while to decide who to put in the cover illustration... (*laugh*)

–Rei Toma

Rei Toma has been drawing since childhood, but she only began drawing manga because of her graduation project in design school. When she drew a short-story manga, *Help Me, Dentist,* for the first time, it attracted a publisher's attention and she made her debut right away. Her magnificent art style became popular, and after she debuted as a manga artist, she became known as an illustrator for novels and video game character designs. Her current manga series, *Dawn of the Arcana,* is her first long-running manga series, and it has been a hit in Japan, selling over a million copies.

DAWN OF THE ARCANA
VOLUME 4
Shojo Beat Edition

STORY AND ART BY
REI TOMA

© 2009 Rei TOMA/Shogakukan
All rights reserved.
Original Japanese edition "REIMEI NO ARCANA"
published by SHOGAKUKAN Inc.

Translation & Adaptation/Kajiya Productions
Touch-up Art & Lettering/Freeman Wong
Design/Yukiko Whitley
Editor/Amy Yu

Printed in the U.S.A.

Published by VIZ Media, LLC
P.O. Box 77010
San Francisco, CA 94107

10 9 8 7 6 5 4 3 2 1
First printing, June 2012

www.viz.com   www.shojobeat.com

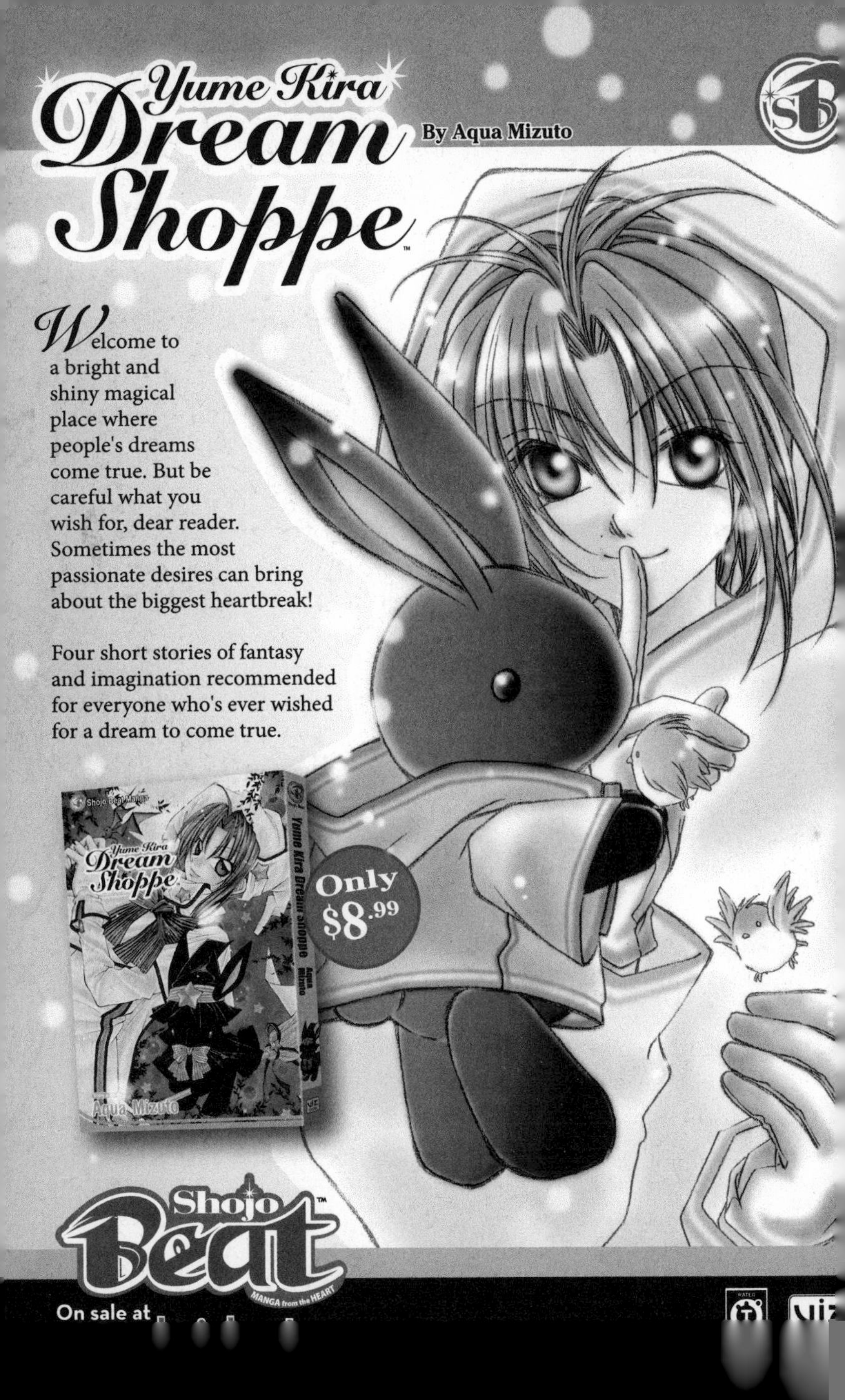

Yume Kira Dream Shoppe™
By Aqua Mizuto
Welcome to a bright and shiny magical place where people's dreams come true. But be careful what you wish for, dear reader. Sometimes the most passionate desires can bring about the biggest heartbreak!
Four short stories of fantasy and imagination recommended for everyone who's ever wished for a dream to come true.
Only $8.99
Shojo Beat Manga
Yume Kira Dream Shoppe
Aqua Mizuto
Shojo Beat™
MANGA from the HEART
On sale at

This is the last page.

In keeping with the original Japanese comic format, this book reads from right to left—so action, sound effects, and word balloons are completely reversed. This preserves the orientation of the original artwork—plus, it's fun! Check out the diagram shown here to get the hang of things, and then turn to the other side of the book to get started!

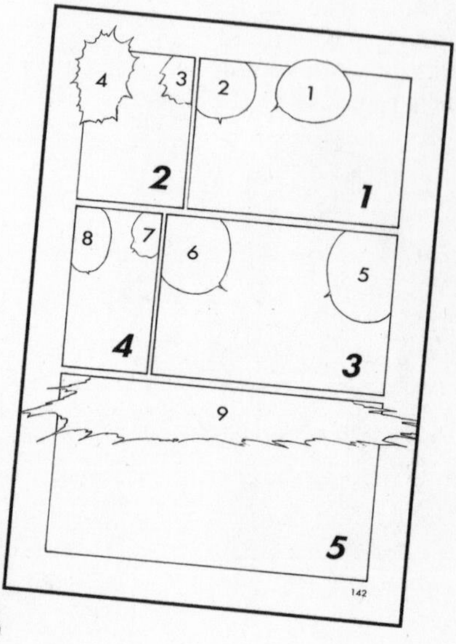
1
2
3
4
1
2
5
6
7
8
3
4
9
5
142

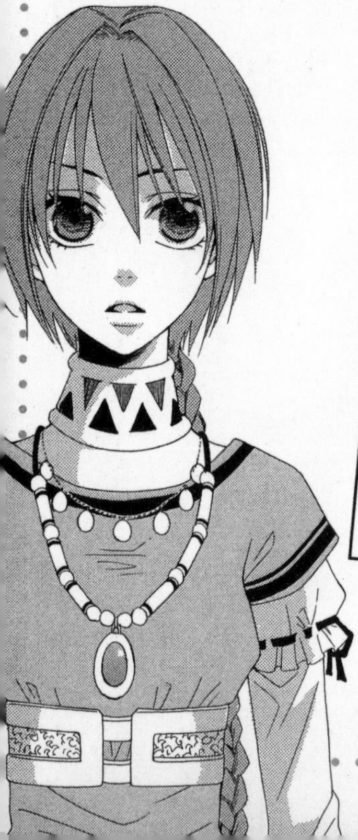